D0147610

Understanding Truth

SCOTT SOAMES

New York   Oxford

Oxford University Press

1999

Oxford University Press

Oxford New York
Athens Auckland Bangkok Bogotá Buenos Aires Calcutta
Cape Town Chennai Dar es Salaam Delhi Florence Hong Kong Istanbul
Karachi Kuala Lumpur Madrid Melbourne Mexico City Mumbai
Nairobi Paris São Paulo Singapore Taipei Tokyo Toronto Warsaw

and associated companies in
Berlin Ibadan

Copyright © 1999 by Oxford University Press, Inc.

Published by Oxford University Press, Inc.
198 Madison Avenue, New York, New York 10016

Oxford is a registered trademark of Oxford University Press.

All rights reserved. No part of this publication may be reproduced,
stored in a retrieval system or transmitted, in any form or by any means,
electronic, mechanical, photocopying, recording, or otherwise,
without the prior permission of Oxford University Press.

Library of Congress Cataloging-in-Publication Data
Soames, Scott.
Understanding truth / Scott Soames.
    p.   cm.
Includes bibliographical references and index.
ISBN 0-19-511151-6; 0-19-512335-2 (pbk.)
1. Truth. I. Title.
BC171.S63 1999
121—dc21   97-38551

9 8 7 6 5 4 3 2 1

Printed in the United States of America
on acid-free paper

UNDERSTANDING TRUTH

To my children,
Greg and Brian,
and
to the memory of my parents,
Bill and Ruth Soames

Acknowledgments

The contents of this book have provided substantial parts of a series of graduate seminars I have taught over a period of many years at several institutions. The first of these was given at Yale University when I was a beginning assistant professor. Thinking that truth was a topic I should know more about, I decided to teach a course on it as a way of learning the material. Two of my senior colleagues at the time, Robert Fogelin and Ruth Marcus, attended the seminar and urged me to publish a book based on the material I presented. Ruth, who was then an editor at Oxford University Press, recommended it to the press, which promptly offered me a contract. Although I declined the offer as premature, I owe to Ruth the idea of submitting the project for publication, and I am grateful for the encouragement she offered at that early stage.

Shortly thereafter I moved to Princeton University and continued giving the seminar there. Representatives of Oxford would come around to ask me to reconsider, and before long I did — with the understanding that any publication would be years away. I continued to work on the material at a leisurely pace. Many other philosophical projects intervened and several times took precedence, but every two or three years, I would give a version of the course in which I would either develop new material or refine old work. During the 1989–90 academic year, when I was on a sabbatical supported by Princeton and a fellowship from the John Simon Guggenheim Memorial Foundation, I completed versions of chapters 1–6 and preliminary discussions of various related topics, only some of which I have been able to include in the present volume. At that point, real life intruded and I underwent five years of personal difficulties, during which time I was unable to concentrate sufficiently to do consistent work on the project. That trying period came to an end during my sabbatical in the spring of 1995 when I produced a draft of chapter 7 and spent nine weeks lecturing on truth (chapters 2–7) as José Gaos lecturer at the Instituto de Investigaciones Filosóficas of the Universidad Nacional Autónoma de Mexico, in Mexico City. I am indebted to the director, Olga E. Hansberg Torres, to Margarita M. Valdes, and to all my friends at the Instituto for their warm hospitality and for the opportunity they provided me to present my work.

In the 1995–96 academic year, I gave the truth seminar again at Princeton and presented chapters 7 and 8 as lectures, the former to the Philosophy Department at Wayne State University and the latter at the ninth conference of the Sociedad Filosófica Ibero Americana in Querétaro, Mexico. In the spring of 1997, I gave the seminar at the Department of Philosophy, Graduate School and University Center of the City University of New York. I would like to thank all the seminar and lecture participants over the years, at Princeton and elsewhere, from whose questions and comments I have benefited. In this respect, one person deserves special mention. In the early 1980s, my friend and then colleague Nathan Salmon attended my seminar, during the course of which he made two important contributions to the book. The first was his interpretation of Alfred Tarski's puzzling notion of an inconsistent language, an interpretation that was crucial in developing the view presented in the final section of chapter 2 on Tarski's argument that English and other natural languages are inconsistent. The second was his suggestion, developed and extended in the first half of chapter 6, that if Saul Kripke's truth predicate is not to succumb to the Strengthened Liar, it must somehow be understood as partially defined more or less along the lines illustrated by my artificial predicate *smidget*. In both cases, his observations played a seminal role in my thinking—though he should not be held responsible for, or even be assumed to endorse, the use I have made of them.

Although material from much of this book, particularly chapters 2, 6, 7, and 8, has been presented as lectures at a number of universities in the United States, Mexico, Canada, England, and Australia, most of it has not previously appeared in print. The exceptions are chapter 8, which appears in slightly modified form as "The Truth about Deflationism," *Philosophical Issues* 8 (1997), 1–44, and chapter 4, which includes material from my "What Is a Theory of Truth?," *Journal of Philosophy* 81, no. 8 (1984) [411–29], and my "T-Sentences," in *Modality, Morality, and Belief: Essays in Honor of Ruth Barcan Marcus*, edited by Walter Sinnott-Armstrong, Diana Raffman, and Nicholas Asher (New York: Cambridge University Press, 1995) [250–270]. Chapter 1 has not appeared before but is based on the classic article by my former teacher Richard Cartwright, "Propositions," in *Analytical Philosophy*, 1st series, edited by R. J. Butler (Oxford: Basil Blackwell, 1962). The appendix to chapter 4 makes reference to material from the Princeton Ph.D. dissertation of Mario Gomez-Torrente, for which I served as an adviser.

Finally, I would like to add a word of thanks to my friends, colleagues, and students at Princeton; to my chairman, Paul Benacerraf, who had to endure far too many "progress reports" on the manuscript; and to my ex-wife Jane Nakashima, whose encouragement and advice during the early stages of the project were a great help to me.

Princeton, New Jersey   S. S.
July 1997

Contents

UNDERSTANDING TRUTH

Introduction

The aim of this book is to illuminate the notion of truth and the role it plays in our ordinary thought, as well as in our logical, philosophical, and scientific theories. The main questions to be investigated include "Why do we need a truth predicate at all?," "What theoretical tasks does it allow us to accomplish?," and "How must we understand the content of any predicate capable of accomplishing these tasks?" The discussion of these questions is organized into three parts. Part I, which consists of chapters 1 and 2, addresses substantive background issues that bear directly on serious philosophical discussions of truth: the identification of the bearers of truth; the basis for distinguishing truth from other notions, like certainty, with which it is often confused; and the formulation of positive responses to well-known forms of philosophical skepticism about truth. Part II, which consists of chapters 3–6, explicates the formal theories of Alfred Tarski and Saul Kripke, including their treatments of the Liar paradox, and evaluates the philosophical significance of their work. Part III, consisting of chapters 7 and 8, extends important lessons drawn from Tarski and Kripke to new domains: vague predicates, the Sorites paradox, and the development of a larger, deflationary perspective on truth.

The end result does not fit neatly into familiar preexisting categories. The book is not a survey of formal work on truth, a critique of informal philosophical speculation on the subject, a textbook on leading approaches, or a fundamentally new theory of my own making, although it contains elements of all four. The main aim of the book is to integrate and extend the most important insights on truth from a variety of sources. A central conviction underlying the discussion is that there is a continuity between the best technical work on truth and the most enlightening philosophical reflection on the topic. My aim has been to bring the two together and to show how each can illuminate the other.

The book is written for a general audience in philosophy. Although I hope some sections will be of interest to specialists, no specific background is presupposed, and I have tried to explain all technical material I use or talk about. Undoubtedly, some previous familiarity with first-order logic, as well as with standard topics in the philosophy of language, would be helpful. However, with a little work, most of the discussion should be accessible to nonspecialists, including graduate students in philosophy and advanced undergraduates with a serious interest in the subject.

I begin in chapter 1 by investigating the question "What sorts of things are true or false?" Different candidates — sentences, utterances, statements (propositions) — are distinguished from one another, and statements (propositions) are identified as the primary bearers of truth; sentences and utterances are deemed to be true insofar as they express true propositions. In chapter 2, five forms of what may broadly be construed as truth skepticism are examined. The first of these, expressed in an argument by Gottlob Frege, is that truth is so fundamental a notion that it is presupposed whenever we say or think anything, and for that reason it is indefinable (since any definition would itself presuppose it). The second form of skepticism holds that truth is epistemologically unattainable and therefore dispensable. In the chapter, I show how this all-too-common view arises from a highly seductive but ultimately fallacious argument that ends up conflating truth with certainty. The third form of truth skepticism sees truth claims as carrying ineliminable metaphysical baggage — about the nature of reality and our relation to it — and so as being scientifically suspect. The fourth form of skepticism has aptly been called "nihilism about truth." This is the view that there is no such property as truth and that truth predicates lack descriptive content. The final form of truth skepticism to be examined is the view that truth is inherently paradoxical and so must be either abandoned or revised. The most intriguing formulation of this view is that of Tarski, who argued that the Liar paradox shows English and other natural languages to be inconsistent because they contain defective and ultimately incoherent truth predicates. In chapter 2, I argue that, based on a precise and plausible interpretation of Tarski's argument (including his puzzling notion of an inconsistent language), the argument turns out to be logically valid but almost certainly unsound, since one of its premises can be seen to be indefensible. Similar results are achieved for each of the other forms of truth skepticism. In each case, the skeptical argument is dismantled, and the skeptical conclusion is shown to be either false or without support.

Once the grounds for truth skepticism have been cleared away, one is in a position to take seriously the idea that informative theories, analyses, and definitions of truth are possible. The first such theory to be examined is Tarski's celebrated definition of truth for certain (restricted) formal languages. In chapter 3, I begin by explaining how he conceived of the problem: (i) how his distinction between the metalanguage, in which the truth predicate is defined, and the object-language, to which the truth predicate is applied, prevents the Liar paradox from arising; (ii) how his criteria of adequacy guarantee that any definition satisfying them introduces a predicate that applies to all and only object-language truths; and (iii) how he approached the technical problem of formulating a definition that would satisfy his condition of material adequacy by allowing the derivation of what he regarded as an appropriate "partial definition" of truth — namely, a sentence of the form *s is true in L iff p* in which 's' is replaced with a name of a sentence of L and 'p' is replaced with a metalanguage paraphrase of that sentence — for each sentence of the object-language. Next I explain in detail the formal techniques employed in Tarski's inductive definitions of truth, the method of turning inductive definitions into explicit definitions (where possible), and the way in which his definitions can be shown to be materially adequate. The chapter concludes with a discussion of the relationship between the notions of truth and proof in the language of arithmetic. There, following an illuminating unpublished lecture by Kripke, I give the outlines of Tarski's theorem of the indefinability in arithmetic of the notion of arithmetical truth and of *Gödel's* first incompleteness theorem, stressing the close relations between them, their ingenious use of the Liar and heterologicality paradoxes, and their implications for our understanding of the notion of truth. In the appendix to chapter 3, I review Tarski's conceptions of quotation and quantification and discuss his fallacious argument against using substitutional quantification into quotes to define truth. The broader issue of the intelligibility of substitutional quantification is briefly addressed, and the value of Tarski's original, nonsubstitutional definition of truth is stressed.

Chapter 4 focuses on the question of whether Tarski's definition can be taken to be an analysis of the notion of truth. Since it is obvious that his formally defined truth predicates do not mean precisely the same thing as our ordinary truth predicate, *is true*, it is clear that the conception of analysis presupposed by the question cannot be one that requires synonymy of *analysandum* with *analysans*. In the chapter, I claim that what is required, if one is to be seen as having provided an analysis of truth, is that one's formally defined truth predicates must be capable of playing the role of truth in all theoretical contexts in which that notion is legitimately required. With this in mind, I argue that although Tarski's truth predicates can play many of the roles demanded of a notion of truth (e.g., see the appendix to chapter 4 for a defense of Tarski's conception of logical truth and logical consequence), there is one role they cannot play — namely, the role of truth in theories of meaning and interpretation. Crucial to the argument is my contention that there is a certain analytic connection between our ordinary notions of truth and meaning, in virtue of which statements of the truth conditions of sentences provide some information about their meanings. Since there is no corresponding connection between Tarski's notion of truth and the notion of meaning, statements of the Tarskian truth conditions of sentences (i.e., biconditionals one side of which involve the application of a Tarskian truth predicate to a sentence) provide no information whatsoever about meaning. The explanation of this difference between ordinary and Tarskian truth predicates is, I suggest, that whereas a sentence is understood to be true in the ordinary sense iff it expresses a true proposition, no such connection to propositions is built into Tarski's truth predicates. The consequences of all this for Donald Davidson's conception of Tarski-style theories of truth as theories of meaning are briefly considered, and the chapter concludes with a discussion of the relationship between analyses of truth on the one hand and the philosophical doctrine of physicalism—that is, the doctrine that all genuine facts, properties, and so on are determined by physical facts, properties, and so on—on the other. I argue that whatever worries the physicalist may have with the ascription of contents to mental states or linguistic expressions, the notion of truth, properly understood, is not the locus of these concerns.

In chapter 5, we return to an especially puzzling form of the Liar paradox. At the end of chapter 3, we prove that the language of arithmetic does not contain its own truth predicate by showing that, for any language, the claim that it both satisfies certain minimal conditions and contains its own truth predicate leads to a contradiction. We now confront the puzzle that it seems obvious both that English satisfies the relevant conditions and that English contains its own truth predicate. Of course this cannot be. In the chapter, different attempted solutions to this paradox are considered, including the well-known view, arrived at through a natural application of Tarski's techniques, that English is really an infinite hierarchy of languages defined by an infinite hierarchy of Tarski-style truth predicates. I explain the construction of the hierarchy and show how, in this view, different versions of the paradox are blocked. I then turn to several problems with the approach, the most serious of which is the irresistible urge to violate the hierarchy's restrictions on intelligibility in the very process of setting it up and describing it. We tend to forget this because we imagine ourselves taking a position outside the hierarchy from which it can be described. However, when we realize that the hierarchy is supposed to apply to the very language we are using to describe it, the paradox returns with a vengeance, threatening to destroy our description of precisely the thing that is meant to avoid it. Because of this, it seems desirable to search for an alternative solution. In that vein, the chapter closes with an explanation of how, if it could be justified, rejecting bivalence—that is, rejecting, in certain cases, both the claim that s is true and the claim that s is not true—would block the paradoxes.

The first half of chapter 6 is devoted to the construction of a philosophical model of partially defined predicates that would vindicate this idea. The crucial contention, originally suggested to me by my former Princeton colleague Nathan Salmon, is that a predicate may be introduced into a language by rules that provide sufficient conditions for it to apply to an object and sufficient conditions for it to fail to apply but no conditions that are both individually sufficient and jointly necessary for it to apply or for it to fail to apply. Because the conditions are mutually exclusive but not jointly exhaustive, there will be objects for which there are no possible grounds for accepting either the claim that the predicate applies to them or the claim that it does not. In the chapter, I illustrate how a language could come to contain such predicates, and I argue that there is a natural way of understanding the truth predicate in which it conforms to this model. In this view, it turns out that there are sentences, including Liar sentences like *This sentence is not true* and Truth Tellers like *This sentence is true*, about which the rules determining whether or not a sentence is true provide no result. Because of this, both the claim that such sentences are true and the claim that they are not true must be rejected, thereby blocking the usual paradoxical results.

The upshot of all this is a philosophical justification of a special kind of "gappy" treatment of the Liar. The justification amounts to an argument that the proposed treatment of the paradox satisfies three important desiderata. First, the gaps are not technical artifacts cooked up just to avoid the paradox; rather, they exist independently in language and arise from a process that applies to semantic and nonsemantic notions alike. Second, the gaps result from a plausible set of instructions for introducing the truth predicate; the gappy character of Truth Tellers and Liars is an automatic and unpremeditated consequence of these instructions. Third, the gaps provide an explanation of how we can (and indeed must) reject the claim that the Liars are true while also rejecting the claim that they are not true (thereby avoiding the Strengthened Liar).

Nevertheless, these results do not, by themselves, constitute a definitive and general solution to the paradox. The reason they do not has to do with its dynamic character; the very activity of solving the paradox in a particular case provides material for re-creating it in a new and strengthened form. In the chapter, I show that even if the truth predicate in a particular language is partially defined in the manner envisioned, once speakers are in a position to describe it as such and to explain how the original version of the Liar is thereby blocked, they will be in possession of conceptual material that can be used to restate the paradox in a form resistant to the original solution. While this does not, in my view, undermine the rationale for taking the ordinary truth predicate to be partially defined, it does limit what can be achieved, philosophically, by such an analysis.

In the second half of chapter 6, I explain Kripke's formal theory of truth and relate it to the philosophical model developed in the first half of the chapter. In my view, this model incorporates and makes explicit the essential philosophical insights guiding his formal construction. However, two factors complicate matters. First, Kripke's logical construction is compatible with several different philosophical interpretations. Second, some of his own remarks invoke a philosophical model quite different from the one I suggest, with a markedly different interpretation of the gaps that characterize crucial sentences containing the truth predicate. I argue that in these brief remarks Kripke uncharacteristically misdescribes the real philosophical import of his own formal construction. More generally, the second half of the chapter consists of (i) an explanation of the basic elements of his formal theory (the minimal fixed point, intrinsic fixed points, the definitions of ungrounded and paradoxical sentences, the construction of his "hierarchy," etc.) and (ii) an argument that the philosophical model of partially defined predicates developed in the first half of the chapter is superior to other interpretations and captures Kripke's most important philosophical insights.

The model of partially defined predicates is put to further use in chapter 7. There I develop a theory of vagueness according to which vague predicates are both partially defined and context-sensitive. Given such a predicate, one begins with a set of things that the rules of the language clearly determine it applies to — its default (determinate-) extension — and a set of things that the rules of the language clearly determine it does not apply to — its default (determinate-) antiextension. Since these sets do not exhaust all cases, speakers have the discretion of adjusting the extension and antiextension so as to include initially undefined cases in the predicate's contextually determined extension and antiextension. Typically this discretion is exercised by characterizing an object for which the predicate is initially undefined as being F or as being not F. When a speaker explicitly characterizes such an object as being F (or not F) and other conversational participants accept this, the extension (or antiextension) of the predicate is conversationally adjusted so as to include it plus all other objects that bear a certain similarity relation to it. Often the relevant similarity relation involves perceptual indistinguishability or something akin to it. Thus when some o object is explicitly characterized as F, the extension of the predicate is adjusted so as to include o plus all other objects indistinguishable or virtually indistinguishable from o.

These are the features of vague predicates on which the Sorites paradox is built. Given the right kind of case, one can construct a chain $x_1, \ldots, x_n$, such that x_1 is definitely F, x_n is definitely not F, and each x_{i+1} bears the relevant similarity relation (of indistinguishability or virtual indistinguishability) to x_i. In this sort of situation, one can often create a sense of puzzlement and cognitive discomfort by walking a subject through the sequence and asking whether successive items are F. One starts with the subject's initial characterization of x_1 as F. The rule governing application of the predicate to new cases will then determine that, by current conversational standards, x_2, which bears the relevant similarity relation to x_1, counts as F as well. When shown x_2 and asked to confirm this, the subject is merely being asked to explicitly characterize something as F that already counts as being F by the previously accepted conversational standards. Once the subject has done this, however, x_3 comes implicitly to be characterized as F, and the process can be repeated indefinitely.

This is the dynamic version of the Sorites paradox. In chapter 7, I argue that there is nothing inherently contradictory, incoherent, or deeply puzzling about it. What it shows is simply that the boundary lines fixing the extensions and antiextensions of certain vague predicates are inherently unstable. Although this is not a practical problem for speakers in ordinary situations and although it does not represent any theoretical incoherence in the semantics of vague terms, it does explain the discomfort one feels when presented with the dynamic version of the Sorites. One is uncomfortable because one feels pressured into establishing stable boundary lines that cannot be maintained. The solution is to recognize that there is no requirement that the boundary lines for the application of vague predicates be stable in this way.

There are, of course, other versions of the Sorites paradox in addition to the dynamic version. In chapter 7, I argue that the proposed theory of vague predicates provides plausible and instructive solutions to them as well. The chapter concludes with a brief discussion of vague predicates that are not Sorites predicates and of so-called higher-order vagueness.

The final chapter, chapter 8, articulates a broad philosophical perspective on truth incorporating important insights of Tarski and Kripke, without their somewhat artificial restrictions on the bearers of truth. Among these insights, none is more important than their essentially deflationist conception of truth. For Tarski and Kripke, truth is not a contentious metaphysical or epistemological notion, and a successful analysis of it should not be laden with controversial philosophical consequences. Rather, the content of the claim that a putative truth bearer is true is equivalent to that of the truth bearer itself, a fact that endows the truth predicate with an important practical and theoretical utility. Because the claim that x is true is equivalent to the claim made by x itself, one can get the effect of committing oneself to each member of a class of putative truth bearers by predicating truth of them, even if one is not able to produce, display, or assert the members of that class one by one.

One of the central points of the chapter is that as powerful and compelling as this idea is, there is no hope of maintaining it as long as the bearers of truth are taken to be sentences. The claim that *Snow is white* is a true sentence of English is simply not equivalent, in a sufficiently strong and interesting sense, to the claim that snow is white. Thus if deflationism about truth is to be maintained, it must be restricted to truth bearers other than sentences. Fortunately this need not be a serious limitation. Since a sentence is true iff it expresses a true proposition, the proper application of deflationism is to propositions. Once this is recognized, the relevant equivalence claim seems extremely plausible: The proposition that snow is white is equivalent, in some appropriately strong sense, to the proposition that it is true that snow is white (or to the claim that the proposition that snow is white is true).

This is not, of course, all there is to be said about the truth of propositions. Among the further questions to be answered are "In precisely what sense is a proposition equivalent to the claim that it is true?," "Is the equivalence identity, so that p and the claim that p is true are the same proposition, or is the equivalence relation something weaker?," "Is truth for propositions definable or eliminable?," "Is the content of the truth predicate for propositions exhausted by the totality propositional equivalences of the form *P iff the proposition that P is true*?," "How precisely are Liar and related pathological propositions to be characterized?," and "Does deflationism about propositional truth have significant philosophical implications?" Although some of these questions can be answered quite straightforwardly, others are more elusive and open ended. In fact, in my view, no existing theory adequately resolves all of them. To illustrate this, I examine a wide range of deflationary theories of truth—including the classical redundancy theory, Peter Strawson's performative theory, and Paul Horwich's minimal theory—and attempt to separate what is correct and worth preserving in them from what is not. Although the end result does not itself add up to a complete and comprehensive theory, I hope that enough is said to clear up many of the most significant philosophical doubts and confusions about truth.

Notation

In what follows I will use either single quotation marks or italics when I want to refer to particular words, expressions, or sentences—for example, 'snow' or *snow*.

Sometimes both will be used in a single example — for example, *'Snow is white' is a true sentence of English iff snow is white*. This italicized sentence refers to itself, a sentence whose first constituent is the quote name of the English sentence that consists of the word 'snow' followed by the word 'is' followed by the word 'white'. In addition to using italics for quotation, sometimes I will use them for emphasis. I trust that in each case it will be clear from the context how they are being used.

In addition, when formulating generalizations about words, expressions, or sentences, I will often use the technical device known as "corner quotes". For example, when explaining how simple formulas of a language L are combined to form larger formulas I use statements like (1a), which has the meaning given in (1b).

    1a.   For any formulas A and B of the language L, ⌜A & B⌝ is a formula of L.
      b.   For any formulas A and B of the language L, the expression which consists of A followed by '&' followed by B is a formula of L.

Given (1), we know that if 'snow is white' and 'grass is green' are formulas of L, then 'snow is white & grass is green' and 'grass is green & snow is white' are also formulas of L.

Roughly speaking a generalization of the sort illustrated by (2a) has the meaning given by (2b).

    2a.   For any (some) expression E of L, ⌜ . . . E . . . ⌝ is so and so.
      b.   For any (some) expression E of L, the expression consisting of ' . . . ' followed by E followed by ' . . . ' is so and so.

One slightly tricky example of this is given in (3).

    3a.   For any name n of L, ⌜'n' refers to n⌝ expresses a truth.
      b.   For any name n of L, the expression consisting of the left-hand quote mark followed by n followed by the right-hand quote mark followed by 'refers to' followed by n expresses a truth.

Particular instances of (3a) are given in (4).

    4a.   *'Brian Soames' refers to Brian Soames* expresses a truth.
      b.   *'Greg Soames' refers to Greg Soames* expresses a truth.

PART I

Foundational Issues

Truth Bearers

'True' is an adjective that, in its central use, functions as a grammatical predicate, taking nouns and noun phrases as subjects:

That is true.
The last sentence on the page is true.
What he just said is true.
The proposition that power corrupts is true.

This grammatical fact encourages us to think that when we assertively utter such a sentence we typically refer to something and say of it that it is true. The thing referred to is called, by philosophers, the *bearer of truth* (falsity). To say of such a thing that it is true (false) is to predicate truth (falsity) of it. In this view, 'true' is a logical as well as a grammatical predicate used to describe or characterize entities as having a certain property—truth.

I will assume, to begin with, that this view is correct; truth is a property and there really are things that are true or false, just as there are things that are uttered, written, published, and purchased.[1] What are these things? Initially, there would appear to be a variety of potential truth bearers. Among the things we ordinarily characterize as being true or false are *statements, beliefs, claims, assumptions, hypotheses, propositions, sentences,* and *utterances.* However, this impression of diversity may be misleading. Even if one assumes that statements, beliefs, claims, and the rest are bearers of truth, it is not obvious without argument that these entities are distinct from one another—for example, that statements are different from beliefs or that propositions are something other than sentences. To the extent that these entities can be identified, one need not worry about different kinds of truth bearers. But can they be identified?[2]

Let us begin with statements. By a statement, I mean *that which one states*, not one's stating of it. The two are clearly different. If one states that all power corrupts, then what one states is that all power corrupts. It would be absurd to say that this, namely, that all power corrupts, was what one did or was one's particular act of doing it. What one did was to *state* that all power corrupts, something that many others have done. The particular act of stating this was something that happened at a certain place and time. What was stated is neither something that is done nor something that happens.

In ordinary speech, the word 'statement' is sometimes used to refer to what one states, as in

Mary and Martin made the same statement, which Bob contradicted.

At other times, it is used to refer to one's stating something, as in

Mary's statement lasted for more than a minute.

I will always use the term 'statement' in the first way, on a par with 'what is said or stated'. In this sense, a statement is what many philosophers have called a proposition.

To state that so-and-so is clearly not the same as to assume, believe, conjecture, or claim that so-and-so. However, *what is stated* can also be assumed, believed, conjectured, claimed, or asserted. Thus statements can be identified with assumptions, beliefs, conjectures, claims, or assertions provided that these terms are taken to refer to what is assumed, believed, conjectured, claimed, or asserted rather than to acts or states of assuming, believing, and so on. Since it is perfectly correct to speak of beliefs, assumptions, and the rest as being true, what might initially have seemed to be a multiplicity of different truth bearers can be reduced substantially.

What kinds of things are statements or propositions? Since statements are things that can be said, one might be tempted to identify them with two linguistic candidates: sentences and utterances or, in different terminology, sentence types and sentence tokens. Sentence types are abstract objects related to but not identical with the particular sounds or marks on paper (tokens) produced by speakers. The distinction between the two can be established in several ways. For example, it is commonly supposed that there are infinitely many sentences of English that will never be uttered. But surely if a sentence S is to be identified with an utterance U, then U must count as an utterance of S (rather than of some other sentence or no sentence at all). Thus the usual supposition about the scope of English carries with it the conclusion that some sentences are not utterances—that is, some sentence types are not sentence tokens.

This conclusion can be strengthened by imagining a case in which two people, x and y, utter (or write) the same sentence. Since the particular sounds (or marks) produced by x and y are different, their utterances (tokens) are numerically distinct. However, the sentence uttered was the same in each case. From this, it follows that either x's utterance is not identical with the sentence x uttered or y's utterance is not identical with the sentence y uttered or both.

Schematically, the argument looks like this:

Premise 1. $U_x \neq U_y$
Premise 2. $S_x = S_y$
Conclusion 1. $\sim(U_x = S_x \ \& \ U_y = S_y)$
                          i.e., $U_x \neq S_x \ v \ U_y \neq S_y$

Could it be that x's utterance (U_x) is identical with the sentence x uttered (S_x) even though y's utterance (U_y) is not identical with the sentence y uttered (S_y)? In light of premise (2), this is possible only if the sentence y uttered is identical with x's utterance—that is, with the particular sounds or marks produced by x. But it would be implausible to claim that what y uttered was a series of sounds or marks that y did not produce. This suggests an additional premise stating that if U is an utterance of a sentence S, then S is identical with an utterance only if it is identical with U.

Premise 3.   (u)(s) [if uRs, then (u')(if s = u', then s = u)]
                      (R is here a relation holding between utterances and sentences they are utterances of.)

Together premises (1)–(3) entail that neither x's nor y's utterance is identical with the sentence uttered.

Conclusion 2. $U_x \neq S_x \ \& \ U_y \neq S_y$

Since a similar argument could be constructed for any sentence, we may conclude that no sentence is identical with any utterance.

The reason for considering this argument in some detail is that it generalizes. For example, to distinguish statements (propositions) from utterances, imagine a case in which x and y assert the same proposition. Since their utterances are different but their statements are the same, either x's utterance is not identical with what x stated or y's utterance is not identical with what y stated or both. To complete the argument, one may note the implausibility of claiming that the statement asserted by one of the speakers was a sequence of sounds (marks) that the speaker did not produce. (Here, 'R' in premise [3] stands for a relation that holds between utterances and propositions asserted by those utterances.)

The same argument can be made for distinguishing statements from sentences. Just as the same statement can be made by different utterances, so utterances of different sentences can result in assertion of the same statement. For example, if x were to assertively utter the English sentence 'Two plus two equals 4' and y were to assertively utter its Russian translation or the synonymous English sentence 'Four equals two plus two', then x and y would say the same thing; they would make the same statement. Similarly, if x were to assertively utter 'Today is sunny in Seattle' on day d and y were to assertively utter the nonsynonymous sentence 'Yesterday was sunny in Seattle' on day d plus 1, then x and y would assert the same proposition. Once this is seen, the schematic argument can be brought into play. The crucial premise (3) needed to complete it rules out the possibility that the proposition one asserts might be a sentence one has not uttered.

Thus there is good reason to distinguish propositions from both sentences and utterances. Whereas the latter are vehicles for expressing beliefs and assertions, the former, propositions, are the things that are believed and asserted. They are also the semantic information that utterances and sentences taken in particular contexts express or encode. In short, they are the information contents of sentences in contexts.

Since it is natural to think of the meaning of a sentence in terms of the semantic information it encodes, this may seem to suggest that meanings are propositions. However, this is not quite right. Although there is a close relationship between the meanings of sentences and the propositions they express, the two cannot always be identified. To see why, we need to consider two different kinds of cases: those in which utterances of sentences with different meanings express the same proposition and those in which utterances of sentences with the same meaning express different propositions.

The first sort of case is illustrated by the following pairs:

1a.   2 is a prime number.
  b.   It is an prime number. (Said referring to 2)
2a.   I am going to win the election. (Said by x)
  b.   You are going to win the election. (Said to x)
3a.   It is sunny today in Seattle. (Said on day d)
  b.   It was sunny yesterday in Seattle. (Said on d + 1)

For each pair, one can specify contexts of utterance C and C' such that the proposition expressed by (a) in C is identical with the proposition expressed by (b) in C'. This is reflected in the way in which utterances of such sentences are reported in indirect discourse. For example, if Bill assertively uttered (1a) and Tom assertively uttered (1b) in answer to the question "What do you know about the number 2?," then it would be correct to report that they said (asserted) the same thing—namely, that 2 is a prime number. Since what is said (asserted) is a proposition, (1a) and (1b) sometimes express the same proposition.

They are not, however, synonymous. If they were, then they would express the same proposition in all contexts of utterance, which they do not. The meaning of (1a) is such that it expresses the same proposition in all contexts of utterance (when taken with its standard meaning). The meaning of (1b) allows it to express different propositions in different contexts. Someone who knows the meaning of (1a) knows what proposition it always expresses; someone who knows the meaning of (1b) knows what (different) propositions it expresses in different contexts.

With this in mind, imagine a situation in which x and y express the same proposition by uttering (1a) and (1b), respectively. We may now run through the first part of the schematic argument and draw conclusion 1: Either the meaning of (1a) is not identical with the proposition x used it to express or the meaning of (1b) is not identical with the proposition y used it to express or both. From this, plus a plausible premise (3a), it follows that some meanings are not propositions.

Premise 3a.   (m) (p)[if pRm, then (p')(if m = p', then p' = p)]
              If proposition p can be expressed by a sentence meaning m, then the only proposition m can be identified with is p. (Given that each meaning can be used to express some proposition, it follows that a meaning m may be identified with a proposition p only if p is the unique proposition m can be used to express.)

However, in order to conclude that no meanings are propositions, one needs premise (3b), which, unlike premise (3a), is not obvious.

Premise 3b.   (m)(p) [if pRm, then (m')(if p = m', then m' = m)]
              If proposition p can be expressed by a sentence meaning m, then the only meaning p can be identified with is m. (Given that each proposition can be expressed using some meaning, it follows that a proposition p may be identified with a meaning m only if m is the unique meaning that can be used to express p.)

The difference between the two can be brought out by comparing two classes of sentences. *Eternal sentences*, like (1a), have meanings that result in their expressing the same proposition in every context of utterance. *Occasion sentences*, like (1b), have meanings that allow them to express different propositions in different contexts. Premise (3a) has the innocuous consequence that meanings of sentences cannot be identified with propositions they are incapable of expressing. It also has the consequence that the meaning of an occasion sentence cannot be identified with any of the many propositions it can be used to express. This, too, is reasonable. If the meaning of (1b) were identical with the proposition that 2 is a prime number, then uses of the sentence to express other propositions—for example, that 3 is a prime number—would be inexplicable. Thus premise (3a) can be accepted, and we may conclude that some meanings—those of occasion sentences—are not propositions.

Premise (3b) is another matter. It has the consequence that if a proposition can be expressed by both an occasion sentence and an eternal sentence, then it cannot be identical with the meaning of either. This is questionable. It is natural to think that what one understands when one understands a sentence is something that allows one to determine what is expressed on a given occasion of utterance from a knowledge of the sentence uttered and the context of utterance. Meanings can then be thought of as functions from contexts of utterance to propositions expressed. The meaning of an occasion sentence is a function that assigns different propositions as values to different contexts as arguments. The meaning of an eternal sentence is a function that assigns the same proposition to every context. Since in this case the function is constant, there would seem to be little harm in overlooking the contexts and identifying the meaning of an eternal sentence with the proposition it (always) expresses. In this view, propositions are the sorts of things that are meanings of eternal sentences, no matter what kinds of sentences are used on various occasions to express them.

There is, of course, another way to construct an instance of the schematic argument that does not rely on premise (3b). The argument is based on cases in which sentences with the same meaning express different propositions in different contexts. For example, if x uses (2a) to make a statement about x and y uses it to make a statement about y, then the meaning of x's sentence is the same as the meaning of y's sentence but the propositions they express are different. Thus we may conclude that either x's meaning is not identical with the proposition x expressed or y's meaning is not identical with with the proposition y expressed or both. Since premise (3a) has already been accepted, we may also draw the following conclusion 1 of the schematic argument,

Conclusion 1. $P_x \neq M_x \ \& \ P_y \neq M_y,$

as well as the more general conclusion that x's meaning is not identical with any proposition.

However, since (2a) is an occasion sentence, this is nothing new. What would be new is the conclusion that no meaning is identical with any proposition. One could draw this conclusion if it were clear that the argument just constructed involving (2a) could be repeated for every meaning, which it cannot. In general, premises corresponding to (1) and (2) will be available only when occasion sentences are involved; when the sentences are both synonymous and eternal, the same proposition will be expressed by x and y. Thus the proposal that propositions are meanings of eternal sentences survives the schematic argument.

Other arguments, of course, may bear on this issue.[3] However, I will not pursue them. I will assume that the meaning of a sentence is a function from contexts of utterance to propositions expressed by the sentence in those contexts. The function is constant in the case of an eternal sentence and nonconstant otherwise. Whether or not one wishes to ignore the difference between the proposition p and a constant function that assigns p to every context will not matter for my purposes. What does matter is the conception of propositions as objects of belief and assertion, as semantic information contents of sentences in contexts, and as fundamental bearers of truth and falsity.

In addition to propositions, utterances, eternal sentences, and occasion sentences taken in contexts (sentence/context pairs) can all be construed as truth bearers. However, the truth of a sentence or utterance depends on the truth of the proposition it expresses. A sentence or utterance cannot be true if it says nothing or expresses no proposition. Rather, it is true because it expresses a true proposition.

This dependence is not symmetrical. Certainly a proposition can be true even if it has never been expressed by any actual utterance. It is also not absurd to suppose that it can be true even if there is no sentence that expresses it. For example, for each of the nondenumerably many real numbers, there is a proposition that it is greater than or equal to zero. If each sentence is a finite string of words drawn from a finite vocabulary, then the number of propositions outstrips the denumerable infinity of sentences available to express them—that is, there are truths with no linguistic expression. Moreover, if languages are man-made constructions, then propositions that are expressed by sentences could have been true even if no sentences had expressed them. For example, the proposition that the sun is a star could have been true even if no one and hence no sentence had existed to express it.

Notes

1. This assumption will be examined in chapter 2.
2. My discussion of this question follows to a considerable degree the illuminating discussion in Richard Cartwright, "Propositions," in *Analytical Philosophy*, 1st ser., ed. R. J. Butler (Oxford: Basil Blackwell, 1962) pp. 81–103.
3. See, for example, ibid., section 12.

TWO

Forms of Truth
Skepticism

A central goal of theories of truth is to provide definitions, analyses, or explications that tell us what truth is by explaining what 'true' means or should mean if it is to function in desired ways in logical, philosophical, mathematical, and empirical theories. However, this assumes that the notion of truth has a significant role to play in such theories and that something useful and informative can be said about it. A striking feature of philosophical thought about truth is the existence of several lines of reasoning questioning this very assumption.

I will refer to these lines of reasoning as forms of *truth skepticism*. As I use it, this term covers a wide variety of skeptical views about truth, including not only skepticism about whether there is such a thing as truth but also skepticism about whether truth is knowable, theoretically fruitful, or definable. In this chapter, I will discuss five forms of truth skepticism:

   i.   Truth is indefinable.
  ii.   Truth is unknowable and epistemologically dispensable.
 iii.   Truth is irreducibly metaphysical and hence not scientifically respectable.
 iv.   There is no such property as truth; truth predicates are trivial and lack content.
  v.   The notion of truth, as we ordinarily understand it, is paradoxical and thus must be either abandoned or revised.

Although, in my view, the arguments for these skeptical conclusions are inconclusive at best, there is much to be learned from a careful consideration of them.

Frege's Argument That Truth Is Indefinable

The idea that truth is indefinable fits naturally into a view of concepts that divides them into two types: simple and complex. Complex concepts are definable in terms of simple concepts, which are indefinable. We can use simple concepts to analyze other things, but they are too fundamental to be analyzed themselves. Rather, they constitute our starting point in analysis; we have no choice but to take them for granted. The question at issue is whether truth is such a concept.

Gottlob Frege seems to have thought that it is. However, there is another part of his basic idea. He seems to have thought that truth has a special status among the concepts—the status of being in a certain sense presupposed by all other concepts, even the simple ones. He expresses this idea in the following passage from his article, "Thoughts": "We cannot recognize a property of a thing without at the same time finding the thought *this thing has this property* to be true. So with every property of a thing there is tied up a property of a thought, namely truth."[1]

This passage expresses the idea that truth is somehow presupposed whenever we say or think that anything has any property whatsoever. Whenever we say or think that something has a certain property P, Frege believes we are, in effect, saying or thinking that a certain thought is true—namely, the thought that the thing does have property P. So whenever we say or think anything, we are implicitly invoking the notion of truth. We have here the germ of an argument that we will examine shortly. In effect, the argument says that if we were to try to define truth in terms of some other concept—call it D (for the defining concept)—then we would find that the definition failed because whenever we tried to apply D to anything, we would be presupposing the notion of truth that we were trying to define.

Before looking in detail at this argument, I want to emphasize two things about what Frege is saying. The passage continues:

> It is also worth noticing that the sentence 'I smell the scent of violets' has just the same content as the sentence 'It is true that I smell the scent of violets.' So it seems, then, that nothing is added to the thought by my ascribing to it the property of truth. And yet is it not a great result when the scientist after much hesitation and laborious research can finally say 'My conjecture is true'? The meaning of the word 'true' seems to be altogether *sui generis*.[2]

The first point I want to call attention to is that according to Frege, truth is a property of thoughts or propositions in the sense discussed in chapter 1. For Frege, sentences are vehicles for expressing information. The thought expressed by a sentence on a given occasion is the information content carried by the sentence on that occasion. When one assertively utters a sentence, typically one says or asserts the thought expressed by the sentence on that occasion. Thus for Frege, assertion is a relation between an agent and a thought. So are other attitudes like belief, knowledge, proof, and so on. Whenever one asserts, believes, knows, proves, or verifies that so-and-so, what one asserts, believes, knows, proves, or verifies is the thought that so-and-so. This shows up in the analysis of sentences used to ascribe assertions, beliefs, and other attitudes to agents. According to Frege, the sentence ⌜α asserts (believes) that S⌝ is true (on a particular occasion of use) iff the individual referred to by α (on that occasion) asserts (believes) the thought referred to by the phrase ⌜that S⌝—which is just the thought expressed by S (on that occasion). In general, when we want to refer to the thought expressed by a particular sentence, we use an expression such as ⌜that S⌝, or ⌜the proposition that S⌝. The use of these expressions indicates that something is being said about a thought (proposition).[3]

This brings us to the issue of the bearers of truth. Clearly, the sorts of things that may be asserted, believed, known, proved, or verified are things that may be true. Thus thoughts or propositions are bearers of truth (and falsity) for Frege. They are not the only things that may be true or false, but they are the primary bearers of truth and falsity. We may speak of a sentence being true (on a particular occasion), but this just means that the thought expressed by the sentence (on that occasion) is true. Thus for Frege, the proper focus for a theory or analysis of the notion of truth lies in its application to thoughts (propositions).

The second thing about the passage I want to call attention to is an important contrast between two different sorts of linguistic environments in which the truth predicate is used to talk about thoughts or propositions.

Environment 1.   It is true that S. / The proposition that S is true.
Environment 2.   Everything John says is true.
                 There are true propositions that are not supported by available evidence.
                 Every proposition is such that either it or its negation is true.

In the passage cited previously, when Frege talks about the sentences 'I smell the scent of violets' and 'It is true that I smell the scent of violets,' he is concerned with a use of the truth predicate in the first kind of environment. When he talks about the scientist's remark 'My conjecture is true,' he is concerned with a use of the truth predicate in the second sort of environment.

Frege's observation is that when we use the truth predicate in the first sort of environment—as when we say ⌜It is true that S⌝—we do not seem to be adding anything significant to what we could say by simply saying S. We may express this, more cautiously than Frege, by saying that ⌜It is true that S⌝ and S are trivially equivalent; hence the biconditional ⌜It is true that S iff S⌝ is necessary, a priori, and knowable by everyone who grasps the notion of truth.[4] Frege also seems to suggest that when the truth predicate is used in the second sort of linguistic environment—as in 'My conjecture is true'—it does add something and is not eliminable without loss of content in the way it is when used in the first kind of environment.

Although Frege does not elaborate on the theoretical significance of this contrast, it turns out to be very significant. We can sum it up this way: Environments of type 2 are important because they provide the only reason we need a truth predicate of thoughts or propositions; environments of type 1 are important because they play a privileged role in explaining what truth consists in.

First consider environments of type 2. These are cases in which we predicate truth of some proposition or set of propositions we do not explicitly assert, display, or produce. For example, we might assert that everything John says is true on the basis of our assessment of John's character and intellect even if we do not know everything he says and hence do not believe the conjunction of everything he has in fact asserted. Similarly, we might claim that every proposition or its negation is true without having to produce an infinite list of disjunctions of a proposition and its negation. In cases like these, we are able to use the truth predicate to say something we would not be in a position to say without it. By contrast, if we never wished to say of a proposition that it is true without displaying it or producing it as we do when we say ⌜It is true that S⌝ or ⌜the proposition that S is true,⌝ then we could get along perfectly well without the truth predicate by just saying S instead. Thus it is the use of the truth predicate in environments of type 2 that provides the theoretical reason why we need a truth predicate.

Now consider environments of type 1. These are involved in equivalences of the form ⌜It is true that S iff S⌝ and ⌜The proposition that S is true iff S⌝. These equivalences are crucial in explaining what truth consists in. For example, in explaining what it is for the proposition that snow is white to be true, one can scarcely do better than to point out that it is true iff snow is white. In explaining what it is for an arbitrary proposition to be true, it would seem to be enough to note that the same sort of explanation could be given in any individual case. Thus in order to know what truth is, it seems to be enough to know that the proposition that snow is white is true iff snow is white, that the proposition that the earth is round is true iff the earth is round, *and so on for any proposition whatsoever.*

In light of this, one might speak of equivalences of the sort illustrated by *It is true that snow is white iff snow is white* and *The proposition that snow is white is true iff snow is white* as definitional of our notion of a proposition (thought) being true—definitional in two senses. First, one might regard any explicit definition

Def.   For all propositions p, p is true iff p is D

to be correct or adequate only if it entails all equivalences of the sort illustrated by these examples. Second, even if it proves to be impossible to formulate such a definition, one might maintain that there is nothing more to the notion of truth than what is given by the totality of such equivalences.

This last position bears important similarities to Frege's own. According to it, truth is, strictly speaking, indefinable, but its use in any particular case can be explained by the relevant equivalence. But why does Frege insist that truth is indefinable, and is it really? We are now in a position to examine his argument in detail.

The argument is given in the first few pages of "Thoughts." There Frege starts out by remarking, "Grammatically, the word 'true' looks like a word for a property."[5] He then goes on to ask what it is predicated of, answering with a heterogeneous list including pictures, ideas, sentences, and thoughts. In the case of pictures, he observes that a picture is true only insofar as it is meant to represent something. "It might be supposed from this that truth consists in a correspondence of a picture to what it depicts." However, he thinks this is wrong. "Now correspondence is a relation. But this goes against the use of the word 'true', which is not a relative term and contains no indication of anything else to which something is to correspond."

The argument to this point is quite simple:

1. Grammatically, 'true' is a predicate applied to individual objects and so ought to stand for a property if it stands for anything at all.
2. Correspondence is a relation holding between at least two objects.
3. Thus truth is not correspondence—that is, the word 'true' does not stand for any correspondence relation (since it does not stand for any relation at all).

This conclusion is both correct and general, applying not just to pictures but to other truth bearers, such as propositions, as well. However, it has no force against correspondence theories of truth. Such theories do not say that 'true' means 'corresponds to' or that the property truth is identical with the relation of correspondence. Rather, they say that truth is a relational property—the property of corresponding to something in reality. Relational properties are very familiar—for example, to be a father is to be a father of someone. The property of being a father, which holds of individuals, is not identical with the relation of fatherhood, which holds between pairs of individuals. Nevertheless, the former can be defined as the property of bearing the latter to some individual. According to correspondence theories, a similar relationship holds between truth and correspondence. Such theories may or may not be correct, but they are not undermined by the observations in (1)–(3).

After making these observations, Frege gives a general argument directed, in the first instance, against all attempts to define truth in terms of correspondence and, by implication, against all definitions of truth whatsoever. He begins by noting that the truth of p cannot involve complete correspondence between p and any fact since complete correspondence is identity and, according to the correspondence theory, a truth is supposed to be distinct from the fact it corresponds to. He goes on:

> But could we not maintain that there is truth when there is correspondence in a certain respect? But which respect? For in that case what ought we to do so as to decide whether something is true? We should have to inquire whether it is *true* that an idea and a reality, say, correspond in the specified respect. And then we should be confronted by a question of the same kind, and the game could begin again. So the attempted definition of truth as correspondence breaks down. For in a definition certain characteristics would have to be specified. And in application to any particular

case the question would always arise whether it were *true* that the characteristics were present. So we should be going round in a circle. It therefore seems likely that the content of the word 'true' is *sui generis* and indefinable.[6]

The argument suggested by this passage can be reconstructed as a reductio ad absurdum:

A. Suppose that truth is definable and that the definition is as follows: For any proposition p, p is true iff p is T.

B. If (A), then to inquire (establish) in any particular case whether a proposition p is true, one must inquire (establish) whether p is T.

C. Therefore, to inquire (establish) whether p is true, one must inquire (establish) whether p is T.

D. To inquire (establish) whether S is to inquire (establish) whether it is true that S, which is to inquire (establish) whether the proposition that S is true.[7]

E. Therefore to inquire (establish) whether a proposition p is true, one must inquire (establish) whether the proposition that p is T is true, which in turn requires one to inquire (establish) whether the proposition that the proposition that p is T is itself T is true, and so on ad infinitum.

The argument can be continued in two different ways, one emphasizing circularity and the other emphasizing regress.

Circularity
F. Since deciding whether a proposition p is true involves deciding whether the proposition that p is T is true, the definition (A) of truth is circular.

G. Since adequate definitions cannot be circular, truth is indefinable.

Regress
F*. So if truth is definable, then deciding whether a proposition p is true requires completing the impossible task of deciding the truth values of infinitely many distinct propositions.

G*. Since we sometimes can decide whether a proposition is true, truth is indefinable.

We begin with an evaluation of the regress argument.[8] For purposes of illustration, let us understand the steps in terms of what is involved in establishing that so-and-so (instead of inquiring that so-and-so). In particular, premise (D) may be understood as follows:

D. To establish whether S is to establish whether it is true that S, which is to establish whether the proposition that S is true.

There is a clear sense in which this is quite plausible. For example, if you have established that snow is white, then you do not have to do anything else to establish that it is true that snow is white. The point is simple. Suppose you have established that S. If you have grasped the notion of truth, then you are in a position to conclude, a priori, that if S, then it is true that S. Hence whatever process you used to establish that S, together with the trivial a priori knowledge that if S, then it is true that S, is sufficient to establish that it is true that S.

It might be objected that even if one has established that S, one may not have explicitly considered the claim that it is true that S, and so one may not have actually drawn that conclusion. Although this is so, it constitutes an objection to (D) only if a necessary condition of one's having established that Q is that one has explicitly drawn the conclusion that Q. That seems too strong; often we credit a person with having established that Q on the grounds that the person has explicitly established something else that has the proposition that Q as a trivial consequence. Still it has to be admitted that one cannot accept the general principle that whenever one has established something (whether explicitly or not), one has established all trivial consequences of it since this principle leads to the unacceptable result that establishing some premise is sufficient for establishing any conclusion that can be derived from it, no matter how long and complex the derivation. With this is mind, one might object that although a person who has explicitly established that S may have thereby (implicitly) established that it is true that S, there is some claim—it is true that it is true that . . . S—that has not been established.

If this objection is correct, then premise (D) is false and the argument fails. However, the contention that (D) is false is not obvious. For this reason, it is worth noting that even if (D) is true, the argument fails for another reason. If (D) is understood in the way we have been interpreting it, then the claim (F*) that there is a vicious regress does not follow from the premises. What (F*) tells us is that we cannot establish whether S until we *first* establish whether it is true that S, and we cannot do that until we *first* establish whether it is true that it is true that S, and so on. This clearly does not follow from the premises, as we are understanding them. For it to follow, we would have to understand premise (D) as saying something quite different—namely, that we cannot ever establish that S without *first* establishing that it is true that S. In such an interpretation, (D) is clearly false. So to sum up, if we understand (D) in a way in which it has a chance of being true, then the regress conclusion does not follow; if we understand it in a way that makes the conclusion follow, then it is not true. Either way the regress argument fails.

A similar point holds for the circularity version of the argument. When we *define* a concept, we explain the grasp of that concept in terms of a *prior* grasp of the defining concepts. A definition is *circular* when our grasp of the defining concepts itself depends on a *prior* grasp of the concept to be defined. In this kind of case, the definition is defeated because it is impossible for both the defining and the defined concepts to be conceptually prior to each other.

Does Frege's argument show that definitions of truth must be circular in this sense? Again we focus on premise (D), using the wording involving what it is to establish that S and accepting, for the sake of argument, the truth of (D), when understood in this way. To show that a definition ⌜For all x, x is Z iff x is D⌝ is circular, one must show that the concept D (T) is defined in terms of the conceptually prior notion Z (truth). If the definition is circular and D (T) does depend on Z (truth), then establishing ⌜n is D (T)⌝ will involve establishing something involving Z (truth). But the converse does not follow: It does not follow that if establishing ⌜n is D (T)⌝ involves establishing something involving Z (truth), then the definition of D (T) *depends on* Z (truth). Hence it does not follow that the definition of Z (truth) in terms of D (T) is circular. The argument from (A) to (E) has the consequence that (i) if p is a proposition that is T, then the proposition that p is T is also T and (ii) establishing that p is T involves establishing that the proposition that p is T is T. In and of itself, there is no more circularity in this than there is in the observation that if we define a *Prop* as *a potential object of belief, assertion, conjecture, and related attitudes* then (i) the claim expressed by ⌜n is a Prop⌝ is a Prop, and (ii) establishing ⌜n is a Prop⌝ involves taking the claim expressed by ⌜n is a Prop⌝ to be the object of an attitude and hence involves (implicitly) establishing that it too is a Prop.

The outcome of the circularity argument is no better if we formulate it so that the issue involves what it is to inquire whether S. In order for the circularity claim (F) to follow from this formulation of the argument, we must interpret premise (D) as saying that we explain what it is to inquire that S in terms of the conceptually prior notion of inquiring whether the claim that S is true. But Frege has given us no reason to think this conceptual priority exists. For one thing, it seems perfectly possible for us to think to ourselves that, say, it was hot today without having before our minds the complex thought that says of that thought that it is true. For another thing, it would be absurd to maintain that the thought that S is true was always conceptually prior to the thought that S; that really would involve an absurd regress—the thought that S is true would be prior to the thought that S, the thought that the thought that S is true would be conceptually prior to both, and so on without end. This is clearly not so. Rather, the biconditional ⌜S iff the thought that S is true⌝ is both necessary and a priori, but the right-hand side does not provide the explanation of what we mean by the left-hand side and so is not conceptually prior. As a result, no matter how we formulate it, Frege's circularity objection to definitions of truth collapses.[9]

Before we leave this issue, two further features of our reconstruction of Frege's argument are worth noting. First, the notion of truth it involves is one that applies to propositions rather than to sentences or utterances. Second, the argument presupposes an attempt to give a completely general definition of truth—one in which the concept of truth to be defined applies to propositions generally, including propositions containing the notion of truth and concepts employed in the definition. Now, just as one might question the possibility of giving a general definition of truth for propositions, so one might question the possibility of defining a general notion of truth applying to sentences.

I have already indicated that I regard propositions as the primary bearers of truth and that sentences are true only in the derivative (but fully legitimate) sense of expressing true propositions. However, not all philosophers accept this, and important theories of truth have been offered that deal with sentences directly without appealing to propositions as intermediaries. Particularly important in this connection are theories of meaning cast in the form of theories of the truth conditions of sentences. A familiar constraint placed on such a theory for a language L is that it entail an instance of the following schema T for each (declarative) sentence of L. (Instances are obtained by replacing 'S' with a sentence of L and 'P' either with that same sentence or with another sentence that expresses the same proposition it expresses and so is a paraphrase of it.)[10]

Schema T.   'S' is true in L iff 'P'

Such theorems are said to give the truth conditions of sentences of L, knowledge of which is supposed to play a central role in understanding the language.

A proponent of such a theory might wonder whether the notion of truth it employs is definable and might even try to show that it is not by constructing a version of Frege's argument applying directly to sentences. For this purpose, steps (A)–(C) could be retained, with occurrences of 'sentence' replacing occurrences of 'proposition' in the original premises. However, the argument would collapse at step (D_s).

D_s.   To inquire whether S is to inquire whether it is true that S, which is to inquire whether the sentence 'S' is true.[11]

To inquire whether S is not to inquire whether the sentence 'S' is true—for example, one who knew no English could inquire whether scientists will find a cure for cancer without making any inquiry about the English sentence 'Scientists will find a cure for cancer' (just as one could be unsure about the truth value of the sentence because one was unsure what it meant even if one had no doubt that cancer would eventually be cured). Moreover, (D_s) cannot be maintained by anyone who subscribes to the view that theories of truth for sentences may qualify as theories of meaning. If it were the case that to inquire whether S were to inquire whether the sentence 'S' is true, then presumably it would also be the case (i) that to know or believe that S would be to know or believe that 'S' is true; (ii) that 'S' *is true iff* S would be a trivial, a priori truth; and (iii) that knowing or believing that S iff Q would be tantamount to knowing or believing that 'S' is true iff Q. However, if knowing that 'S' is true iff S is to play a central role in understanding what 'S' means, then it cannot be a priori, and it cannot be known simply by knowing that S iff S.[12] Thus (D_s) must be rejected by anyone who expects the notion of truth being defined to play a central role in a theory of meaning.

But it might be thought that circularity is already lurking in (C_s) before we even reach later stages in the argument.

C_s.   To inquire whether a sentence s is true, one must inquire whether s is T.[13]

If the notion of truth in question is one used in a truth-conditional theory of meaning and if knowledge of truth conditions plays a central role in understanding the meanings of sentences, then understanding the meaning of the sentence 'S' *is T* must be based on knowing that the sentence 'S' *is T* is true iff 'S' is T.[14] Thus to understand the definiens used to define the truth predicate, one must already grasp the notion of truth one is trying to define.

Although one might loosely describe such a situation as involving a kind of circularity, it is not the sort that would make the definition illegitimate. It has not been shown that the expression 'T' or any expression needed to define it must contain the word 'true' or any other word that expresses the property of being a true sentence. Thus we have no argument that the definition is objectionably circular. What has been shown is this: If (i) there is an unrestricted notion of truth applying to sentences of arbitrary languages and (ii) understanding a sentence is always based on knowing the conditions in which it is true in this sense, then a grasp of this notion of truth is necessary for understanding any sentence, including any definition. Thus if truth is definable, the notion of truth so defined must be one that everyone already grasps in the absence of any definition.

Although interesting, this conclusion is only as strong as the assumptions (i) and (ii) on which it is based and which there are reasons to doubt. Although I will not go into those reasons here,[15] the position reached should seem somewhat implausible. The notion of a sentence is a fairly sophisticated one that children acquire after they have succeeded in understanding a substantial amount of language; even more so the notion of a true sentence. In fact, one explains to children what 'true' means by saying things like "If I say, 'Greg was born in New Haven,' and Greg was born in New Haven, then what I say is true"; "If I say, 'Brian was born in New Haven,' and Brian was not born in New Haven, then what I say is not true"; and so on. But to understand such an explanation, the child must already understand sentences like 'Greg was born in New Haven'. In general, we explain sentences containing the word 'true' by appealing to sentences that do not contain it. Thus it seems as if a child acquires the concepts of truth and a true sentence after he or she has already mastered lots of language.

One could, of course, reject this commonsense way of looking at things as so much misleading appearance and maintain instead that the child merely acquires a word to express a concept he or she has had all along. However, there appears to be little to recommend this apart from a desire to preserve a strict and contentious truth-conditional theory of meaning and understanding.

Truth as Epistemologically Unattainable

At the end of chapter 3 of *Experience and Prediction*, Hans Reichenbach summarizes his findings and presents the following view about truth:

> Throughout the first chapter we entertained the presupposition that propositions about concrete physical facts, which we called observation propositions, are absolutely verifiable. A more precise analysis showed that this conception is untenable, that even for such statements only a weight can be determined. With the object of obtaining more reliable statements, we then introduced impression propositions; throughout the second chapter we upheld the supposition that at least these propositions are capable of absolute verification. We have discovered now that even this is not tenable, that impression propositions also can only be judged by the category

of weight. Thus there are left no propositions at all which can be absolutely verified. *The predicate of truth-value of a proposition, therefore, is a mere fictive quality; its place is in an ideal world of science only, whereas actual science cannot make use of it.* Actual science instead employs throughout the predicate of weight. We have shown, in the first place, that this predicate takes the place of the truth-value in all cases in which the latter cannot be determined; so we introduced it for propositions about the future, so long as their events are not yet realized, and for indirect propositions, which remain unverified for all time. We see now that all propositions are, strictly speaking, of the latter type; that all propositions are indirect propositions and never exactly verifiable. *So the predicate of weight has entirely superseded the predicate of truth-value and remains our only measure for judging propositions.*

If we, nevertheless, speak of the truth-value of a proposition, this is only a schematization. We regard a high weight as equivalent to truth, and a low weight as equivalent to falsehood; the intermediate domain is called 'indeterminate'.[16]

The focus of Reichenbach's discussion is his contention that empirical propositions cannot be established with absolute certainty (where by 'certainty' one means not just an overwhelming feeling of confidence but a state in which one's basis for thinking p rationally guarantees p). At most, Reichenbach thinks, experience can render such a proposition highly probable; however, nothing can rule out the possibility that further experience and reflection will require its rejection. Once he considers himself to have established this, Reichenbach immediately jumps to the skeptical conclusion about truth expressed in the passage. This is puzzling. Why should the claim that certainty is unattainable lead one to think predications of truth or falsity have no place in actual science?

Although Reichenbach offers no argument to link the alleged unattainability of certainty to the supposed inapplicability of a truth predicate, the tendency to infer the one from the other is distressingly familiar. The following line of reasoning illustrates how seductive that inference can be.

1. If the proposition that P is an empirical proposition, then what one is committed to in virtue of assertively uttering

   a. It is true that P / The proposition that P is true

   is stronger than what one is committed to in virtue of assertively uttering

   b. It is highly probable/confirmed/supported/verified that P.

   In each case, one is expected to have strong supporting evidence that P. But in the case of (a), this is not enough since the speaker is also committed to the proposition that P. If it turns out that it is not the case that P, then one who has assertively uttered (a) has made a mistake; this is not always the case with (b).

2. Thus the statement expressed by (a) is stronger than the statement expressed by (b).

3. The strongest statement one can justifiably make regarding any empirical proposition is that it is highly probable, confirmed, supported, or verified. (One reason for holding this is the widely held view that it is a feature of our scientific methodology that no empirical proposition can ever be es-

tablished with complete certainty but rather must be regarded as a more or less probable hypothesis whose acceptance is a function of its role in our total and changeable scientific worldview.)

4. Thus one is never justified in making the statement expressed by (a). Since empirical truth is unattainable, the truth predicate has no legitimate place in empirical science.

Before analyzing where this argument goes wrong, it is important to note at the outset that its conclusion is far too sweeping. We know a priori that it is true that P iff P and that the proposition that P is true iff P. So if we were never justified in asserting that the proposition that P is true, then we would never be justified in asserting that P for any empirical proposition. In short, if scientific methodology excludes truth, then it excludes all empirical statements. Since this is absurd, the conclusion of the argument is clearly false.

The problem with the argument is its confusion of truth with certainty—that is, the limiting case of high probability. This implicit identification cannot be correct. For any proposition p, p is probable or confirmed to degree n iff the proposition that p is true is probable to degree n.[17] This is not the case with certainty. For example, the probability that the coin in my hand will come up heads the next time it is flipped is, we may assume, .5. Thus the probability that it is true that the coin in my hand will come up heads the next time it is flipped is also .5. By contrast, the probability that it is certain that the coin in my hand will come up heads the next time it is flipped is clearly *not* .5. Therefore truth must be distinguished from certainty.

Where then does the argument go wrong? The first serious error occurs in step (2). *The act of asserting* that it is true that P commits one both to having good evidence for the proposition that P, and to the proposition that it is true that P. However, *what one asserts*—namely, the proposition that it is true that P—does not entail anything about one's evidence. The proposition asserted neither entails nor is entailed by the proposition that one has good evidence that P.[18] In this sense, neither of these two propositions is stronger than the other; they are just different. Thus (2) in the argument is false.

Step (3) is also problematic. Even if we accept the contentious claim that no empirical proposition is ever known with certainty,[19] we need to ask what it is supposed to mean for a statement q to be *stronger than* the statement that it is highly probable that P. One might say that for all statements q and r, q is stronger than r iff q entails but is not entailed by r—that is, iff it is impossible for q to be true without r being true but not vice versa. However, if this is what is meant by strength, then (3) is clearly unjustifiable. If the proposition that P is an empirical proposition, then the proposition that it is highly probable that P and (moreover) P entails but is not entailed by the proposition that it is highly probable that P. But surely it is sometimes justifiable to assert not only that it is highly probable that P but also that P (even though the latter is not absolutely certain).

Thus, in this interpretation, (3) is untenable. Perhaps, however, all that is intended by (3) is the claim that no empirical proposition can ever be established with complete certainty. As a result, it might be maintained, one can never justifiably say of such a proposition that it is certain; the most one can claim in this regard is that it is highly probable or confirmed. In this interpretation, the notion of strength in (3) is one involving probability or degree of confirmation—a statement q about an empirical proposition p is stronger than a statement r about p iff q attributes to p a higher probability or degree of confirmation than r does. However, in this interpretation, (3) need not be contested; since the notion of strength in (3) differs from that in (1) and (2), the argument suffers from equivocation and the conclusion, (4), does not follow from the preceding steps.

We have, then, no good argument that predications of truth are illegitimate or that truth is epistemologically unattainable. The key to recognizing this is the observation that it is both necessary and a priori that P iff it is true that P iff the proposition that P is true. Once this is noted, it is obvious that truth is distinct from certainty and that the supposed unattainability of the latter does not undermine the legitimacy or utility of the former.[20]

Is Truth Metaphysical?

Different metaphysical and epistemological views have often been thought to arise from different notions of truth. One illustration of this involves the dispute between realists and antirealists over whether claims about the world that transcend our ability to verify them can nevertheless be regarded as true. For present purposes, we may imagine that (1) and (2) are such claims.

1.   There is a duplicate of the sun in an inaccessible region of space.
2.   There is not a duplicate of the sun in an inaccessible region of space.

Whereas realists maintain that either (1) is true or (2) is true, even if we can never gather sufficient evidence to establish either one, antirealists deny this. To many, this denial seems to fly in the face of the commonsense observation that the existence of stars does not depend on us. However, sensible antirealists contend that the issue is not whether we are causally (or ontologically) necessary for the existence of the stars—we are not—but whether we can mean anything by a claim we cannot verify. For them, the realists' contention violates the hardheaded view that we cannot attach any real sense to a claim that outstrips all possible evidence for it.

It is often thought that this dispute arises from a disagreement about the nature of truth. Whereas realists are seen as proponents of the correspondence theory of truth, antirealists are taken to be opponents of that theory. According to the correspondence theory, whether or not something is true depends not on us, on what it is rational for us to believe, or on what we can support with evidence but on the world. In short, truth is correspondence with reality. By contrast, opponents of this theory maintain that whether or not something is true depends on the available grounds for believing it. According to them, truth is something like the property of being rationally supportable or confirmable in light of possible evidence. Thus realists are said to view truth as a transcendent, nonepistemological concept, whereas antirealists take it to be an immanent, epistemological notion.

If this diagnosis of the dispute between realists and antirealists were correct, then truth would seem to be a metaphysically contentious notion, the use of which would commit one to realism if realists are right about truth or antirealism if antirealists are right. This result could easily give rise to a kind of skepticism about truth in which nonmetaphysically minded thinkers (e.g., scientists and scientifically minded philosophers) attempted to dispense with the notion entirely in order to avoid unwarranted metaphysical assumptions. For this reason, it is important to look more carefully at the diagnosis to determine whether or not it is correct.

The view that the dispute between realists and antirealists arises from a fundamental disagreement about the nature of truth is encouraged by the frequent use of the notion in stating the dispute — for example, as involving whether or not an unverifiable claim like (1) or (2) can nevertheless be true. However, this use is inessential and does nothing to establish the correctness of the diagnosis. The same disagreement that occurs over the assertion of (3) or (4), which make use of the notion of truth, also occurs over the assertion of (5), which does not.

3.   Either the proposition that there is a duplicate of the sun in an inaccessible region of space is true, or the proposition that there is not a duplicate of the sun in an inaccessible region of space is true.
4.   Either 'There is a duplicate of the sun in an inaccessible region of space' is true (in English), or 'There is not a duplicate of the sun in an inaccessible region of space' is true (in English).
5.   Either there is a duplicate of the sun in an inaccessible region of space, or there is not a duplicate of the sun in an inaccessible region of space.

An essential task of theories of truth is to explain the connection between examples like (3) and (4) on the one hand and examples like (5) on the other. However, once this connection is established, any dispute about one will carry over to the others. Thus if the fundamental disagreement between realists and antirealists is over examples like (5), then it is possible that both parties share the same notion of truth. Although the intimate connection between P, ⌜'P' is true⌝, and ⌜The proposition that P is true⌝ allows the dispute to be expressed using the notion of truth, the dispute itself may not be fundamentally about truth at all.

The utility of the truth predicate in stating the dispute is due to its role in formulating certain kinds of generalizations. The dispute between realists and antirealists is not specifically about proposition (3), (4), (5), or any other particular proposition. Rather, there are some generalizations that realists accept and antirealists reject.

The standard means of expressing generalizations in English involve quantificational idioms *some so-and-so, every so-and-so*, and the like. For example, if one thinks that either

   i.   John's mother said that John solved the problem, or
  ii.   Bill's mother said that Bill solved the problem, or
 iii.   Harry's mother said that Harry solved the problem,

and so on for each man, then one can express the appropriate generalization by substituting the quantifier phrase *some man* for the first occurrence of the singular term *John* in (i) and replacing the remaining occurrence of *John* with a pronoun functioning as a variable bound by the quantifier phrase.

6.   Some man's mother said that he solved the problem.
       ($\exists$x: Man x)(x's mother said that x solved the problem)

The realist thinks that either

a.   there is a duplicate of the sun in an inaccessible region of space even though we cannot obtain sufficient evidence to show that there is (a duplicate of the sun in an inaccessible region of space), or
b.   there is not a duplicate of the sun in an inaccessible region space even though we cannot obtain sufficient evidence to show that there is not (a duplicate of the sun in an inaccessible region of space), or
c.   there is intelligent life elsewhere in the universe even though we cannot obtain sufficient evidence to show that there is (intelligent life elsewhere in the universe),

and so on for every proposition. Here the appropriate generalization would seem to be one that quantifies over propositions. Thus if we follow the normal procedure for introducing quantifiers in English, it would seem that we should substitute the quantifier phrase *some proposition* for the first occurrence of *there is a duplicate of the sun in an inaccessible region of space* in (a) and replace its second occurrence with a pronoun bound by that quantifier phrase. However, the result of this is not an appropriate generalization but rather an ungrammatical sentence of English.

7.   *Some proposition even though we cannot obtain sufficient evidence to show that it.[21]

The reason for this involves a crucial difference between (i)–(iii) and (a)–(c). In the former case, the quantifier phrase replaces a *singular term* that names one of the individuals in its range. In the latter case, the quantifier phrase replaces a *sentence* that expresses (rather than names) one of the propositions in its range. Since quantifier phrases like these are noun phrases in English, neither they nor the pronouns they bind can occupy the position of sentences in English.[22] To turn (*7) into a grammatical sentence, we need to add a predicate taking *some proposition* and *it* as subjects, thereby transforming the expressions flanking *even though we cannot obtain sufficient evidence to show that* into complete sentences. To ensure that the resulting sentence expresses the intended generalization of (a)–(c), the predicate must be a truth predicate.

8. Some proposition is true even though we cannot obtain sufficient evidence to show that it is true.

This generalization guarantees that either

a'. The proposition that there is a duplicate of the sun in an inaccessible region of space is true even though we cannot obtain sufficient evidence to show that it is true, or

b'. the proposition that there is not a duplicate of the sun in an inaccessible region of space is true even though we cannot obtain sufficient evidence to show that it is true, or

c'. the proposition that there is intelligent life elsewhere in the universe is true even though we cannot obtain sufficient evidence to show that it is true,

and so on. Elements in the sequence (a'), (b'), (c'), and so on are connected to elements in the sequence (a), (b), (c), and so on by the trivial, a priori, and necessary equivalences that are instances of the schema (9).

9. The proposition that P is true iff P.

As a result, (8) is an acceptable generalization of (a), (b), (c), and so on.[23]

So what we have is this: The (infinite) disjunction of instances of the sort (a)–(c) constitutes the core of the realist's position. In English, the truth predicate is used to formulate a compact, finite statement of this position. However, the utility of the truth predicate in stating the issue separating realists from antirealists does not show that the dispute between them is a dispute over the nature of truth. The fundamental disagreement is over examples like (5), which do not mention truth at all. Whereas realists typically accept instances of

10. Either P or Not P

in cases in which they reject the corresponding instances of

11. Either it is possible to show that P or it is possible to show that Not P,

antirealists do not. Unless this difference can somehow be traced to a prior disagreement about truth, there is nothing here to support the suspicion that truth is a metaphysically loaded notion, the use of which carries with it a commitment to contentious philosophical doctrines like realism or antirealism.

As already indicated, antirealism is, at base, a philosophically motivated theory of meaning. Roughly put, its central contentions are that a sentence is meaningful iff it is capable of being verified (or falsified) and that to understand a sentence is to know how to go about verifying (or falsifying) it. Thus if (1) and (2) are unverifiable (and unfalsifiable), they will be rejected by antirealists as meaningless. This, in turn, will lead to a rejection of (5), either on the grounds that it too is meaningless (by virtue of containing meaningless constituents) or on the basis of a verificationist reading of 'or' in which a disjunction is assertable only if one of its disjuncts is.

The realist response is simply to reject verificationism as a theory of meaning. In and of itself, such a rejection need not involve any special doctrine about truth.[24] Of course, if verificationism is rejected, the task of constructing a positive theory of meaning will remain. To show that the realist's position arises from metaphysical assumptions about the nature of truth, one must show that the only nonverificationist theory of meaning capable of supporting the realist's assertion of examples like (5) is one based on such assumptions.

Michael Dummett sketches an argument for antirealism that illustrates how it is that assumptions about truth might be regarded as central in this way:

> The claim made earlier, that a grasp of the meaning of a sentence is to be identified with an apprehension of the condition under which an assertion made by means of it is correct was an intentionally vague one. It is evident that it is fundamental to the notion of an assertion that it be capable of being either correct or incorrect; and therefore, in so far as assertion is taken to be the primary mode of employment of sentences, it is fundamental to our whole understanding of language that sentences are capable of being true or false, where a sentence is true if an assertion could be correctly made by uttering it, and false if such an assertion would be incorrect. But, within this general framework, many different conceptions of what it means to say of an assertion that it is correct, and therefore of the appropriate notion of truth for our sentences, are possible. It is an essential feature of any theory of meaning that will yield a semantics validating classical logic that each sentence is conceived as possessing a determinate truth-value, independently of whether or not we know it or have at our disposal the means to discover it. . . .
>
> If it is agreed that an understanding of a sentence consists in an awareness of the condition under which a correct assertion may be made by the utterance of that sentence, it becomes indisputable that such an understanding may be represented as consisting in a knowledge of the condition for the sentence to be true. But, now, let us ask what it means to ascribe such knowledge to someone. One case in which the ascription of such knowledge is quite unproblematic is that in which his knowledge consists in the capacity to *state* the condition for the truth of the sentence in some non-circular manner, that is, when the knowledge in question is explicit or verbalizable knowledge. It is, however, evident that we cannot take explicit knowledge of this kind as a model, of universal application, for the grasp of the meanings of words, expressions, and sentences of a language: it is impossible to have a non-circular system of verbal explanations for all the words of a language, and the mastery of the language could not possibly consist in the ability to give circular explanations. Hence, if the understanding of a language consists in the ability to derive, for each sentence of the language, a knowledge of the condition for its truth, such knowledge must, for many of the sentences, be merely implicit knowledge; and so we need to inquire what it means to ascribe to someone an implicit knowledge of the condition for the truth of a sentence. If we take for granted that we can determine, from a person's linguistic or other behavior, when he manifests an acceptance of a sentence as true, then there will be no difficulty in saying what is required for someone to know the condition for a sentence to be true, provided that the condition in question is one which he is capable of recognizing as obtaining whenever it in fact obtains,

namely that he should, whenever the condition obtains, accept the sentence as true. For very few sentences is it possible to make such a claim; but, when a sentence is decidable, then, although we shall not always recognize the condition for its truth as obtaining whenever it does obtain, we are able, at will, to get ourselves into a position in which we can recognize whether it obtains or not; so, in such a case, we may identify someone's knowledge of the condition for the sentence to be true as consisting in his readiness to accept it as true whenever the condition for its truth obtains and he is in a position to recognize it as obtaining, together with his practical knowledge of the procedure for arriving at such a position, as manifested by his carrying out that procedure whenever suitably prompted. . . .

In short: since ex hypothesi, from the supposition that the condition for the truth of a mathematical statement, as platonistically understood, obtains, it cannot in general be inferred that it is one which a human being need be supposed to be even capable of recognizing as obtaining, we cannot give substance to the conception of our having an implicit knowledge of what that condition is, since nothing that we do can amount to a manifestation of such knowledge.

The solution is to abandon the principle of bivalence, and suppose our statements to be true just in case we have established that they are.[25]

Dummett's argument can be reconstructed roughly as follows:

A. The meaning of a sentence consists in its truth conditions. To understand a sentence is to know the conditions in which it is true; such knowledge explains understanding.

B. The notion of truth required by realism is one that may apply to sentences independently of our ability to recognize it as applying.

C. If truth is understood in the manner required by realism, it will be impossible to explain what it means for a speaker to know the truth conditions of unverifiable sentences.

D. Because of this, the realist theory of meaning fails.

E. Since (A) is correct, the verification-transcendent conception of truth required by realism must be rejected in favor of a verificationist conception.

Steps (C) and (D) are likely targets of realist attack, depending on what *explaining what it means* for a speaker to know the truth conditions of a sentence is supposed to amount to. If it means giving a behaviorist reduction of such knowledge in terms of observable linguistic behavior, then (C) might safely be granted whereas (D) is denied.[26] If it means something else, then (C) itself may be the focus of contention.

Another main point of contention is (A). One who takes it for granted that a theory of linguistic meaning and understanding is a theory of truth conditions will naturally be inclined to interpret fundamental disputes about meaning like that between verificationists and realists as disputes about the notion of truth that is central to the framework.[27] However, truth-conditional theories of meaning and understanding are highly debatable and need not be accepted by realists.[28] Although I will not argue the point here, I believe that strict truth-conditional theories of meaning and understanding are insupportable on independent grounds.[29] If that is right, then the main contention in the line of reasoning linking the dispute between realism and antirealism to special assumptions about the nature of truth will be undermined.

In fact, the case for the independence of this dispute from special assumptions about truth is stronger still. Even if (A) were accepted, realism could not be generated from it using a verification-transcendent notion of truth. According to the truth-conditional account, understanding 'not', 'or', (1), and (5) involves understanding that

i.   ⌜Not S⌝ is true (in English) iff S is not true,
ii. ⌜S or R⌝ is true (in English) iff either S is true or R is true (in English),
iii. Sentence (1) is true (in English) iff there is a duplicate of the sun in an inaccessible region of space, and
iv. Sentence (5) is true (in English) iff either there is a duplicate of the sun in an inaccessible region of space or there is not a duplicate of the sun in an inaccessible region of space.

None of this guarantees the assertability of (5) or any other example of the form *Either P or Not P* in which the sentence replacing *P* is intelligible but unverifiable.

These results will be forthcoming if (1) and (2) are accepted as meaningful and one also accepts the axiom schema (10) — that is, one accepts instances of *Either P or Not P* in which *P* is replaced by a meaningful, even if unverifiable, sentence.[30] But note that this addition to the truth-conditional semantics needed to derive the realist's conclusion encompasses the very conclusion that was to be derived. Thus realism does not arise from but rather supplements the semantic theory. In particular, insofar as acceptance of instances of schema (10) with unverifiable disjuncts is crucial to accepting realism, this position cannot be traced to assumptions about the notion of truth employed in clauses (i) and (ii) of such a theory. Realists' willingness to accept such instances may be due to their conceptions of negation and disjunction, but it is not due to a special conception of truth.

It is also due to their attitude toward (1), (2), and other unverifiable sentences. What does the truth-conditional theory tell us about such sentences? It says that understanding (1), for example, involves realizing that (1) is true (in English) iff there is a duplicate of the sun in an inaccessible region of space. Presumably no one can realize that P iff Q without being able to apprehend the proposition that Q, inquire whether Q, believe that Q, doubt that Q, and so on. Thus anyone who claims that to understand 'S' is to realize that 'S' is true (in English) iff Q, even though the latter is unverifiable, must hold that it is possible to believe that Q, doubt that Q, and so on, even though it is unverifiable that Q. Such an application of a truth-conditional theory of meaning to an unverifiable sentence *presupposes* the availability of the claim made by the sentence as a potential object of belief, assertion, and other propositional attitudes.[31]

This presupposition is conceptually prior to the truth-conditional theory of meaning and does *not* arise from it. Given any notion of truth, one could easily construct a truth-conditional theory having (12) as a consequence.

12. 'The gleep flumped me rick' is true (in English) iff the gleep flumped me rick.

The reason no one would construct such a theory is that everyone recognizes in advance that the sentence quoted in (12) is meaningless and that it would be sheer nonsense to say that someone believed that the gleep flumped me rick or knew that some sentence was true iff the gleep flumped me rick. Conversely, the reason that those realists who endorse truth-conditional theories of meaning are willing to apply them to (1) is that they accept in advance that (1) is meaningful and that it is perfectly intelligible to suppose that someone believes that there is a duplicate of the sun in an inaccessible region of space or realizes that (1) is true iff there is a duplicate of the sun in an inaccessible region of space. These theorists are not realists because they apply truth-conditional theories of meaning to unverifiable sentences; rather, they are willing to apply such theories to unverifiable sentences (in part) because they are realists.

In sum, realists accept instances of schema (10), *Either P or Not P*, even in cases in which the sentence replacing *P* is not verifiable. Their willingness to do this arises from (i) a conception of negation and disjunction that leads them to accept instances of (10) in which the sentence replacing *P* expresses a potential object of belief, assertion, and so on[32] and (ii) a willingness to treat unverifiable sentences as expressing such objects of potential belief, assertion, and so on. Both (i) and (ii) are *preconditions* of realist versions of truth-conditional theories of meaning that must be evaluated prior to the adoption of such theories. As a result, realism does not arise from special assumptions about the nature of truth built into these theories.

There are, then, strong reasons for thinking that the dispute between realists and antirealists is not fundamentally about truth after all. If this conclusion is correct, then we have no grounds for supposing that truth is a metaphysically suspect notion.

Nihilism about Truth

Up to now, I have assumed that there is such a thing as truth; that truth is a property of things that are said, asserted, and believed (as well as other things); and that we use the predicate *is true* to describe such things as having this property. However, some philosophers dispute this. According to them, there is no such property as truth and the predicate *is true* is not used to describe anything. They maintain that to say ⌜It is true that S⌝ or ⌜The proposition that S is true⌝ is just to choose a redundant or long-winded way of saying S. In this view, adding the words *it is true that* or *is true* to a sentence does not change the proposition it expresses; S, ⌜It is true that S⌝, and ⌜The proposition that S is true⌝ all express the very same proposition. The word *true* in these sentences may have the practical function of signaling to one's audience that one is agreeing with something that has already been said or conceding a point in advance that one expects to come up. However, it does not play any logical role, has no descriptive content of its own, and so does not contribute to the content of what is said.

This view, referred to by Alfred Tarski as "the nihilistic approach to the theory of truth,"[33] is also known as the redundancy theory of truth. In order to evaluate it, one must distinguish two different linguistic environments in which the word *true* appears: *it is true that* . . . and . . . *is true.* If attention is limited to the first sort of environment, the redundancy theory could be made plausible by taking *it is true that* to be a sentential operator, on a par with negation. Although the two operators are of the same grammatical type, the truth operator could plausibly be seen as logically redundant, whereas negation cannot. The result of applying negation to a sentence is a new sentence whose logical status is markedly different from the original unnegated sentence; the result of applying the truth operator is a new sentence whose logical status appears indistinguishable from that of the sentence to which the operator was applied. Thus if *true* occurred only in the environment *it is true that* . . . , it might be plausible to argue that it is logically empty.

As we have seen, however, this is not the only environment in which it occurs. What makes it interesting is its ability to function as an independent predicate, as in (1).

1a.   The proposition that men are mortal is true.
 b.   The proposition Bill denied is true.
 c.   Everything Maria asserted is true.
 d.   Something Harry believes is not true.
 e.   Church's thesis is true.

The main problem for the redundancy theory is posed by examples like (1b)–(1e), in which the sentence containing the truth predicate does not display that which it is predicated of.

For example, (1c) clearly cannot be analyzed as the conjunction of all the propositions that Maria asserted but rather is equivalent to the quantification in (2).[34]

2.   (p)(if Maria asserted p, then p is true)

Instances of this generalization are obtained by erasing the quantifier and replacing the two occurrences of the variable with occurrences of a singular term referring to a proposition.

3.   If Maria asserted the proposition that power corrupts, then the proposition that power corrupts is true.

However, since (2) contains a truth predicate, redundancy theorists cannot accept it as an analysis of (1c). Nor can the truth predicate simply be erased. Since the quantification in (2) is first order, the variable 'p' is a singular term and hence cannot occupy the position of a sentence. Thus

2*.   (p)(if Maria asserted p, then p)

is ill formed due to the application of the two-place sentential connective *if, then* to a pair consisting of a sentence and a singular term. Instances of (2*)—which arise from replacing occurrences of the variable with occurrences of a constant singular term referring to a proposition—are similarly ill formed.

3*.   If Maria asserted the proposition that power corrupts, then the proposition that power corrupts.

Instead of the *first-order quantification* over propositions illustrated by (2), redundancy theorists typically resort to the kind of *higher-order quantification* found in (4).

4.   (P)(if Maria asserted that P, then P)

Here, variables occupy the position of sentences rather than that of names or singular terms. As a result, instances of (4) are formed not by replacing variables with names of propositions but rather by replacing variables with sentences.

5.   If Maria asserted that power corrupts, then power corrupts.

Although (4) is perfectly well formed, care must be taken in indicating how it is to be understood. There are two standard types of quantification: objectual and substitutional. In the case of the objectual interpretation, variables are associated with ranges of objects. A universal quantification

6.   For all V(... V ...)

is true iff the formula

7.   (... V ...)

is true for all assignments of objects in the range of V to the variable. In the case of substitutional quantification, a variable is associated not with a range of objects but with a substitution class of expressions. In this interpretation, (6) is true iff each substitution instance obtained by replacing occurrences of the variable V in (7) with occurrences of an expression in the substitution class is true.

In certain cases, there is no significant difference between an objectual and a substitutional reading of a quantified sentence. For example, if (i) R is a set of objects, (ii) N is a set of names of (all and only) objects in R, and (iii) a sentence ⌜F(n)⌝ is true iff n names an object that has the property expressedly F, then an interpretation of ⌜For all x F(x)⌝ in which x ranges over the objects in R will have the same truth value as one in which x is associated with the substitution class N. However, in cases in which these conditions are not fulfilled, the two interpretations may result in different truth values. Thus if objects in the range of an objectual quantifier outstrip expressions available to refer to them, as is arguably the case in (8),

8. Some real numbers have no names
   Some x (x is a real number and x has no name)

then an objectual interpretation of the sentence may express a truth even though substitutional interpretations do not. Similarly, if some members of the substitution class fail to refer but can nevertheless occur in true instances of a quantified sentence, as is arguably the case with (9),

9. Some things I have dreamed about do not exist
   Some x (I dreamed about x and x does not exist)

then a substitutional interpretation may express a truth while objectual interpretations do not.

For this reason, it is important to determine whether the proposed redundancy analysis (4) of the English (1c) is to be understood objectually or substitutionally. In asking this question, it is essential to keep a fundamental point in mind. We are not asking whether redundancy theorists wish to *define* the higher-order quantifier in (4) in accord with the explanation of objectual quantification just given or to *define* it in accord with the explanation of substitutional quantification. A key feature of these explanations was their heavy use of the notion of truth; the difference between the two kinds of quantifiers was explained in terms of the different truth conditions they give rise to. Since the quantifier in (4) is part of the proposed redundancy *analysis* of truth, the notion of truth cannot be used by redundancy theorists to define or analyze the quantifier, which should be taken to be a primitive or undefined concept. The question at issue is whether this primitive quantifier is substitutional or objectual.[35]

There are serious problems with the substitutional interpretation of (4) as an analysis of the English (1c). The first has to do with inherent limitations on the substitution class associated with the variable 'P'. Since (1c) is an English sentence, that class must itself be a set of English sentences.[36] However, there are a variety of reasons to think that English, like every other human language, does not have the resources to express every proposition. The most powerful of these derive from the semantic paradoxes and will be discussed in chapters 5 and 6.[37] But there are also commonplace limitations that are more easily grasped. For example, at any given time many objects are not named by any proper name in English and many properties are not expressed by any English predicate. If L is a language that contains names for some of these objects or predicates for some of these properties, then some propositions expressible by speakers of L will not be expressible by English speakers.[38]

Thus it is safe to assume that some propositions are not expressed by any sentence in the substitution class associated with 'P' in the redundancy analysis (4) of (1c). Suppose now that Maria asserted one of these propositions. If she did, then (10a) and (10b) will be true, even though the substitutional construal of (11) may be false.

    10a.   Maria asserted something.
       b.   Maria asserted some proposition.
    11.   (Some P)(Maria asserted P)

Thus the substitutional reading of (11) cannot be a correct analysis of (10a) or (10b). But if the quantification in these examples is not substitutional, then surely the quantification in (1c), as well as (1b) and (1d), is not substitutional either.

The second problem with substitutional interpretations of these examples involves propositions which, although expressed by sentences of English that are candidates for membership in the substitution class, are expressed by different sentences on different occasions. This creates difficulties in cases in which we want to say that a person continues to believe something that person asserted or believed at an earlier time. If the quantification in such an ascription ranges over propositions, then the ascription may be true even if there is not any English sentence S such that ⌜At t x asserted (believed) S⌝ and ⌜x now believes S⌝ are jointly true. However, if the quantification is substitutional, the truth of ⌜x now believes something x previously asserted (believed)⌝ will require such a sentence. The facts of English seem to indicate that no such sentence is required, thus indicating that the kind of quantification found in these examples is not substitutional.

In order to show this, it is necessary to make explicit certain assumptions about temporal semantics. The first assumption is that an ordinary tensed sentence like

    12.   Clinton is about to be elected president

expresses different propositions at different times. On November 4, 1996, it expressed the true proposition that Clinton was then about to be elected president; at present, it expresses the false proposition that he is now about to be elected president.[39]

The second assumption involves past tense examples like (13).

    13.   On November 4, 1996, Clinton was about to be elected president.

Example (13) is true at a time t iff (i) November 4, 1996, is earlier than t and (ii) the proposition expressed by (12) on November 4, 1996, is true. Following the standard practice in temporal semantics, we may take tenses to be sentential operators. In the case of (13), we have a specific past tense operator, which we may represent as (*on November 4, 1996 + Past*). This is attached to the tenseless matrix *Clinton be about to be elected president* to form the logical representation (14) of (13).

    14.   (On November 4, 1996 + Past)(Clinton be about to be elected president)

The logical form (14) is true at a time t iff (i) November 4, 1996, is earlier than t and (ii) the proposition expressed by the tenseless matrix relative to November 4, 1996, is true.[40]

Now consider the examples in (15).

15a.   On November 4, 1996, Al believed that Clinton was about to be elected president.
  b.   Al now believes everything he believed on November 4, 1996.

Given our assumptions, we may take the logical forms of these sentences to be given in (16).[41]

16a.   (On November 4, 1996 + Past)(Al believe that Clinton be about to be elected president)
  b.   For all P [if (on November 4, 1996 + Past)(Al believe P), then (Now + Present)(Al believe P)]

The first thing to notice about these examples is that (15a) and (15b) do not in fact entail (15c).

15c.   Al now believes that Clinton is about to be elected president.

However, if (i) the quantification in (16b) is substitutional and (ii) the untensed matrix *Clinton be about to be elected president* is in the substitution class of the quantifier, then (16a) and (16b) entail (16c).

16c.   (Now + Present)(Al believe that Clinton be about to be elected president)

Since (16c) is the logical form of (15c), it follows that either the quantification in (16b) is not substitutional or the matrix *Clinton be about to be elected president* is not in the substitution class of the quantifier.[42]

Next notice that if the quantification in (16b) is objectual and propositions are temporally indexed, then there is no problem blocking the inference from (16a) and (16b) to (16c). The truth of (16a) tells us that on November 4, 1996, Al believed the proposition expressed by *Clinton be about to be elected president* relative to that date. That proposition is one that attributes to Clinton the property of being then about to be elected (where 'then' refers to the date in question). The truth of (16b) ensures that Al continues to believe this proposition. However, it does *not* require the proposition to continue to be expressed by the same sentence and so does not license the inference to (16c).

If we now want to express the proposition that Al believed earlier and continues to believe, the most natural choice is (17a), whose logical form is (17b) (where 'then' refers to November 4, 1996).

17a.   Clinton was then about to be elected president.
  b.   (Then + Past)(Clinton be elected president)

The proposition now expressed by these sentences is trivially equivalent to the proposition expressed by *Clinton be about to be elected president* relative to November 4, 1996. Provided that Al recognizes this equivalence (and accepts that then was earlier than now), the truth of (16a) and (16b) will ensure the truth of (16d).

16d.   (Now + Present)[Al believe that (then + Past)(Clinton be about to be elected president)]

Since this is the logical form of (15d),

15d.   Al now believes that Clinton was then about to be elected president,

an objectual interpretation of quantification can be used to explain the natural inference from (15a) and (15b) to (15d).

The same cannot be said for a substitutional interpretation of the relevant quantification. Recall that the substitution class for the quantifier in (16b) must not include the untensed sentence *Clinton be about to be elected president* found in (16a). What about the clause (17b) embedded under *believe* in (16d)? If it is to play a role in justifying an inference to (16d) from (16a) plus a substitutional interpretation of (16b), then there must be reason to think that it expresses, relative to November 4, 1996, something Al believed at that time. In other words, the presence of (17b) in the substitution class of the substitutional quantifier will legitimate the inference only if there is reason to think that (18) is true if (16a) is (where 'then' refers to November 4, 1996).

18.   (On November 4, 1996 + Past)[Al believe that (then + Past) (Clinton be about to be elected president)]

However, there is every reason to think that (18) is false. In order for it to be true, (17b) must express, relative to the time November 4, 1996, something Al then believed. However, what (17b) expresses relative to that time is a trivial necessary falsehood. According to our assumptions, the proposition expressed by this sentence relative to November 4, 1996, is true iff (i) November 4, 1996 is earlier than November 4, 1996 and (ii) the proposition expressed by *Clinton be about to be elected president* relative to that time is true. Since there is nothing to suggest that Al believed this absurdity, there is still no explanation of the inference from (16a) and (16b) to (16d) in the substitutional interpretation.

Nor will one be forthcoming unless we can find a sentence that expresses, relative to every time, the proposition expressed by *Clinton be about to be elected*, relative to the particular time November 4, 1996. Since it is doubtful that there is any such sentence of English, it is doubtful that the quantifier in the English

(15b) is substitutional.[43] However, if the quantifier in (15b) is not substitutional, then surely the quantifiers in (1b), (1c), and (1d) are not either.

These problems strongly suggest that no redundancy analysis of these examples involving higher-order substitutional quantification can be correct. This in turn indicates that they contain either ordinary first-order quantification over propositions plus a truth predicate or higher-order quantification over propositions without a truth predicate. Only the second of these alternatives is compatible with the redundancy theory.

There is, however, a very serious problem with this analysis from the point of view of that theory. Ironically, the problem arises directly from the commitment to propositions carried by the objectual quantifiers. Historically, the main proponents of the redundancy theory—for example, F. P. Ramsey, Peter Strawson, Arthur Prior, and Dorothy Grover—adopted it not only as a means of eliminating the property truth but also as part of an overall program of avoiding commitment to the existence of propositions. In fact, there is good reason for these projects to be linked; once one admits that there are propositions, one is hard pressed to deny that there is a property of precisely the true ones.

This point can be illustrated by considering the views of Frege, who, in his article "On Sense and Reference," denied that truth was a property despite his vigorous defense of the reality of propositions.[44] Frege saw this denial as dictated by systematic considerations involving meaning and reference. According to him, the meaning or sense of an expression is distinct from its referent; for example, *the founder of formal logic and most famous student of Plato* and *the teacher of Alexander the Great who was born in Stagira* have different meanings or senses even though both refer to Aristotle. Of course, sense and reference are not entirely unrelated; rather, the sense of an expression determines its reference. Thus two expressions with the same sense must have the same reference, but two expressions with the same reference may have different senses. Frege also maintained that sense and reference are governed by strict compositional principles—the sense (reference) of a complex expression is a function of the senses (referents) of its parts. Thus substitution of coreferential expressions in a complex expression should not change the reference of the whole, and substitution of synonyms should not change meaning or sense.

Frege was guided by these principles in extending his distinction between sense and reference to sentences. He observed that substitution of coreferential expressions with different senses standardly changes the proposition expressed whereas substitution of synonymous expressions does not, and as a result, he identified the proposition expressed by a sentence with its sense or meaning. Impressed by the wide range of cases in which substitution of coreferential expressions does not change truth value (e.g., if A and B are coreferential, then ⌜A is a philosopher⌝ is true iff ⌜B is a philosopher⌝ is true), he took the truth value of a sentence to be its referent.[45]

Frege recognized two truth values, the True and the False. He thought that since they were referents, they were therefore objects and hence not the sort of things that could be senses of expressions or constituents of propositions. In particular, they could not be senses or meanings of the predicates *is true* and *is false* and could not be constituents of the propositions expressed by sentences containing them. This led him to hold that *is true* is not a genuine predicate and that the proposition expressed by (19a) is the same as the proposition expressed by (19b).

19a.   The thought that 5 is a prime number is true.
   b.   5 is a prime number.

Frege expressed this view in the following passage from "On Sense and Reference":

> One might be tempted to regard the relation of the thought to the True not as that of sense to reference, but rather as that of subject to predicate. One can, indeed, say: 'The thought, that 5 is a prime number, is true'. But closer examination shows that nothing more has been said than in the simple sentence '5 is a prime number'. The truth claim arises in each case from the form of the declarative sentence, and when the latter lacks its usual force, e.g., in the mouth of an actor upon the stage, even the sentence, 'The thought that 5 is a prime number is true' contains only a thought, and indeed the same thought as the simple '5 is a prime number'. It follows that the relation of the thought to the True may not be compared with that of subject to predicate. Subject and predicate (understood in the logical sense) are indeed elements of thought; they stand on the same level for knowledge. By combining subject and predicate, one reaches only a thought, never passes from sense to reference, never from a thought to its truth value. One moves at the same level but never advances from one level to the next. A truth value cannot be a part of a thought, any more than, say, the Sun can, for it is not a sense but an object.[46]

Many will find Frege's argument for the redundancy theory unpersuasive because they do not accept his premises about the sense and reference of sentences. It should be noted, however, that the argument is unsuccessful even if the premises are accepted. Given the True as a referent determined by certain thoughts, one can define a truth predicate, trivially, as follows: x is true iff x is a thought that determines the True as referent. If *true* is defined in this way, then the thought expressed by (19a) will be one in which the property of being true (i.e., the property just defined) is predicated of the thought expressed by (19b). Consequently, (19a) and (19b) will express different but necessarily equivalent thoughts.

It is, of course, somewhat strange to maintain that there is both an object the True and a property of being true. However, since the property is definable in terms of the object, this position is no stranger than one that talks only of the mysterious object—the True. Thus it should be clear that Frege has no real argument for the redundancy theory.

Frege's problem illustrates a more general point. If redundancy theorists acknowledge the existence of propositions, they will have a hard time denying that there is a property of precisely the true ones. For example, if the quantification in the redundancy analysis

4.   (P)(if Maria asserted that P, then P)

of the English

1c.   Everything Maria asserted is true

is objectual, with the variable ranging over propositions, then the same sort of higher-order objectual quantification over propositions can be used to define the property of being a true proposition.

20.   For all propositions x [x is true iff $(\exists P)(x = $ the proposition that P & P)].

Here we set the range of the ordinary first-order variable x to be the same as the higher-order existential quantifier over propositions. Although some may question this definition because they question the legitimacy of the higher-order propositional quantification, redundancy theorists who offer (4) as an analysis of (1c) cannot be among them. However, once the quantification is allowed, the property of being true is definable in terms of it.[47] And surely if there is a property of being true, then the predicate *is true* stands for that property, thus falsifying the central tenet of the redundancy theory.

To sum up, the redundancy or nihilistic theory of truth denies that truth is a property and that *is true* is a genuine predicate. The theory may look plausible when attention is limited to examples like ⌜It is true that S⌝ or ⌜The proposition that S is true⌝, in which what is said to be true is directly displayed. However, the theory apparently cannot handle the cases that make the truth predicate useful and interesting—sentences containing *true* that do not display anything said to be true. The most significant of these are quantificational sentences in which the truth predicate is used to express generalizations. In attempting to dispense with this predicate, redundancy theorists are forced to treat the quantification in these sentences as higher order. A substitutional interpretation of this quantification fails to capture the intended meanings of the sentences and is therefore inadequate. An objectual interpretation in which the higher-order quantifiers range over propositions provides the means for defining a truth predicate after all.

There are other, related problems with the redundancy theory. One familiar kind of case in which *true* is used is one in which we refer demonstratively to a proposition and say, "That's true." Typically in such cases, the proposition said to be true is expressed by an assertive utterance or inscription present in the context, so it is transparent what proposition we have referred to. In these cases, the redundancy theory may seem tempting. However, not all cases of referring to a proposition and saying that it is true are like this.

Just as we can refer to a proposition using an ordinary demonstrative, so, it would seem, we can nondemonstratively refer to a proposition using a proper name. Suppose that a proposition p gets named *Extensionality*, duly inscribed in *The Encyclopedia of Philosophical Logic*. It would seem that we could then use the sentence *Extensionality is true* to predicate truth of the proposition p even in contexts in which there is no assertive utterance or inscription expressing that proposition. It is a common feature of proper names that one can use a name to assert a proposition about the individual it refers to even if one cannot identify or uniquely and noncircularly describe that individual without the help of experts. If this general feature of names carries over to names of propositions, then it should be possible to use the name *Extensionality* to assert a proposition about its referent even if one cannot state, identify, or noncircularly and uniquely describe Extensionality without the help of experts. And if this is possible, then one should be able to use the sentence *Extensionality is true* to predicate truth of Extensionality — the proposition p — even in cases in which one is not in a position to state or assert that proposition.[48] Since in such a case one has asserted the proposition that Extensionality is true without asserting the proposition p, the two propositions, though necessarily equivalent, cannot be identical, and the redundancy analysis of typical uses of *That's true* cannot be extended to this type of case.

Thus it appears that sentences in which proper names of propositions are grammatical subjects of the truth predicate pose an additional difficulty for the redundancy theory. If names were equivalent to definite descriptions, this might not be so since they might then be assimilated to the quantificational case. However, the convincing refutation of descriptive theories of names by Saul Kripke[49] and others makes this strategy unpromising. Thus the difficulty involving names seems to go beyond those already noted involving quantification.

Because of these difficulties, the redundancy theory cannot be accepted. A central aspect of our use of the phrase *is true* is its use with names and quantifiers in cases in which what is said to be true is not directly displayed or presented. To account for such cases, *is true* must be treated as a genuine predicate expressing the property truth. Once this is admitted, the analysis carries over to cases like *That's true*, ⌜The proposition that S is true⌝, and ⌜It is true that S⌝ as well. In short, there is such a thing as truth; it is a property of things that are said, asserted, and believed (among other things); and the predicate *is true* is used to describe things as having this property.

Truth and Paradox

The final form of truth skepticism to be considered holds that truth, as we ordinarily understand it, leads inevitably to paradox and is therefore incoherent. The feature of our ordinary notion of truth thought to be responsible for this result is its apparent universality. The predicates *is true* and *is not true* seem capable of applying not just to a restricted range of statements but to any statement one might make. Since these predicates are themselves used in making statements, it follows that they may be applicable to the very statements they are used to make. This leads to various versions of the *Liar paradox*, as when one says that what one is saying is not true.

There are many ways to reconstruct the paradox. Some involve apparent instances of *propositions* that say of themselves that they are not true, whereas others involve *sentences* that attribute untruth to themselves. Although there are important parallels between sentential and propositional versions of the Liar, there are also potential differences. As it happens, most formal and philosophical work on the paradox—including the seminal contributions of Tarski and Kripke (to be discussed in later chapters)—have concerned truth predicates applying to sentences. For this reason, we will concentrate primarily on sentential rather than propositional versions of the Liar.

A simple example of a Liar-paradoxical sentence is (1).

1.   Sentence (1) is not true.

Here, the expression *sentence* (1) is to be understood as synonymous with (and an abbreviation for) *the sentence that is the first numbered example in the section "Truth and Paradox" in chapter 2 of the book by Scott Soames on truth.* Since this example is made up of English words in accordance with the normal rules of English grammar, it is clearly a grammatical sentence of the language. It also appears to be perfectly meaningful. One indication of this is the fact that a person not familiar with this section of the book would experience no difficulty comprehending what it says. Another indication of the meaningfulness of sentence (1) is the fact that what it says (the proposition it expresses) would clearly have been true if the first numbered example in this section of the book had been, say, 2 + 2 = 5. But if sentence (1) says something (expresses some proposition) that would have been true had certain circumstances obtained, then it says something (expresses some proposition) and so is meaningful.

What makes this sentence paradoxical is that a contradiction can be derived from apparently incontrovertible assumptions about it.

Version 1 of the Liar
P1.   'Sentence (1) is not true' is true iff sentence (1) is not true.
P2.   Sentence (1) = 'Sentence (1) is not true'.
C1.   Sentence (1) is true iff sentence (1) is not true.
C2.   Sentence (1) is true and sentence (1) is not true.

(C1) is derived by substituting the expression *Sentence (1)* for the quote-name 'Sentence (1) is not true' in (P1) on the basis of the identity (P2). Since the truth of (P2) ensures that these expressions are coreferential, the substitution is clearly truth preserving and the derivation is legitimate. (C1), in turn, tautologically implies (C2) for surely either sentence (1) is true or it is not. Since each of these alternatives leads, together with (C1), to the conclusion that it is both true and not true, it follows that sentence (1) is both true and not true. Thus we have derived a contradiction from (P1) and (P2).

Since we cannot accept a contradiction, it would seem that we must reject either (P1) or (P2). But (P2) can be established by simple inspection and is incontrovertible. And (P1) is an instance of the schema T,

Schema T.   'S' is true iff S,

the correctness of which seems central to our notion of truth. Indeed it seems impossible for any instance of this schema to be false. After all, a claim ⌜A iff B⌝ can be false only if (i) A is true and B is false or (ii) A is false and B is true. Where A is ⌜'S' is true⌝ and B is S, these combinations cannot occur, for (i) if S is false, then the claim that it is true cannot be true and (ii) if S is true, then the claim that it is true cannot be false. But if no instance of the schema can be false, then (P1) cannot be false, and so, it would seem, (P1) cannot be denied.

Moreover, schema T seems to incorporate a linguistic rule essential to understanding the truth predicate. Suppose, for example, one were asked to explain the meaning of a truth predicate applying to English sentences to someone who already understood a lot of English but was not acquainted with the word *true* or any synonym for it. One could scarcely do better than to say something like the following: "The sentence 'Snow is white' is true iff snow is white, the sentence 'Bill Clinton was elected president in 1996' is true iff Bill Clinton was elected president in 1996, and so on for every English sentence." But if conveying the meaning of the truth predicate of English sentences involves conveying the acceptability of all instances of schema T, then it is hard to see how anyone competently employing the predicate could reject any such instance.

This, then, is the paradox. We have derived a contradiction from a pair of seemingly incontrovertible premises using apparently unassailable logical rules. Since we cannot accept a contradiction, we must reject either one of the premises or one of the rules. But it is hard to see how any of these could be incorrect.

It is important to emphasize that what we have so far is simply a puzzle, albeit a deep and interesting one. Nothing in the statement of the puzzle by itself constitutes an attack on the legitimacy or coherence of our ordinary notion of truth. Nevertheless, the intractability of the paradox could be used as the basis for such an attack. One line of reasoning to this effect might be put roughly as follows: The notion of truth, as we ordinarily understand it, requires all instances of schema T to be true. However, version 1 of the Liar paradox shows that this leads to contradiction. Therefore, the notion of truth, as we ordinarily understand it, is incoherent, and it is a defect of English that it contains such an incoherent predicate.

Something close to this line of reasoning is suggested in the following passage by the great semanticist, logician, and truth theorist, Alfred Tarski:

> A characteristic feature of colloquial language (in contrast to various scientific languages) is its universality. It would not be in harmony with the spirit of this language if in some other language a word occurred which could not be translated into it; it could be claimed that 'if we can speak meaningfully about anything at all, we can also speak about it in colloquial language'. If we are to maintain this universality of everyday language in connexion with semantical investigations, we must, to be consistent, admit into the language, in addition to its sentences and other expressions, also the names of these sentences and expressions, and sentences containing these names, as well as such semantic expressions as 'true sentence', 'name', 'denote', etc. But it is presumably just this universality of everyday language which is the primary source of all semantical antinomies, like the antinomies of the liar or of heterological words. These antinomies seem to provide a proof that every language which is uni-

versal in the above sense, and for which the normal laws of logic hold, must be inconsistent. This applies especially to the formulation of the antinomy of the liar which I have given . . . and which contains no quotation-function with variable argument. If we analyze this antinomy in the above formulation we reach the conviction that no consistent language can exist for which the usual laws of logic hold and which at the same time satisfies the following conditions: (I) for any sentence which occurs in the language a definite name of this sentence also belongs to the language; (II) every expression formed from (2) [*x is a true sentence iff p*] by replacing the symbol 'p' by any sentence of the language and the symbol 'x' by a name of this sentence is to be regarded as a true sentence of this language; (III) in the language in question an empirically established premise having the same meaning as (α) ['*c is not a true sentence' is identical with c*] can be formulated and accepted as a true sentence.

If these observations are correct, then the very possibility of a consistent use of the expression 'true sentence' which is in harmony with the laws of logic and the spirit of everyday language seems to be very questionable.[50]

Tarski's argument has the following structure:

A. Any language that satisfies certain conditions is inconsistent.
B. English and other natural languages satisfy these conditions.
C. Therefore English and other natural languages are inconsistent.

The conditions cited by Tarski are

0.   The usual laws of logic hold for the language.
0.5. The language contains a truth predicate applying to its own sentences.
I.   The language contains names of all its sentences.
II.   All instances of schema T are true sentences of the language.
III. An empirical premise analogous to (P2) in version 1 of the Liar is a true sentence of the language.

We may take it that conditions (0), (0.5), and (I) ensure the existence in the language of paradoxical sentences such as sentence (1). Let us assume that one of the things guaranteed by condition (0) is the existence of normal logical operators in the language, including ordinary (classical) negation. The combination of this plus (0.5) ensures the availability of a complex *untruth predicate* that applies to a sentence of the language iff it is not true. Finally, condition (I) should be construed liberally. If quote-names were the only way of referring to sentences in a language, then paradoxical sentences in the style of sentence (1) could not be constructed. However, this is not the situation envisioned by Tarski. Instead, he should be understood as assuming that sentences of the language are freely nameable or describable in the language, either by descriptions of the sort *sentence that occurs in such and such a place, is uttered at such and such a time by so-and-so*, and so on or by arbitrary names like *sentence (1)*. If these conditions are met, the language will contain paradoxical sentences analogous to sentence (1).

We may take this as the first assumption of a second version of the Liar paradox, reconstructable from Tarski's remarks.

A1. 'Sentence (1) is not true' is a sentence of English.

The second and third assumptions are given by Tarski's conditions (II) and (III).

A2. All instances of schema T are true in English.[51]
A3. The sentence *Sentence (1)* = '*Sentence (1) is not true*' is a true sentence of English.

The relationship between these assumptions and (P1) and (P2) of version 1 of the Liar should be clear. Instead of appealing to a specific instance, (P1), of schema T version 2 makes the metalinguistic claim that all instances of schema T are true. Since (A1) ensures that (P1) is such an instance, (A1) and (A2) together yield the metalinguistic result that the sentence (P1) is true. (A3) is just the claim that sentence (P2) is true. Thus version 2 of the Liar is a metalinguistic reformulation of version 1 based on the claim that the premises of version 1 are true sentences of English. Since these premises were used in version 1 to derive a contradiction, one would expect the assumptions in version 2 to be used to derive the metalinguistic conclusion that a contradictory sentence is true in English.

However, in order for Tarski's remarks about the inconsistency of natural languages to be reconstructable in this way, two additions to (A1)–(A3) are needed. Here I follow the sensible and insightful suggestions made by my former colleague Nathan Salmon.[52] The first thing we need is an interpretation of Tarski's condition (0) to the effect that the normal laws of logic hold for English. Salmon suggests that this be interpreted as asserting that all standard logically valid inferences are truth preserving in English. The idea is (i) that we can recognize in English certain expressions corresponding to logical operators in standard (classical) systems of logic; (ii) that because of this we can recognize certain sequences of English sentences as being instances of logically valid patterns of inference; and (iii) that if a sequence of English sentences $S_1, \ldots, S_n$ corresponds to the premises of a logically valid inference $P_1, \ldots, P_n$ / C and S_c is an English sentence that corresponds to C, then S_c will be true in English if $S_1, \ldots, S_n$ are. This is both a plausible suggestion of what it might mean to say that the normal laws of logic hold for English and an addition to (A1)–(A3) that is needed to derive the metalinguistic conclusion that the contradictory (C2) of version 1 of the paradox is a true sentence of English.

The final addition needed to complete our reconstruction of Tarski's remarks is some interpretation of his puzzling notion of an inconsistent language. On the face of it, it is far from clear what it could possibly mean to say that a language is inconsistent. Certainly the existence of inconsistent or contradictory sentences in the language is not sufficient. Any language with negation contains inconsistent sentences, and any language with both negation and conjunction contains contradictory sentences. However, far from being a defect, which inconsistency is supposed to be, having resources sufficient to allow the construction of inconsistent or contradictory sentences is a virtual prerequisite for a language to be rich enough to be of significant interest.

Salmon's suggestion is that Tarski's notion of an inconsistent language be understood as one in which some sentence and its negation are jointly true in the language and hence as a language in which at least one contradiction is a true sentence. This interpretation has the virtue of (i) making some sense of the application of the notion of inconsistency to a language while (ii) making Tarski's conclusion that natural languages are inconsistent follow from his premises.[53]

With this in mind, we can reconstruct Tarski's argument that English is inconsistent as follows:

Version 2 of the Liar
A1. Sentence (1) is a sentence of English.
A2. All instances of schema T are true in English.
A3. 'Sentence (1) = "Sentence (1) is not true" ' is true in English.
A4. The usual laws of logic hold in English—that is, all standard logically valid patterns of inference are truth preserving in English.
C1. ' "Sentence (1) is not true" is true iff sentence (1) is not true' is true in English. (From [A1], [A2], and the definition of what it is to be an instance of schema T)
C2. 'Sentence (1) is true iff sentence (1) is not true' is true in English. (From [C1], [A3], and [A4]'s guarantee of the truth-preserving character of the law, substitutivity of identity)
C3. 'Sentence (1) is true and sentence (1) is not true' is true in English. (From [C2] and [A4]: tautological consequence)
C4. 'Sentence (1) is true' is true in English and 'Sentence (1) is not true' is true in English. (From [C3] and [A4]: simplification of conjunction)
A5. 'Sentence (1) is not true' is a negation in English of 'Sentence (1) is true'.
Def. A language is inconsistent iff some sentence and its negation are both true in the language.
C5. English is inconsistent.

This metalinguistic version of the Liar parallels the earlier nonmetalinguistic version and, on the face of it, would seem to call for a similar response. In the case of version 1, we derived a contradiction. Since no one can rationally accept a contradiction, we must reject at least one premise or rule of inference used in the derivation. In the case of version 2, we did not derive a contradiction, but we did derive the conclusion that a contradiction is true. (In fact, since classically valid patterns of inference allow one to derive anything from a contradiction, we can also derive that s is true for every English sentence s.) However, this result seems no more acceptable than the result of version 1. Thus it seems that here too we must reject either a premise or a rule of inference. But this means that we cannot draw the conclusion that English is inconsistent or that the notion of truth it contains is incoherent. Rather than seeing the paradox as a source of truth skepticism, we should regard it as the impetus for replacing initially plausible but ultimately inaccurate assumptions about the truth predicate with an acceptable theory of how the predicate really works in the language.

However, this was not Tarski's attitude toward the metalinguistic version of the Liar. Whereas he clearly did not accept the premises, rules of inference, and conclusions of version 1 of the paradox, he apparently was willing to do so in the case of version 2.[54] Thus instead of rejecting paradox-creating assumptions about English and other natural-language truth predicates, he rejected the languages themselves as inadequate for the construction of serious theories of truth and proposed that they be replaced, for these purposes, by formalized languages for which restricted truth predicates could be defined in a way that made the construction of Liar-paradoxical sentences impossible.

Although Tarski is justly famous for his ground-breaking results on truth in formalized languages, his position regarding truth in English and other natural languages is very hard to accept. It is very hard to accept the claim that a contradictory sentence is true in English or that English contains a sentence and its negation that are jointly true, let alone the astounding conclusion that every English sentence is true. One reason these conclusions seem so unacceptable may be that our understanding of what we mean by *true* and *negation* is such that no sentence s' that is true when s is also true could possibly count as the negation of s. Another reason may have to do with the centrality of disquotation to our notion of truth. One of the most important and useful features of the truth predicate is its role in allowing one to pass from the metalinguistic ⌜'S' is true⌝ to the nonmetalinguistic S and vice versa. But one who says, in English, that a certain contradictory sentence of English is true can avoid contradicting oneself only if one denies this disquotational inference. The problem is that such a denial seems incoherent if the word 'true' is being used with its standard meaning.

It should be noted that this problem is not restricted to cases in which the inference involves a paradoxical example like sentence (1). Since Tarski's premises entail that all English sentences are true, one who accepts those premises can avoid explicitly contradicting oneself only if one also denies either (i) that 'Snow is white' is true in English iff snow is white or (ii) that 'Snow is not white' is true in English iff snow is not white or both (and so on for every pair of a sentence and its negation). In addition to being difficult to accept, such denials tend to undermine the rationale for the crucial assumption, (A2), that all instances of schema T are true. The pretheoretic intuition that instances of this schema are true is tied to the view that they are assertable. As a result, once assertability is rejected, the claim that instances of schema T are true loses its intuitive justification and the argument that English is inconsistent becomes untenable. Although the conclusion is not formally inconsistent, the argument is scarcely credible.

It is reasonable to suppose, then, that there must be other, more plausible diagnoses of what the Liar paradox shows about natural languages — diagnoses that involve rejecting one or more of the premises and rules of inference used in the paradoxical arguments. We will consider two such diagnoses in chapters 5 and 6. However, before we do, we need to examine Tarski's definition of truth for formalized languages and discuss its philosophical significance. This will be done in chapters 3 and 4. As we will see, Tarski insulates his definition from paradox by using a metalanguage M to specify a formal object-language L and then defining within M a restricted truth predicate T applying to sentences of L. Since L does not contain a truth predicate, no Liar-paradoxical sentences are constructable in it. Since any sentence S of M containing the predicate T is not a sentence of L, the truth predicate contained in S is not one that applies to S itself, and thus the sentence cannot be seen as asserting or denying its own truth. (The process can be repeated by defining a truth predicate for M in a "higher" metalanguage M' and so on ad infinitum.) Thus Liar-paradoxical sentences are excluded by Tarski's construction.

There is, then, no question about the coherence or legitimacy of restricted truth predicates of the sort defined by Tarski. Although the situation is less clear with our ordinary notion of truth, expressed in natural language, we have still found no basis for fundamental skepticism. In undermining Tarski's argument that English is inconsistent, we have eliminated a potentially significant rationale for regarding our ordinary notion of truth as incoherent. The price we pay for this reassurance is the recognition of our ignorance about certain fundamental principles involving that notion. No matter how plausible the assumptions made about truth in versions 1 and 2 of the Liar may seem, they are jointly incoherent and hence unacceptable. Thus the task of finding more accurate and acceptable principles remains.

Notes

1. Gottlob Frege, "Der Gedanke. Eine logische Untersuchung," in *Beitrage zur Philosophie des deutschen Idealismus* 1 (1918): 58–77, translated into English as "Thoughts" by P. Geach and R. H. Stoothoff in *Collected Papers on Mathematics, Logic, and Philosophy* ed. B. McGuinness (Oxford: Basil Blackwell, 1984), 351–72, reprinted in *Propositions and Attitudes*, ed. N. Salmon and S. Soames (New York: Oxford University Press, 1988), 33–55, at 36.

2. Ibid., 36, 37.

3. The most natural way to treat the expressions 'that—' and 'the proposition that—' is as intensional term-creating operators. To say they are intensional is to say that their extensions are functions from the intensions of their arguments to the extensions of the compound terms they form. In this view, expressions within the argument (i.e., in the complement sentence) retain their ordinary reference or extension, but the operator does not look at these extensions. The virtue of this way of treating these expressions is that it allows us to have what is often tendentiously called "semantic innocence" within a theory that is Fregean in spirit. This is important because, given semantic innocence, one can apply ordinary rules of coreference or anaphoric dependencies to interpret a pair of noun phrases, one of which is inside a *that* clause and the other of which is outside such a clause.

Although this is possible in a theory that is Fregean in spirit, such a theory does not conform to all aspects of Frege's stated views. In particular, he did not treat complement clauses in this way. For him, the expressions in a sentence occurring as the complement of a belief predicate, for example, do not, in that environment, refer to their customary referents; rather, they refer to their customary meanings or senses. This allows him to preserve the principle that the referent (extension) of a compound expression is always a function of the referents (extensions) of its parts, at the expense of construing the reference relation not as one that holds between expressions and the things they designate but as one that holds between occurrences of expressions (within other expressions) and the things designated. Although this view is one of the technical possibilities open to a theorist, it is not conceptually required by any proper conception of reference, extension, or compositionality or by Frege's basic distinction between sense and reference.

4. Frege suggests that S and ⌜It is true that S⌝ may express the very same thought. This is a suggestion I want to resist for reasons that will become clear later.

5. Frege, "Thoughts," 34, 35.

6. Ibid., 35; emphasis in original.

7. Unlike the other premises in this argument, (D) is a premise schema (each of whose instances may be used as a premise) rather than an independent statement in its own right. An instance is obtained by replacing occurrences of the schematic letter 'S' with occurrences of a declarative sentence of English. For example, one such instance is *To inquire (establish) whether Princeton is in New Jersey is to inquire (establish) whether it is true that Princeton is in New Jersey, which is to inquire (establish) whether the proposition that Princeton is in New Jersey is true.*

8. One premise worth calling attention to is (B). It sets a high standard for definition—namely, that an expression Y qualifies as a definiens for a definiendum X only if Y is substitutable for X without changing truth value in sentences generally, including propositional attitude constructions such as *Jones says (that), believes (that), wonders whether . . . X. . . .* Many philosophical analyses aim at providing necessary and sufficient conditions for the application of a concept without attempting to meet this higher standard implicit in premise (B). For present purposes, I will accept the standard and concentrate on independent difficulties in the argument.

9. This being said, one qualification needs to be added. There is a view, for which Frege gives an independent argument elsewhere, according to which truth is not a property at all and the sentences ⌜It is true that S⌝ and ⌜The thought (proposition) that S is true⌝ express the very same thought (proposition) as the sentence S. If this view is correct, then there is no property or concept of truth to be defined, and (D) is unproblematically correct. In fact, both this view and the argument for it are defective, as will be shown in "Nihilism about Truth" later in this chapter.

10. For example,

i.   'Firenze é una bella città' is true in Italian iff Florence is a beautiful city

and

ii.   'Florence is a beautiful city' is true in English iff Florence is a beautiful city

are instances of schema T for Italian and English, respectively. Each expresses a nontrivial a posteriori linguistic fact and so must be distinguished from an example like

iii.   Florence is a beautiful city iff Florence is a beautiful city,

which expresses a trivial a priori nonlinguistic fact and is *not* an instance of schema T.

11. Like (D), this is a premise schema each instance of which can be regarded as a premise. For example, one such instance is *To inquire whether scientists will find a cure for cancer is to inquire whether it is true that scientists will find a cure for cancer, which is to inquire whether (the English sentence) 'Scientists will find a cure for cancer' is true.*

12. To know that 'S' is true iff S is to know that which is expressed by the theorem in a truth-conditional theory of meaning for L that "gives the meaning of" 'S'. (It makes no difference whether the theorem has the form 'S' *is true iff* S or the form 'S' *is true iff P*

since both will express the same proposition when 'P' is a paraphrase of 'S'.) Believing the proposition expressed by this theorem is supposed to provide one with nontrivial, a posteriori information about meaning. By contrast, one can believe that S iff S without understanding 'S' at all (e.g., a speaker of Italian can believe that Florence is a beautiful city iff Florence is a beautiful city without having any idea what the English sentence 'Florence is a beautiful city' means). Since believing that S iff S provides one with no information about meaning, it cannot be sufficient for believing anything that does provide such information.

13. Here 's' is a bound variable rather than a schematic letter, and the entire statement is a premise rather than a premise schema.

14. In this sentence, 'S' is again being used as a schematic letter.

15. See Scott Soames, "Direct Reference, Propositional Attitudes, and Semantic Content," *Philosophical Topics* 15 (1987):47–87, reprinted in Salmon and Soames, *Propositions and Attitudes*, 197–239; "Direct Reference and Propositional Attitudes," in *Themes from Kaplan*, ed. J. Almog, J. Perry, and H. Wettstein (New York: Oxford University Press, 1989), 393–419; "Semantics and Semantic Competence," *Philosophical Perspectives* 3 (1989): 575–96; and "Truth, Meaning, and Understanding," *Philosophical Studies* 65 (1992): 17–35.

16. Hans Reichenbach, *Experience and Prediction* (Chicago: University of Chicago Press, 1938), 187–88; emphasis added. For Reichenbach, the theory of weight and the theory of probability are one and the same.

17. Here I use lowercase 'p' as a variable over propositions. This contrasts with the previous use of uppercase 'P' as a schematic sentential letter in expressions like *The proposition that P is true* and *It is true that P*.

18. I will say that a proposition q entails a proposition r iff it is impossible for q to be true without r being true.

19. This is not to say that it is never known at all.

20. In his classic article, "Truth and Confirmation," in *Readings in Philosophical Analysis*, ed. H. Feigl and W. Sellars (New York: Appleton-Century-Crofts, 1949), 119–27, Rudolph Carnap uses similar observations to distinguish Alfred Tarski's semantic conception of truth from certainty.

21. The counterpart of (*7) in first-order logic is

i. ($\exists$p)(p even though we cannot obtain sufficient evidence to show that p)

This too is ungrammatical since variables in first-order logic are restricted to singular terms and so cannot occupy the position of sentences. This restriction is relaxed in higher-order logic. (See n .22)

22. This fact about English and other natural languages is not shared by familiar artificial languages employed in symbolic logic. In such languages, quantifiers are treated as sentential operators and in some cases may be used to bind variables of different syntactic types, including sentences as well as singular terms. In such systems, there is no formal bar to quantifications of the sort illustrated by (i).

i. ($\exists$P)(P even though we cannot obtain sufficient evidence to show that P)

Later we will consider interpretations of such quantification and their bearing on issues in the theory of truth. For the present, it is sufficient to note that if quantification of this sort is legitimate, it can be used to characterize the dispute between realists and antirealists without using a truth predicate.

23. There is a technical complication here that may be worth noting. On the assumption that English contains a denumerable infinity of sentences, each of finite length, the number of propositions exceeds the number of English sentences. Consequently, an un-

derstanding of (8) in which the quantifier ranges over all propositions is one in which it goes beyond what is expressed by the sequence (a), (b), (c), and so on, if members of the sequence are restricted to sentences of English. However, this should not affect the philosophical point at issue—the sorts of propositions expressible in English are sufficient to express the dispute between realists and antirealists. If one wanted to close the potential gap between (8) and the sequence (a), (b), (c), and so on, one could either take the range of the quantifier phrase in (8) to be restricted to propositions expressed by English sentences or understand the *and so on* used in presenting the sequence to include possible additions to English as well as actual English sentences. One could also quantify over sentences instead of propositions, which would result in (i) rather than (8).

  i. Some sentence (of English) is true even though we cannot obtain sufficient evidence to show that it is true.

24. See Alonzo Church's review of the second edition of A. J. Ayer's *Language, Truth, and Logic* in *Journal of Symbolic Logic* 14 (1949): 52–53; and Carl G. Hempel's "Problems and Changes in the Empiricist Criterion of Meaning," *Revue Internationale de Philosophie* 4 (41–63), 1950, reprinted as "The Empiricist Criterion of Meaning" in *Logical Positivism*, ed. A. J. Ayer (Glencoe, Ill.: Free Press, 1959), 108–29.

25. Michael Dummett, *Elements of Intuitionism* (Oxford: Oxford University Press, 1977), 371–75; emphasis in original. Although Dummett's argument is specifically directed against realism in the philosophy of mathematics, he emphasizes that it is based on general considerations about meaning that apply across the board.

26. See John Burgess, "Dummett's Case for Intuitionism," *History and Philosophy of Logic* 5 (1984):177–94.

27. In *Truth and Other Enigmas* (Cambridge: Harvard University Press, 1978), xxi, Michael Dummett described what he took to be the status of truth-conditional theories among philosophers as follows: "The idea that a grasp of meaning consists in a grasp of truth-conditions was [in 1959], and still is, part of the received wisdom among philosophers."

28. Burgess stresses this point in "Dummett's Case for Intuitionism," in which he defends realism in mathematics while rejecting truth-conditional theories of meaning and understanding.

29. See the articles mentioned in note 15.

30. Often realists will accept all such instances, although this is stronger than what is needed. For example, in chapters 6 and 7, I will argue that there are meaningful but *indeterminate* sentences P such that ⌜Either P or Not P⌝ may be rejected (without threat to realism).

31. It presupposes that the theorist takes it to be possible to believe that, assert that, or inquire whether Q even though the theorist recognizes that it is unverifiable that Q. It should be noted that 'Q' in this formulation may stand in either for the sentence of English whose truth conditions are being stated or for a paraphrase of that sentence that expresses the same claim that it does.

32. The qualification in note 30 also applies here. The realist need not accept instances of (10) in which the sentence replacing P expresses an *indeterminate* object of potential belief, assertion, and so on.

33. Alfred Tarski, "Truth and Proof,"*Scientific American*, June 1969, 63–77, at 66.

34. The use of the unrestricted quantifier (over propositions) in (2) rather than the restricted quantifier in

  i. [For all p: Maria asserted p](p is true)

is intended solely to simplify the discussion. In my view, the quantifier in the English (1c) is restricted, even though the sentence as a whole may be treated as equivalent to (2). In what follows, I set aside the differences between restricted and unrestricted quantification in evaluating the redundancy theory.

There is, however, one potential difference worth noting. Restricted quantification is ubiquitous in English, as is illustrated by examples like

iia.   Every graduate student in the class will be disappointed.
  b.   Not every graduate student in the class will be disappointed.
iiia. Many graduate students in the class will be disappointed.
  b.   Not many graduate students in the class will be disappointed.

It has often been noted that all these sentences carry some sort of presumption that there are graduate students in the class (or at least one). One proposed analysis sees this presumption as a logical consequence of each of the sentences, even though the (b) sentences are negations of the (a) sentences. As a result, the analysis claims that there are "truth-value gaps." The negation of a sentence is taken to be true iff the sentence is false; a restricted quantification, for example, $[Qx:Fx](Gx)$, is said to be true iff there is at least one F and Q—all/ many/ . . . —of the F's are G; and it is said to be false iff there is at least one F and not Q—not all/ not many/ . . . —are G. In this proposal, the negation of a sentence S—for example, the negation of (iia) or (iiia)—is not always equivalent to the claim ⌜It is not true that S⌝ or ⌜That S is not true⌝ (since the latter claims may be true when S and its negation are not). It follows that if the proposition expressed by ⌜It is not true that S⌝ (⌜That S is not true⌝) is the negation of the proposition expressed by ⌜It is true that S⌝ (⌜That S is true⌝), then the proposition expressed by ⌜It is true that S⌝ (⌜That S is true⌝) is not identical with the proposition expressed by S. In general, redundancy theories of truth are incompatible with semantic analyses that give rise to "truth-value gaps" of this kind.

35. The primitiveness of the quantifier has nothing to do with the truth conditions it gives rise to. If it is a primitive substitutional quantifier, then sentences containing it will have the substitutional truth conditions sketched previously; if it is a primitive objectual quantifier, then sentences containing it will have the indicated objectual truth conditions. The fact that the quantification is not defined by the truth conditions is not necessarily an objection to the redundancy theory. For example, ordinary first-order objectual quantification is not defined by a statement of truth conditions either. It is not obvious—without further argument—that a similar status for other quantifiers is objectionable.

36. Or it must be a set of logical forms of English sentences.

37. There is also a purely "arithmetical" argument. If sentences of English are finitely long strings constructed from a finite vocabulary, then the totality of propositions will greatly exceed the denumerable infinity of English sentences.

38. It does not help if some of the objects unnamed in English are denoted by English descriptions since sentences containing descriptions do not express the same propositions as corresponding sentences containing proper names. How about demonstratives? Certainly it is sometimes true that we refer to individuals using English demonstratives like *this, that, he, she,* and so on even though we do not have any name for the individual. However, it is plausible to suppose that for a given context of utterance C and agent i, there will typically be many objects that are not demonstratively referred to in C and that i is not able to refer to demonstratively in C. If this is right, then an agent i might truly utter *Maria asserted some proposition* in C even though i had no means of expressing in C the proposition that Maria asserted because it directly concerned an object both unnamed in English and beyond i's demonstrative reach. (In a case like this, Maria may either have spoken another language or have demonstratively referred in English to something beyond i's demonstrative

reach in C.) Such a result would be sufficient to show that the quantification in *Maria asserted some proposition* is not substitutional in the standard sense.

39. According to this assumption, the proposition expressed by (12) at t is the temporally indexed proposition that Clinton is about to be elected president at t. This proposition does not change truth values over time even though sentence (12), which expresses it, expresses different propositions (with different truth values) at different times. Arguments for this assumption and developments of it can be found in Mark Richard, "Temporalism and Eternalism," *Philosophical Studies* 39 (1981): 1–13, and "Tense, Propositions, and Meanings," *Philosophical Studies* 41 (1982): 337–51; and Nathan Salmon, "Tense and Singular Propositions," in Almog, Perry, and Wettstein, *Themes from Kaplan*, 331–92. The assumption, which is part of the traditional view of propositions in philosophy, is also endorsed in Frege, "Thoughts," 53; G. E. Moore, "Facts and Propositions," in *Philosophical Papers* (New York: Collier, 1962), 60–88, at 71; and Richard Cartwright, "Propositions," in *Analytical Philosophy*, 1st ser., ed. R. J. Butler (Oxford: Basil Blackwell, 1962), 81–103, at 92–94.

40. See Salmon, "Tense and Singular Propositions," for further details.

41. In representing (15a), I have treated the *that* clause as semantically tenseless despite the fact that it contains the past tense form of the verb *to be*. A different alternative with equivalent semantic import would be to view the *that* clause as containing a semantic present tense operator, as in (i) or (ii).

i.   (On November 4, 1996 + Past)[Al believe that (Present)(Clinton be about to be elected)]
ii. (On November 4, 1996 + Past)[Al believe that (then + Present)(Clinton be about to be elected)]

The idea is to express the fact that the time at which Al held the belief was the same as the time he held the belief about (to the effect that Clinton was then about to be elected president). Since this is the interpretation of (15a) we are interested in, we cannot represent it as (18), for reasons discussed later in the text.

18. (On November 4, 1996 + Past)[(Al believe that (then + Past)(Clinton be about to be elected president)]

Examples like (15a) have often been analyzed by linguists as resulting from the operation of *sequence of tense* syntactic or morphological rules that require subordinate clauses to agree in morphological but not semantic tense with superordinate clauses. Another putative example of the same phenomenon is (iii).

iii. Last month I thought that I would spend my next sabbatical in California.
     (Last month + Past)[(I think that (Future)(I spend my next sabbatical in California)]

Here *would* is seen as a morphologically past tense version of *will*, agreeing with the past tense form in the matrix clause. As in the case of (15a), the result is a difference between the grammatical form of the subordinate clause and its semantic force.

42. This argument is an adaptation of the argument given in Richard, "Temporalism and Eternalism," for the conclusion that propositions are temporally indexed. See also Mark Richard, *Propositional Attitudes*, (New York: Cambridge University Press, 1990), chap. 2.

43. Similar problems are posed by the following examples:

i.   On October 10, the ambassador will tell the newspapers that his meeting on October 8 was a great success.

> (On October 10 + Future)[the ambassador tell the newspapers that (Past)(his meet-ing on October 8 be a great success)]

   ii.   The ambassador now believes everything he will tell the newspapers on October 10.

> (P)[if (on October 10 + Future)(the ambassador tell the newspapers P) then [now + Present)(the ambassador believe P)]

   iii.   The ambassador now believes that his meeting on October 8 was a great success.
(Now + Present)[the ambassador believe that (Past)(his meeting on October 8 be a great success)]

   iv.   The ambassador now believes that his meeting on October 8 will be a great success.
(Now + Present)[the ambassador believe that (Future)(his meeting on October 8 be a great success)]

If the context of utterance for these examples is October 9, the inference from (i) and (ii) to (iii) is acceptable. However, if the context of utterance is before October 8, the inference to (iii) must be blocked and the inference to (iv) allowed. A substitutional interpretation of the quantification in (ii) provides no apparent means of getting these results.

We could define a formal language with substitutional quantification in which these problems did not arise. However, the relevance of such an enterprise to the task of inter-preting English is highly dubious.

44. Gottlob Frege, "On Sense and Reference," in *Translations from the Philosophical Writings of Gottlob Frege*, ed. Peter Geach and Max Black (Oxford: Basil Blackwell, 1970), 56–78.

45. To handle apparent counterexamples—such as *George IV wondered whether Scott was the author of* Waverly and *George IV wondered whether Scott was Scott*—in which substitution of coreferential terms changes truth value, Frege appealed to his doctrine of indirect reference. According to the doctrine, a term that ordinarily refers to a person, for example, switches its reference and comes to refer, when embedded under a verb like *wonder*, to its ordinary sense or meaning. Since *Scott* and *the author of* Waverly have different ordinary senses, they are taken to have different referents in the sentences about George IV. As a result, the fact that substitution of one for the other in these sentences changes truth value was not seen by Frege as a refutation of the conjunction of his com-positional principle about reference with his characterization of truth values as referents of sentences.

46. Frege, "On Sense and Reference," 64.

47. For present purposes, I am ignoring restrictions needed to block the Liar and related paradoxes. Such restrictions are needed not only for (20) but also for examples like (4). Given appropriate restrictions, (20) will define a restricted notion of truth.

48. A similar case, discussed in a little more detail, is found in Soames, "Semantics and Semantic Competence."

49. Saul Krikpe, *Naming and Necessity* (Cambridge: Harvard University Press, 1980).

50. Alfred Tarski, "The Concept of Truth in Formalized Languages," in *Logic, Seman-tics, and Metamathematics*, 2d ed., ed. John Corcoran (Indianapolis, Ind.: Hackett, 1983), 152–278, at 164–65.

51. An instance is obtained by replacing the two occurrences of the letter 'S' in the schema with corresponding occurrences of any meaningful declarative sentence of English.

52. Salmon made these suggestions at my Princeton seminar on truth on April 2, 1981.

53. Another, well-known interpretation of Tarski's notion of an inconsistent language is also worth considering. According to it, an inconsistent language is to be understood as analogous to an inconsistent theory—that is, a theory with inconsistent theorems. The

difficulty with this view is that it seems to be merely a confusion to identify a language with a theory. Theories are true or false; languages are neither. Theories are defective if they contain both a sentence and its negation; languages are defective if they fail to contain any such pair. Theories contain specific sentences labeled as axioms; languages contain a multiplicity of sentences from which speakers are free to select any sentences they wish to play the role of axioms of theories expressible in the language.

Nevertheless, an analogy between theories and languages might be exploited in attempting to make sense of the notion of an inconsistent language. Theories are often spoken of, perhaps metaphorically, as asserting their theorems. By extension, we might regard them as asserting that their theorems are true. Languages, on the other hand, are often said to contain analytic sentences—that is, sentences true in virtue of meaning. Such sentences are sometimes said to be true in virtue of the semantic rules of the language. Given this, one might naturally describe an analytic sentence as one whose truth is required by the rules of the language and hence as a sentence whose truth is asserted by the language itself. An inconsistent language could then be characterized as one whose set of analytic sentences is inconsistent.

This interpretation of Tarski's contention that English and other natural languages are inconsistent was first presented by Hans Herzberger in "The Logical Consistency of Language," *Harvard Education Review* 35 (1965) (469–80). (Herzberger rejected the contention on the grounds that it is impossible for a set of truths to be inconsistent.) A related interpretation is endorsed by Tyler Burge in the following passage from "Semantical Paradox," *Journal of Philosophy* 76 (1979): 169–98, at 169–70: "The best ground for dissatisfaction [with Tarski] is that the notion of a natural language's harboring contradictions is based on an illegitimate assimilation of natural language to a semantical system. According to that assimilation, part of the nature of a 'language' is a set of postulates that purport to be true by virtue of their meaning or are at least partially constitutive of that 'language'. Tarski thought that he had identified just such postulates in natural language as spawning inconsistency. But postulates are contained in theories promoted by people. Natural languages, *per se*, do not postulate anything. What engenders paradox is a certain naive theory or conception of the natural concept of truth. It is the business of those interested in natural language to improve on it."

A point in favor of interpretations of Tarski along these lines is the fact that he sometimes did conflate languages and theories, indicating, for example, that in order to specify a language one must specify its axioms, rules of inference, and theorems. For example, see Tarski, "The Concept of Truth in Formalized Languages," section 2, 166; see also Alfred Tarski, "The Semantic Conception of Truth," *Philosophy and Phenomenological Research* 4 (1944): 341–75, reprinted in *Semantics and the Philosophy of Language*, ed. Leonard Linsky (Urbana: University of Illinois Press, 1952), 13–47, at sections 6–8, pp. 18–21. Thus Tarski's tendency to conflate languages and theories may have contributed to his readiness to regard the notion of an inconsistent language as clear and unproblematic.

Nevertheless, there is a fundamental problem with interpreting Tarski's conclusion that English is inconsistent as the claim that the set of sentences of English that are true in virtue of meaning is inconsistent. The problem is that Tarski's premises, given in the passage from "The Concept of Truth in Formalized Languages" quoted in the text, do not entail that the set of sentences of English that are true in virtue of meaning is inconsistent. Note that Tarski's condition (II) does not say instances of schema T are true in virtue of meaning; it just says they are true. Moreover, the empirical premise—(P2)—mentioned in condition (III) could not possibly be true in virtue of meaning. Thus the purported inconsistency reached as a consequence of these premises cannot be one involving truths in virtue of meaning.

However, it can be one involving truths of the language, as suggested by Salmon. Since any sentence that is true in virtue of meaning is true, the Salmon interpretation of the inconsistency claim can be seen as a consequence of the Herzberger interpretation, stripped of its problematic features.

Another possible interpretation of Tarski is one in which he views a language as a set of sentences plus instructions as to when the various sentences of the language are properly assertable. In this view, it is somehow built into the nature of English that certain sentences are assertable without proof, others are assertable only when derived by recognized rules of inference from sentences of the first sort, and still others are assertable only when empirical and perhaps observable conditions obtain. (See in particular Tarski, "The Semantic Conception of Truth," section 6.) In this interpretation, the rules of English dictate that each instance of schema T is assertable and perhaps also that (P2) is assertable, given observable facts about sentence (1). (See Tarski, "The Semantic Conception of Truth," section 8, p. 20.) The language could then be considered inconsistent on the grounds that it sanctions the assertion of inconsistent sentences.

This interpretation of Tarski will yield significantly different results from the ones suggested by Herzberger and Salmon only if it is maintained that the rules of a language can dictate the assertability of a sentence that is not true in the language. But how could that be? It is hard to imagine that it should be a condition of my speaking English that I be willing to assert things that are not true. Moreover, Tarski nowhere explicitly states that a language can dictate the assertability of a sentence that is not true. In fact, his formulations of the conditions under which languages are supposed to be inconsistent indicates that he thinks the opposite. As we have noted, in Tarski, "The Concept of Truth in Formalized Languages," the premises leading to inconsistency assert that instances of schema T, including (P1), are *true* and that an empirical premise, such as (P2), is also *true*. Essentially the same argument is given in Tarski, "The Semantic Conception of Truth," section 8, except there the premises leading to inconsistency include the claims (i) that "all sentences which determine the adequate usage of [*true*]," by which Tarski means all instances of schema T, "can be *asserted* in the language" (20) and (ii) that an empirical premise such as (P2) is *assertable* in the language. Tarski's apparent willingness to regard these two formulations as equivalent versions of the same argument indicates that he did not distinguish between truth in a language and assertability in a language in a way that would give rise to an interpretation significantly different from those of Herzberger and Salmon.

Finally, no matter what Tarski may actually have had in mind, it seems to me that the rules of English do not dictate that English speakers accept the premises and rules of inference used in the Liar paradox to derive a contradiction. Whether or not it is *correct* to reject (P1) or the claim that either sentence (1) is true or sentence (1) is not true, one *can* reject them while still speaking English.

54. In "The Semantic Conception of Truth," Tarski has this to say about version 1 of the paradox: "In my judgment, it would be quite wrong and dangerous from the standpoint of scientific progress to depreciate the importance of this and other antinomies, and to treat them as jokes or sophistries. It is a fact that we are here in the presence of an absurdity, that we have been compelled to assert a false sentence (since (3) ['S' *is true iff* 'S' *is not true*] as an equivalence between two contradictory sentences, is necessarily false). If we take our work seriously, we cannot be reconciled with this fact. We must discover its cause, that is to say, we must analyze premises upon which the antinomy is based; we must then reject at least one of these premises, and we must investigate the consequences which this has for the whole domain of our research" (20).

Two Theories of Truth

THREE

Tarski's Definition
of Truth

Tarski's Strategy

As we have seen, Tarski took the Liar paradox to show that ordinary truth predicates occurring in natural language are incoherent and hence that no coherent definitions of such predicates are possible.[1] In his view, the source of the paradox is the universality of natural languages and the unrestricted semantic predicates they contain. The universality of natural languages ensures that they contain predicates like *true, refers to,* and *denotes,* as well as a rich system of naming or otherwise talking about their own expressions. The unrestrictedness of these ordinary semantic predicates makes them capable of applying to expressions containing the predicates themselves and hence gives rise to the Liar paradox. To avoid the paradox, Tarski proposed that we construct tightly circumscribed nonuniversal languages and replace our ordinary unrestricted semantic predicates with carefully restricted substitutes whose application is limited to the sentences and expressions of those languages.

For example, suppose that L is a language that contains no semantic predicates and no means of explicitly referring to (or quantifying over) its own expressions. (Suppose also that it contains no indexicals or other context-sensitive expressions whose content varies from one context of utterance to another.) Let M be a richer language that contains L as a subpart plus the means of studying L. In particular,

M contains the conceptual resources needed to refer to (and quantify over) (i) expressions and sets of expressions (including sentences) of L and (ii) arbitrary sets of n-tuples of the objects about which the sentences of L make claims. Given an *object-language* L and a *metalanguage* M related in this way, Tarski showed how to construct a definition *in* M of a predicate T that applies to all and only the true sentences *of* L. Since the truth predicate T is part of M but not L, no sentence containing it is one to which it applies. Thus no Liar-paradoxical sentences are constructible in either M or L.

Prior to presenting his definition, Tarski laid down certain characteristics that it and the truth predicate it introduces ought to have. His most important requirement involves the disquotational character of the predicate. Suppose, for example, that 'Snow is white' is a sentence of L, with the meaning that it has in English — namely, that snow is white. If T is a truth predicate for L, then (1) should be assertable (and true) in M.

1.   'Snow is white' is T in L iff snow is white.

More generally, if T is a truth predicate for L, then all instances of schema T must be assertable (and true) in M, where instances are obtained by replacing the letter 'X' in the schema with a name of a sentence of L and the letter 'P' either with that same sentence or with a paraphrase of it.[2]

Schema T.   X is T in L iff P.

In fact, Tarski regarded the truth and assertability of all instances of schema T to be not merely a necessary condition for T to be a truth predicate for L but a sufficient condition as well. The reason for this may be illustrated by appealing to another, closely related schema.[3]

Schema TM.   If X means in L that P, then X is true in L iff P.

This schema states an obvious connection between our ordinary notions of truth and meaning. Anyone who understands *true*, *means*, and the other expressions in the schema is in a position to recognize its correctness. Now notice that for each genuine instance of schema T (in which 'P' is replaced by a sentence that is a paraphrase of and hence means the same thing as the sentence of L whose name replaces 'X'), there is a corresponding instance of schema TM with a true (and assertable) antecedent. Thus for each instance of schema T, we have both ⌜X is T in L iff P⌝ and ⌜X is true in L iff P⌝ and hence ⌜X is T in L iff X is true in L⌝. Since any predicate T for which all instances of schema T hold is a predicate that applies to a sentence *s* of L iff *s* is true in L, Tarski was willing to characterize any such predicate as a truth predicate for L.

The importance of schema T for Tarski is further illustrated by his characterization of individual instances like (1) as "partial definitions" of truth. In "Truth and Proof," he puts this as follows:

Thus (1) ['*Snow is white*' *is true iff snow is white*] and (1') ['*Snow is white*' *is false iff snow is not white*] provide satisfactory explanations of the meaning of the terms 'true' and 'false' when these terms are referred to the sentence 'snow is white'. We can regard (1) and (1') as partial definitions of the terms 'true' and 'false', in fact, as definitions of these terms with respect to a particular sentence.[4]

This characterization of individual instances of schema T has consequences for more general definitions of truth. If such instances are thought of as partial definitions, then the task of defining truth for an entire language may be seen as that of finding a way of generalizing the "partial definitions" so as to cover every sentence of the language.

Tarski expressed this idea by requiring that a definition of truth for L must logically entail an instance of schema T for each sentence of L. Any proposed definition of truth satisfying this condition is said to be *materially adequate*. If, in addition, it is *formally correct*—that is, if it satisfies the usual formal rules for constructing definitions—then Tarski would regard it as a satisfactory definition of truth. Finally, since other semantic terms, such as *refers to, denotes, applies to,* and so on, raise problems similar to those involving truth, Tarski was interested in definitions that did not employ any undefined semantic terms. He noted that if this condition is satisfied, then the definition of truth "will fulfill what we intuitively expect from every definition; that is it will explain the meaning of the term being defined in terms whose meaning appears to be completely clear and unequivocal. And, moreover, we have then a kind of guarantee that the use of semantic concepts will not involve us in any contradictions."[5]

Tarski's problem, then, was to find a way to generalize the "partial definitions of truth" provided by instances of schema T, without appealing to undefined semantic primitives, in a way that would satisfy his conditions of material adequacy and formal correctness. As he points out, in the special case in which the object-language has only finitely many sentences, the problem has a trivial solution.[6] For example, let L be the fragment of English consisting of the following 100 sentences:

1 is an even number.
2 is an even number.

> .
> .
> .

100 is an even number.

A definition of truth for L satisfying Tarski's requirements can be constructed as follows:

2. For all sentences s of L, s is true in L iff either
     s = '1 is an even number', and 1 is an even number, or
     s = '2 is an even number', and 2 is an even number, or

.
.

. , or
s = '100 is an even number', and 100 is an even number.

Although Tarski regards this sort of definition as perfectly satisfactory, he notes that it can be given only in the rather artificial case in which a definite, finite number of specifiable sentences exhausts an entire language. Since this condition is typically not met by the languages for which we would like to have truth definitions, some other method of generalizing the "partial definitions" provided by schema T is needed.

One method that might initially seem attractive involves replacing the two occurrences of 'Snow is white' in (1) with a sentential variable bound by a universal quantifier.

   3.   For all S, 'S' is true in L iff S.

One minor problem that Tarski finds with this proposal is that it does not have the proper form, as in

   4.   For all sentences x of L, x is true in L iff . . . ,

of a general definition of truth. Whereas a definition of the form (4) specifies the conditions under which the predicate *is true* will apply to a sentence, no matter how that sentence is designated, (3) deals explicitly only with cases in which the predicate is combined with a quote-name. However, as Tarski notes, if each sentence of L has a quotation-mark name in M, then this difficulty can easily be remedied by reformulating (3) as (5).[7]

   5.   For all sentences x of L, x is true in L iff for some S, x = 'S' and S.

Tarski's real objection to both (3) and (5) is that they embody an erroneous conception of the interaction of quotation and quantification. It is important in this connection to distinguish the two different kinds of quantificational variables that occur in these formulas. The variable 'x' in (5) is a first-order objectual variable that is associated with a range of objects—the sentences of L—about which the sentence as a whole makes claims. In constructing an instance of (5), one erases the quantifier *for all sentences x of L* and replaces the remaining (free) occurrences of 'x' with a name of one of the objects in its range. By contrast, the variable 'S' in (3) and (5) is a higher-order substitutional variable. Instead of being associated with a range of objects, a substitutional variable is associated with a substitution class of expressions—in this case, the set of sentences of L. A substitutionally quantified formula is not about the expressions in its substitution class, and an instance of such a formula is obtained by erasing the quantifier and directly substituting a member of the substitution class (rather than the name of a member) for remaining (free) occurrences of the substitutional variable.

Tarski's objection to (3) and (5) is an objection to quantification into quotation-mark names. According to him, a quote-name is a syntactically simple term that names whatever expression occurs within the quotation marks — no matter whether that expression is a name, variable, sentence, or sequence of unrelated symbols. In this conception, there is no bindable occurrence of the variable 'S' in the quotation-mark name " 'S' " any more than there is such an occurrence in the word 'snow'. Thus (3) is materially equivalent to (3'), one of whose instances is (1').

3'.   For all S, the 19th letter of the alphabet is true in L iff S.
1'.   The 19th letter of the alphabet is true in L iff snow is white.

Since no letter of the alphabet is a true sentence of L, these claims are obviously false. Analogous remarks apply to (5). Thus Tarski concluded that one cannot construct truth definitions by generalizing individual instances of schema T along the lines of (3) and (5).[8]

Faced with this result, Tarski turned to a different method to achieve the desired definition. Roughly put, his strategy was to formulate a definition that applies to the simplest sentences of L and then to extend it to the remaining sentences of L by specifying principles that assign truth values to compound sentences on the basis of the truth values of their parts. This strategy is illustrated in the following two sections.[9]

A Simple Tarskian Truth Definition

The first step in giving a truth definition is to give a precise specification of the object-language L for which truth is to be defined. We will restrict our attention to languages of the first-order predicate calculus. To characterize such a language, one needs to specify its logical and nonlogical vocabulary plus the rules for constructing compound expressions — terms, formulas, and sentences — from simpler expressions of the language. The general form of such a characterization is as follows:[10]

Vocabulary
   Nonlogical vocabulary:
      a.   A finite number of predicates, with an indication for each as to whether it is a one-place predicate, a two-place predicate, and so on
      b.   A finite number of function symbols, with an indication for each as to whether it is one-place, two-place, and so on
      c.   A finite number of names
   Logical symbols:[11]
      '&' (and), '~' (not), '∃', plus infinitely many variables 'x_1', 'x_2', and so on; for any variable v_i, $\ulcorner \exists v_i \urcorner$ is a quantifier (meaning 'there is at least one')

Terms
  a.   Names and variables are terms.
  b.   If $t_1, \ldots, t_n$ are terms and f is an n-place function symbol, then the result of combining f with $t_1, \ldots t_n$ is a term.[12]
  c.   Nothing else is a term.

Formulas
  a.   The combination of an n-place predicate with n terms is an atomic formula.[13]
  b.   If A and B are formulas, so are $\ulcorner(\sim A)\urcorner$ and $\ulcorner(A \ \& \ B)\urcorner$.
  c.   If A is any formula and v_i is any variable, then $\ulcorner(\exists v_i \ A)\urcorner$ is a formula.
  d.   Nothing else is a formula.

Sentences
  a.   A sentence is a formula containing no free occurrences of any variable.
  b.   An occurrence of a variable v_i in a formula A is free in A iff it is not within the scope of any occurrence in A of a quantifier using v_i.
  c.   The scope of an occurrence of a quantifier is the quantifier itself plus the (smallest complete) formula immediately following it.

Let the *language of arithmetic* be the language of this type whose nonlogical vocabulary consists of (i) a single two-place predicate '='; (ii) a single name '0'; (iii) a single one-place function symbol 'S'; and (iv) a pair of two-place function symbols '+' and '*'. We will understand the quantifiers of the language as ranging over the natural numbers; '=' as standing for the identity relation; '0' as naming the number zero; 'S' as standing for the function that assigns to each natural number its successor; '+' as standing for the addition function on natural numbers; and '*' as standing for the multiplication function.
   The first step in defining truth for this language is to define denotation for variable-free terms and application for predicates.

  1.   *The Denotation of a Variable-Free Term*
       A variable-free term α denotes a number n iff (i) α is the symbol '0' and n is the number zero; (ii) α is the term $\ulcorner S(\beta)\urcorner$ for some term β and n is the successor of the number denoted by β; (iii) α is the term $\ulcorner(\gamma + \delta)\urcorner$ for some terms γ and δ and n is the sum of the numbers denoted by γ and δ; or (iv) α is the term $\ulcorner(\gamma * \delta)\urcorner$ for some terms γ and δ and n is the product of the numbers denoted by γ and δ.
  2.   *The Application of a Predicate*
       A two-place predicate P applies to a pair of numbers <n, m> iff P is the symbol '=' and m is the same number as n.

In the case of predicates, the definition is a simple stipulation. In the case of variable-free terms, it is an inductive definition that first stipulates the denotation of the simplest variable-free term and then indicates how the denotation of each compound term is determined by the denotations of the simpler terms from which it is constructed. The end result is a definition that fixes the denotation of every variable-free term in the language.

The next step is to use the notions of denotation and application to define truth in the language. Again the definition is inductive, with an initial clause defining truth for atomic sentences followed by clauses assigning truth values to complex sentences on the basis of the truth values of simpler sentences.

3. *Inductive Definition of Truth for the Language of Arithmetic*
    a. An atomic sentence $\ulcorner\alpha = \beta\urcorner$ is true iff '=' applies to the pair of numbers $<n, m>$ denoted by α and β, respectively.
    b. A sentence $\ulcorner(\sim A)\urcorner$ is true iff A is not true.
    c. A sentence $\ulcorner(A\ \&\ B)\urcorner$ is true iff A is true and B is true.
    d. A sentence $\ulcorner(\exists v_i\ A)\urcorner$ is true iff there is some true sentence $A(\alpha)$ that arises from $\ulcorner(\exists v_i\ A)\urcorner$ by erasing $\ulcorner\exists v_i\urcorner$ and replacing all free occurrences of v_i in A with occurrences of some variable-free term α.

The material adequacy of this definition may be illustrated by (informally) deriving a representative instance of schema T from it.

A. '$\sim(\exists x_1\ (S(S(0))\ *\ x_1) = S(S(S(0))))$' is true iff '$(\exists x_1\ (S(S(0))\ *\ x_1) = S(S(S(0))))$' is not true. (From [3b])

B. '$(\exists x_1\ (S(S(0))\ *\ x_1) = S(S(S(0))))$' is true iff $\ulcorner(S(S(0))\ *\ \alpha) = S(S(S(0)))\urcorner$ is true for some variable-free term α. (From [3d])

C. $\ulcorner(S(S(0))\ *\ \alpha) = S(S(S(0)))\urcorner$ is true iff '=' applies to the pair of numbers $<n, m>$ denoted by $\ulcorner(S(S(0))\ *\ \alpha)\urcorner$ and '$S(S(S(0)))$', respectively. (From [3a])

D. $\ulcorner(S(S(0))\ *\ \alpha) = S(S(S(0)))\urcorner$ is true iff the number denoted by '$S(S(S(0)))$' is the same as the number denoted by $\ulcorner(S(S(0))\ *\ \alpha).\urcorner$ (From [C] and [2])

E. $\ulcorner(S(S(0))\ *\ \alpha) = S(S(S(0)))\urcorner$ is true iff the successor of the successor of the successor of zero is the same as the number denoted by $\ulcorner(S(S(0))\ *\ \alpha)\urcorner$—that is, iff $\ulcorner(S(S(0))\ *\ \alpha)\urcorner$ denotes the number 3. (From [D] plus clauses [i] and [ii] of [1])

F. $\ulcorner(S(S(0))\ *\ \alpha) = S(S(S(0)))\urcorner$ is true iff the product of the successor of the successor of zero and the denotation of α is the number 3—that is, iff 2 times the denotation of α is 3. (From [E] and clauses [i], [ii], and [iv] of [1])

G. '$(\exists x_1\ (S(S(0))\ *\ x_1) = S(S(S(0))))$' is true iff there is a term α such that 2 times the denotation of α is 3. (From [B] and [F])

H. '$(\exists x_1\ (S(S(0))\ *\ x_1) = S(S(S(0))))$' is true iff there is a natural number n such that 2 times n is 3. (From [G] plus the fact that every natural number n is denoted by some term of L)

I. '$\sim(\exists x_1\ (S(S(0))\ *\ x_1) = S(S(S(0))))$' is true iff there is no natural number n such that 2 times n is 3. (From [A] and [H])

Since the metalanguage sentence on the right-hand side of 'iff' in (I) may be regarded as a paraphrase of the object-language sentence on the left, (I) qualifies as an instance of schema T. A similar derivation can be provided for each object-language sentence. Thus the definition of truth is materially adequate.

It will be noticed that although the definition fixes the truth value of each sentence of the language, it does not have the form of (4),

4. For all sentences s of L, s is true in L iff . . . ,

that Tarski requires of a formally correct definition of truth. Instead of being a universally quantified biconditional in which the formula on the right-hand side of the connective 'iff' is an expression that defines the notion of being a true sentence of L, the "inductive definition" given above is a set of four axioms that fixes the extension of 'true' without providing an equivalent expression that can be substituted for it.

Nevertheless, it is a simple matter to convert the inductive definition to an explicit definition of the required form.

5. *Explicit Definition of Truth for the Language of Arithmetic*
    For all sentences s of the language L_A of arithmetic, s is true in L_A iff there is a set T_{LA} such that s is a member of T_{LA} and for all sentences z of L_A, z is a member of T_{LA} iff (i) z is an atomic sentence $\ulcorner \alpha = \beta \urcorner$ and '=' applies to the pair of numbers $<n, m>$ denoted by α and β, respectively; (ii) z is the sentence $\ulcorner (\sim A) \urcorner$ for some sentence A of L_A, and A is not a member of T_{LA}; (iii) z is the sentence $\ulcorner (A \& B) \urcorner$ for some sentences A and B of L_A, both of which are members of T_{LA}; or (iv) z is the sentence $\ulcorner (\exists v_i A) \urcorner$ for some variable v_i and formula A of L_A and there is some sentence $A(\alpha)$ of L_A that is a member of T_{LA} and that arises from $\ulcorner (\exists v_i A) \urcorner$ by erasing $\ulcorner \exists v_i \urcorner$ and replacing all free occurrences of v_i in A with occurrences of a variable-free term α.

This definition is both formally correct and materially adequate. It does, however, contain semantic terms — *denotes* and *applies to* — and so one might wonder whether it meets Tarski's goal of defining truth without the use of any undefined semantic terms. We have already given what amounts to an explicit definition of what it is for the one and only predicate of L_A to apply to something, plus an inductive definition of denotation for variable-free terms. All that remains is to convert that inductive definition to an explicit definition.

6. *Explicit Definition of the Denotation of a Variable-Free Term*
    For all variable-free terms α of the language L_A of arithmetic and natural numbers n, α denotes n in L_A iff there is a set D_{LA} of which $<\alpha, n>$ is a member and for all x and y $<x, y>$ is a member of D_{LA} iff (i) x is the symbol '0' and y is the number zero; (ii) x is the variable-free term $\ulcorner S(\beta) \urcorner$ for some term β and y is the successor of a number m such that $<\beta, m>$ is a member of D_{LA}; (iii) x is the variable-free term $\ulcorner (\gamma + \delta) \urcorner$ for some terms γ and δ and y is the sum of numbers m and o such that $<\gamma, m>$ and $<\delta, o>$ are members of D_{LA}; or (iv) x is the variable-free term $\ulcorner (\gamma * \delta) \urcorner$

for some terms γ and δ and y is the product of numbers m and o such that $<\gamma, m>$ and $<\delta, o>$ are members of D_{LA}.

Tarski regarded such definitions as making it theoretically possible to reduce the semantic notions of denotation and truth in L to nonsemantic notions. To eliminate 'true' from the metalanguage in favor of a nonsemantic definiens, one simply proceeds as follows: Start with the right-hand side of the definition, (5), of truth—*there is a set T_{LA} such that s is a member of T_{LA} and for all sentences z of L_A,*. . . . Next rewrite clause (i) in that expression as *z is an atomic sentence $\ulcorner \alpha = \beta \urcorner$, α denotes a number n, β denotes a number m, and '=' applies to the pair of numbers $<n, m>$*. Then substitute for α *denotes a number n* the right-hand side of (6)—*there is a set D_{LA} of which $<\alpha, n>$ is a member and for all x and y,*. . . . Next perform a similar operation on β *denotes a number m* (with appropriate relettering of variables in [6]). Finally, substitute '=' *is the symbol '=' and m is the same number as n* for '=' *applies to the pair of numbers $<n, m>$*, on the basis of (2). The end result is a Tarskian truth predicate for L_A that applies to precisely the truths of L_A, even though it contains no semantic terms.

Tarskian Truth Definitions: The General Case

The method employed in defining truth for the language of arithmetic was first to characterize what it is for an atomic sentence to be true, and then to define the truth of complex sentences in terms of the truth values of simpler sentences. Although this method is perfectly adequate for the language of arithmetic, it is insufficiently general, since it cannot be applied to languages that lack variable-free terms for some of the objects they are used to talk about. If L is such a language, we cannot in general characterize a sentence $\ulcorner (\exists v_i A) \urcorner$ of L as true iff some sentence A(t) is true that results from erasing the quantifier and substituting a variable-free term t for free occurrences of v_i. Intuitively, the problem is this: The sentence $\ulcorner (\exists v_i A) \urcorner$ "says that" there is at least one object that has the characteristics expressed by A. However, this may be true even if none of those objects are denoted by variable-free terms of L. Thus, Tarski had to find some other way of characterizing what it means for a sentence $\ulcorner (\exists v_i A) \urcorner$ to be true.

The natural solution to this problem is to introduce a mechanism that allows variables to serve as temporary names of objects. One can then say that $\ulcorner (\exists v_i A) \urcorner$ is true iff there is an object o such that the formula $A(v_i)$ that results from erasing the quantifier is true when v_i is treated as a name of o—that is, $\ulcorner (\exists v_i A) \urcorner$ is true iff there is an object o such that $A(v_i)$ is true relative to an assignment of o as the denotation of v_i. This was essentially Tarski's strategy, though not his terminology. Instead of talking about "an assignment of objects to variables," Tarski spoke of ordered "sequences of objects"; and instead of characterizing formulas as being "true relative to a sequence," he spoke of "a sequence satisfying a formula." However Tarski's sequences are designed solely to provide assignments of objects to variables, and the relation of satisfaction holding between sequences and formulas is just the converse of the relation of truth-relative-to holding between a formula and a sequence—that is, a sequence satisfies a formula iff the formula is true relative to the sequence.

Tarski's notion of a sequence can be thought of as follows: Let D be the class of objects that sentences of L are used to talk about (the domain of L). A sequence is an infinite arrangement of objects from D.[14] In effect, it amounts to a (totally defined) function that assigns each positive integer exactly one object from D. The ith member of a sequence is simply the object that is assigned to the integer i. There is no requirement that every element of D occur in every sequence and there is no limit on the number of times a single element of D can occur in a sequence—that is, if Q is an individual sequence and o is a particular object, Q may assign o to no integers, to every integer, or to any combination of integers. Since the variables of L can be arranged in a fixed, infinite list, each sequence can be seen as assigning each variable an object as value. The object a sequence assigns to the ith variable is just the object it assigns to the integer i—in other words, the ith member of the sequence.

With this means of providing variables with denotations relative to sequences we can define what it is for a formula to be true relative to a sequence using the same technique that allowed us to define the truth of sentences of the language of arithmetic. Whereas before we defined truth for *atomic sentences*, and then extended the definition by characterizing the truth (or untruth) of *complex sentences* in terms of the truth (or untruth) of simpler *sentences*, this time we define truth relative to a sequence for *atomic formulas*, and extend the definition by characterizing the truth (or untruth) of *complex formulas* relative to sequences in terms of the truth (or untruth) of simpler *formulas* relative to sequences.

As before, we begin with denotation—this time relativized to sequences.

1. *Inductive Definition of the Denotation of a Term relative a Sequence*
    a. For all i, the ith variable v_i of L denotes an object o relative to a sequence Q iff o is the ith member of Q.
    b. A name n in L denotes an object o relative to a sequence Q iff
        i.   n is the name 'a' and o is Alfred; or
        ii. n is the name 'b' and o is Brian; or
             (and so on, stipulating the denotation of each name in L).
    c. A term $\ulcorner f(\beta) \urcorner$ consisting of a one-place function symbol f and a term β denotes an object o relative to a sequence Q iff
        i.   f is the symbol 'm' and o is the mother of the denotation of β relative to Q; or
        ii. f is the symbol 'g' and o is the father of the denotation of β relative Q; or (and so on for each one-place function symbol of L)
    d. Similar clauses for arbitrary n-place function signs until all the function symbols in L are exhausted.

The relativization of denotation to sequences affects variables and complex terms containing variables, but not names. Clause (b) of the definition ensures that the denotation of a name is fixed independently of sequences, and so does not change from one to another. The only reason for mentioning sequences in connection with names is to have a single concept—the denotation of a term relative to a sequence—that applies to terms of all types.

The definition of application for predicates proceeds exactly as before, with a stipulation for each predicate in the language.

2. *The Application of Predicates*
    a. A one-place predicate P applies to an object o iff
        i.   P is the symbol 'F' and o is female; or
        ii. P is the symbol 'M' and o is male;
             (and so on for each one-place predicate in the language)
    b. A two-place predicate P applies to a pair of objects $<o, o'>$ iff
        i.   P is the symbol 'L' and o loves o'; or
             (and so on for each two-place predicate in the language)
    c. Similar stipulations for arbitrary n-place predicates of L.

The notions of application and denotation relative to a sequence can now be used to define truth relative to a sequence.

3. *Inductive Definition of Truth Relative to a Sequence*
    a. An atomic formula ⌜$P(\alpha, \ldots, \delta)$⌝ consisting of an *n*-place predicate followed by n terms is true relative to a sequence Q iff P applies to the *n*-tuple of objects $<o_\alpha, \ldots, o_\delta>$ denoted relative to Q by $\alpha, \ldots,$ δ, respectively.
    b. A formula ⌜$(\sim A)$⌝ is true relative to a sequence Q iff A is not true relative to Q.
    c. A formula ⌜$(A \& B)$⌝ is true relative to a sequence Q iff A is true relative to Q and B is true relative to Q.
    d. A formula ⌜$(\exists v_i A)$⌝ is true relative to a sequence Q iff there is a sequence Q* that differs from Q at most in the ith place and the formula $A(v_i)$ which arises from ⌜$(\exists v_i A)$⌝ by erasing ⌜$\exists v_i$⌝ is true relative to Q*.

Next we must define the unrelativized notion of truth applying to *sentences* of L in terms of the notion of a *formula* of L being true relative to a sequence. We have two choices. We could say that a sentence of L is true iff it is true relative to some sequence; or we could say that a sentence of L is true iff it is true relative to all sequences. In fact, it makes no difference which of these we select since a *sentence* of L is true relative to one sequence iff it is true relative to all sequences.

This can be shown by verifying the commonsensical point that the only denotations assigned by a sequence that are relevant to determining whether a formula is true relative to the sequence are denotations of variables that have free occurrences in the formula. This thesis is expressed by (4).

4. If a formula of F of L is true (not true) relative to a sequence Q, then F is true (not true) relative to all sequences that differ from Q at most in what they assign variables that do not have free occurrences in F.

Since sentences have no free occurrences of variables, it follows from (4) that a sentence is true relative to one sequence iff it is true relative to all sequences.

Thesis (4) can be established by simple induction on the complexity of formulas. (Let atomic formulas have complexity 0, $\ulcorner(\sim A)\urcorner$ and $\ulcorner(\exists v_i A)\urcorner$ have the complexity 1 + the complexity of A, and let $\ulcorner(A \& B)\urcorner$ have the complexity 1 + the complexity of its most complex conjunct.) The truth of thesis (4) is transparent for atomic formulas. Suppose now that it holds for all formulas of complexity less than or equal to n, and that F is a formula of complexity n + 1. If F is the formula $\ulcorner(\sim A)\urcorner$, or $\ulcorner(A \& B)\urcorner$, then the thesis holds for F, since, by supposition, it holds for A and B. If F is the formula $\ulcorner(\exists v_i A)\urcorner$, and F is true relative to a sequence Q, then there is a sequence Q^* that differs from Q at most in the ith place such that A is true relative to Q^*. By supposition, it follows that A is true relative to all sequences $Q^{*\prime}$ that agree with Q^* on assignments to variables (including v_i) free in A. Now let Q' be any sequence that agrees with Q in what it assigns variables free in F. For each such Q' there will be a $Q^{*\prime}$ that differs from Q' at most in the ith place which is such that A is true relative to $Q^{*\prime}$. Thus, by (3d), F is true relative to Q'. In other words, thesis (4) holds for F, since if F is true relative to Q, then it is true relative to all Q' that differ from Q at most in what is assigned to variables that do not have free occurrences in F.

In light of this result truth can be defined as follows:

5. *Definition of Truth*
   For all sentences s of L, s is true in L iff s is true relative to some sequence Q (which in turn holds iff s is true relative to all sequences).

Although the definition of truth for this language is a little more complicated than the definition of truth for the language of arithmetic, the method used in constructing it is basically the same as the one employed earlier, augmented with the means of assigning (temporary) denotations to variables, and of evaluating formulas containing free occurrences of variables relative to such assignments.

The only aspect of the definition that may not appear completely transparent is clause (3d) of the definition of truth relative to a sequence. One might wonder why the truth of $\ulcorner(\exists v_i A)\urcorner$ relative to a sequence Q is defined in terms of the truth of A relative to *some sequence that may differ from* Q, rather than Q itself. In effect, one might wonder why the clause in the definition for quantified formulas isn't (3d'), rather than (3d).

3d'. A formula $\ulcorner(\exists v_i A)\urcorner$ is true relative to a sequence Q iff the formula $A(v_i)$ which arises from $\ulcorner(\exists v_i A)\urcorner$ by erasing $\ulcorner\exists v_i\urcorner$ is true relative to Q.

The problem with (3d') is best illustrated by its consequences for the definition of the unrelativized notion of truth applying to sentences of L. If (3d') were substituted for (3d), thesis (4) would be falsified, and it would no longer be the case that a sentence is true relative to one sequence iff it is true relative to all sequences. Thus, we would have to choose whether to say that a sentence of L is true iff it is true relative to some sequence, or that a sentence of L is true iff it is true relative to all sequences. Moreover, neither choice would be correct. Selecting the former alternative would allow us to derive pseudo-T-sentences of the sort (6), and prevent us from deriving genuine T-sentences of the sort (7); selecting the latter alternative would allow us to derive pseudo-T-sentences of the sort (8), and prevent us from deriving genuine T-sentences of the sort (9).[15]

6. $\ulcorner \sim (\exists v_i\ A) \urcorner$ is true in L iff at least one object (in the domain of L) "isn't A".
7. $\ulcorner \sim (\exists v_i\ A) \urcorner$ is true in L iff no object (in the domain of L) "is A".
8. $\ulcorner (\exists v_i\ A) \urcorner$ is true in L iff every object (in the domain of L) "is A".
9. $\ulcorner (\exists v_i\ A) \urcorner$ is true in L iff at least one object (in the domain of L) "is A".

Thus, if (3d') were substituted for (3d), the resulting definition would not be materially adequate, and so would not be a correct definition of truth for L.

The material adequacy of the original definition (using (3d)) is illustrated by the following derivation (assume for simplicity that the domain of L is restricted to human beings):

A. '$(\exists x_1\ (\sim (\exists x_2\ (Lx_1x_2))))$' is true in L iff it is true relative to some sequence. [From (5)]

B. '$(\exists x_1\ (\sim (\exists x_2\ (Lx_1x_2))))$' is true relative to a sequence Q iff there is a sequence Q^* that differs from Q at most in the first place and '$(\sim (\exists x_2\ (Lx_1x_2)))$' is true relative to Q^*. [From (3d)]

C. '$(\sim (\exists x_2\ (Lx_1x_2)))$' is true relative to Q^* iff '$(\exists x_2\ (Lx_1x_2))$' is not true relative to Q^*. [From (3b)]

D. '$(\exists x_2\ (Lx_1x_2))$' is not true relative to Q^* iff there is no sequence $Q^{*\prime}$ that differs from Q^* at most in the 2nd place such that '(Lx_1x_2)' is true relative to $Q^{*\prime}$. [From (3d)]

E. '(Lx_1x_2)' is true relative to $Q^{*\prime}$ iff 'L' applies to the pair $<o, o'>$ consisting of the denotation of 'x_1' relative to $Q^{*\prime}$ followed by the denotation of 'x_2' relative to $Q^{*\prime}$. [From (3a)]

F. 'L' applies to the pair $<o, o>$ consisting of the denotation of 'x_1' relative to $Q^{*\prime}$ followed by the denotation of 'x_2' relative to $Q^{*\prime}$ iff the first member o of $Q^{*\prime}$ loves the second member o' of $Q^{*\prime}$. [From (1a) and (2b)]

G. '(Lx_1x_2)' is true relative to $Q^{*\prime}$ iff the first member o of $Q^{*\prime}$ loves the second member o' of $Q^{*\prime}$. [From (E) and (F)]

H. '$(\exists x_2\ (Lx_1x_2))$' is not true relative to Q^* iff there is no sequence $Q^{*\prime}$ that differs from Q^* at most in the 2nd place such that the first member of $Q^{*\prime}$ loves the second member of $Q^{*\prime}$. [From (D) and (G)]

I. '$(\exists x_2\ (Lx_1x_2))$' is not true relative to Q^* iff there is no individual o' who is loved by the first member of Q^*. [From (H) and the characterization of sequences]

J. '$(\sim (\exists x_2\ (Lx_1x_2)))$' is true relative to Q^* iff there is no individual o' who is loved by the first member of Q^*. [From (C) and (I)]

K. '$(\exists x_1 \ (\sim (\exists x_2 \ (Lx_1x_2))))$' is true relative to a sequence Q iff there is a sequence Q^* that differs from Q at most in the first place whose first member o loves no one. [From (B) and (J)]

L. '$(\exists x_1 \ (\sim (\exists x_2 \ (Lx_1x_2))))$' is true relative to a sequence Q iff someone loves no one. [From (K) and the characterization of sequences]

M. '$(\exists x_1 \ (\sim (\exists x_2 \ (Lx_1x_2))))$' is true in L iff someone loves no one. [From (A) and (L)]

This derivation also illustrates the importance of the restriction on Q^* in (3d) to sequences that *differ from Q at most in the ith place*. If this restriction were dropped and (3d-) were substituted for (3d), then step (D) would be replaced by (D-), and (M-) rather than (M) would be derived.

(3d-)   A formula $\ulcorner(\exists v_i A)\urcorner$ is true relative to a sequence Q iff the formula $A(v_i)$ which arises from $\ulcorner(\exists v_i A)\urcorner$ by erasing $\ulcorner \exists v_i \urcorner$ is true relative to some sequence Q^*.

D-. '$(\exists x_2 \ (Lx_1x_2))$' is not true relative to Q^* iff there is no sequence $Q^{*\prime}$ such that '(Lx_1x_2)' is true relative to $Q^{*\prime}$.

M-. '$(\exists x_1 \ (\sim (\exists x_2 \ (Lx_1x_2))))$' is true in L iff no one loves anyone.

Thus, the restriction on Q^* in Tarski's clause (3d) is needed to ensure the material adequacy of the definition.

All that remains to fulfill Tarski's requirements is to convert the inductive definitions of denotation and truth relative to a sequence to explicit definitions.

10. *The Denotation of a Term Relative to a Sequence*
For all terms α of L, objects o and sequences Q, α denotes o relative to Q iff there is a set D_L of which $<\alpha, \text{o}, Q >$ is a member and for all expressions e, objects o', and sequences Q', $<\text{e}, \text{o}', Q'>$ is a member of D_L iff (i) for some i, e is the ith variable v_i and o' is the ith member of Q'; or (ii) e is the name 'a' and o' is Alfred, or e is the name 'b' and o' is Brian, or . . . (and so on, for each name in L); or (iii) for some one-place function symbol f and term β, e is the expression $\ulcorner f(\beta)\urcorner$ and f is the symbol 'm' and o' is the mother of an individual o^* such that $<\beta, \text{o}^*, Q'>$ is a member of D_L, or f is the symbol 'g' and o' is the father of an individual o^* such that $<\beta, \text{o}^*, Q'>$ is a member of D_L, or . . . (and so on for each one-place function symbol of L); or (iv) . . . (similar clauses for arbitrary n-place function signs until all the function symbols in L are exhausted).

11. *Truth Relative to a Sequence*
For all formulas F of L and sequences Q, F is true relative to Q iff there is a set T_s of which $<F, Q>$ is a member and for all formulas G and sequences Q', $<G, Q'>$ is a member of T_s iff (a) G is an atomic formula $\ulcorner P(\alpha, \ldots, \delta)\urcorner$ consisting of an n-place predicate followed by n terms and P applies to the n-tuple of objects $< \text{o}_\alpha, \ldots, \text{o}_\delta>$ denoted relative to Q'

by $\alpha, \ldots, \delta$, respectively; or (b) G is the formula $\ulcorner(\sim A)\urcorner$, for some formula A of L, and $<A, Q'>$ is not a member of T_s; or (c) G is the formula $\ulcorner(A\&B)\urcorner$, for some formulas A and B of L, and $<A, Q'>$ and $<B, Q'>$ are both members of T_s; or (d) G is the formula $\ulcorner(\exists v_i\, A)\urcorner$, for some variable v_i and formula A of L, and there is a sequence Q^* that differs from Q' at most in the ith place and a formula $A(v_i)$ that arises from $\ulcorner(\exists v_i\, A)\urcorner$ by erasing $\ulcorner\exists v_i\urcorner$ such that $< A(v_i), Q^*>$ is a member of T_s.

The relationship between inductive definitions and explicit definitions is straightforward. Inductive definitions employ the term being defined—for example, denotation relative to a sequence, or truth relative to a sequence—in clauses that specify its application to new cases in terms of its application to previously defined cases. To turn such a definition into an explicit definition, one trades such occurrences of the term being defined for occurrences of a set variable, and rewrites the clauses so that they specify set-membership conditions for new cases in terms of set-membership conditions for previously specified cases. The conversion is completed by putting the definition in the form of a universally quantified biconditional with an explicit quantification over sets (to bind the newly introduced set variable) immediately following 'iff'.[16]

This technique for converting an inductive to an explicit definition will work whenever the existence of the set required by the explicit definition is guaranteed. One will have this guarantee whenever the domain of the object-language is a set, and the meta-language contains quantifiers that range over arbitrary sequences of elements of that set. However when the quantifiers of the object-language range over all sets—and hence the domain of the language is not a set[17]—no explicit definition of denotation, or truth, relative to a sequence is possible.

To see this, let L be such an object-language and imagine a proposed explicit definition of denotation relative to a sequence for L of the sort given in (10). If there were a set D_L of the kind required by the definition, it would be in the domain of the object-language, and would therefore occur as ith member of various sequences. We could then derive (12) and (13), which are necessarily false.[18]

12. $<D_L, v_i, Q>$ is a member of D_L iff D_L is the ith member of Q.
13. $<D_L, v_i, Q>$ is a member of D_L.

Thus, there is no set D_L of the sort required by an explicit definition of denotation relative to a sequence for L. Fortunately this does not mean that we cannot speak of terms of L denoting things relative to sequences. For although no explicit definition of denotation relative to a sequence can be given, there is no difficulty in providing an inductive definition along the lines of (1). Such a definition can be thought of as a set of axioms that fixes the application of the notion being defined, without requiring the existence of a set of all and only those things that it applies to. Analogous points hold for definitions of truth relative to a sequence for object-languages whose domains include all sets.

Truth and Proof

An important point to notice about Tarski's definition of truth for a language is that although it may be viewed as saying what it is for a sentence of the language to be true, it does not provide a criterion that can be used to determine which sentences are true. If one understands an object-language sentence but is uncertain whether it is true, Tarski's definition won't help to resolve one's uncertainty. Thus it remains desirable to formulate criteria of truth in addition to Tarski's definition of truth.

In some cases such criteria are already well developed. A good example is the language of arithmetic specified earlier. To determine whether or not a sentence of arithmetic is true one attempts to derive it from arithmetical sentences already known to be true. This procedure is standardly formalized in well-known systems of proof. Such a system consists of a (decidable) set of sentences drawn from the language to play the role of axioms, plus a set of purely mechanical rules of inference that allow one to derive formulas of certain specified forms from formulas of other, related forms. A proof is then defined as any finite sequence of formulas of the language each of which is either an axiom or a formula that follows by one of the rules of inference from earlier formulas in the sequence. A sentence of the language is provable iff it is the last formula of some proof.

In order to fulfill their intended purpose, the axioms selected should be transparently true, and the rules of inference should be clearly truth-preserving. If these conditions are met, then we have a guarantee that any provable sentence is true, and the system of proof provides an effective positive test for truth. Since there is no other test for arithmetical truth, it may seem that a sentence of the language of arithmetic is true iff it is provable. But if that is so, then a definition of provability in the language could be taken to be a definition of truth, and Tarski's own definition might seem superfluous.

Of course, Tarski's definition of truth is not superfluous. Although he understood the temptation of identifying truth with provability in mathematics, he did not think that a definition should presuppose the existence of a complete, effective positive test for truth—a point of view shown to be correct by Kurt Gödel's demonstration that the set of arithmetical truths is not coextensive with the set of provable sentences of any axiomatizable theory of arithmetic. Thus, Tarski could not have used proof to define truth, but had to proceed essentially along the lines just described.

Although the demonstration that truth and proof do not coincide is too complex to be given here, its basic outlines are easily grasped and are worth going into. The central idea is an application of two closely related paradoxes—the Liar, in which a sentence can be seen as asserting its own untruth, and the heterologicality paradox, in which a predicate is said to be heterological iff it does not apply to itself. For example the predicate 'is a person' is heterological because it is not a person, whereas the predicate 'is an expression' is not heterological because it is an expression. The paradox arises when one asks whether the predicate 'heterological' is, or is not, heterological.

The paradox can be avoided — and in fact made to do important logical work — by confining the heterologicality predicate to the meta-language. To this end, we let L be a particular object-language, and (1) be a meta-language definition of what it is for an object-language predicate to be heterological.

1.   For all predicates P of L, P is heterological iff P does not apply to itself.

We further assume (2).

2.   For all predicates P of L, either P applies to itself or P does not apply to itself, but not both.

We then conclude that L doesn't contain its own heterologicality predicate — that is, L doesn't contain any predicate that applies exactly to those predicates of L that are heterological. For if it did, then the predicate would both apply to itself and not apply to itself, which is impossible.

We next notice the connection between heterologicality and untruth. Suppose, for the moment, that L contains names for its expressions. For any predicate P of L, and name [p] in L of P, call the sentence P[p] in which P is combined with a name of itself a self-ascription of P. Now consider the claim (3).

3.   A self-ascription of P is untrue.

Intuitively, this says that P does not apply to itself, and hence that P is heterological. In effect, we have used the two-place predicate, *is a self-ascription of* and the one-place predicate *is untrue* to define *heterological*. Thus, we should be able to show that L can't contain both its own self-ascription predicate, and its own untruth predicate.

To do this, we assume (4) and stipulate that a predicate of L is any formula of L containing a single free variable.

4.   Every sentence of L is either true or untrue (but not both).

Now suppose that L contains its own self-ascription and untruth predicates. Then it will also contain formula (5).[19]

5.   ∃y (y is a self-ascription of x & y is untrue)

Since this is a formula of L with one free variable, it is a predicate of L. Indeed, it is a heterologicality predicate. But since L can't contain its own heterologicality predicate, either L doesn't contain its own self-ascription predicate, or it doesn't contain its own untruth predicate. In other words, if L contains its own self-ascription predicate, then it cannot contain its own untruth predicate.

To see how this relates to the Liar, consider the sentence (6) of L that arises from (5) by replacing the variable 'x' with a name [v] of the predicate (5).

6.   ∃y (y is a self-ascription of [v] & y is untrue)

Notice that (6) is a self-ascription of (5). If it is the only self-ascription of (5) (i.e., if [v] is the only name in L for (5)), or if all self-ascriptions of a predicate have the same truth value, then (6) can be taken to say that it is untrue — and so is a Liar sentence of the form (7) in which the predicate P applies to the sentence itself.

7.   ∃y (Py & untrue y)

Liar sentences of this form are important in languages which may allow names for its sentences, but which don't allow any sentence to contain a name of itself. This is the sort of situation that confronted Gödel and Tarski in their proofs about arithmetic.

To apply this reasoning to the language L_A of arithmetic it is necessary to adopt a convention according to which certain statements in L_A about the natural numbers can be used to simulate corresponding statements about the formulas of L_A. The convention is based on a system of Gödel numbering in which each expression of L_A is assigned a unique Gödel number. The system is a 1-1 mapping between expressions of L_A and a subset of the natural numbers. The mapping is effective in the sense that there is a purely mechanical procedure for determining, given an expression of L_A, its unique Gödel number, and, conversely, for determining, given a natural number, the expression of L_A, if any, that it is a Gödel number of.

One such system is illustrated in (8).

8.   A System of Gödel Numbering

(	1	0	5
)	19	S	6
∼	2	+	7
&	29	*	79
∃	3	=	8
x_1	4		
x_2	49		
x_3	499		
etc.			

The Gödel number of a compound expression is the number denoted by the Arabic numeral resulting from concatenating the Arabic numerals of the Gödel numbers of the symbols that make it up. For example, the Gödel number of $\sim (\exists x_1\ 0 = S(x_1))$ is 2134586141919. It may be noted that although every sentence of L_A has a Gödel number which is named by some term of L_A, no sentence of L_A contains a name of its own Gödel number.

The system of Gödel numbering allows us to interpret certain sentences of the language of arithmetic as making claims about expressions whose Gödel numbers are the official subject matter of those sentences. For example, suppose we stipulate that any open sentence with exactly one variable free is a predicate of L_A, that '0' is a numeral of L_A, and that if α is a numeral of L_A, then $\ulcorner S(\alpha) \urcorner$ is also a numeral of L_A. We then stipulate that where P is any such predicate, a self-ascription of P is the sentence that results from P by substituting the numeral that names the Gödel number of P for all occurrences of the free variable in P. Next consider the numerical relation that holds between n and m iff m is the Gödel number of a predicate P of L_A, and n is the Gödel number of a self-ascription of P. This relation is effectively decidable, since given any pair of numbers we can always determine which expressions of L_A, if any, they are Gödel numbers of, and given any pair of expressions of L_A we can always decide if one of them is a predicate and the other is a self-ascription of that predicate. Now, an important result about the language of arithmetic is that every effectively decidable relation is definable within it—that is, for every such k-place relation R there is a formula of L_A which is true of an arbitrary k-tuple of numbers[20] iff that k-tuple is an instance of R. Thus, *y is the Gödel number of a self-ascription of a predicate with Gödel number x* is definable in L_A. But this means that *y isn't the Gödel number of a true sentence of L_A* cannot be defined in L_A, since if it were, then L_A would, in effect, contain its own heterologicality predicate;[21] and that, as we have seen, is impossible.

It should be recalled that we are assuming that every sentence of L_A is either true or not true, but not both. We also know that for all formulas F of L_A, F is true relative to a sequence iff $\ulcorner(\sim F)\urcorner$ is not true relative that sequence. Thus, if L_A contained a predicate T that was true of precisely those numbers that are Gödel numbers of true sentences of L_A, then $\ulcorner(\sim T)\urcorner$ would be a predicate that was true of precisely those numbers that are not Gödel numbers of true sentences of L_A. Since L_A cannot contain such an untruth predicate $\ulcorner(\sim T)\urcorner$, while it does contain (classical) negation, it also cannot contain its own truth predicate T. This is Tarski's well-known result establishing the arithmetical indefinability of arithmetical truth.

The distinction between truth and proof is established by specifying a system of proof, consisting of a decidable set of axioms drawn from L_A plus a set of rules of inference. Since a proof is just a finite sequence of formulas of L_A, the system of Gödel numbering of formulas can be used to assign a unique Gödel number to each proof. To get the Gödel number of a proof just think of the sequence of formulas being arranged horizontally, one after another, and treat the result as a complex expression whose Gödel number is computed in the usual way. Now consider the numerical relation that holds between a pair of numbers n and m iff n is the Gödel number of a proof of a sentence with Gödel number m. This relation is effectively decidable, since (i) we can always decide, given any pair of numbers, whether one is the Gödel number a sentence S and the other is the Gödel number of a sequence of formulas, the last member of which is S, and (ii) given any sequence of formulas of L_A, we can always determine whether it is a proof—in other words, whether each of its formulas is either an axiom or a consequence of earlier formulas via one of the rules of inference. But then, since the relation is effectively decidable, it is also definable in L_A. Thus, there is a formula, *Proof (x_1, x_2)*, of L_A that is true of a pair of numbers n and m iff n is the Gödel number of a proof of the sentence whose Gödel number is m. But this means that the formula $\ulcorner \exists x_1$ Proof $(x_1, x_2)\urcorner$ is true of precisely the Gödel numbers of provable sentences of L_A.[22]

Since the set of provable arithmetical sentences is definable in the language of arithmetic, whereas the set of arithmetical truths is not, the set of truths is not identical with the set of provable sentences. It follows that if the system of proof is formulated so as to prove only truths, then there must be some arithmetical truths (in fact infinitely many of them) that are not provable in the system. This result is perfectly general, and applies to all formalized systems of proof for arithmetic. All such systems that prove only truths are incomplete in that they leave many arithmetical truths unproven. This is the simplest (and weakest) version of Gödel's First Incompleteness Theorem.[23] In light of this result Tarski could not use proof to define truth, but rather had to devise an entirely different way of proceeding.

Appendix: Tarski on Truth, Quotation, and Substitutional Quantification

In the section "Tarski's Strategy," I noted that Tarski rejected the definition (1) of truth involving substitutional quantification into quotes.

1.   For all sentences x of L, x is true in L iff for some S, x = 'S' & S.

Tarski's objection was based on his understanding of quotation-mark names:

> Quotation-mark names may be treated like single words of a language, and thus like syntactically simple expressions. The single constituents of these names—the quotation marks and the expressions standing between them—fulfill the same function as the letters and complexes of successive letters in single words. Hence they can possess no independent meaning. Every quotation-mark name is then a constant individual name of a definite expression (the expression enclosed by the quotation marks) and in fact a name of the same nature as the proper name of a man. For example, the name " 'p' " denotes one of the letters of the alphabet. With this interpretation, which seems to be the most natural one and completely in accordance with the customary way of using quotation marks, partial definitions of the type (3) ['It is snowing' is a true sentence iff it is snowing] cannot be used for any significant generalizations. In no case can the sentences (5) [For all p, 'p' is a true sentence iff p] or (6) [For all x, x is a true sentence iff, for a certain p, x is identical with 'p', and p] be accepted as such a generalization. In applying the rule of substitution to (5) we are not justified in substituting anything at all for the letter 'p' which occurs as a component of a quotation-mark name (just as we are not permitted to substitute anything for the letter 't' in the word 'true').[24]

In this conception of quotation, variables do not have genuine (grammatically significant) occurrences within quotes and so are not bindable from without. However, one might wonder whether Tarski's conception of quotation is correct.

Suppose that there are infinitely many expressions and hence infinitely many quote-names. If, as Tarski insists, these names are "single words," and hence "syntactically simple expressions," then it may seem as if the language must contain infinitely many primitive expressions that a speaker must master, even though they are not related by any linguistic rule. And if there is no linguistic rule relating them, then presumably they must be learned one by one. But this is impossible. Thus, it might be argued, Tarski's conception of quotation is unacceptable.

Although this objection is ultimately unsuccessful, it must be conceded that it is not entirely without merit. The occurrence of 'cat' in the quote-name " 'cat' " is certainly no orthographic accident in the way in which its occurrence in 'cattle' is. Rather, quotation is a productive process governed by rules of roughly the following sort:

2. For any expression e, the expression consisting of the left-hand quote mark followed by e followed by the right-hand quote mark is a singular term.
3. Any singular term consisting of the left-hand quote mark followed by an expression e followed by the right-hand quote mark denotes e.

However, this constitutes an objection to Tarski's view of quotation only if it is assumed that there can be no productive rules for generating and assigning referents to individual words or lexical items. If (2) is taken to be a rule that generates an infinite number of single-word names from a finite base and (3) is seen as assigning referents to those names based on their lexical structure, then Tarski's view of quote-names can be maintained.

There seems to be no principled basis for excluding such a view. For example, consider an analogous case with variables. Surely one could introduce and evaluate variables by rules of the sort (2') and (3').

2'. The letter 'x' is a variable, and for any expression e, if e is a variable, then the expression that consists of e followed by a superscripted star is a variable. (So 'x', 'x*', 'x**', and so on are variables.)
3'. The denotation of 'x' relative to a sequence is the first member of the sequence. If $\ulcorner e* \urcorner$ is a variable and the denotation of e relative to a sequence s is the ith member of s, then the denotation of $\ulcorner e* \urcorner$ relative to s is the ith + 1st member of s.

Although these rules could be seen as generating and interpreting infinitely many variables, each variable is a syntactically simple unit. Surely we do not want to say that the variable 'x*' contains a grammatically significant occurrence of the variable 'x', which is bindable and open to substitution via the usual logical laws. But if we allow (2') and (3') to be lexical rules governing variables, it should be possible to formulate a Tarski-like conception of quotation governed by lexical rules (2) and (3).[25] In such a conception, quantification into quotation is impossible, and Tarski's objection to (1) stands.

However, this is not the end of the matter. Although Tarski's conception of quotation is acceptable, it is not the only such conception. Indeed, just as it is possible to formulate legitimate quotation operators that are impervious to quantification, so it is possible to formulate legitimate quotation operators that allow quantifying-in. If such operators are needed for generalizations of the sort illustrated by (1), then there is no problem providing them.

For example, we may let 'Quote' be a one-place functor which when prefixed to any constituent α (term, predicate, formula, sentence, etc.) produces a complex singular term ⌜Quote(α)⌝ that denotes α. We next distinguish a set of substitutional variables that we wish to use to quantify into such constructions. Where v is such a variable, ⌜Some v F(v)⌝ is true iff one of its substitution instances F(α) is true, where α is an expression in the substitution class of v and F(α) arises from F(v) by replacing all free occurrences of v with α. Since in this conception of quantification variables have genuine occurrences within quotation, nothing else needs to be said in order to make sense of sentences like (4), where (4) is just like the proposed truth definition (1) except for containing the quotation functor 'Quote' instead of the usual quotation marks.[26]

4.   For all sentences x of L, x is true in L iff for some S, x = Quote(S) & S.

Given this conception of quotation and quantification, one can easily establish the material adequacy of putative truth definitions of the sort illustrated by (4). For this purpose, let L be a fragment of English, let 'x' be an objectual variable in the metalanguage ranging over sentences of L, and let 'S' be a substitutional variable in the metalanguage whose associated substitution class is the set of sentences of L (also 'P' and 'Q'). What follows is an informal derivation of a representative instance of schema T. In addition to the proposed truth definition (4), the derivation appeals to the axiom (5), which expresses a basic feature of our quotation functor, plus the elementary theorem (6) of the syntax of L.

5.   (P)(Q)((Quote(P) = Quote(Q)) ⊃ (P iff Q)).
6.   Quote(John is bald) = Quote(John is bald).

Derivation of "Quote(John is bald) is true in L iff John is bald"
A.   If Quote(John is bald) is true in L, then for some S (Quote(John is bald) = Quote(S) & S). (From [4])
B.   If Quote(John is bald) is true in L, then John is bald. (From [A] and [5])
C.   If John is bald, then (Quote(John is bald) = Quote(John is bald) & John is bald). (From [6])
D.   If John is bald, then for some S (Quote(John is bald) = Quote(S) & S). (From [C])
E.   If John is bald, then Quote(John is bald) is true in L. (From [D] and [4])
F.   Quote(John is bald) is true in L iff John is bald. (From [B] and [E])

Tarski realized that an attempt along these lines could be made to rescue proposed substitutional definitions of truth by appealing to quotation functors of the sort illustrated by 'Quote'.

> In order to rescue the sense of sentences (5) [*For all p, 'p' is a true sentence iff p*] and (6) [*For all x, x is a true sentence iff for a certain p, x is identical with 'p' and p*] we must seek quite a different interpretation of the quotation-mark names. We must treat these names as syntactically composite expressions, of which both the quotation marks and the expressions within them are parts. Not all quotation-mark

expressions will be constant names in that case. The expression " 'p' " occurring in (5) and (6), for example, must be regarded as a function, the argument of which is a sentential variable and the values of which are constant quotation-mark names of sentences. We shall call such functions *quotation functions*. The quotation marks then become independent words belonging to the domain of semantics, approximating in their meaning to the word 'name', and from the syntactical point of view they play the part of functors.[27]

However, Tarski thought that such an attempt to rescue the proposed substitutional definitions could not succeed because the required conception of quotation was indefensible. Although he raised a number of quibbles, the only objection with any real force was his contention that quantification into quotation leads inevitably to paradox. According to him,

> the use of the quotation functor exposes us to the danger of becoming involved in various semantical antinomies, such as the antinomy of the liar. This will be so even if—taking every care—we make use only of those properties of quotation-functions which seem almost evident. In contrast to that conception of the antinomy of the liar which has been given above, we can formulate it without using the expression 'true sentence' at all, by introducing the quotation-functions with variable arguments.[28]

Tarski's reasoning on this point can be reconstructed as follows. First we introduce sentence c.

c.   (S) (c = Quote(S) ⊃ ~ S).

Given our proposed truth definition (4), which is equivalent to (4'),

4'.   For all sentences x of L, x is true in L iff ~ (S) (x = Quote(S) ⊃ ~ S)

sentence c says that c is not true in L. Next we present two incontrovertible premises.

P1.   c = Quote((S) (c = Quote(S) ⊃ ~ S)).
P2.   (P)(Q)((Quote(P) = Quote(Q)) ⊃ (P iff Q)).

(P1) is established by simple inspection. (P2) is just our axiom (5). In addition to expressing an essential feature of the 'Quote' functor, it is needed to establish the material adequacy of the proposed truth definition (4) and so cannot be given up without conceding Tarski's claim about the inadequacy of such definitions. The problem is that, according to Tarski, "by means of elementary logical laws we easily derive a contradiction from [these] premises."[29]

Although Tarski did not present such a derivation, it seems clear what he had in mind.

A. Assume: (S) (c = Quote(S) ⊃ ~ S).

B. c = Quote((S) (c = Quote(S) ⊃ ~ S)) ⊃ ~ (S) (c = Quote(S) ⊃ ~ S). (Universal Instantiation on [A], substituting *(S) (c = Quote(S) ⊃ ~ S)* itself for 'S')

C. ~ (S) (c = Quote(S) ⊃ ~ S). (From [P1] and [B])

D. Since assumption (A) leads, together with (P1), to its own negation, we may take (C) as having been established by (P1) alone.

E. Some S (c = Quote(S) & S). (From [C] by logical consequence)

F. Some S (Quote((S) (c = Quote(S) ⊃ ~ S)) = Quote(S) & S). (From [E] by substitution of *Quote((S) (c = Quote(S) ⊃ ~ S))* for c on the basis of [P1])

G. (Q)((Quote((S) (c = Quote(S) ⊃ ~ S)) = Quote(Q)) ⊃ ((S) (c = Quote(S) ⊃ ~ S) iff Q)). (From [P2] by Universal Instantiation, substituting *(S) (c = Quote(S) ⊃ ~ S)* for 'P')

H. (S) (c = Quote(S) ⊃ ~ S). (From [F] and [G])

I. (S) (c = Quote(S) ⊃ ~ S) & ~ (S) (c = Quote(S) ⊃ ~ S). (From [C] and [H])

The moral that Tarski seems to have drawn from this is that since a contradiction can be derived from (P2) together with the clearly correct (P1), (P2) must be rejected. But then the putative truth definition (4) cannot be shown to be materially adequate. More fundamentally, since (P2) must be true if substitutional quantification into quotation is to have its intended sense, such quantification must not make sense after all.

This conclusion is mistaken for the elementary reason that, contra Tarski, (P1) and (P2) do not entail a contradiction. The illusion that they do is fostered by fallacious applications of the rule Universal Instantiation at steps (B) and (G). What the rule allows is substitution of any member of the substitution class associated with a variable for occurrences of the variable that become free as a result of erasing the universal quantifier. If, "taking every care," we stipulate that the substitutional variables are members of the metalanguage only and that the members of their substitution classes are object-language sentences, then no sentence containing such a variable can be introduced by Universal Instantiation and no contradiction can be derived.[30]

As a result, Tarski's objections to substitutional definitions of truth of the sort illustrated by (4) collapse. Such definitions are both formally correct and materially adequate in Tarski's sense. Do they satisfy his third requirement of defining truth without presupposing any undefined semantic terms? Some philosophers have thought not. For example, in his book *Ways of Meaning*, Mark Platts considers the possibility of using the generalization *(p) ('p' is true iff p)* to define truth. About this, he says the following:

> Everything now hangs upon the interpretation of the quantifier. First, it might be read objectually, so that '(p)' is tantamount to 'for each and every object p'; but with this reading, the generalization is ill-formed. . . . But suppose we try the alternative,

substitutional reading. It is not clear that this will keep the logic clean, but it will not work anyway. We are attempting to define the truth-predicate as part of the enterprise of defining truth. Yet consider the interpretation of the substitutional quantifier. The interpretation of the existential quantification '(∃x) (Fx)' is this: there is a name which, when concatenated with the predicate 'F', produces a *true* sentence. The interpretation of the universal quantification '(x) (Fx)' is this: all names, when concatenated with the predicate 'F', produce a *true* sentence. The problem is clear: substitutional quantification is defined in terms of truth, and so cannot itself be used to define truth.[31]

This view embodies a subtle but fundamental mistake about the nature of substitutional quantification. If 'x' is a substitutional variable with an associated substitution class of proper names, then the quantification '(∃x) (Fx)' *is true* iff there is a name which, when concatenated with the predicate 'F', produces a *true* sentence. However, '(∃x) (Fx)' *does not mean* that there is a name which, when concatenated with the predicate 'F', produces a *true* sentence. The proposition that is expressed by the quantification is not a metalinguistic proposition about expressions at all. To suppose otherwise is to confuse substitutional quantification with objectual quantification over expressions.

This point is illustrated by the following concrete examples.

7.   The sun is hot.
8.   Some n (n is hot).

Imagine that 'the sun' is a name and that 'n' is a substitutional variable whose substitution class contains 'the sun' and other English names. Sentence (8) is a logical consequence of sentence (7), and the proposition expressed by (8) can be inferred directly from the proposition expressed by (7). Now, it is clearly possible for a person to believe the proposition expressed by (7)—that is, to believe that the sun is hot—without believing anything about sentence (7) or any other English expressions. Since the proposition expressed by (8) can be inferred from the proposition expressed by (7), it too can be believed without believing anything about English (or other) expressions. Thus the proposition expressed by (8) is not a metalinguistic proposition about the expressions that constitute its substitution instances. Moreover, if expressions can mean different things in different possible worlds (because of how they are used by speakers in those worlds), then the proposition (actually) expressed by (8) may be true at a world w in which the sun is hot even if the metalinguistic proposition (actually) expressed by (9) is false at w.

9.   There is a name which, when taken as the subject of the predicate 'hot', produces a *true* sentence.

Thus the proposition expressed by a substitutional quantification may not even be necessarily equivalent to the associated metalinguistic proposition about its substitution instances.

One reason for confusion about this is that substitutional quantifiers, like other logical operators, are often introduced and explained by appeal to truth conditions. This may encourage one to think that if substitutional quantification is described by saying that ⌜Some n (Fn)⌝ "is true iff there is a name which, when concatenated with the predicate F, produces a *true* sentence," then one has been given a meaning-preserving analysis or paraphrase of the substitutionally quantified sentence. But this is no more true of substitutional quantification than it is of other logical operators. Conjunction may be described by saying that ⌜P & Q⌝ is true iff true P is true and Q is true, but this does not mean that a conjunctive sentence expresses a metalinguistic proposition about the truth of its (sentential) conjuncts. Similarly, the objectual quantifier ⌜∃v⌝ is often introduced and explained by saying that ⌜∃v Fv)⌝ is true iff Fv is true relative to an assignment of an object o to v, despite the fact that the metalinguistic claim on the right-hand side of the 'iff' is no paraphrase of the objectually quantified sentence mentioned on the left.[32]

What proposition, then, is expressed by a substitutionally quantified sentence? It should not be surprising to learn that there is no way of paraphrasing such a sentence without using substitutional quantification, just as there is no way of paraphrasing an objectually quantified sentence without using objectual quantification and no way of paraphrasing a truth-functional compound without using truth-functional operators. Like these logical operations, substitutional quantification is primitive, if it is legitimate at all.

But is it legitimate? Do we really understand it? I am inclined to think we do, even though the point is not easily established by direct argument and I have no conclusive proof to offer. One strategy is to find readily comprehensible generalizations in English that apparently are not objectual—for example, *I have recently discovered that several things I have always wanted do not exist, He is several things that I am not,* and so on. If the best account of some of these sentences is one that views them as substitutional, then substitutional quantification must make sense.[33]

Thus it looks as if there is at least some possibility that Tarski could have satisfied all three of his stated requirements—formal correctness, material adequacy, and freedom from primitive semantic concepts—with a substitutionally quantified definition of truth. Nevertheless, it is fortunate that he did not take this route for substitutional definitions fail to satisfy an unstated fourth requirement that his actual definition brilliantly fulfills: theoretical fruitfulness. By linking the truth or falsity of a sentence to semantic properties of its structurally significant parts (the domain of the quantifiers; the denotations of names, predicates, and function symbols; and the truth or falsity—relative to assignments—of constituent clauses), Tarski's definition both allows one to prove in the metalanguage a variety of highly significant theorems about the truths of the object-language, and provides the basis for a semantic account of notions like logical truth and logical consequence. In short, Tarski's structural, nonsubstitutional definition of truth supplies the resources needed for a substantive semantic metatheory of object-language sentences. This will be the point of departure for our discussion of the significance of Tarski's theory of truth in chapter 4.

Notes

1. Tarski required a definition of truth for L to entail all instances of Schema T. However in the case of natural languages the totality of these instances is inconsistent with obvious facts about the language. Hence definitions meeting Tarski's requirements cannot be correct.

2. Here and in what follows I will assume that the names that replace the letter 'X' in schema T are either quote names or names that share with quote names the characteristic that the expressions they refer to can be constructed from an understanding of the names themselves (e.g., *the word consisting of the string of letters Es, En, O and Double-U*). When in the text I say that if T is a truth predicate all instances of schema T are true and assertable, what I say is to be understood as follows: For any expression T, if T is a truth predicate of L, then all instances of the scheme $\ulcorner$X is T in L iff P$\urcorner$ are true and assertable.

3. Instances may be obtained by replacing 'X' with the name of any sentence of L and 'P' with any sentence of the meta-language whatsoever.

4. Alfred Tarski, "Truth and Proof," *Scientific American*, June 1969, 63–77, at p. 64..

5. "The Semantic Conception of Truth," op. cit. p. 23.

6. "Truth and Proof," op. cit. p. 65.

7. Alfred Tarski, "The Concept of Truth in Formalized Languages," in *Logic, Semantics, and Metamathematics*, 2nd ed., ed. John Corcoran (Indianapolis, Ind: Hackett, 1983), 152–278, at 159.

8. One might wonder whether a different conception of quotation, which allowed bindable occurrences of substitutional variables inside of quotes, could be used to construct a truth definition. In "The Concept of Truth in Formalized Languages" Tarski considers and rejects this possibility on the grounds that such a conception of quantification "exposes us to the danger of becoming involved in various semantical antinomies, such as the antinomy of the liar. This will be so even if—taking every care—we make use only of those properties of quotation-functions which seem almost evident. In contrast to that conception of the antimony of the liar which has been given above, we can formulate it without using the expression 'true sentence' at all, by introducing the quotation functions with variable arguments." (pp. 161–2) Tarski's reasoning on this point is presented and criticized in the appendix to this chapter.

9. The truth definitions in the next two sections follow Tarski's leading ideas, while departing somewhat (for the purpose of simplification and clarification) from Tarski's own discussions in matters of organization and detail.

10. Here, and throughout the specification of the truth definitions, I employ variables of the meta-language that range over expressions of the object-language. For example in

    i.   If A and B are formulas of L, then $\ulcorner$(A & B)$\urcorner$ is also a formula of L

'A' and 'B' range over expressions of L, and for any assignment of particular expressions to the variables, $\ulcorner$(A & B)$\urcorner$ is the expression of L that consists of the left-hand parenthesis, followed by the expression assigned to the variable 'A', followed by '&', followed by the expression assigned to the variable 'B', followed by the right-hand parenthesis.

11. Since negation, conjunction and existential quantification are sufficient to define all the familiar logical constants of the predicate calculus, the others need not be listed here.

12. Strictly speaking one needs to specify the method of combination of function symbols with terms in order to precisely characterize the language. Often the function symbol is simply prefixed to the result of enclosing the terms in parentheses—$\ulcorner$f(t$_1$, . . . t$_n$)$\urcorner$. How-

ever, in some cases, as when '+' is used as a 2-place function symbol for the addition function, a different means of combination is used — $\ulcorner(t_1 + t_2)\urcorner$.

13. Again, one needs to specify the manner of combination of predicates with terms in order to precisely characterize the language. Often the predicate is simply prefixed to the terms — $\ulcorner P\ t_1 \ldots t_n \urcorner$. However, sometimes, as when '=' is used as a two-place predicate standing for the identity relation, the predicate is typically placed between the terms — $\ulcorner t_1 = t_2 \urcorner$.

14. It is not strictly required that D be a set — for example the domain of objects for a given language could be stipulated to include all sets. Since there is no set of all sets, the domain of such a language would not be a set. This would not affect our ability to give an inductive definition of truth for the language. However, as we shall see, it would prevent us from turning the inductive definition into an explicit definition.

15. Sentences (6) and (8) are pseudo-T-sentences because the meta-language sentences on the right-hand sides of 'iff' have different truth conditions from the object-language sentences mentioned on the left-hand sides of the biconditionals; and so the meta-language sentences are not paraphrases of the object-language sentences. By contrast, sentences (7) and (9) are genuine T-sentences because the meta-language sentences on the right-hand sides of these biconditionals are acceptable paraphrases of their object-language counterparts.

16. The exercise is a little more cumbersome in cases in which one has the sort of simultaneous recursion on terms and formulas that one finds in languages the contain definite descriptions as terms. Suppose, for example that (i) were added to the specification of terms given in the previous section.

    i.   If v_i is a variable, and F is a formula, then $\ulcorner(\text{the } v_i\ F)\urcorner$ is a term.

The inductive definition of denotation relative to a sequence would then be augmented as follows:

    ii.   A term $\ulcorner(\text{the } v_i\ F)\urcorner$ denotes an object o relative to a sequence Q iff o is the unique object such that F is true relative to a sequence Q* that differs from Q at most in having o as its ith member.

The inductive definition of denotation would then depend on the inductive definition of truth, and vice versa. It is worth noting that although this makes the conversion to explicit definitions more complicated, it does not make it impossible. The exercise is left to the reader.

17. Since there is no set of all sets.

18. Under the assumptions (i) that n-tuples are set theoretic constructions, and (ii) that no set can be a member of itself, or a member of a member of itself, and so on.

19. Here I assume for convenience that the self-ascription predicate in L is 'is a self-ascription of' and the untruth predicate is 'is untrue'.

20. To say that the formula is true of a k-tuple of numbers is to say that the formula is true relative to a sequence in which the elements of the k-tuple are assigned as values to the k free variables in the formula.

21. More precisely, it would include a predicate P that was true of precisely the Gödel numbers of predicates of L_A, including P, that do not apply to their own Gödel numbers.

22. Note, the set of provable sentences of L_A is definable in L_A even though it is not an effectively decidable set. Although there is a decision procedure for determining whether an arbitrary finite sequence of formulas of L_A is a proof of a given sentence s, there is no upper bound on the number of such sequences that need to be checked in order to determine whether s is a provable sentence. Thus, there is a complete, effective positive test for provability, but no complete, effective negative test, and so no decision procedure.

Nevertheless, the set of provable sentences in L_A is definable in L_A by virtue of simple existential generalization on a formula that defines the proof relation in the language.

23. This sketch of the outlines of the Gödel-Tarski results is based on an introductory portion of Saul Kripke's presentation in his Princeton seminar on truth, September 29, 1982. The relationship between it and Gödel's own way of proceeding can be seen by comparing formulas (5) and (6) above with (i) and (ii) below. ('[k]' in (ii) is the numeral denoting the Gödel number of (i).)

   i. $\exists x_2$ (x_2 is a self-ascription of x_1 & $\sim \exists x_3$ Proof (x_3, x_2))
   ii. $\exists x_2$ (x_2 is a self-ascription of [k] & $\sim \exists x_3$ Proof (x_3, x_2))

Just as (5) is a predicate that applies to those predicates that are not true of themselves, so (i) is a predicate that applies to those predicates that are not provable of themselves. Just as (6) can be seen as saying that it is not true, so (ii) can be seen as saying that it is not provable. We saw that the language of arithmetic cannot contain its own untruth predicate, and so cannot contain any predicate corresponding to (5). However, since it does contain its own self-ascription and unprovability predicates, it does contain a predicate corresponding to (i)—that is, a predicate true of precisely the Gödel numbers of predicates of the language whose self-ascriptions are not provable in the designated system of proof. It therefore contains a sentence corresponding to (ii)—that is, one which is true iff its Gödel number is not the Gödel number of a sentence that is provable in the system. Since (ii) in effect "says" that it is unprovable, it is either true and unprovable, or false and provable. Thus, if the system is set up so that only truths are provable, it follows that (ii) is unprovable, and the system is incomplete.

24. Alfred Tarski, "The Concept of Truth in Formalized Languages," op. cit., at 159–60.

25. Such a conception is developed and defended by Mark Richard in "Quotation, Grammar, and Opacity," *Linguistics and Philosophy* 9 (1986): 383–403. Among other things, Richard argues that Arabic numerals are single-word names that are generated and evaluated by productive lexical rules. This provides an explanation of why one cannot quantify into numerals—*$\exists x$ ($x56 = 16^2$)—and why substitution of an ordinary singular term for one of the digits of an Arabic numeral fails to preserve well formedness—29, *2the number of planets, *2(7 + 2).

26. I take no stand here on whether our ordinary understanding of quotation marks is one that allows quantifying-in with substitutional quantifiers. Whatever one may think about that, 'Quote' is a quotation functor that allows such quantification.

With a little effort, one could even make sense of objectual quantification into the scope of 'Quote'. To do so, we would need to distinguish the class of objectual variables used for quantifying-in and relativize the denotation of ⌐Quote(α)⌐ to assignments of objects to these variables. Where α does not contain such variables, the denotation of ⌐Quote(α)⌐ is just α and does not vary from assignment to assignment. Where α is one of the variables, we would need to specify the denotation of ⌐Quote(α)⌐ relative to an assignment of an object o to α—for example, the pair <α, o>. The idea could be extended so that, where α is a formula containing free occurrences of the objectual variables, the denotation of ⌐Quote(α)⌐ relative to an assignment is a structured complex made up of constituents that are either expressions or pairs of variables and objects. (The idea is analogous to David Kaplan's arc quotes except for opting for what Kaplan calls *associative valuation* of quoted expressions containing variables rather than *substitutional valuation*. See David Kaplan, "Opacity," in *The Philosophy of W. V. Quine*, ed. Lewis E. Hahn and Paul A. Schilpp [La Salle, Ill.: Open Court, 1986], 229–89, at 243–45.) In such a conception, the putative "law" (i) of standard quantification theory would fail in the specific case of (ii).

    i. $(x)(y)(x = y \supset (\Phi x \supset \Phi y))$
    ii. $(x)(y)(x = y \supset (Quote(x) = Quote(x) \supset Quote(x) = Quote(y)))$

However, (i) is not essential to objectual quantification but rather is a parochial truth that holds when Φ contains no quotational or quasi-quotational operators. See Mark Richard, "Quantification and Leibniz's Law," *Philosophical Review* 96 (1987): 555–78. ([i] and [ii] also come out true if the denotation of $\ulcorner Quote(v) \urcorner$ relative to an assignment of a value to the variable v is taken to be the value of v rather than the pair consisting of the variable and its value. This is what Kaplan calls *substitutional valuation* of quoted formulas containing bindable occurrences of objectual variables.)

27. Tarski, "The Concept of Truth in Formalized Languages," 161–62.

28. Ibid.

29. Ibib.

30. This point is made by Ruth Marcus in "Quantification and Ontology," *Nous* 6 (1972): 240–50, at 246–47, and by Saul Kripke in "Is There a Problem about Substitutional Quantification?," in *Truth and Meaning*, ed. Gareth Evans and John McDowell (Oxford: Oxford University Press, 1976), 325–419, at 367–68.

In fairness to Tarski it should be added that in the section in which he gives his argument he is concerned with natural languages like English. If the object language, for which a definition of truth is needed, is English, then it might be maintained that there could be no plausible grounds for excluding sentence (c) (and other sentences containing substitutional variables) from the substitution classes associated with sentential variables. If one took this position, then Tarski's argument would go through, and the substitutional definition of truth for English as a whole would be defeated.

If this was Tarski's position, then he was not guilty of any basic logical mistake. However, on this interpretation, his position leaves open the possibility of giving substitutional definitions of truth for fragments of English, formulated in higher metalanguages containing substitutional variables whose associated substitution classes do not include sentences containing those very variables. One might then ask whether there is reason to prefer the kinds of truth definitions that Tarski actually provided to definitions such as these.

Thanks to Mario Gomez-Torrente for discussion of the material in this note.

31. Mark de Bretton Platts, *Ways of Meaning* (London: Routledge and Kegan Paul, 1979), 14–15.

32. Another reason why someone might think that the substitutional quantification in the proposed truth definition (4) presupposes the notion of truth it is supposed to define may derive from the observation that a truth characterization for the metalanguage containing the usual clause for the substitutional quantifier in (4) will appeal to an antecedently given notion of object-language truth. However, it is hard to see that there is any objectionable circularity in this. Perhaps the thought that there is derives from the further thesis that to understand the sentences of a language is to know that which is expressed by a theory of truth for the language. If this thesis were accepted, it might be maintained that to understand a sentence like (4), which expresses a substitutional definition of truth, one must already grasp the notion of truth that (4) is supposed to define. There are several points to make about this. First, the thesis that understanding meaning is knowing that which is expressed by a truth theory is itself problematical and subject to strong objections. Second, as we shall see in chapter 4, Tarski would reject the thesis since in his conception of truth, it is clearly false. More generally, the view that knowledge of meaning equals knowledge of truth conditions does not lead to the result that substitutional definitions of truth are circular. Instead, it gives rise to the conclusion that any proposed definition that is materially adequate in Tarski's sense cannot be a correct definition of truth since if a

definition of truth is materially adequate, then instances of schema T, which follow from it, will be a priori on the assumption that definitions are a priori. But knowledge of linguistic meaning is empirical, not a priori. Thus there is no special objection to substitutional definitions of truth. Moreover, if one accepts Tarski's constraints on truth definitions, one will reject the thesis that equates knowledge of truth conditions with knowledge of meaning. More on this in chapter 4.

33. For a useful discussion, see Joseph Camp Jr., "Truth and Substitutional Quantifiers," *Nous* 9 (1975): 165–85.

FOUR

The Significance of
Tarski's Theory of Truth

Is Tarski's Definition an Analysis of Truth?

If we focus on a particular object-language L, it is clear that Tarski's definition provides us with a predicate that applies to all and only the true sentences of L. Many philosophers have thought that it also provides a philosophically revealing analysis of the nature of truth as it has classically been understood. It is, of course, widely recognized that Tarski's truth predicate does not have precisely the same meaning as the English word 'true'. In fact, the two predicates do not even apply to the same class of things. Whereas Tarski's truth predicate applies only to sentences, the English word 'true' is normally predicated of propositions, as in (1).

    1a.   The proposition that the earth revolves around the sun is true.
      b.   Church's theorem is true.
      c.   Everything he asserted is true.

Moreover, even when the English word 'true' is predicated of sentences, it is not subject to Tarskian restrictions. Whereas Tarski's predicate applies only to sentences of a single object-language (which contains neither it nor any predicate coextensive with it), the word 'true' can be predicated of arbitrary English sentences (including those containing 'true'), as well as of sentences of other lan-

98

guages. Thus we can say in English that a sentence of English is true, that a sentence of Japanese is true, and even that the first sentence uttered in the twenty-fifth century or its negation will be true (without having any idea what language will be used). This suggests that if English does contain a truth predicate of sentences, then it is not a restricted Tarskian truth predicate but rather an unrestricted relational predicate, *true in L*, for variables 'L'.[1]

Given these differences, one might wonder how anyone could take Tarski's definition to be an analysis of our ordinary notion of truth. To understand this, one must remember that according to Tarski and many others, our ordinary notion of truth is defective precisely because its unrestrictedness gives rise to paradox. The sort of analysis of truth that Tarski attempted to provide is one that would eliminate this alleged defect while preserving the central and useful features of the notion. In effect, Tarski tried to specify not how 'true' is actually understood but how it ought to be understood if it is to function in our logical, mathematical, and scientific theories in the ways normally intended.

Analyses of this kind are often called "explications." In general, an explication of some pretheoretically understood concept C consists in the definition of a related concept C' that (i) applies to those things that are clear and central instances of the concept C; (ii) is precise and well defined; (iii) is free of difficulties and obscurities present in the original concept C; and (iv) may play the role of C in all theoretical contexts in which that notion is legitimately required. The claim that Tarski's definition provides an analysis of truth can be understood as the claim that the definition satisfies these criteria.

If we restrict our attention to the sorts of object-languages for which Tarski provided truth definitions, then the material adequacy and formal correctness of the definitions will ensure that the first two of these criteria are satisfied. More interesting issues are raised by the third and fourth criteria. In order to evaluate the proposed analysis against these criteria, we must determine what difficulties and obscurities in the ordinary notion of truth are eliminated by Tarski's definition, and how well Tarski's truth predicates play the theoretical roles truth predicates are required to fulfill.

For Tarski, the paramount difficulty involving the ordinary notion of truth was the Liar paradox. This paradox and the lessons to be drawn from it will be taken up in chapters 5 and 6. However, at this point it is worth noting that the Liar paradox was not the only difficulty philosophers had with the notion of truth. At the time Tarski wrote, a number of leading philosophers were skeptics about truth on the basis of various alleged epistemological and metaphysical difficulties of the sort illustrated in chapter 2.[2] Historically, Tarski's work was very effective in sweeping away the bases of such skepticism. It is easy to see why. Tarski showed how to explicitly define truth predicates for certain languages L, presumed to be adequate for science and mathematics, using only notions already expressible in L plus elementary syntax and set theory. As a result, if syntax, set theory, and L are all unparadoxical and philosophically unproblematic, then adding a Tarskian truth predicate cannot possibly lead either to paradox or to any philosophically objectionable consequences. This is illustrated by the fact that if 'TRUE' is a Tarskian truth predicate and S is a sentence in the language to which it applies, then ⌜'S' is TRUE⌐ is equivalent, in the presence of elementary syntax and set theory, to S. Thus if, prior to Tarski, one had been philosophically inclined toward truth skepticism without perhaps seeing clearly how to get along without the notion of truth entirely, then Tarski's theory might well have appeared to provide a philosophically liberating analysis of what had seemed to be a problematic notion.[3]

This brings us to the final criterion for judging Tarski's definition as an explication of truth: theoretical fruitfulness. Truth is an important metatheoretical notion used in the investigation and evaluation of theories of widely diverse types. Very often we want to know whether the claims made by a particular theory are true, whether there are truths not captured by the theory, and whether there are other theories that do better than the given theory in telling the truth about a specific domain. Similarly, it is important to be able to characterize as precisely as we can the cases in which the truth of a set of sentences of a certain sort guarantees the truth of other, related sentences. The spectacular success of Tarski's theory of truth is due in large part to its fruitfulness in metatheoretical investigations of this sort. The important point in this connection is not just that Tarski's definition applies to all object-language truths but that the way in which it is formulated is revealing and theoretically productive.[4]

The Fruitfulness of Tarski's Definition

A striking feature of Tarski's truth definition is that it not only specifies a predicate that applies to all and only object-language truths but also links the truth or falsity of a sentence to semantic properties of its structurally significant parts—the domain of the quantifiers, the denotations of the nonlogical vocabulary, and the truth or falsity, relative to assignments, of constituent clauses. Because of this, the definition provides the formal tools needed to systematically investigate in the metalanguage a variety of highly significant propositions about structurally related sentences of the object-language. For example, where L is one of the languages we have been concerned with, the following theorem can be established.

1. For any singular terms α and β of L, if ⌐$\alpha = \beta$⌐ is true in L and if s and s' are sentences of L that differ only in the substitution of one of these terms for the other, then s is true in L iff s' is true in L.

Similarly, given a system of proof and a metalanguage definition of what constitutes a proof in that system, one can often provide conclusive answers to questions like (2),(3), and even (4).

2. Is every provable sentence of the system true in L?
3. Is every truth in L provable in the system?
4. If it is not the case that all and only the truths of L are provable in the given system, is there any other system in which all and only the truths of L are provable?

Tarski's definition also provides the basis for an account of notions like logical truth and logical consequence. Roughly put, a logical truth is a sentence that comes out true (in Tarski's sense) no matter what nonempty domain of quantification is chosen and no matter what denotations from that domain are selected for the nonlogical vocabulary of the sentence. Similarly, a sentence c is a logical consequence of a set s of sentences iff every choice of a nonempty domain of quantification plus denotations for the nonlogical vocabulary that makes each member of s true also makes c true (in Tarski's sense).

Standardly, the word 'model' is used to designate any choice of a nonempty domain of quantification together with an assignment of denotations from the domain to nonlogical vocabulary. The denotation of a name in a model is an individual member of the domain of the model; the denotation of an n-ary predicate is the set of n-tuples of individuals (drawn from the domain) that the predicate applies to; and the denotation of an n-ary function symbol is an n-place function from the set of n-tuples of individuals (drawn from the domain) into the domain. Given this basis, we can abstract a definition of *truth in a model* from Tarski's truth definition by (i) stipulating that the sequences mentioned in the definition be sequences of objects from the domain of the model and (ii) replacing the original clauses that specified the denotations of particular nonlogical vocabulary items with generic clauses like those in (5).

5a.   A name n denotes an object o in a model M (relative to a sequence Q) iff o is the object that M assigns to n.

b.   An n-ary predicate P applies to an n-tuple of objects in a model M iff that n-tuple is a member of the set that M assigns to P.

c.   If f is an n-ary function symbol and $t_1, \ldots t_n$ are terms, the term $\ulcorner f(t_1, \ldots, t_n)\urcorner$ denotes an object o in a model M, relative to a sequence Q, iff o = $g(o_1, \ldots, o_n)$, where g is the function that M assigns to f and o_i is denoted by t_i in M, relative to Q, for each i.

Aside from these differences, the definition of truth in a model for the languages we have been concerned with is just like Tarski's original definition of truth. Given the definition of truth in a model, we can then characterize a logical truth as one that is true in all models and a logical consequence c of a set s of sentences as a sentence that is true in all models in which the members of s are true. Other logical properties and relations can be given similar characterizations.[5]

Such characterizations have considerable philosophical, as well as mathematical, import. To see this, it is instructive to compare the "semantic," model-theoretic characterizations of logical notions with alternative "syntactic" characterizations in terms of formal derivability from specified (logical) axioms and/or rules of inference. Although both are mathematically precise, the semantic characterizations are much better candidates for *analyses* of pretheoretic notions like logical consequence and logical truth than the syntactic characterizations are. Intuitively, if Q is a logical consequence of P, then the truth of Q should in some sense be guaranteed by the truth of P, independent of anything that depends on the special subject matter of P and Q. If we require that Q be true in every model in which P is true, then this condition would seem to be met since the truth of P will be enough to determine the truth of Q independent of any special features of the domain of quantification or the denotations of the nonlogical vocabulary. Moreover, if Q is false in some models in which P is true, then it would seem that one must appeal to special facts about the subject matter of P and Q (involving the domain of quantification or the denotations of the nonlogical vocabulary) to get from the truth of P to the truth of Q, thus disqualifying Q from being a genuine logical consequence of P. For these reasons, the model-theoretic characterizations are strong candidates for being analyses of the logical notions and have been widely treated as such.

By contrast, whenever a formal system of derivability is presented, it is always a significant question whether all and only the proper derivations it defines are genuine instances of logical consequence. By accepting the model-theoretic analysis of logical consequence, one can formulate and investigate such questions with mathematical precision. For example, just as, in the case of a theory of some particular subject matter, one can mathematically investigate and provide answers to questions like (2)–(4), so in the case of the logical notions one can mathematically investigate and provide answers to questions like (6)–(8).[6]

6. Is it the case that for all sentences P and Q, if Q is derivable from P in system S (where S is some specified system of proof), then Q is true in all models in which P is true? (Is S "sound"?)
7. Is it the case that for all sentences P and Q, if Q is true in all models in which P is true, then Q is derivable from P in S? (Is S "complete"?)
8. If it is not the case that for all sentences P and Q, Q is derivable in S from P iff Q is true in all models in which P is true, is there any other system in which the equivalence does hold?

The upshot of these considerations is that Tarski's definition of truth has proven to be a very fruitful one in a variety of metatheoretical investigations. If one looks at Tarski's definition as an *explication* of our pretheoretic notion of truth, then the theoretical fruitfulness of his proposed *explicans* lends weight to the view that the explication is a good one.[7]

Truth and Meaning

Another area in which the notion of truth has been put to theoretical use is semantics or the theory of meaning. A common view among philosophers, logicians, and linguists is that the meaning of an expression consists in the contribution it makes to the meanings of sentences that contain it, and the meaning of a sentence consists in its truth conditions. Moreover, since the meaning of a sentence is identified with its truth conditions, it is typically maintained that to understand a sentence is to know the conditions in which it is true. In this view, a theory of meaning for a language is a theory that specifies the truth conditions of sentences on the basis of the semantically significant properties (denotation, application, etc.) of its constituent parts.

The simplest and most fundamental version of this view takes the truth conditions of sentences to be that which is expressed by ordinary instances of schema T and casts theories of meaning for a language L in the form of Tarskian theories (definitions) of truth in L.[8] Such a conception is reflected in the familiar distinction in formal semantics between uninterpreted and interpreted languages. The former are said to result from syntactic specifications of well-formed sentences; the latter are typically characterized as the result of adding "an interpretation"—that is, a model, which, when combined with a definition of truth in a model, yields a Tarskian theory of truth.

This view is endorsed and extended to natural languages by Donald Davidson in the following passage from his influential article, "Truth and Meaning":

> (T) s is T iff p
>   What we require of a theory of meaning for a language L is that without appeal to any (further) semantic notions it place enough restrictions on the predicate "is T" to entail all sentences got from schema T when 's' is replaced by a structural description of a sentence of L and 'p' by that sentence.
>   Any two predicates satisfying this condition have the same extension, so if the metalanguage is rich enough, nothing stands in the way of putting what I am calling a theory of meaning into the form of an explicit definition of a predicate "is T." But whether explicitly defined or recursively characterized, it is clear that the sentences to which the predicate "is T" applies will be just the true sentences of L, for the condition we have placed on satisfactory theories of meaning is in essence Tarski's Convention T that tests the adequacy of a formal semantical definition of truth.
>   The path to this point has been tortuous, but the conclusion may be stated simply: a theory of meaning for a language L shows "how the meanings of sentences depend upon the meanings of words" if it contains a (recursive) definition of truth-in-L. And, so far at least, we have no other idea how to turn the trick. It is worth emphasizing that the concept of truth played no ostensible role in stating our original problem. That problem, upon refinement, led to the view that an adequate theory of meaning must characterize a predicate meeting certain conditions. It was in the nature of a discovery that such a predicate would apply exactly to the true sentences. I hope that what I am doing may be described in part as defending the philosophical importance of Tarski's semantical concept of truth. . . .
>   There is no need to suppress, of course, the obvious connection between a definition of truth of the kind Tarski has shown how to construct, and the concept of meaning. It is this: the definition works by giving necessary and sufficient conditions of the truth of every sentence, and to give truth conditions is a way of giving the meaning of a sentence. To know the semantic concept of truth for a language is to know what it is for a sentence—any sentence—to be true, and this amounts, in one good sense we can give to the phrase, to understanding the language.[9]

If this view were correct, then the notion of truth defined by Tarski could play the central role in theories of meaning for various languages, thereby providing further vindication of his definition as an adequate explication or analysis of truth. However, the view is not correct. To see this, imagine that 'e' is a name of the earth, that 'R' is a predicate applying to round things, that 'T in L' is a Tarskian truth predicate, and that (1) is an instance of schema T derivable in the meta-language from the characterization of truth for the object-language.

  1.   'Re' is T in L iff the earth is round.

Since 'T in L' is the Tarskian truth predicate, nothing is lost by replacing it with its explicit definition, which results in something of the form (2).

  2.   [There is a set T_L such that 'Re' is a member of T_L and for all sentences s of L, s is a member of T_L iff (i) s = $\ulcorner P\ t \urcorner$ for some one-place predicate P and term t, and there is an object o such that t denotes o and P applies to o, or (ii) . . .] iff the earth is round.

Since 'Re' is a sentence consisting of a one-place predicate and a term, we can simplify (2) by dropping the extraneous clauses (ii). . . . We must also replace *denotes* and *applies* with their Tarskian definitions, thereby producing something of the form (3).

  3.   [There is a set T_L such that 'Re' is a member of T_L and for all sentences s of L such that s = $\ulcorner P\ t \urcorner$ for some one-place predicate P and term t, s is a member of T_L iff there is an object o such that (i) t = 'e' and o = the earth, or t = 'm' and o = Mars, or . . . (one disjunct for each name in L) . . . , and (ii) P = 'R' and o is round, or . . . (one disjunct for each one-place predicate in L) . . .] iff the earth is round.

The only information about 'Re' that this provides is expressed by (4), which is trivially equivalent to (5).

  4.   [There is a set T_L such that (i) 'Re' is a member of T_L and (ii) 'Re' is a member of T_L iff 'Re' = 'Re' and 'e' = 'e' and 'R' = 'R' and there is an object o such that o = the earth and o is round] iff the earth is round.
  5.   There is an object o such that o = the earth and o is round iff the earth is round.

The crucial point to recognize is that none of these biconditionals (1)–(5) say anything that constrains the meaning of 'Re' in any way. One could know that which they express without knowing the first thing about what 'Re' means or does not mean. Suppose, for example, that one did not know that 'Re' means in L that the earth is round and was considering the hypothesis that it means in L that the earth is not round. Given the biconditionals (1)–(4) plus an instance of Tarski's a priori constraint (6) regarding what predicates qualify as truth predicates, one could conclude that either 'T in L' in (1) is not a truth predicate for L (and that T_L is not the set of truths in L) or 'Re' does not mean in L that the earth is not round.

6.   If 'T in L' is a truth predicate for a language L (i.e., if it applies to precisely the true sentences of L) and if, moreover, s means in L that P, then s is T in L iff P.

However, without knowing the meanings of the sentences of L, one could not determine whether 'T in L' is a truth predicate for L (or whether T_L is the set of truths of L). Similarly, without knowing that 'T in L' is a truth predicate (and that T_L is the set of truths), one could determine nothing about the meaning of sentences of L.[10]

The crucial point for theories of truth as theories of meaning is that instances of (7a), which contain our ordinary pretheoretic notion of truth, are obvious and knowable a priori, whereas instances of (7b), which contain a Tarskian truth predicate for L, are anything but obvious and are not knowable a priori.

7a.   If s means in L that P, then s is true in L iff P.
  b.   If s means in L that P, then s is T in L iff P.

It is precisely the obviousness and availability of (7a) that allows claims of the form *s is true in L iff P* to provide information about meaning. For example, if one knew that 'Re' is true in L iff the earth is round, then one could immediately eliminate the hypothesis that 'Re' means in L that the earth is not round since given that hypothesis, one could derive the contradictory result that the earth is round iff 'Re' is true in L iff the earth is not round. The unavailability of (7b) prevents similar conclusions from being drawn from claims of the form *s is T in L iff P*. As a result, claims of this form provide no information about meaning.

The point may be put by noting that the obvious and a priori nature of instances of (7a) is due to the fact that there is a conceptual or analytic connection between our ordinary notions of truth and meaning that does not hold between the notion of meaning and Tarski's concept of truth. The basis of this connection is, I suggest, the primacy of propositions as bearers of truth in the ordinary sense. The bearers of truth are, in the first instance, what is said and believed, which in turn are the semantic contents of sentences. Sentences are true derivatively—just in case they express true propositions. Consequently, when we are told that a sentence is true in the ordinary sense, we are given information about the proposition it expresses and thereby about its meaning.

This may be seen by noting that when no indexicality is involved and a sentence expresses the same proposition on different occasions of use, talk about its meaning is, for all intents and purposes, interchangeable with talk about the proposition it expresses. In such cases, instances of (7a) are tantamount to instances of (8), which wear their triviality on their sleeves.

8.   If s expresses the proposition that P in L, then the proposition expressed by s in L is true iff P.

The "analytic connection" between truth and meaning is the result of three facts: (i) to say that a sentence s means in L that P is to say that s expresses the proposition that P in L; (ii) to say that s is true in L is to say that the proposition expressed by s in L is true; and (iii) instances of the propositional schema

PT. The proposition that P is true iff P

are trivial, a priori, and necessary. If this is right, then the information about meaning carried by statements that give the truth conditions of sentences comes from and is explained by the implicit commitment to propositions carried by our ordinary notion of truth.

Tarski's truth predicate 'T in L', on the other hand, is defined independently of propositions. As a result, the claim that it applies to a sentence s gives us no information about the meaning of s. The predicates 'T in L' and 'true in L' do, of course, apply to precisely the same sentences of L. However, they do not express the same concept, and because of this, sentences containing them do not carry the same information.[11]

This means that the notion of truth defined by Tarski cannot play the central role in a truth-conditional theory of meaning in the manner envisioned by Davidson in the passage quoted previously. Given an object-language L of the appropriate sort, one can use Tarskian techniques to construct a characterization of truth in L. However, there are two diametrically opposed ways in which the characterization can be understood. Following Tarski, one may take it to be a definition that introduces and gives content to a new predicate. If one takes this route, the resulting truth definition provides no information about meaning. Alternatively, following Davidson, one may take the truth characterization to contain our ordinary, antecedently understood notion of truth. If one takes this route, the resulting theory states the truth conditions of object-language sentences in a way that provides information constraining their meaning.[12] Since these two construals of the truth characterization are mutually exclusive, we cannot have both.

This creates a potential problem for the view that Tarski's definition is a successful analysis or explication of truth. We already know that Tarski's notion of truth differs in certain respects from our ordinary notion. If truth is required to play an important theoretical role and if that role can be played by our ordinary notion but not by Tarski's, then the definition cannot be accepted as an adequate analysis; whatever its other merits, it does not tell us all we need to know about what truth is.

So far, of course, the result is only conditional. If truth conditions play a significant role in interpreting sentences, then Tarski's definition is not an adequate analysis of truth. Although I believe that, in the end, we should accept the negative assessment expressed by the consequent of this conditional, it is important to be clear about the grounds for doing so. At a minimum, one should not simply assume that the meaning of a sentence consists in its truth conditions, that a theory of meaning for a language consists in a theory of the truth conditions of its sentences, or that Tarski's proposed analysis is inadequate *because* it fails to provide a notion of truth validating this view of meaning.

In fact, our discussion so far has touched on a serious problem with precisely this view. We have seen that the notion of truth required by this view of meaning cannot be a newly introduced theoretical construct, defined by some Tarski-like procedure. We have also seen that it must be conceptually connected to the notion of meaning in a way that makes instances of *If s means in L that P, then s is true in L iff P* turn out to be a priori necessities. Our ordinary notion of truth satisfies this condition because it applies primarily to propositions and only derivatively to sentences in virtue of the propositions they express. But if propositions are the semantic contents of sentences, then surely we want a theory of meaning to tell us which propositions the various sentences of a language express. Davidsonian theories, which state the truth conditions of sentences in the form of instances of schema T, do not do this. As a result, the very notion of truth required by such theories carries an implicit commitment to propositions that can be used to cast doubt on the theories themselves.

In other work, I have developed this embryonic objection by arguing that the proposition expressed by a sentence cannot be defined in terms of the circumstances in which the sentence is true, that theories of meaning cannot successfully be identified with theories of truth conditions, and that understanding a sentence cannot successfully be analyzed as knowing the conditions in which it is true.[13] If these arguments are correct, then the mere fact that Tarski's truth predicates cannot be used in theories of meaning and understanding of this kind does not in itself doom the analysis. What does doom the analysis is its failure to supply a truth predicate of propositions, needed for a proper theory of meaning and understanding. However, I will not try to reconstruct the demonstration of this here. For present purposes, we may rest content with the more limited conclusion that Tarski's definition of truth is at odds with a familiar view linking truth conditions with meaning, and that the tension between the two threatens the adequacy of the definition as an analysis or explication of truth.[14]

Truth and Physicalism

A final issue that arises in assessing the adequacy of a proposed analysis of a given concept involves the question of its compatibility with one's general philosophical and methodological commitments.[15] One such commitment that many philosophers have found attractive is physicalism. Roughly put, physicalism is the doctrine that all genuine facts, all objects, and all properties are in principle reducible to or determined by physical facts, physical objects, and physical properties. Physicalism requires that all biological differences between organisms, all psychological differences between individuals, and all cultural and institutional differences between societies be grounded ultimately in terms of differences of the sort described in theoretical physics. According to some, it also requires one to reject any concept in one of the special sciences that is not replaceable in principle by a concept definable in physical theory.

This includes semantic concepts like truth, reference, and meaning. Some physicalists maintain that these concepts play legitimate roles in science only if they are physicalistically definable. One who seems sympathetic to this view is Willard van Orman Quine. He maintains that certain semantic notions are not physicalistically definable and so are not scientifically legitimate. In particular, he claims that the totality of all physical facts fails to determine alleged facts about meaning, synonymy, translation, and the proposition expressed by a sentence (as well as the propositions asserted and believed by speakers). Because of this, he claims that there really are no semantic facts of this sort and that notions like meaning, synonymy, and the like have no legitimate role to play in a scientific description of the world.[16]

This raises the question of whether truth is a notion that physicalists like Quine can accept. In an influential article on Tarski, Hartry Field points out that in the early 1930s a number of leading philosophers — including Rudolf Carnap and Karl Popper — were physicalists who were skeptical of semantic notions such as truth and denotation.[17] However, after Tarski presented his definition, the notion of truth was accepted by these previously skeptical philosophers.[18] Even Tarski seems to have thought that compatibility with physicalism was a desirable feature of his definition of truth. Although producing an analysis with this feature was not one of his leading motivations, he does mention it once in his writings as a positive element.

Tarski's discussion occurs in a section of his article "The Establishment of Scientific Semantics" in which he gives reasons for preferring explicit definitions of truth over inductive definitions (where possible).[19] He characterizes the latter as introducing semantic terms as metalanguage primitives whose extensions are determined by a specified set of axioms. He regards this method as less than optimal because (i) it requires us to raise and resolve the question of the consistency of the axioms governing the semantic notions; (ii) it takes as primitive those concepts that have historically been subject to repeated misunderstandings; and (iii) "should this method prove to be the only possible one and not be regarded as merely a transitory stage, it would arouse certain doubts from a general philosophical point of view." In particular, he maintains that "it would then be difficult to bring this method into harmony with the postulates of the unity of science and of physicalism (since the concepts of semantics would be neither logical nor physical concepts)."[20] By contrast, if truth and other semantic terms are explicitly defined, then (i) the question of consistency does not arise; (ii) the semantic terms do not have to be taken as primitive; and (iii) they are thus "reduced to purely logical concepts, the concepts of the language being investigated and the specific concepts of the morphology of language."[21]

It is perhaps worth pointing out that the version of physicalism apparently envisioned in Tarski's remark is an expansive one, allowing both physical and logico-mathematical elements without requiring the latter to be reduced to the former. We may take it that this "expansive physicalism" asserts that (i) all facts are physical or logico-mathematical facts; (ii) all scientific (or descriptive) claims are reducible to claims about the physical and logico-mathematical characteristics of things; and (iii) all scientific (or descriptive) concepts are definable in terms of physical and logico-mathematical concepts. Tarski's remarks seem to suggest that this doctrine requires truth to be eliminable via an explicit, physicalistic definition. Anything else — for example, taking truth to be a primitive whose extension is fixed by a set of axioms — was deemed at least somewhat suspect.[22]

At first glance, it would certainly seem as if Tarski succeeded in reducing truth to physicalistically acceptable terms. What he showed is that for certain languages L, adequate for natural science and mathematics, one can define a truth predicate using only notions already expressible in L plus certain syntactic and set-theoretic apparatus. Thus if L is physicalistically pure and if syntax and set theory are un-problematic, then defining a metalanguage truth predicate cannot introduce any difficulties.

Nevertheless, this conclusion has been challenged. In his well-known critique of Tarski, Field argues that Tarski's proposed replacements for the notions of de-notation and application are not physicalistically acceptable reductions of our pretheoretic notions. Because Field takes Tarski to have reduced truth to deno-tation and application, he concludes that Tarski has not legitimated the notion of truth for physicalists.[23]

Field does not, of course, dispute the fact that Tarski's definitions are exten-sionally correct. He maintains, however, that extensional correctness is not enough. In addition, he requires that any genuine reduction must show semantic facts about expressions to be identical with physical facts about their users and the environments in which they are used. Tarski's definitions do not do this.

This can be seen by considering a simple example. Suppose that 'Re' is a sentence of L and that the relevant semantic facts about it are given in (1).

   1a. 'e' denotes the earth (in L).
    b. 'R' applies (in L) to an object iff it is round.
    c. 'Re' is true in L iff the earth is round.

If Tarski's definitions really specify the physicalistic content of semantic notions, then in each case we ought to be able to substitute the physicalistic definiens for the semantic definiendum without changing the physical fact thereby specified. Performing this substitution and simplifying the results, we obtain

   2a. 'e' = 'e' and the earth = the earth.
    b. For all objects o, 'R' = 'R' and o is round iff o is round.
    c. 'Re' = 'Re' and there is an object o such that o = the earth and o is round iff the earth is round.

But there is a problem in identifying these facts with those in (1). As Field points out, it is natural to suppose that the expressions of a language have semantic properties only in virtue of the ways they are used by speakers. Thus he holds that the facts given in (1) would not have obtained if speakers' linguistic behavior had been different.[24] Since the facts in (2) are not speaker-dependent in this way, Field concludes that they are not semantic facts and that Tarski's attempted reduction fails. Tarski's truth predicate is both physicalistic and coextensive with 'true in L', but it is not, according to Field, a physicalistic conception of truth.

In Field's view, Tarski's truth characterization inherits its inadequacy as a re-duction from the pseudoreductions that constitute its base clauses. Thus Field's strategy for solving the problem is to provide genuine reductions for the notions of denotation and application, based on something like the model of the causal-historical theory of reference. The picture that emerges from his discussion is one in which an adequate definition of truth is a two-stage affair. Stage 1 is Tarski's reduction of truth to denotation and application. Stage 2 is the imagined causal-historical reduction of the notions of a term denoting and a predicate applying to an object in a language.[25] If the physical facts that determine denotation in one language do so in all, then these relations will hold between expressions and objects for variable 'L'. When logical vocabulary and syntax are kept fixed, the result is a notion of truth that is not language-specific but is itself defined for variable 'L'.

Although the resulting picture appears rosy, there are several potential problems with it. One concerns reference to abstract objects, for which a causal account seems problematic. Another involves Quinean worries about the (alleged) failure of physical facts to determine claims about reference. These, of course, are obstacles to a physicalistic reduction of denotation and application. However, other difficulties become clear when one notices that Field has understated his objection to Tarski. If the alleged dependence of semantic facts on facts about speakers shows that Tarski has not reduced denotation and application to physical facts, then the very same point shows that he has not reduced truth to denotation and application.

This can be seen by considering a pair of elementary examples. Imagine two languages, L_1 and L_2, that are identical except that in L_1 the predicate 'R' applies to round things, whereas in L_2 it applies to red things. Owing to this difference, certain sentences will have different truth conditions in the two languages.

3a.   'Re' is true in L_1 iff the earth is round.
 b.   'Re' is true in L_2 iff the earth is red.

Under Tarski's original definition, this difference will be traceable to the base clauses of the respective truth definitions, where the applications of predicates are simply listed.

Field's objection to this is that although Tarski's definitions correctly *report* that 'R' applies to different things in the two languages, they do not *explain* how this difference arises from the way in which speakers of the two languages use the predicate. What Field fails to point out is that exactly the same objection can be brought against Tarski's treatment of logical vocabulary and syntax in the inductive part of his definition.

This time let L_1 and L_2 be identical except for their treatment of 'v'.

4a.   A formula $\ulcorner(A \lor B)\urcorner$ is true in L_1 (with respect to a sequence s) iff A is true in L_1 or B is true in L_1 (with respect to s).
 b.   A formula $\ulcorner(A \lor B)\urcorner$ is true in L_2 (with respect to a sequence s) iff A is true in L_2 and B is true in L_2 (with respect to s).

Owing to this difference, sentences containing 'v' will have different truth conditions in the two languages. In order to satisfy Field's requirements on reduction, it is not enough for a truth characterization to report such differences. Rather, such differences must be explained in terms of the manner in which speakers of the two languages treat 'v'.[26] Since Tarski's truth definitions do not say anything about this, their inductive clauses should be just as objectionable to the physicalist as the base clauses.

This means that Field's strategy of achieving a genuine reduction of truth by supplementing Tarski with nontrivial definitions of denotation and application cannot succeed. The reason it cannot is that, given Field's strictures on reduction, Tarski has not reduced truth (for standard first-order languages) to denotation and application. At best he has reduced it to the class of semantic primitives listed in (5).[27]

5. The notion of a term denoting an object
   The notion of a predicate applying to objects
   The notion of a formula consisting of the application of an n-place predicate P to an n-tuple of terms $t_1 \ldots, t_n$
   The notion of a formula A being a negation of a formula B
   The notion of a formula A being a disjunction of formulas B and C
   The notion of a formula A being an existential generalization of a formula B with respect to a variable u and a domain D of objects

This way of looking at things requires a restatement of every clause in Tarski's truth definition. For example, the clause for negation, which had been given by (6a), must now be restated as (6b).

6a. If B = $^\ulcorner(\sim A)^\urcorner$, then B is true in L (relative to a sequence Q) iff A is not true in L (relative to Q).
   b. If B is a negation of a formula A, then B is true (relative to a sequence Q) iff A is not true in L (relative to Q).

The resulting abstraction extends the generality of the truth definition to classes of first-order languages that differ arbitrarily in syntax plus logical and nonlogical vocabulary.

Although this generality is appealing, it has a price. Whereas the original definitions simply stipulated that $^\ulcorner(\sim A)^\urcorner$ is a negation, $^\ulcorner(A \lor B)^\urcorner$ is a disjunction, and $^\ulcorner(\exists x\, Ax)^\urcorner$ is an existential generalization over a range D of objects, the revised definition does not provide a clue about which formulas fall into these categories. Moreover, Field's physicalist now has to provide reductions of each of these semantic notions.

How might this be done? Field cannot define negation as a symbol that attaches to a formula to form a new formula that is true (relative to a sequence) iff the original is false (relative to that sequence), for that would make the reduction of truth to the notions in (5) circular. Nor can he take negation to be primitive and stipulate that $^\ulcorner(\sim S)^\urcorner$ is to be the negation of S, for that would fail to specify the facts about speakers that explain the semantic properties of $^\ulcorner(\sim S)^\urcorner$. Although there are alternative approaches, none appears to be clearly successful.[28] The problems involved in reducing denotation and application to physical facts are hard enough; adding the logical notions makes the job that much harder.

As I have stressed, the source of this difficulty is the demand that semantic facts be reducible to physical facts about speakers. In effect, this demand limits acceptable definitions to those that legitimate substitution for semantic notions in claims like (7) and (8).

7.　If L-speakers had behaved differently (or been differently constituted), then 'e' would not have denoted the earth (in L), and 'R' would not have applied (in L) to round things, and $\ulcorner(A \vee B)\urcorner$ would not have been true (in L) iff A is true (in L) or B is true (in L).

8.　The fact that L-speakers behave as they do (and are constituted as they are) explains why 'e' denotes the earth (in L), why 'R' applies (in L) to round things, and why $\ulcorner(A \vee B)\urcorner$ is true (in L) iff either A is true (in L) or B is true (in L).

Field's critique of Tarski is based on the conviction that there ought to be a way of spelling out (7) and (8) so that they come out true when physicalistic substitutes replace semantic terms and their initial clauses are construed as expressing contingent, empirical physical possibilities.[29] As we have seen, Tarski's definition does not have this character.

It should be emphasized that this critique of Tarski is based on two contentious assumptions. The first is Field's version of physicalism. The second is the contention that there is a genuine theoretical need for a truth predicate, tied to the behavior of speakers, of a kind not provided by Tarski. Presumably, the idea is that there is some explanatory task involving the thought and action of speakers that requires a truth predicate that is physicalistic but non-Tarskian.

Field addresses this point in the last section of his article, in which he discusses the reasons why we want a notion of truth:

> The notion of truth serves a great many purposes, but I suspect that its original purpose—the purpose for which it was first developed—was to aid us in utilizing the utterances of others in drawing conclusions about the world. To take an extremely simple example, suppose that a friend reports that he's just come back from Alabama and that there was a foot of snow on the ground there. Were it not for his report we would have considered it extremely unlikely that there was a foot of snow on the ground in Alabama—but the friend knows snow when he sees it and is not prone to telling us lies for no apparent reason, and so after brief deliberation we conclude that probably there *was* a foot of snow in Alabama. What we did here was first to use our evidence about the person and his situation to decide that he probably said something true when he made a certain utterance, and then to draw a conclusion from the truth of his utterance to the existence of snow in Alabama. In order to make such inferences, we have to have a pretty good grasp of (i) the circumstances under which what another says is likely to be true, and (ii) how to get from a belief in the truth of what he says to a belief about the extralinguistic world.
>
> If this idea is right, then two features of truth that are intimately bound up with the purposes to which the notion of truth are put are (I) the role that the attempt

to tell the truth and the success in doing so play in social institutions, and (II) how to get from a belief in the truth of what he says to a belief about the extralinguistic world. It would then be natural to expect that what is involved in communicating the meaning of the word 'true' to a child or to a philosopher is getting across to him the sorts of facts listed under (I) and (II).[30]

Field's view seems to be that we use truth to interpret and draw conclusions from the utterances of others and that we need a physicalistically acceptable but non-Tarskian notion of truth to play an important theoretical role in explaining what goes on in such cases. However, it is not obvious precisely what that role is. Three things seem to be going on in the sort of case Field has in mind. First, the hearer determines what has been asserted by the speaker's utterance. Second, the hearer assesses the likelihood that what the speaker has asserted is true. Last, the hearer draws a conclusion about the world from the assumption that the speaker has asserted a truth.

At this point, we need to ask a fundamental question. What are the things that are asserted by speakers and assessed for truth or falsity by hearers? If, as I maintain, they are propositions, then the three tasks involved in Field's example are (i) determining that a certain utterance — that is, a certain sequence of sounds — is an assertion of the proposition that there is a foot of snow on the ground in Alabama; (ii) assessing the likelihood that the assertion is true; and (iii) concluding that there is a foot of snow on the ground in Alabama from the assumption that the proposition that there is a foot of snow on the ground in Alabama is true.

In this view, Tarski's notion of truth is inadequate because it does not apply to propositions. However, this has nothing special to do with physicalism. Suppose, for example, that we had a characterization of truth for propositions analogous to Tarski's characterization of truth for sentences. We may imagine that, like Tarski's characterization, it says nothing about the behavior of speaker-hearers and nothing about the role of asserting truths in our lives. Moreover, just as Tarski's definition has instances of schema T as consequences, so, we may imagine, our truth characterization for propositions has instances of schema PT as consequences.

9. Schema PT. The proposition that P is true iff P.

Given speakers' grasp of such a truth predicate, one could easily explain their drawing conclusion (iii) that there is a foot of snow on the ground in Alabama from the assumption that the proposition that there is a foot of snow on the ground in Alabama is true.[31] What about (i) and (ii)? If one is a physicalist, one will, of course, demand that physical facts — including facts about speakers' use of language — determine what proposition is asserted by various utterances.[32] Although a physicalist may for this reason demand that there be some sort of physicalistic grounding of the notion of assertion, it is not obvious that any specification of truth in terms of physical facts about speakers is required. Absent the demonstration of such a requirement, (i) provides no reason for unhappiness with a truth characterization for propositions that does not mention speaker-hearers at all.

This leaves only (ii) — the task of assessing the likelihood that a given assertion of a particular proposition is true. A purely formal characterization of truth, which says nothing about truth being the goal of assertions, can be expected to categorize the claim that a particular (empirical) assertion is true as being an ordinary empirical statement whose acceptability in a given case depends on the empirical evidence at hand. However, this is no objection to such a definition since such claims are in fact empirical and do depend on empirical evidence for support.

It may be objected that what the definition cannot account for is the necessary and a priori character of a certain presumption that is involved in assessing the likelihood that a given assertion is true—namely, the presumption that in most cases people try to speak the truth. In reply, it should be pointed out that it is not obvious that this presumption really is a necessary and a priori truth. Moreover, even if one accepts the claim that something like the presumption is necessary and a priori, this does not preclude one from also accepting a formal characterization of truth that makes no mention of truth as the goal of assertion. The presumption that in most cases people try to speak the truth is tantamount to the presumption that in most cases people say what they believe—that is, in most cases people assert p only if they believe p. If this is a conceptual or a priori necessity, then there may be some conceptual and a priori connection between the notions of assertion and belief. Given such a connection, plus the trivial, a priori necessities that are the instances of schema PT, one may conclude a priori that most instances of (10) are true.

10.   One who asserts that P believes that the proposition that P is true.

Since some conclusion like this is all that might be reasonably required as an a priori presumption in assessing the likelihood that a particular assertion is true, task (ii) noted previously does not require a notion of truth defined in terms of facts about speakers and hearers.

Indeed, none of the tasks do. Thus if one takes propositions to be things asserted by speakers and assessed for truth or falsity by hearers, then it is by no means clear that we need a notion of truth defined in terms of properties of language users. If one is a physicalist, one may want physicalistic accounts of what it is for an agent to believe or assert a proposition, as well as what it is for an utterance to express a proposition. However, the pressure for a physicalistic reduction will be on these notions rather than on the (non-Tarskian) notion of truth as a property of propositions.

This is evidently not the picture that Field has in mind. Unlike the view just outlined, Field does not take the required notion of truth to apply to propositions. Unlike Tarski, he also does not take it to apply to sentences (i.e., sentence types). Instead, Field's notion of truth applies to utterances—particular sounds or marks on paper. Thus in describing the physicalist's position, he says:

> People utter the sounds 'Electrons have rest mass but photons don't' . . . , and we apply the word 'true' to their utterances. We don't want to say that it is a primitive and inexplicable fact about those utterances that they are true, a fact that cannot be explicated in non-semantic terms; this is as unattractive to a physicalist as supposing that it is a primitive and inexplicable fact about an organism at a certain time that it is in pain.[33]

In effect, Field criticizes Tarski for not providing a physicalistically acceptable truth predicate of utterances.

But this is strange. Tarski was not concerned with utterances. Moreover, a theory of truth applying directly to utterances is not needed in order to answer Field's question about the factors determining whether or not an utterance is true. Confronted with the question

11.   In virtue of what are certain sounds true?

the natural response is to break it up into two subsidiary questions:

12a.   In virtue of what are those sounds the expression of a certain proposition?
  b.   In virtue of what is that proposition true?

Answering the first of these questions may be a daunting challenge to the physicalist; answering the second need not be.

Even if propositions are not invoked, essentially the same strategy of dealing with (11) is open to Tarski. Thus, confronted with (11), Tarski's response ought to be to replace it with the subsidiary questions in (13).

13a.   In virtue of what are the sounds an utterance of a certain sentence in L?
  b.   In virtue of what are sentences (of L) true in L?

Whereas Tarski provided an answer to the second question, the first was no part of his task.[34]

It is hard to see how Field himself could avoid some such division of labor. At one point, he suggests that in order to handle ambiguous and indexical expressions, truth definitions should be formulated in terms of tokens rather than types.[35] The idea is that utterances are contextually disambiguated and that semantic notions should apply to unambiguous entities. Field takes this to indicate that all clauses in a (Tarski-style) truth definition should be formulated so as to apply to tokens. To this end, he reformulates the clause for negation as (14).

14.   A token of $\ulcorner \sim e \urcorner$ is true (relative to a sequence) iff the token of e that it contains is not true (relative to the sequence).[36]

However, this will not do. As I indicated earlier, Field cannot accept any truth definition in which a certain syntactic form is simply stipulated to be a negation, for to do this would be to fail to explicate the facts about speakers in virtue of which negative constructions have the semantic properties they do. Instead, (14) must be replaced with something along the lines of (15).

15.   A token of a formula B, which is a negation of a formula A, is true (relative to a sequence) iff some designated token of A is not true (relative to the sequence).

But now there is a problem. Even if the notion of a formula B being a negation of a formula A can be given a physicalistic definition in terms of facts about how it is used by speakers, there there is no clear way of specifying the relevant token of A needed in (15); indeed, there is no way of ensuring that it will exist.

If we could count on utterances of negative sentences always containing, as proper parts, utterances of the sentences they are negations of, then the problem would not arise. Although this is a feature of certain artificial languages, it is not a characteristic of natural languages actually spoken by people. In order to avoid arbitrarily restricting truth definitions to (utterances involving) this subset of artificial languages, we need some way of eliminating undue dependence on empirically unreliable tokens. The most straightforward way of doing this is to define truth for a more reliable class of entities—either propositions expressed by utterances (as I would urge) or the sentence types that particular tokens are utterances of (as others might prefer).[37] Once this is done, the theorist is free to accept truth definitions in the Tarski style applying to sentence types or analogous characterizations of truth for propositions, while leaving it open whether the relations between speakers, utterances, expressions, sentence types, and propositions are purely physicalistic.

Conclusion

The upshot of this is that physicalism does not pose a direct challenge to theories of truth and does not provide an additional objection to the view that Tarski's definition is an adequate analysis of truth. Rather, the real problems for that view lie elsewhere. Despite the evident virtues of Tarski's definition and its demonstrated utility in metatheoretical investigations, it falls short of what might be expected from an analysis of truth in a number of respects. We have seen that his truth predicate differs significantly in meaning from natural-language predicates like 'true'. In addition, his technique for defining truth was designed for relatively simple artificial languages lacking many of the syntactic and semantic features of natural languages. Although various extensions and modifications of that technique have been applied to richer formal languages,[38] no treatment of English as a whole (or any other natural language) has been forthcoming. Most important, Tarski's notion of truth does not apply to propositions and (because of this) cannot be used to state truth conditions of sentences in a way that provides information about their meanings. Since there seems to be a genuine need for a notion of truth with these characteristics, it would appear that Tarski's definition should not be regarded as an analysis of truth.

Nevertheless, the definition is a valuable analytical tool that can be used to shed considerable light on a variety of issues involving the notion of truth. One of the most important of these is the Liar paradox and the lessons it holds for our understanding of both formal and natural languages. We will turn to this topic in chapter 5.

Appendix: A Defense of Tarski's Model-Theoretic Analysis of Logical Truth and Logical Consequence

In discussing the fruitfulness of Tarski's definition of truth in this chapter, I emphasized how Tarski was able to generalize his definition so as to provide a precise characterization of the notion of the truth of a sentence in a model, which serves as the basis of the now widely accepted analyses of logical consequence and logical truth.

> *Model-Theoretic Definitions of Logical Consequence and Logical Truth*
> A sentence c is a logical consequence of a set s of sentences iff there is no model in which all the sentences in s are true and c is false.
> A sentence s is a logical truth iff s is true in every model (which interprets all of the nonlogical vocabulary in s).[39]

These definitions are intended to be applied to a variety of formal languages, including languages of the standard first-order predicate calculus illustrated in chapter 3.

A further important application involves languages of the second-order predicate calculus. These languages are simple extensions of first-order languages with the single addition that they contain variables that count syntactically as predicates and function terms, along with those that are singular terms. Just as the first-order variables range over individuals of the domain (that can serve as potential denotations of singular terms), so the new second-order variables range over sets of n-tuples of elements drawn from the domain (that can serve as potential denotations of n-place predicates) and (total) functions from n-tuples of the domain into the domain (that can serve as potential denotations of n-ary function signs).

The standard notion of a model of a second-order language is just like that of a first-order language: the selection of a nonempty set of individuals to serve as the domain plus an assignment of appropriate denotations to each nonlogical symbol in the language. The definition of truth in a model is also the same, except for the addition of the following clauses for the new second-order quantifiers.

> *Truth in a Model (Relative to an Assignment) for Formulas with Second-Order Quantifiers*
> A formula ⌜(∀P F)⌝ or ⌜(∀f F)⌝ is true in a model M relative to an assignment A (of appropriate values to all first-and second-order variables) iff F is true in M relative to all assignments A' that differ at most from A in what denotation is assigned to the second-order predicate variable P or to the second-order function variable f. [Where v is any variable — whether first or second-order — ⌜∀v⌝ and ⌜(v)⌝ are equivalent notations for the universal quantifier.]
> A formula ⌜(∃P F)⌝ or ⌜(∃f F)⌝ is true in a model M relative to an assignment A (of appropriate values to all first-and second-order variables) iff there is some

assignment A' that differs at most from A in what it assigns to the second-order predicate variable P or to the second-order function variable f and F is true in M relative to A'.[40]

For example, if P is a one-place predicate variable and v is an individual variable, the sentence $\ulcorner(\exists P \forall v\ Pv)\urcorner$ is true in a model M iff there is some subset of the domain of M of which every individual in the domain is a member. Since the domain always counts as a subset of itself, this sentence is true in all models and so is a logical truth according to the model-theoretic account.

Despite the fact that Tarski's model-theoretic definitions of logical consequence and logical truth have been very widely accepted as analyses of these notions, this position has recently been challenged by John Etchemendy in his book *The Concept of Logical Consequence*.[41] Etchemendy presents two sorts of criticisms. The first questions various historical details of Tarski's discussion in "On the Concept of Logical Consequence"[42] and the relation between his original definitions and the now-familiar model-theoretic definitions given previously. The second attacks the model-theoretic definitions directly and argues that they cannot serve as philosophical analyses. The historical criticisms include (i) the claim that Tarski's original definitions differ from the now-standard model-theoretic definitions in that they were not intended to allow variations in domain from one model to another; (ii) the claim that Tarski recognized the need to demonstrate that if Q is a logical consequence of P, then it is a necessary truth that if P is true then Q is true, and he gave a fallacious argument that this result follows from his definition of logical consequence; (iii) the claim that no such demonstration can be given if Tarski's analysis is accepted; and (iv) the claim that Tarski's discussion of the relevance of ω-incomplete theories of arithmetic to a proper account of logical consequence is confused. In my view, all of these essentially historical criticisms have been refuted by a variety of scholars, with the most thorough and penetrating refutation I am aware of being given by Mario Gomez-Torrente in his dissertation, "Tarski's Definition of Logical Consequence: Historical and Philosophical Aspects."[43] I will therefore treat Tarski's original accounts of logical consequence and logical truth as equivalent to the standard model-theoretic characterizations given previously, and I will confine my attention to Etchemendy's arguments that these cannot serve as philosophical analyses of the notions in question. For simplicity, I will follow him in focusing exclusively on logical truth since the points made in his arguments and the objections I will make to them can easily be carried over to a discussion of logical consequence.[44]

Etchemendy's two most important arguments link the model-theoretic characterization of logical truth to potentially controversial claims in set theory. The central idea behind the arguments is that for certain sentences s, the model-theoretic definition of logical truth makes the characterization of s as a logical truth or as not a logical truth depend on substantive, nonlogical considerations about the size of the set-theoretic universe. In the case of first-order logic, there are first-order sentences that are not genuine logical truths but that would be true in all models if the set-theoretic universe (available for constructing models) were finite. Thus if the model-theoretic definition of logical truth is accepted, then the only way to avoid extensional incorrectness is to postulate an infinite set-theoretic universe. However, according to Etchemendy, there is still a problem. Since this strategy makes the logical status of certain first-order sentences depend on the claim that the set-theoretic universe is infinite, the strategy is forced to mischaracterize the set-theoretic claim as itself being a logical truth. For this reason, he concludes that the model-theoretic account cannot be accepted as an adequate *analysis* of the notion of logical truth.

The argument is similar in the second-order case, except that here the criticism is sharper since Etchemendy contends that there is no avoiding extensional incorrectness. In this case, there is a controversial nonlogical hypothesis CH about the size of the set-theoretic universe which is such that (i) if CH is true, then there is some second-order sentence that will be true in all models because CH is true and (ii) if CH is not true, then there is a different second-order sentence that will be true in all models because CH is not true. In either case, some sentence gets declared to be a logical truth by the model-theoretic definition because a certain nonlogical fact obtains. But no genuine logical truth can depend on a nonlogical truth in this way. Hence, whether CH is true or not, the model-theoretic definition will wrongly characterize as logically true some second-order sentence that is not a genuine logical truth.

As we will see, these arguments presuppose some grasp of the notion of logical truth that is independent of and antecedent to the usual model-theoretic definitions. This presupposition is bolstered by the fact that logicians prior to Tarski did, of course, make use of the concepts of logical truth and logical consequence. In fact, it was common in the period just prior to his article on the subject to regard a sentence as logically true just in case it is true in all models. As Tarski himself notes, his contribution was to make this notion precise by showing how the notion of truth in a model could be formalized and made mathematically tractable using the concepts from his earlier definition of truth.[45] Thus it is not surprising that he was confident that he did capture the preformal notion that working logicians had in mind.

However, this is not all there is to the story. Etchemendy maintains that there are certain constraints on what logic is and hence on what a truth of logic should be. Although these constraints are implicitly accepted by practitioners of logic, Etchemendy thinks they are missed or violated by the usual model-theoretic treatment. He does not spend a great deal of time clarifying and making precise exactly what these constraints are. However, it appears from his discussion that they include the following:[46]

C1.   If s is logically true, then s is a necessary truth.
C2.   If s is logically true, then s is knowable a priori.
C3.   If s is logically true, then s is analytic.

Etchemendy seems to lay most weight on (C3), which involves the notion of analyticity. Although the notion is never precisely defined, the general idea seems to be roughly as follows. A sentence s is analytic iff s is true in virtue of meaning — that is, iff someone who understands s thereby possesses information that, in principle, makes it possible to recognize its truth. Let us further characterize the claim (proposition) expressed by an analytic sentence as analytic. In doing so, we grant that the reasoning required to recognize the truth of an analytic sentence, given the information that comes from understanding it, may in certain cases be complex and challenging. Thus analytic sentences need not be obvious, and someone can understand such a sentence at a certain time and still not recognize it to be true at that time. Still, what is needed for someone to recognize its truth is not further information.

At crucial points in his discussion, Etchemendy focuses on a special subclass of analytic truths—namely, those that are true solely in virtue of the meanings of the logical constants they contain (the universal and existential quantifiers, the identity predicate, plus the usual truth-functional connectives). As the following passage indicates, he suggests that a sentence is a genuine logical truth, in the "ordinary" preformal sense, iff it is true solely in virtue of the meanings of its (standard) logical constants:

> What we have here is a perfectly understandable notion that could well pass for a relativized version of logical truth, for the notion of logical truth *with respect to an arbitrary selection of fixed terms*. Of course, it seems most natural to apply the term *logical* truth when this concept is relativized to expressions of traditional interest to logicians, expressions like 'or' and 'everyone'. When the collection includes such expressions as 'is a man' and 'is a bachelor', we might want to revert to a term like *analytic*; "logical truth" seems a bit of a stretch. But what is important is that the basic idea, the idea of a sentence that owes its truth to nothing more than the meanings of some (perhaps proper) subset of its expressions, is easily extended to the general case. The concept that results is something like this. Certain sentences are true merely by virtue of the meanings of their expressions. With some of these sentences, this fact will depend on the meanings of all of the sentence's constituent expressions equally. But with others, including all the examples we have looked at, the fact depends only on the specific meanings of certain of those expressions, plus very general assumptions about the semantic categories of the remaining expressions. This is what gives rise to an intuitive relativization of our concept of logical truth, what makes sense of the notion of a sentence being logically true with respect to an arbitrary selection of expressions. The selected expressions are those whose specific meanings, as opposed to general semantic category, are relevant to the sentence's analytic truth.
>
> When the selected expressions include only those of a traditional "logical" sort— connectives, quantifiers, and so forth—this relative notion coincides with one standard conception of logical truth. The basic idea of this conception is often described as follows: a sentence is *logically* true if it is true *solely by virtue of the meaning of the logical vocabulary it contains.*[47]

Etchemendy goes on to ask whether Tarski's model-theoretic definition captures this notion of logical truth. He argues that it does not, devoting chapter 8 to the case of languages of the first-and second-order predicate calculus, where the logical vocabulary is taken to consist of the standard set of quantifiers and connectives plus the identity predicate. In what follows, we will consider these cases one at a time.

Etchemendy's Argument That First-Order Logical
Truth Cannot Be Analyzed as Truth in All Models

The argument in the first-order case involves sentences of the following sort.

σ_2 $\exists x \, \exists y \, (x \neq y)$
σ_3 $\exists x \, \exists y \, \exists z \, (x \neq y \, \& \, y \neq z \, \& \, x \neq z)$

For each sentence σ_n in this series and each model M, σ_n is true in M iff there are at least n objects in the domain of M.[48] Thus if we consider the negations of these sentences, we find that $\neg\sigma_n$ is true in M iff there are fewer than n objects in the domain of M.

$\neg\sigma_2$ $\neg\exists x \, \exists y \, (x \neq y)$
$\neg\sigma_3$ $\neg\exists x \, \exists y \, \exists z \, (x \neq y \, \& \, y \neq z \, \& \, x \neq z)$

What interests Etchemendy about this last sequence of sentences is that if the set-theoretic universe were to turn out to be finite, then for some finite n, every model would have a domain with fewer than n elements and $\neg\sigma_n$ plus all sentences following it in the sequence would be true in all models, and hence would be characterized by the model-theoretic definition as logical truths. But surely, Etchemendy argues, this would be wrong, since whether or not something is a logical truth should not depend on the size of the set-theoretic universe.

Etchemendy states his view as follows:

> For each n, $\neg\sigma_n$ says that there are fewer than n objects in the universe. Once again, none of these should come out logically true, no matter how large or small the universe happens to be. But consider how the standard account assesses these sentences. . . . If the universe is finite, the present account will mistakenly pronounce an infinite number of the sentences $\neg\sigma_2$, $\neg\sigma_3$, . . . logically true. Of course, if the universe is infinite, none of these sentences will be declared logically true. But is that because the account has captured our ordinary notion of logical truth? After all, these sentences are not *in fact* logically true, but neither would they *be* logically true if the universe were finite. . . .
>
> How does the standard semantics deal with this problem? After all, the sentences $\neg\sigma_2$, $\neg\sigma_3$, . . . do not come out logically true according to the usual, model-theoretic account, at least as it is ordinarily presented; if they did the analysis would have few, if any, defenders. Exactly what feature of the standard semantics assures us that none of these is declared a logical truth? . . .
>
> Now in the standard presentation the only thing that assures us that none of the above sentences comes out logically true is the axiom of infinity assumed in the underlying set theory. It is this axiom that guarantees the existence of infinite models (that is, infinite restriction sets for interpreting our quantifiers), and so that guarantees interpretations of $\exists$ in which all these sentences come out false. . . .
>
> It is important to see exactly what is going on here. The basic problem to be addressed is this. Our assessments of the logical status of $\neg\sigma_2$, $\neg\sigma_3$, . . . are dependent on a non-logical feature of the world, the size of the universe. So long as this de-

pendence remains, our definition clearly has not captured the ordinary concept of logical truth, nor do we have any internal guarantee of its extensional adequacy. For none of these sentences is a logical truth, and neither would any of them *be* logical truths if the universe were finite.[49]

In this argument, Etchemendy is not saying that the standard model-theoretic account wrongly classifies any first-order sentence as a logical truth that is not a genuine logical truth. Nor does he claim that it wrongly classifies any first-order sentence as not being a logical truth that really is. Hence he is not arguing that the model-theoretic account is extensionally incorrect for first-order languages. Rather, he is saying that the account does not qualify as an *analysis* of the notion of first-order logical truth because it wrongly makes the classification of certain sentences as not being logical truths depend on a nonlogical fact about the size of the set-theoretic universe. He has no quarrel with the claim that there are infinitely many sets—for example, the empty set, the set containing the empty set, the set containing the previous two, the set containing the previous three, and so on. Hence he has no quarrel with the claim that there are models with infinite domains in which each sentence in $\neg\sigma_2, \neg\sigma_3, \ldots$ is false. What he objects to, as he puts it, is the idea that if the set-theoretic universe *were* finite, then some of these sentences *would be* logical truths. Since, in his view, taking the model-theoretic account as an analysis commits one to this idea, he takes himself to have shown that the account does not provide an adequate *analysis* of first-order logical truth.

At this point, it may be useful to clear away a bothersome but ultimately irrelevant objection. If one looks at each $\neg\sigma_n$, one may notice that it contains more than n expressions. Because of this, any situation in which fewer than n things of any kind exist in the whole universe is a situation in which the sentence $\neg\sigma_n$ does not itself exist. But surely, it might be objected, if the sentence does not exist in the situation, it will not incorrectly be classified as a logical truth in the situation and so the situation will not count as a counterexample to the model-theoretic analysis of logical truth.[50]

Fortunately, there is no need to speculate about how Etchemendy might respond to this objection since his point can be made with sentences that do not have this special peculiarity. For example, consider sentence (1).

1. $\forall x [\sim Rxx \ \& \ \exists y \ Rxy] \ \& \ \forall x \ \forall y \ \forall z \ [(Rxy \ \& \ Ryz) \supset Rxz]$

One can see, from understanding the logical vocabulary of (1)—the universal quantifier, the existential quantifier, conjunction, and material implication—plus from understanding what it means for a sentence to be true in a model, that (1) is true only in models in which some subset of the domain contains infinitely many members. For the same reason, one can see that the negation, (2), of (1) is false only in models in which some subset of the domain has infinitely many members.

2. $\sim (\forall x [\sim Rxx \ \& \ \exists y \ Rxy] \ \& \ \forall x \ \forall y \ \forall z \ [(Rxy \ \& \ Ryz) \supset Rxz])$

THE SIGNIFICANCE OF TARSKI'S THEORY OF TRUTH   123

Because of this, (2) can play the role of the sentences in $\neg\sigma_2$, $\neg\sigma_3$, ... in Etchemendy's argument. Just as none of the sentences in $\neg\sigma_2$, $\neg\sigma_3$, ... is a genuine logical truth, neither is (2). Just as accepting the existence of infinite sets allows the model-theoretic account correctly to classify the sentences in $\neg\sigma_2$, $\neg\sigma_3$, ... as not being logical truths, so it allows the account correctly to classify (2) as not being a logical truth. The problem, as Etchemendy sees it, is that taking the model-theoretic account to be an *analysis* commits one to the incorrect claim that if the universe *were* finite, then (2) *would be* a logical truth.

At this point, there is another objection to Etchemendy's argument that appears to be telling. Not only are there infinitely many sets, but also it is necessarily true that there are. After all, in any possible state of the world, no matter what else existed, the empty set would exist. But then the set whose only member is the empty set would exist, as would the set containing both the empty set and the set whose only member is the empty set, and so on ad infinitum. Thus not only is the set-theoretic universe not finite, but also it could not have been finite. This means that in the model-theoretic account, the sentences in $\neg\sigma_2$, $\neg\sigma_3$, ... are not logical truths and *could not* have been logical truths.[51] But then we have no objection to taking the model-theoretic account to be an *analysis* of first-order logical truth.

Etchemendy is well aware of this objection to his argument, and he has a reply to it:

> The problem these sentences bring out remains even if we consider the finitist to be necessarily wrong—that is even if we take the axiom of infinity to be a necessary truth. All we need recognize is that the axiom of infinity, and its various consequences, are not *logical* truths. This is all that is required to see that the output of Tarski's account is still influenced by extralogical facts—in this case by the set-theoretic fact expressed by the axiom of infinity. . . .
>
> Now if we still want to claim that the standard semantics avoids the intuitive defect . . . , there seems only one recourse available. We must claim that the axiom of infinity does not express an "extralogical" claim, and so that our account is not, at least on this score, subject to extralogical influence. But this response is implausible in the extreme. For if it is a logical truth that there are infinitely many objects, then it must equally be a logical truth that there are at least twenty-seven. So to execute this defense consistently we would have to argue that, contrary to our initial impressions, all of the σ_n really *should* be judged logically true.[52]

Etchemendy's contention, I take it, is that the only way to defend the model-theoretic account as an *analysis* of logical truth is to maintain that it is *logically true* that there are infinitely many things. However, not only is this defense extremely implausible, but also it is self-defeating since it requires classifying each σ_n as a logical truth, despite the fact that the standard account routinely treats it as nonlogical.

Although it is clear that Etchemendy thinks this, it is not obvious why he does. What needs to be shown is that the model-theoretic account can provide a correct analysis of the notion of logical truth only if the claim that there are infinite sets is a logical truth. Although Etchemendy asserts this, he does not offer any argument for it. Consequently, we need to try to reconstruct a line of reasoning that might make this seem plausible.

The following seems like a good place to begin.

S1.   If Tarski's model-theoretic definition of logical truth is a correct analysis of that notion, then for any sentence s, the claim that s is a logical truth is analytically equivalent to the claim that s is true in all models, and the claim that s is not a logical truth is analytically equivalent to the claim that there is a model in which s is false.

The justification for this first step in the argument comes from our conception of what an analysis is. As I pointed out earlier in the chapter in connection with Tarski's definition of truth, the aim of his analyses was not to produce exact synonyms of the informal, pretheoretic notions under analysis. Rather, his definitions should be viewed as explications of the concepts under investigation. In general, an explication of some pretheoretically understood concept C consists in the definition of a related concept C' that (i) applies to those things that are clear and central instances of the concept C; (ii) is precise and well defined; (iii) is free of difficulties and obscurities present in the original concept C; and (iv) may play the role of C in all theoretical contexts in which that notion is legitimately required. The claim that the model-theoretic definition of logical truth provides an analysis of that notion should be understood as the claim that it satisfies these criteria. If this claim is correct, then we can take the notion of logical truth employed in any theoretical context to be identical with the model-theoretic notion. Treating (S1) as itself providing such a theoretical context, we see that accepting the model theoretic account as an analysis commits us to (S1).

What about the claim that sentence (2) is false only in models in which some subset of the domain has infinitely many members? Is it analytic? Let us take this question to be about the following sentence.

3.   '~ ($\forall$x [~Rxx & $\exists$y Rxy] & $\forall$x $\forall$y $\forall$z [(Rxy & Ryz)$\supset$ Rxz])' is false only in models in which some subset of the domain has infinitely many members.

Whether or not (3) is analytic depends on the status we accord to the characterization of truth in a model used in Tarski's analysis of logical truth. We are assuming, for the sake of argument, that the characterization of logical truth as truth in all models is an analysis and so gives us an analytic equivalence. At issue now are the precise formulation and status of Tarski's "definition" of truth in a model. One alternative is to take it to be a genuine definition that introduces and fully specifies the content of the two-place predicate S is true in model M, without the use of any undefined semantic primitives. If we think of it in this way, then it is natural to formulate the clauses as making specific reference to various logical symbols, as in (4).

4a. ⌜F & G⌝ is true in a model M (relative to an assignment A of values to variables) iff both F and G are true in M (relative to A).

b. ⌜∀x S(x)⌝ is true in a model M relative to an assignment A iff S(x) is true in M relative to all assignments that differ from A at most in what they assign to 'x'.

If the "definition" of truth in a model is understood and constructed in this way, mentioning the various symbols occurring in sentence (2), then (3) may be considered analytic.

However, there is another way of interpreting the characterization of truth in a model. Instead of seeing it as a genuine definition that introduces and gives content to a new semantic predicate, S *is true in model M*, we can see it as a substantive characterization of the truth conditions of sentences *when the expressions of the language are interpreted as indicated by the model*—that is, when the names are treated as *referring to* the objects assigned to them in the model, when the predicates are treated as *applying to* members of the sets assigned to them in the model, and so on. To view the characterization of truth in a model in this way is to see it as invoking the ordinary notions of truth, reference, and application in a fashion analogous to the way in which a proponent of Donald Davidson's conception of theories of meaning is required to view Tarski's original characterization of truth.

If one takes this approach, then it is natural to go a step further and formulate the clauses in the characterization of truth in a model in a general way that does not mention particular expressions, as in (5).

5a. The conjunction of formulas F and G is true in a model M (relative to assignment A of values to variables) iff both F and G are true in M (relative to A).

b. The universal generalization of a formula S(x) is true in a model M relative to an assignment A iff S(x) is true in M relative to all assignments that differ from A at most in what they assign to 'x'.

The difference between (4) and (5) is that the latter leaves it open precisely how conjunctions and universal generalizations are formed, whereas the former mentions the particular symbols involved. If the style of (5) is followed throughout, then the characterization of truth in a model will not mention any particular symbols and the application of the definition to any specific (first-order) language must be supplemented with an indication of which symbols stand for the universal and existential quantifiers in the language, the identity predicate, plus the usual truth-functional operators. In this conception, (3) is not analytic since one could fully understand the sentence without having the information that '&' is the symbol for conjunction, '∀x' is the symbol for universal quantification, and so on needed to verify that (3) is true.[53]

For the purpose of evaluating Etchemendy's argument, it is not crucial to decide between these two ways of understanding the characterization of truth in a model. However, we do need an extension of the notion of analyticity for characterizing (3) if the second way of understanding truth in a model is presupposed. Let us say that a sentence s is *virtually analytic* just in case someone who understands s and all expressions quoted or otherwise named in s thereby possesses information that in principle (with sufficient reasoning and reflection), makes it possible to recognize the truth of s. Then all analytic sentences are virtually analytic. In addition, (3) may reasonably be taken to be virtually analytic in this sense (in either construal of the notion of truth in a model).

We may now continue our reconstruction of Etchemendy's argument against Tarski's model-theoretic analysis of logical truth for first-order logic. The next steps in the argument are as follows:

> S2.   It is (virtually) analytic that (2) is false only in models in which some subset of the domain has infinitely many members.
>
> S3.   So if Tarski's model-theoretic account is a correct analysis, then it is (virtually) analytic that if (2) is not a logical truth, then there are sets with infinitely many members (infinite sets).
>
> S4.   In point of fact, we know that (2) is not a logical truth. (Let us take this to be a constraint on any adequate analysis.)

So far we have reached the intermediate result that if one takes Tarski's definition to be an adequate analysis, one is committed to both of the following: (i) it is (virtually) analytic that if (2) is not a logical truth, then there are infinite sets, and (ii) (2) is not a logical truth. If we could validly conclude

> A.   It is (virtually) analytic that Q

from P plus

> B.   It is (virtually) analytic that [if P then Q],

then (S3) and (S4) would assure us that to take Tarski's definition to be an analysis would be to commit ourselves to the claim that *it is virtually analytic, and hence analytic, that there are infinite sets*.[54] This seems close to the reductio ad absurdum that Etchemendy is looking for.

However, there is an obvious problem that must be confronted. To conclude (A) from (B) plus P would be to commit a modal fallacy; to validly conclude (A) from (B), one needs the supplementary premise (C).

> C.   It is (virtually) analytic that P.

Consequently, what we need if our reconstruction of Etchemendy's argument is to succeed is not simply the claim

> 6.   (2) is not a logical truth,

but rather the claim

7.   It is (virtually) analytic that (2) is not a logical truth.

Etchemendy does not provide an argument for this premise or even seem to notice that one is needed. How might it be established? Consider the principles in (S5).

S5a.   For all sentences s, if s is a logical truth, then it is virtually analytic that s is a logical truth.
  b.   For all sentences s, if s is not a logical truth, then it is virtually analytic that s is not a logical truth.

One might attempt to defend the application of (S5a) to first-order logic along something like the following lines: The completeness proof for first-order logic guarantees that if s is a first-order logical truth, then s can be proved using purely logical principles. But if one has proved, on the basis of logic alone, that s is true, then merely by reflecting on what one has done, one can come to know that s is a truth that can be proved by logic alone and hence that s is a logical truth. Recall now that Etchemendy supposes that the logical principles needed to prove s are analytic and can be known on the basis of one's understanding of the logical vocabulary. It would seem to follow that understanding the meaning of the logical vocabulary is sufficient, in principle, to allow one to establish that s is true and then, by reflecting on how one established this, to conclude that s is a logical truth. If this is right, then for any first-order logical truth s, it is virtually analytic that s is a logical truth. This would give us (S5a).

Of course, what we need for our reconstruction of Etchemendy's argument is a justification of (S5b). Suppose, for the sake of argument, that we had one. Then, from (S3), (S4), and (S5b), we could validly infer (S6).

S6.   If Tarski's model-theoretic definition is a correct analysis of the notion of logical truth, then the claim that there are sets with infinitely many members is analytic.

Finally, if the claim that it is analytic that there are infinite sets is truly indefensible, then one could agree with Etchemendy that Tarski's model-theoretic definition of logical truth cannot be taken to be an analysis of the informal, pretheoretic notion.

There are, however, two crippling problems with this argument. First, no compelling justification can be given either for the general principle (S5b) or for the particular claim that it is virtually analytic that (2) is not a logical truth. Second, even if the conclusion that it is analytic that there are sets with infinitely many members could be derived, it is not obvious that this would constitute a reductio ad absurdum of the model-theoretic analysis. What Etchemendy actually claims to be absurd is the view that it is a *logical truth* that there are infinite sets and hence that the axiom of infinity of standard (first-order) set theory is a logical truth. Certainly this axiom is not normally regarded as a logical truth nowadays. Etchemendy thinks that it should not be so regarded since he believes that our intuitive notion of logical truth is a restricted subcase of analyticity — a sentence is a logical truth iff it is true solely in virtue of the meanings of those of its expressions that are taken to be part of the *logical* vocabulary. In the case of a first-order sentence, this means that a sentence is a logical truth in the intuitive sense only if it is true solely in virtue of the meanings of the truth-functional connectives, the universal and existential quantifiers (excluding any assumptions about their range),[55] plus the identity sign. Since any sentence that might play the role of an axiom of infinity in first-order set theory is one whose truth depends on the meaning given the nonlogical symbol 'ε' (for set membership), plus a special interpretation of the quantifiers as ranging over sets, it is obvious that this axiom is not a logical truth.[56] However, even if such a sentence is not true solely in virtue of the meanings of its logical vocabulary, it might still be true solely in virtue of its logical and non-logical vocabulary together and thus be analytic. To get a reductio, what one must show is that there is a sense of analyticity that both validates the argument (S1)–(S6) and renders the claim that it is analytic that there are sets with infinitely many members absurd. As we will see, it is extremely implausible to suppose that this can be done.

Let us begin with (S5b). Whether or not one accepts the above defense of (S5a), it is clear that a similar defense cannot be given of (S5b). Since first-order logic is complete but not decidable, there is no effective procedure which when given a sentence that is not a logical truth, will always be able to show that it is not a logical truth. Given any first-order sentence s, one could, if one chose to do so, start running through all legitimate proofs of first-order sentences looking for a proof of s. The problem with doing this, however, is that there is no general upper bound for how long one might have to look before concluding that s is not provable and so is not a logical truth. Hence we have no guarantee that any sentence that is not a logical truth can be shown not to be a logical truth "by logic alone."

With this mode of justification closed to us, we must ask whether (S5b), or even just the particular claim (7), can be established. The prospects of this are exceedingly dim. Recall the conception of analysis invoked earlier to justify (S1). According to this conception, the model-theoretic definition will qualify as an analysis iff its definiens — that is *s is true in all models* — could, in principle, serve all legitimate theoretical functions of *is a logical truth*. Suppose we think that it does qualify as an analysis in this sense. Then we may take claims (6) and (7) to have precisely the same content as (6_A) and (7_A).

6_A.   It is not the case that (2) is true in all models.

7_A.   It is (virtually) analytic that it is not the case that (2) is true in all models.

Is (6_A) virtually analytic or not? The answer is not transparent. One might, for example, make the following case that it is. Anyone who understands (6_A) is in a position to infer that it is true iff there are models in which (2) is false. If one also understands (2), one is in a position further to infer that there are models in which (2) is false only if there are sets with infinitely many members. Are there such sets? It is very natural to think not only that there are but also that the claim that there are is both necessary and a priori. But if the claim that there are sets with infinitely many members is a priori, then it is in principle possible for our subject, who understands both (6_A) and (2), to come to know that there are without being given any information beyond that which the subject already possesses. Putting all this together, we may conclude that (6_A) is virtually analytic since someone who understands both (6_A) and (2) can, in principle, establish a priori that it is true. However, this result is of no help in providing the reductio that Etchemendy desires since the same reasoning used to show that (6_A) is virtually analytic establishes that the claim that there are sets with infinitely many members is itself analytic.

It might be objected that this result presupposes a conception of analyticity that is too broad since it includes all necessary, a priori truths. Perhaps there is a more restrictive conception that would serve Etchemendy's purposes better. Since such a conception is nowhere spelled out, this speculation is tentative in the extreme. However, perhaps some idea like the following could be made out. Call a sentence *analytically obvious* iff failure to recognize its truth is sufficient to show that one does not understand it. Call a sentence *strongly analytic* iff it can be established by a valid proof, each line of which is analytically obvious. Finally, imagine in the preceding argument that we replace references to analyticity (and virtual analyticity) with references to strong analyticity (and virtual strong analyticity).

It is arguable that someone who understands the notion of a set and grasps the argument that there are sets with infinitely many members might nevertheless deny the conclusion of that argument. In my opinion, and I take it in Etchemendy's, such a person would be wrong—even necessarily wrong and a priori wrong. Still one might maintain that when such a person uses the word *set* in a sentence, that person means what we mean and expresses the same proposition we do. If this position is correct, then the claim that there are sets with infinitely many members is *not* strongly analytic. However, again this is no help in producing a reductio of the model-theoretic analysis of logical truth since in this account, (6_A) will not be (virtually) strongly analytic either.

Indeed, it seems clear that there is no reasonable conception of analyticity that makes (7_A) true and the claim that it is analytic that there are sets with infinitely many members false. In my view, this dooms Etchemendy's attempt to give a reductio of the model-theoretic analysis. The only possible strategy remaining for salvaging the reductio is to claim that there is an informal, pretheoretic sense of *logical truth* and a reasonable sense of *analyticity* with the following two features:

i.   In these senses, the claim that (6) is virtually analytic is true whereas the claim that it is analytic that there are sets with infinitely many members is false.
ii. Nothing can count as an adequate analysis of logical truth unless it preserves (i) (given the same sense of analyticity).

But there is no reason to think that these two conditions can jointly be satisfied. If, as is commonly believed, the claim that there are infinitely many sets is both necessary and a priori, then the notion of analyticity required to satisfy (i) must be such that claims that are both necessarily and a priori equivalent may fail to be analytically equivalent.[57] But then the satisfaction of (ii) will have the effect that even a formally correct, noncircular, and otherwise acceptable analysis of logical truth in which the *analysans* is necessarily and a priori equivalent to the *analysandum* (the informal notion of logical truth), as well as being able to do all the theoretical work required of the *analysandum*, may be judged to be inadequate on the grounds that *analysandum* and *analysans* are not analytically equivalent in the requisite sense. This is unreasonable. Philosophically interesting analyses are not attempts to produce synonyms or anything approaching this very strong, imagined sense of analytic equivalence. Hence the notion of analyticity needed for (i) undermines (ii), and we may conclude that Etchemendy's attempt to show that the model-theoretic account fails to provide an analysis of first-order logical truth does not succeed.

Etchemendy's Argument That the Model-Theoretic Definition of Logical Truth Is Extensionally Incorrect for Second-Order Logic

Etchemendy's argument regarding second-order logic is an application of a line of reasoning very similar to that used in the first-order case. With respect to first-order logical truth, he admits that the model-theoretic definition is extensionally correct; it picks out the right class of sentences. However, it succeeds in doing so only by its dependence on substantive assumptions about the size of the set-theoretic universe. In particular, it is only the assumption of infinite domains that allows the definition to avoid wrongly characterizing certain sentences as logical truths. Etchemendy thinks that this dependence shows something illegitimate about the definition—namely, that it is forced to treat a substantive assumption about the set-theoretic universe as if it were a logical truth. We have seen that this is untrue. The ability of the model-theoretic definition to avoid classifying the relevant sentences as logical truths *does not require* classifying assumptions about the size of the set-theoretic universe as *logically true* or even as *analytic* in any sense in which such a claim would be objectionable.

In the second-order case, Etchemendy argues that certain unavoidable facts about the size of the set-theoretic universe combined with the model-theoretic definition lead to the classification of certain second-order sentences as logical truths that, in fact, are not logical truths. Hence he claims that the definition is extensionally incorrect. The argument is based on two "equivalences":

E1.   It is a fact about second-order logic that there is a second-order sentence A that is false in a model M iff some subset of the domain of M is larger than the set of natural numbers but smaller than the set of all sets of natural numbers (the power set of the set of natural numbers).[58] There is an unproved hypothesis in set theory, called the continuum hypothesis, that says that there is no set of such an intermediate size.[59] Thus, the relevant second-order sentence A is such that the claim that it is true in all interpretations and hence qualifies under the model-theoretic definition as a logical truth is, in a certain sense, "equivalent to" the continuum hypothesis in set theory.[60]

E2. It is also a fact about second-order logic that there is a second-order sentence B that is false in a model M iff the domain D of M is the same size as the power set of natural numbers but D has no subsets of intermediate size—larger than the set of natural numbers but smaller than the power set. If the continuum hypothesis is false—and hence its negation is true—such a domain will always have such intermediate subsets. So if the continuum hypothesis is false, then there is no model falsifying B, and B gets classified as a model-theoretic logical truth. In short, the claim that B is true in all models and hence is a model-theoretic logical truth is "equivalent to" the negation of the continuum hypothesis.

In a nutshell, Etchemendy's argument based on these "equivalences" is as follows. Neither the continuum hypothesis nor its negation is a logical truth. Thus nothing "equivalent" to either is a logical truth. This means that neither the claim that A is true in all models nor the claim that B is true in all models is a logical truth. Etchemendy takes this as showing that neither A nor B can themselves be genuine logical truths. But since either the continuum hypothesis or its negation is true, it follows that either A is true in all models or B is true in all models. Either way, we have a sentence that is true in all models but is not a genuine logical truth. Hence the model-theoretic definition is extensionally incorrect.[61]

The argument may be reconstructed as follows:

The Basic Argument

S1. A is true in all models iff the continuum hypothesis is true.
S2. B is true in all models iff the negation of the continuum hypothesis is true.
S3. Neither the continuum hypothesis nor its negation is a logical truth.
S4. So neither the claim that A is true in all models nor the claim that B is true in all models is a logical truth.
S5. For all s, if s is a logical truth, then the claim that s is true in all models is a logical truth.
S6. Thus neither A nor B is a logical truth.
S7. Either the continuum hypothesis is true or its negation is true.
S8. But this means that either A is true in all models or B is true in all models.
S9. So if the model-theoretic definition of logical truth is extensionally correct, then either A is a logical truth or B is a logical truth.
S10. Since the consequent of (S9) contradicts (S6), the model-theoretic definition of logical truth is not extensionally correct.

The first problem with this argument is that (S4) does not follow from (S1)–(S3). Rather, it follows from (S3) together with the claims that (S1) and (S2) are logical truths. But they are not logical truths, nor, as they stand, are they regarded as such by anyone. There are two alternatives for dealing with this difficulty. The first alternative follows the pattern used in the first-order case, substituting the claim that (S1) and (S2) are virtually analytic for the claim that they are logical truths. In this construal, the argument becomes:

First Reformulation of the Argument

$S1_1$.   It is virtually analytic that A is true in all models iff the continuum hypothesis is true.

$S2_1$.   It is virtually analytic that B is true in all models iff the negation of the continuum hypothesis is true.

$S3_1$.   Neither the continuum hypothesis nor its negation is an analytic truth.

$S4_1$.   So neither the claim that A is true in all models nor the claim that B is true in all models is virtually analytic.

$S5_1$.   For all s, if s is a logical truth, then the claim that s is true in all models is virtually analytic.

S6–S9.   As before.

In this way of viewing the argument, one needs a conception of analyticity that validates $(S1_1)$–$(S3_1)$. Sentences A and B are rather complex, and the reasoning connecting their being true in all models with the truth or falsity of the continuum hypothesis is quite complicated. Because of this, it is surely possible for someone to understand A, B, (S1), and (S2) without recognizing the truth of (S1) and (S2). On the other hand, the reasoning establishing (S1) and (S2) can be broken down into fairly obvious steps, each of which is both necessary and recognizable a priori. It is not obvious that this is true of the continuum hypothesis or its negation. Perhaps there is even some stronger sense of analyticity according to which (S1) and (S2) are virtually analytic because they can be established by a series of steps, each of which is tied in some close way to an understanding of the meanings of the relevant terms, whereas this is not true of the continuum hypothesis or its negation. Consequently, although this has not by any means been proved, it might turn out that there is a defensible sense of analyticity that validates $(S1_1)$–$(S4_1)$.

This is one way of getting to (a version of) (S5). Mario Gomez-Torrente has pointed out that there is a second way of construing the argument that allows us to reach a similar result.[62] The first step is to formulate the continuum hypothesis and its negation as sentences in standard first-order set theory, CH and ~CH. Next, by a system of coding analogous to Gödel numbering, we can formulate a sentence CODE(VALID A) of that language which has the form

8. $\forall x$ (x is a model of [A] $\supset$ [A] is true in x)—where '[A]' refers to the set that codes sentence A

and which is true in the intended interpretation of set theory iff the second-order sentence A is true in all models. Ditto for B and CODE(VALID B). It can then be shown that

9a.   CODE(VALID A) iff CH
  b.   CODE(VALID B) iff ~CH

are theorems provable in standard (Zermelo-Fraenkel) set theory and hence that CODE(VALID A) and CODE(VALID B) are provably equivalent in ZF set theory to CH and ~CH, respectively.

The question now arises, "Can we get from this equivalence, plus the observation that neither CH nor ~CH is a logical truth, to the claim that neither CODE(VALID A) nor CODE(VALID B) is a logical truth?". The answer, of course, is that we cannot. If such an inference were valid, then a similar inference could be used to establish the absurd conclusion that there are no logical truths, for where s is any undisputed logical truth — for example, *If p then p* — s is provably equivalent in ZF to any theorem of ZF. Since many of these theorems are not logical truths, the relevant inference would tell us that s is not either. Consequently, another route to (S4) in Etchemendy's argument must be found.

Gomez-Torrente observes that reformulating the argument in the following way will do the trick.

Second Reformulation of the Argument

S1₂.   CODE(VALID A) iff CH is a theorem of ZF.

S2₂.   CODE(VALID B) iff ~CH is a theorem of ZF.

S3₂.   CH is independent of the axioms of ZF. There are models that make all the axioms of ZF true while making CH false (and its negation true), and there are models that make all the axioms true that make CH true (and its negation false).

S4₂.   So neither CODE(VALID A) nor CODE(VALID B) is a theorem of ZF and neither is a logical truth since there are interpretations in which they are false.

S5₂.   For all S, if S is a logical truth, then CODE(VALID S) is a logical truth (or a theorem of ZF).

S6–S9.   As before.

When the argument is formulated this way, the first four steps are unobjectionable.

This means that in both reformulations of Etchemendy's argument, the key question concerns (S5). In neither case is this step self-evident, nor does he give an argument for it.[63] Here, it should be noted that (S5₁) and (S5₂) are analogous to the principle (S5a) discussed in connection with Etchemendy's argument concerning first-order logical truth. In the first-order case, I mentioned that one might try to defend (S5a) by saying that if s is first-order logical truth, then it is possible in principle to prove s using only assumptions that are themselves logical truths. One might then reflect on the fact that one has proved s by logic alone and so come to know by logic alone that s is a logical truth. But if one can know by logic alone that s is a logical truth, then, it might be maintained, it is a logical truth (or at any rate it is virtually analytic) that s is a logical truth. Moreover, since Etchemendy thinks that it is part of the concept of logical truth that such a truth is true independently of the interpretations of its nonlogical vocabulary, it is virtually analytic that s is true in all models.[64]

However, this argument clearly cannot be applied to the second-order case. Whatever else may be wrong with it, one cannot assume that if s is a logical truth of second-order logic, then it can be proved by logic alone since, given prevailing notions of logical consequence and logical truth, second-order logic is incomplete. That is, any formalization of second-order logic whose theorems include only sentences that are true in all models is a formalization in which many sentences that are true in all models cannot be proved. Given the model-theoretic definition of logical truth, one gets the standard result that no legitimate system of proof for second-order logic allows one to prove all second-order logical truths. In arguing against the model-theoretic account, one cannot simply assume the correctness of some other conception of logical truth that violates this result without begging the question. Consequently, if Etchemendy's argument is to succeed, some other justification for $(S5_1)$ or $(S5_2)$ must be given.

First consider $(S5_1)$ and its two salient instances.

$S5_1$.   For all s, if s is a logical truth, then the claim that s is true in all models is virtually analytic.

$S5_{1A}$.   If A is a logical truth, then the claim that A is true in all models is virtually analytic.

$S5_{1B}$.   If B is a logical truth, then the claim that B is true in all models is virtually analytic.

In order for the first reformulation of Etchemendy's argument to succeed, it must be shown that there is some sense of analyticity validating $(S1_1)$–$(S4_1)$ that also validates at least the last two of these three principles. Now, the only reason for thinking that there might a sense of analyticity validating $(S1_1)$–$(S4_1)$ is the observation that (i) it has proven very difficult, and perhaps may turn out to be impossible, to establish conclusively either the continuum hypothesis or its negation, whereas (ii) we can establish, using a priori principles plus information about what A and B mean, that A is true in all models iff the continuum hypothesis is true and B is true in all models iff the negation of the continuum hypothesis is true. In this situation, the only grounds for accepting both $(S3_1)$ and $(S5_1)$ must come from a belief that if s is a second-order logical truth, then it cannot turn out to be as difficult to establish that s is true in all models as it is to establish the continuum hypothesis or its negation. But why should one accept this? The defender of the model-theoretic definition of logical truth, who holds that there is no sound, complete proof procedure for second-order logical truth, does not share this belief. Since this defender has been given no reason to accept it, the first attempt to reformulate Etchemendy's argument against the extensional correctness of the model-theoretic characterization of second-order logical truth does not succeed.

Essentially the same is true of the second reformulation of the argument. In this case, the defender of the model-theoretic account can give an independent argument against $(S5_2)$ in either of its forms.

$S5_2$.   For all S, if S is a logical truth, then CODE(VALID S) is a logical truth (or a theorem of ZF).

The argument against $(S5_2)$, due to Gomez-Torrente, is as follows:[65]

i.   For any sentence S in the language of arithmetic, it is provable in ZF that S is true in arithmetic iff it is a model-theoretic consequence of the second-order Peano axioms for arithmetic.
    CODE(VALID (PA$_2$ ⊃ S)) ↔ STAR(S) is a theorem of ZF.

Here, CODE(VALID (PA$_2$ ⊃ S)) is sentence of first-order ZF set theory which, through a system of coding, can be taken to say that the conditional whose consequent is the sentence S of arithmetic and whose antecedent is the conjunction of the second-order axioms for Peano arithmetic is true in all models. In other words, CODE(VALID (PA$_2$ ⊃ S)) is true in the intended interpretation of set theory iff S is a model-theoretic consequence of the second-order Peano axioms. STAR(S) is the set-theoretic translation of the arithmetical sentence S—arithmetic can be done within set theory, and STAR(S) is the sentence in that system that corresponds to S.

ii. Since ZF is a theory in which arithmetic can be done, Gödel's first incompleteness theorem applies to it—there is a sentence STAR(G) of set theory about the natural numbers as construed in ZF that is true in the intended interpretation of ZF but is not provable in ZF. Since it is not provable, STAR(G) is false in some models of ZF.

iii. By (i) it follows that CODE(VALID (PA$_2$ ⊃ G)) is false in some models of ZF and hence is neither a theorem of ZF nor a logical truth.

iv. But since STAR(G) is true in the intended interpretation of ZF, G is a truth of arithmetic.

v.   It is a well-known metatheoretical result that all truths of arithmetic are model-theoretic consequences of the second-order Peano axioms for arithmetic. Thus PA$_2$ ⊃ G is true in all models.

vi. Therefore PA$_2$ ⊃ G is a sentence that is a model-theoretic logical truth, even though CODE(VALID (PA$_2$ ⊃ G)), which represents the claim that it is a model-theoretic logical truth, is neither a model-theoretic logical truth nor a theorem of ZF.

This argument shows that if *logical truth* in (S5$_2$) is understood according to the model-theoretic account, then it is demonstrably false. Thus the only way to salvage the second attempted reconstruction of Etchemendy's argument would be to give some alternative characterization of logical truth validating (S5$_2$) and to show that this alternative characterization ought to be preferred to the model-theoretic account. Etchemendy does not do this, and there is no reason to think it can be done. In fact, as Gomez-Torrente points out, one of the factors motivating the development of second-order logic was the assumption that second-order Peano arithmetic is complete—that is, that all arithmetical truths are logical consequences of the axioms, in the sense of *logical consequence* employed by working logicians and mathematicians. If this is taken as a constraint on any acceptable account of logical consequence, then there is no hope of validating (S5$_2$).

It may be, of course, that Etchemendy has a different intuitive conception of logical consequence in mind that is not subject to this constraint. His emphasis on the analyticity of logical truths may be an indication of this, especially if one thinks of analytic truths as knowable solely on the basis of reflecting on their meaning. There is at the outset some tension between the conception of second-order logical truths as analytic and the familiar result that for any sound system of proof there will be second-order logical truths not provable in the system. Someone committed to the idea that logical truths must all be knowable by us might be skeptical of any conception of logical truth for which sound and complete proof procedures are impossible. However, if this is to be the basis of attacking Tarski's model-theoretic conception, then no complicated cardinality arguments of the sort given by Etchemendy are needed. Moreover, any such attack would be highly revisionary of the practice of most logicians, both pre and post-Tarski. Etchemendy has done little to motivate such a revision.

Summary

We have seen that Etchemendy's arguments against the model-theoretic analyses of logical truth and logical consequence do not succeed. Since these analyses make crucial use of Tarski's definition of truth, we have (partially) vindicated the claim in this chapter that Tarski's definition of truth was theoretically fruitful in important contexts in which we need a notion of truth. This does not, of course, change our overall assessment that Tarski did not provide an adequate analysis of the notion of truth since there are some theoretical tasks—related to theories of meaning and interpretation—for which a notion of truth other than Tarski's is needed. This negative conclusion is related, in the end, to how we should understand his positive achievement in providing model-theoretic analyses of logical truth and logical consequence. The characterization of truth in a model upon which these analyses are based is best and most naturally viewed as playing the role of *interpreting* sentences in models, and so as employing the ordinary (non-Tarskian) semantic notions of truth and denotation. When Tarski's formal machinery is understood in this way, there is good reason to accept the resulting model-theoretic definitions of logical truth and logical consequence as analyses.[66]

Notes

1. Presumably this predicate is definable in terms of the three-place relational predicate *x expresses a proposition p in L* plus the standard English truth predicate of propositions.

2. See, for example, C. G. Hempel, "On the Logical Positivists' Theory of Truth," *Analysis* 2 (1935): 49–59; Hans Reichenbach, *Experience and Prediction* (Chicago: University of Chicago Press, 1938), section 22; and Otto Neurath, "Sociology and Physicalism" and "Protocol Sentences," in *Logical Positivism*, ed. A. J. Ayer (Glencoe, Ill.: Free Press, 1959). 282–317, and 199–208.

3. For example, in *The Logic of Scientific Discovery* (New York: Harper Torchbook, 1965), 274, Karl Popper describes the impact of Tarski's theory of truth on his philosophy as follows: "It cannot be too strongly emphasized that Tarski's idea of truth (for whose definition with respect to formalized languages Tarski gave a method) is the same idea which Aristotle had in mind and indeed most people (except pragmatists): the idea that

truth is correspondence with the facts (or with reality). But what can we possibly mean if we say of a *statement* that it corresponds with the *facts* (or with reality)? Once we realize that this correspondence cannot be one of structural similarity, the task of elucidating this correspondence seems hopeless; and as a consequence, we may become suspicious of the concept of truth, and prefer not to use it. Tarski solved this apparently hopeless problem (with respect to formalized languages), by reducing the unmanageable idea of correspondence to a simpler idea (that of 'satisfaction' or 'fulfillment').

Owing to Tarski's teaching, I am no longer hesitant in speaking of 'truth' and 'falsity'. And like everybody else's views (unless he is a pragmatist), my views turned out, as a matter of course, to be consistent with Tarski's theory of absolute truth. Thus although my views on formal logic and its philosophy were revolutionized by Tarski's theory, my views on science and its philosophy were unaffected."

Another philosopher who found Tarski's conception of truth liberating was Rudolf Carnap. See in particular his "Intellectual Autobiography," in *The Philosophy of Rudolf Carnap*, ed. P. A. Schilpp (LaSalle, Ill.: Open Court, 1963), 60–61. There Carnap discusses the widespread skepticism about truth in leading philosophical circles in Tarski's time, his own surprised but positive reaction to Tarski's definition, and his subsequent efforts to overcome the truth skepticism of others by using Tarski's definition to illustrate the need to distinguish truth from notions like knowledge, certainty, and confirmation.

In understanding the liberating effect of Tarski's work on philosophers concerned with truth, it is of course necessary to distinguish difficulties and obscurities in various pre-Tarskian philosophical conceptions of truth from difficulties and obscurities inherent in the ordinary notion. The fact that philosophers have harbored various confusions about truth does not show that there are inherent difficulties in the ordinary notion. Thus the success of Tarski's theory in overcoming various forms of truth skepticism does not in itself show that our ordinary notion is defective and in need of replacement by a Tarskian substitute.

4. As compared, for example, with the relatively uninteresting truth definition given in the appendix to chapter 3.

5. Tarski discusses these matters, somewhat informally, in his 1936 essay, "On the Concept of Logical Consequence," reprinted in *Logic, Semantics, and Metamathematics*, 2d ed., ed. John Corcoran (Indianapolis, Ind.: Hackett, 1983), 409–420. When I speak of a sentence being true in all models I will mean true in all models that interpret all of its nonlogical vocabulary; similarly for the claim that a sentence c is true in all models in which the sentences in set s are true.

6. A similar point can be made about logical truth. A syntactic (proof-theoretic) characterization of logical truth is said to be sound just in case every sentence it characterizes as a logical truth is true in all models; it is complete just in case every sentence that is true in all models is shown to be a logical truth by the syntactic characterization. Unsoundness is regarded as a fatal defect; incompleteness is seen as a limitation to be corrected in cases in which complete characterizations are possible. In short, the syntactic characterizations are seen as tests for the presence of the model-theoretically defined notions, which in turn are typically taken to be analyses of the informal and pretheoretic logical notions.

7. The widely accepted claim that Tarski's model-theoretic definitions of logical truth and logical consequence constitute adequate explications of these notions has been challenged by John Etchemendy in *The Concept of Logical Consequence* (Cambridge: Harvard University Press, 1990). I discuss this challenge in the appendix to this chapter.

8. Another version of the same view relativizes truth to circumstances, characterizes the truth conditions of a sentence as the set of circumstances in which it is true, and issues in claims of the sort illustrated by (i).

i. 'Snow is white' is true in C iff snow is white in C.

(Circumstances are typically taken to be alternative total states of the world or "possible worlds," but other choices, such as partial states of the world or "situations," are also possible.) Although the relativization of truth to circumstances is not strictly Tarskian, the theories are essentially extensions of Tarski's techniques. Like the theories discussed in the text, these theories will also be subject to the philosophical point made later about the mismatch between Tarski's project of defining (and legitimating) truth and the enterprise of using truth to characterize meaning.

9. Donald Davidson, "Truth and Meaning," *Synthese* 17 (1967): 304–23, reprinted in *The Philosophy of Language*, ed. A. P. Martinich (New York: Oxford University Press, 1985), 72–83, at 75–76.

10. This was no problem for Tarski since he did not take definitions of truth to be theories of meaning. Rather, he assumed that an understanding of the object-language was a prerequisite for demonstrating the adequacy of a definition of truth for it.

11. In chapter 8, a diagnosis is offered for the widespread failure to recognize the far-reaching difference in meaning between Tarski's truth predicate and our ordinary notion of truth. The key to this diagnosis is the illusion that instances of the schema 'S' *is true in English iff* S, containing our ordinary truth predicate, are trivial, analytic sentences, known to be such by competent speakers of English. If this were the case, then it might seem tempting to argue as follows: (i) Suppose that T_E is a Tarskian truth predicate for English (or some relevant subpart of English) for which a materially adequate definition could be given; (ii) since the definition of T_E is analytic, the instances of 'S' *is* T_E *iff* S that follow from it must also be analytic; (iii) since instances of 'S' *is true in English iff* S are themselves analytic, each instance of 'S' *is* T_E is analytically equivalent to the corresponding instance of 'S' *is true in English*; (iv) but then since the claim that a sentence is Tarski-true is analytically equivalent to the claim that it is true in the ordinary sense, Tarski's truth predicate must have essentially the same meaning as our ordinary truth predicate (restricted to the relevant object-language for Tarski's predicate), and so Tarski's truth predicate must be capable of playing any legitimate theoretical role that our ordinary truth predicate is capable of playing. In this chapter, we have already shown that the conclusion of this argument is false. In chapter 8, the fallacies in the argument for this conclusion are exposed.

12. Davidson seems to have gotten this point almost exactly backward in "Truth and Meaning." In a passage overlapping the one quoted previously, he says: "A theory of meaning for a language L shows 'how the meanings of sentences depend upon the meanings of words' if it contains a (recursive) definition of truth-in-L. And, so far at least, we have no other idea how to turn the trick. It is worth emphasizing that the concept of truth played no ostensible role in stating our original problem. That problem, upon refinement, led to the view that an adequate theory of meaning must characterize a predicate meeting certain conditions. It was in the nature of a discovery that such a predicate would apply exactly to the true sentences. I hope that what I am doing may be described in part as defending the philosophical importance of Tarski's semantical concept of truth. But my defense is only distantly related, if at all, to the question whether the concept Tarski has shown how to define is the (or a) philosophically interesting conception of truth, or the question whether Tarski has cast any light on the ordinary use of such words as 'true' and 'truth.' It is a misfortune that dust from futile and confused battles over these questions has prevented those with a theoretical interest in language—philosophers, logicians, psychologists, and linguists alike—from recognizing in the semantical concept of truth (under whatever name) the sophisticated and powerful foundation of a competent theory of meaning" (75–76). Here Davidson suggests that in constructing a theory of truth as a theory of meaning, one

employs the concept of truth defined by Tarski while ignoring its relation to our ordinary notion of truth. In fact, however, the only chance of success in such an enterprise comes from employing the ordinary notion (in a formal theory structurally isomorphic with Tarski's) while ignoring the concept of truth Tarski actually defined.

Davidson's confusion on this point seems to have been shared by Rudolf Carnap in *Introduction to Semantics* (Cambridge: Harvard University Press, 1943), section 7, and *Meaning and Necessity* (Chicago: University of Chicago Press, 1947), 5–6. The unsuitability of Tarski's truth predicate for truth-conditional theories of meaning and the need for an antecedently understood notion of truth have been noted in many places, including Michael Dummett, *Truth and Other Enigmas* (London: Duckworth, 1978), xx–xxi, 7–8; J. A. Foster, "Meaning and Truth Theory," in *Truth and Meaning*, ed. Gareth Evans and John McDowell (New York: Oxford University Press, 1978), 8–9; Scott Soames, "What Is a Theory of Truth?," *Journal of Philosophy* 81 (1984): 411–29, at 422–24; and John Etchemendy, "Tarski on Truth and Logical Consequence," *Journal of Symbolic Logic* 53 (1988): 51–79. Davidson also seems to have explicitly recognized the point in work subsequent to "Truth and Meaning." See, for example, "Radical Interpretation," *Dialectica* 27 (1973): 313–28, at 321.

13. See Scott Soames, "Direct Reference, Propositional Attitudes, and Semantic Content," *Philosophical Topics* 15 (1987): 47–87, reprinted in *Propositions and Attitudes*, ed. Nathan Salmon and Scott Soames (New York: Oxford University Press, 1988); 197–239; "Semantics and Semantic Competence," *Philosophical Perspectives* 3 (1989): 575–96; and "Truth, Meaning, and Understanding," *Philosophical Studies* 65 (1992): 17–35.

14. Could Tarski's analysis be saved by taking a theory of meaning for a language L to consist of the definition of a Tarskian truth predicate for L plus infinitely many instances of schema (7b)? Orthodox Davidsonians would object on the grounds that (i) the theory fails to be finitely axiomatizable and (ii) by invoking the notion of meaning, it fails to provide an analysis of meaning in terms of the extensional notion of truth. I would add that apart from these concerns, it would not provide enough information about the interpretation of sentences. Although the information it would provide in this respect is essentially the same as the information provided by a Davidsonian truth theory employing our ordinary notion of truth, this information is insufficient to determine the meaning of object-language sentences. See Soames, "Truth, Meaning, and Understanding."

15. This section is based largely on Soames, "What Is a Theory of Truth?," parts of which are repeated below.

16. The doctrine of physicalism stated in the text—as well as by Quine himself—is ambiguous depending on how one characterizes the notion of determination (which is supposed to obtain between physical facts and all other genuine facts) or the notion of reduction (which is supposed to hold between physical theory and all other legitimate theories). According to certain characterizations of these relations, the doctrine of physicalism is rather weak and it is doubtful that it rules out very much of what we would ordinarily take to be legitimate; according to other characterizations, the doctrine turns out to be so strong as to have little independent plausibility. When these ambiguities are eliminated, it is far from clear that physicalism represents a genuine threat to any of our ordinary semantic notions. These issues are taken up in Scott Soames, "Skepticism about Meaning: Indeterminacy, Normativity, and the Rule-Following Paradox," in *Meaning and Reference*. The Canadian Journal of Philosophy, Supplementary vol. 23, ed. Ali A. Kazmi (1998).

17. Hartry Field, "Tarski's Theory of Truth," *Journal of Philosophy* 69 (1972): 347–75.

18. It is an interesting historical question to determine the extent to which the skeptical doubts about truth harbored by these scientifically minded philosophers were due to physicalism as opposed to other factors. If one looks at the literature of this period, it is hard to

resist the conclusion that factors other than physicalism were the main pre-Tarskian grounds for truth skepticism. For example, Hans Reichenbach's skepticism about truth seems to have been the result of confusing truth with certainty, as was pointed out in chapter 2. Moreover, if one looks at Carl Hempel's useful pre-Tarski survey, "On the Logical Positivists' Theory of Truth," one does not find physicalism cited as one of the causes of skepticism about traditional conceptions of truth. Instead, one finds a debate between such philosophers as Rudolf Carnap, Otto Neurath, Moritz Schlick, and Hempel regarding whether traditional correspondence theories of truth make sense and whether they should be replaced by so-called coherence theories of truth.

The starting position in the debate seems to have been Ludwig Wittgenstein's view in the *Tractatus* that all meaningful sentences are either atomic or truth-functional compounds of atomic sentences. (Wittgenstein had an extended view of truth-functional compounds that encompassed his own conception of quantification. See Scott Soames, "Generality, Truth Functions, and Expressive Capacity in the *Tractatus*," *Philosophical Review* 92 (1983): 573–89.) An atomic sentence was supposed to be true iff it pictured an atomic fact. The truth of nonatomic sentences was determined by the truth values of the atomics. In effect, one could characterize the theory in traditional terms by saying that it consisted in a correspondence theory of truth for the atomic sentences plus a kind of coherence (with atomic sentences) theory of truth for the nonatomic sentences.

Many positivists regarded the correspondence part of the theory as an embarrassment to be eliminated. One factor contributing to this seems to have been the doctrine, held over from the *Tractatus*, that saw attempts to talk about the relationship between language and the world as instances of unintelligible metaphysics and therefore to be avoided. Another closely related point seems to have been the thought that correspondence theories of truth inevitably require metaphysically questionable, pseudo-material counterparts—namely, facts—for sentences to correspond to. Finally, one sees in the debate much talk about whether it makes sense to suppose that it is possible to *compare* "propositions" (usually thought of as sentences or sentence tokens by these philosophers) with facts in order to determine their truth or falsity.

The crucial contrast here seems to have been between determining truth by "comparing propositions with facts" and determining truth by "comparing propositions with other (already accepted) propositions." It is striking that both sides in the dispute seem to have accepted essentially the following line of reasoning: (i) If the truth of a proposition p consists of its correspondence with reality, then it must be possible to determine that p is true by comparing it directly with reality, without relying on any auxiliary background assumptions (for that would involve comparing p with other propositions). (ii) If it is possible to determine that p is true by comparing it directly with reality, then it must be possible to be certain that p is true on the basis of the experience of comparing it with reality, since given the experience, no possible auxiliary assumptions can undermine it. In short, it seems to have been thought that the correspondence theory of truth requires a class of incorrigible propositions to which the theory applies directly (with the truth of other propositions determined by the extent to which they are coherent with or supported by the basic incorrigible propositions).

For example, Moritz Schlick, who argued against pure coherence theories, pinned his case for a limited version of the correspondence theory on the existence of incorrigible "basic propositions." (See Moritz Schlick, "The Foundation of Knowledge," in Ayer, *Logical Positivism*, 209–27, and "Facts and Propositions," *Analysis* 2 [1935]: 65–70.) On the other hand, Carnap, Neurath, and Hempel rejected incorrigible basic or "protocol" statements and took this to imply the rejection of the correspondence theory of truth in favor of a coherence theory. Hempel sums up their positive view in the following remarks: "So

THE SIGNIFICANCE OF TARSKI'S THEORY OF TRUTH 141

also the concept of truth may be characterized in this formal mode of speech, namely, in a crude formulation, as a sufficient agreement between the system of acknowledged protocol-statements and the logical consequences which may be deduced from the statement and other statements which are already adopted. . . . The system of protocol statements which we call true, and to which we refer in every day life and science, may only be characterized by the historical fact, that it is the system which is actually adopted by mankind, and especially by the scientists of our culture circle; and the 'true' statements in general may be characterized as those which are sufficiently supported by that system of actually adopted protocol statements" ("On the Logical Positivists' Theory of Truth," 54, 57).

Several observations about this debate are in order. First, insofar as the proponents of the coherence theory were skeptics about the ordinary notion of truth, it was because they uncritically took that notion to encompass what they took to be discredited doctrines about knowledge, certainty, and confirmation, as indicated by the fact that the concept they ended up characterizing was not truth but something like "is a proposition that, at a given time, is highly confirmed by actual observation and experience." Second, the primary reasons for their skepticism seem to be either unrelated to physicalism or only distantly related. (Perhaps the worry that talk about the relationship between language and the world must be objectionably metaphysical had some connection with the inability to see how that relationship could be physical. However, this was typically not stressed.) Third, much of the apparent skepticism was the result of the unwarranted importation of epistemological (and metaphysical) doctrines into questions about the nature of truth and even of elementary confusions of truth with notions like certainty and confirmation. Fourth, Tarski's discussion of truth, including his emphasis on the centrality of schema T, was effective in clearing up these confusions and in disentangling contentious epistemological (and metaphysical) doctrines from the analysis of truth. I would maintain that it is in this way that Tarski had his main effect in legitimating truth for previously skeptical philosophers. For an example of this effect, see Rudolf Carnap, "Truth and Confirmation," in *Readings in Philosophical Analysis*, ed. H. Feigl and W. Sellars (New York: Appleton-Century-Crofts, 1949), 119–27.

19. Alfred Tarski, "The Establishment of Scientific Semantics," in Corcoran, *Logic, Semantics, and Metamathematics*, 401–8.

20. Ibid., 406.

21. Ibid.

22. This is a very strong conception of reducibility and one that, I suspect, many committed physicalists would not be willing to accept. One of its odd consequences is that it condemns as illegitimate Tarskian truth predicates for languages containing quantifiers ranging over all sets since explicit definitions are impossible in this case. But why should the fact that one "runs out of sets" with which to construct explicit definitions threaten the physicalistic acceptability of truth predicates for such languages?

23. Field, "Tarski's Theory of Truth," 350.

24. I use the phrase "linguistic behavior" in a broad sense to include all facts about speakers relating to their use of language.

25. I am ignoring here, for simplicity, the denotation of function signs.

26. Presumably speakers of L_1 differ in some way from speakers of L_2 regarding their beliefs, intentions, attitudes, brain states, or overt linguistic behavior involving 'v'.

27. Field partially anticipates this point in "Tarski's Theory of Truth," nn. 5, 10. In note 5 (page 351), he comments that in model theory quantifiers are given an "unusual" semantics in which they range over the members of some specified set rather than over all (actually existing) things. In such a case, Field claims, Tarski has reduced truth to deno-

tation, application, and the notion of the range of the quantifiers. (For Tarski, this constituted the usual case since it is only when the range of quantifiers is restricted that explicit
truth definitions can be given for languages with a certain minimal richness.) In note 10
(page 353), Field mentions, without specifying, the existence of problems that must be
faced when the definition of truth is generalized so as not to contain a particular logical
vocabulary.

28. For example, in *The Roots of Reference* (La Salle, Ill.: Open Court, 1974), Willard
van Orman Quine attempts to characterize truth-functional operators in terms of communitywide dispositions to assent and dissent. He ends up concluding that indeterminacy
between classical and intuitionist construals of the connectives is inevitable. Although
Quine's argument is effectively criticized by Alan Berger in "Quine on 'Alternative Logics'
and Verdict Tables," *Journal of Philosophy* 77, no. 5 (1980): 259–77, it is evident that the
task of providing the kind of physicalistic reductions of logical notions required by Field's
project is a difficult one. (An interesting approach that appeals to mentalistic notions like
belief can be found in Gilbert Harman, "Beliefs and Concepts: Comments on Brian Loar,"
Proceedings of the Philosophy of Science Association 2 [1983] 654–61; also Gilbert Harman,
"(Nonsolipsistic) conceptual role semantics," *New Directions in Semantics*, ed. E. LaPore
(London: Academic Press, 1987), 55–81.)

29. In stating this requirement in terms of the replacement of a semantic term by its
physicalistic definiens, I have tacitly relied on Tarski's emphasis on explicit definition.
However, I do not think the philosophical point of the requirement depends on this. In
cases in which only an axiomatic treatment is possible, Field could require that the axioms
governing 'true', together with contingent, empirical facts about speakers and their environments, have statements of type (7) and (8) as consequences.

30. Field, "Tarski's Theory of Truth," 370–71.

31. By contrast, it is not easy to see how speakers' inferences involving beliefs that
certain claims are true could be explained by a physicalistic definition of truth. If D were
the definiens of such a definition, it would have to be highly theoretical and would have
a sense very different from that of the word 'true', as used by ordinary speakers in the kind
of example Field has in mind. As a result, the proposition expressed by *s is D* would not
be the same as the proposition expressed by *s is true*, as used by such speakers. Thus even
if a biconditional relating these propositions was physically or metaphysically necessary, it
would be possible for an agent to believe one without believing the other. Indeed, it seems
highly unlikely that ordinary speakers have any acquaintance with the proposition that s is
D. But then since such speakers never draw conclusions from the claim that something is
D, it is hard to see how this supposed physicalistic conception of truth could be said to
play any explanatory role in their reasoning at all.

32. As I have already mentioned, Quine is one physicalist who thinks that the totality
of physical facts does not determine what proposition is expressed by a sentence or utterance. In "Skepticism about Meaning: Indeterminacy, Normativity, and the Rule-Following
Paradox," I argue that there is an important sense of *determine* in which Quine is wrong
about this and hence that there is an important sense in which physicalists can accept talk
about propositions.

33. Field, "Tarski's Theory of Truth," 359.

34. In this way of defending Tarski, a language may be identified with an abstract object
whose Tarski-defined semantic properties are independent of empirical facts about speakers.
For example, one way to think of a standard first-order language L is as a triple, $<S_L, D_L, F_L>$, where S_L is a family of sets representing the various categories of well-formed expressions of L; D_L is a domain of objects; and F_L is a function that assigns objects in D_L to the
names of L, subsets of the domain to one-place predicates of L, and so on. Let J be the

class of such languages. Truth can now be defined in nonsemantic terms for variable 'L' in J in a straightforward Tarskian fashion. The only significant change from before is that the notions of Tarski-denotation and Tarski-application are no longer given language-specific list definitions but rather are defined for variable 'L' using the "interpretation" functions built into the languages. In particular, a name n refers to an object o in a language L iff $F_L(n) = o$. (Since F_L is a purely mathematical object—a set of pairs, if you like—it does not incorporate any undefined semantic notions.) The resulting truth predicate is just what is needed for metatheoretical investigations of the nature, structure, and scope of a wide variety of theories.

What the truth definition does not do is tell us anything about speakers. In this conception, languages are abstract objects that can be thought of as bearing their Tarski-defined semantic properties essentially. There is no possibility that expressions of a language might have Tarski-denoted something other than what they do denote or that sentences of a language might have had different Tarski-truth conditions. Any variation in Tarskian semantic properties (across times or worlds) is a variation in languages. Thus semantic properties are not contingent on anything, let alone facts about speakers.

In this picture, what is contingent on facts about speakers is which language a person or population speaks and which expression a given utterance is an utterance of. Let L_1 and L_2 be two languages in J that are identical except for the interpretations of certain nonlogical vocabulary—perhaps the color words in L_1 are shape words in L_2. We can imagine a situation in which it is correct to characterize L_1 rather than L_2 as the language of a given community. In this view, to ask what such a characterization amounts to and what would justify it is to ask not a semantic question about the languages but a pragmatic question about their relation to speakers.

Although Tarski had nothing to say about this relation, other philosophers have had something to say. In "Language and Languages," in *Minnesota Studies in the Philosophy of Science*, vol. 7, ed. K. Gunderson (Minneapolis: University of Minnesota Press, 1975), 3–35, David Lewis invokes a different but equally abstract conception of a language and proposes an analysis of what it is for a community to speak such a language in terms of a convention of truthfulness and trust. Discussions of what Donald Davidson calls "radical interpretation" can also be reconstructed as dealing with this issue. For physicalists, the crucial question is whether any purely physical grounding of such an explication can be given. If so, the physicalist can accept both Tarski-style semantic notions that apply to sentences and related semantic/pragmatic notions that apply to utterances. If not, then either the latter or physicalism itself must be abandoned. What is not problematic, in this conception, is the physicalist's acceptance of Tarski's semantic notions applying to sentence types and other expressions.

35. Field, "Tarski's Theory of Truth," 351–53.

36. Ibid., 352.

37. Field's concern that truth definitions should apply to unambiguous entities is met if propositions are taken to be the (primary) bearers of truth. If sentence types are chosen, ambiguity might be treated as a case of homonymy. For example, instead of thinking that English contains a single (ambiguous) word type 'bank', one can take English to contain two different words, 'bank$_1$' and 'bank$_2$', whose tokens are phonologically indistinguishable. The contextual factors that Field relies on to disambiguate tokens might then be thought of as determining whether particular utterances are tokens of the type 'bank$_1$' or the type 'bank$_2$'.

38. Extensions of Tarski's techniques have been applied to languages involving indexicality and various kinds of intensionality. Typically these extensions of Tarski's methods yield definitions of multirelativized notions of truth—for example, truth *in a model, relative*

to a context of utterance and circumstance of evaluation. Although these notions of truth are highly useful, they are quite different from more familiar unrelativized notions.

39. For a model to interpret all the nonlogical vocabulary in s is for it to assign a denotation from the domain to each name in s, a set of n-tuples of elements in the domain to each n-place predicate in s (except '=' when it is treated as a logical symbol), and a (total) function from n-tuples in the domain to elements in the domain to each n-ary function symbol in s. From now on, when I speak of a logical truth as a sentence that is true in all models, I will take it to be understood that this means that the sentence is true in all models that interpret its nonlogical vocabulary.

40. In both cases, the value assigned by A' to the second-order variable must, of course, be of the appropriate sort based on the domain D—that is, a set of n-tuples of elements of D to an n-place predicate variable and a function from n-tuples of D into D to an n-ary function variable.

41. Etchemendy, *The Concept of Logical Consequence.* See also his "Tarski on Truth and Logical Consequence."

42. "On the Concept of Logical Consequence" was first given by Tarski as an address at the International Congress of Scientific Philosophy in Paris in 1935. It was published in Polish, then in German in 1936 and later in English in *Logic, Semantics, and Meta-mathematics.*

43. Mario Gomez-Torrente, "Tarski's Definition of Logical Consequence: Historical and Philosophical Aspects" (Ph.D. diss., Princeton University, 1996). See also his "On a Fallacy Attributed to Tarski," *History and Philosophy of Logic* (forthcoming), and "Tarski on Logical Consequence," *Notre Dame Journal of Formal Logic* 37, no. 1 (1996): 125–51. In addition, see M. Garcia-Carpintero, "The Grounds for the Model-Theoretic Account of the Logical Properties," *Notre Dame Journal of Formal Logic* 34 (1993): 107–31; V. McGee, review of Etchemendy, *Journal of Symbolic Logic* 57 (1992): 254–55; and G. Sher, *The Bounds of Logic* (Cambridge: Massachusetts Institute of Technology Press, 1991), and "Did Tarski Commit 'Tarski's Fallacy'?," *Journal of Symbolic Logic* 61 (1996) 653–86.

44. Note that in the model-theoretic account, a sentence is a logical truth iff it is a logical consequence of every set of sentences.

45. See Tarski, "On the Concept of Logical Consequence," 414.

46. Etchemendy, *The Concept of Logical Consequence,* 102–6.

47. Ibid., 102–3; emphasis in original.

48. We are taking the identity predicate to be a logical constant, the interpretation of which does not vary from model to model.

49. Etchemendy, *The Concept of Logical Consequence,* 113–15; emphasis in original.

50. For the same reason, it is hard to understand Etchemendy's comment in ibid., 113, that "if the universe is finite, the present account will mistakenly pronounce an infinite number of the sentences $\neg\sigma_2$, $\neg\sigma_3$, . . . logically true." This, of course, invites the reply that if there really are infinitely many such sentences, then obviously the universe is not finite.

51. I am here following Etchemendy in ignoring the possibility that the symbols in the sentences in $\neg\sigma_2$, $\neg\sigma_3$, . . . could have been used with different meanings. Such scenarios are irrelevant to the point Etchemendy is trying to make.

52. Etchemendy, *The Concept of Logical Consequence,* 116–17; emphasis in original.

53. It is possible to understand the sentence 'Si y solo si' *is a Spanish phrase* or '*La nieve es blanca si y solo si Princeton esta en Nueva Jersey' is a true sentence of Spanish* without knowing what *si y solo si* means and hence without knowing that it is the Spanish equivalent of 'if and only if'.

54. There is no difference between virtual analyticity and analyticity when applied to claims that do not mention any expressions.

55. Except that the range is nonempty.

56. One of the troublesome features of Etchemendy's discussion is his frequent use of the locution *it is a logical truth that* without explanation. The predicate *is a logical truth* is typically regarded as a predicate of sentences—sentences, not the propositions they express, are standardly regarded as logical truths. One could extend the notion of logical truth (as we have extended the notion of analyticity in the discussion of Etchemendy's argument) so that a proposition can be characterized as logically true iff some sentence that expresses it is a logical truth. We could then use the usual locutions of indirect discourse in talking about logical truth—that is, we could say that it is a logical truth that such and such. However, we would then have to confront the possibility that there might be some proposition that is expressed by two sentences, one a logical truth and one not. Such a proposition would, of course, have to be counted as a logical truth. Thus according to this way of speaking, to say that it is not a logical truth that such and such is to say that none of the sentences expressing the proposition that such and such is a logical truth.

This is relevant to the question of whether it is a logical truth that there are sets with infinitely many members. The claim that there are sets with infinitely many members can be expressed (in a variety of ways) in standard first-order set theory. The argument given in the text shows that none of these first-order sentences is a logical truth in Etchemendy's sense. Suppose, however, that the claim that there are sets with infinitely many members can be expressed in some other ways as well. In fact, it is possible to express essentially this claim in second-order logic using a sentence that does not contain 'ε' or any other non-logical symbol. Should this second-order sentence be regarded as a logical truth in Etchemendy's intuitive sense? No, because in order to determine that the sentence is true, special assumptions have to be made about the range of the quantifiers. So, even considering this possibility, we conclude that it is not a logical truth that there are infinitely many sets.

57. If this were not so, then the conjunction of (6) with the claim that there are sets with infinitely many members would be analytically equivalent to (6) itself since they are necessarily and a priori equivalent. But if that conjunction were analytically equivalent to (6), then the claim that there are sets with infinitely many members would have to be an analytic consequence of (6), which contradicts the assumption that (6) is virtually analytic whereas the claim about sets is not analytic.

58. Here, to say that a set A is larger than a set B is to say (i) that B can be put into a one-to-one correspondence with some subset of the set A but (ii) it is impossible to put the whole of A into a one-to-one correspondence with B.

59. This hypothesis is independent of the standard axioms of set theory. That is, there are models that make all the standard axioms true while making the continuum hypothesis false, as well as models that make all the standard axioms true while making the continuum hypothesis true. For this reason, the truth or falsity of the continuum hypothesis is often thought of as an open question in set theory.

60. Etchemendy does not specify precisely what the nature of this equivalence is. As we will see, doing so is of central importance to his argument.

61. Etchemendy, *The Concept of Logical Consequence*, 123, 124.

62. Mario Gomez-Torrente, "Tarski, Etchemendy, and Logical Consequence," paper presented at my truth seminar, Princeton University, 1995.

63. There is, I believe, a reason for this oversight that is illuminated by the following passage: "What we have is a sentence of our second-order language, call it C, whose logical status is being tied to the ordinary truth or falsity of a certain generalization, say, (10) $\forall v_1$ ... $\forall v_n$ [C'] It turns out, though, that the facts described by (10) are of an entirely extralogical sort: whether (10) is true depends on nothing more nor less than the continuum

hypothesis—and clearly, neither it nor its negation is a logical truth. . . . The mere truth of a universal generalization can only guarantee that its instances are true; it cannot guarantee that they are logically true. Of course, if the generalization itself is *logically* true, then the instances will be logically true as well. . . . *But if the generalization is not logically true, if it makes say, a substantive historical or physical or set-theoretic claim, then neither will its instances be logical truths*" (Etchemendy, *The Concept of Logical Consequence*, 123–24; emphasis on the final sentence added).

In order to understand this passage, one must understand the incautious way in which Etchemendy chooses to represent the claim that a sentence is true in all models. He assumes that for any sentence S, the claim that S is true in all models can be represented by and even identified with the claim $\ulcorner \forall v_1, \ldots, \forall v_n \, S(e_1, \ldots, e_n/v_1, \ldots v_n) \urcorner$. Here, $e_1, \ldots, e_n$ are the nonlogical expressions occurring in S, and $S(e_1, \ldots, e_n/v_1, \ldots, v_n)$ is the (higher-order) formula that results from replacing each occurrence of a nonlogical expression e_i in S with a corresponding occurrence of a variable of the appropriate type. A suitably expansive domain is assumed, and each universal quantifier is taken to range over a class of objects that constitute alternative appropriate interpretations of expressions in the relevant category—individuals if e_i is a singular term, sets of individuals if e_i is a one-place predicate, and so on. The idea is that $\ulcorner \forall v_1, \ldots, \forall v_n \, S(e_1, \ldots, e_n/v_1, \ldots, v_n) \urcorner$ is supposed to be true (in Etchemendy's intended interpretation) iff any assignment of an appropriate interpretation to the nonlogical constants of S make it true. This is the justification for taking $\ulcorner \forall v_1, \ldots, \forall v_n \, S(e_1, \ldots, e_n/v_1, \ldots, v_n) \urcorner$ to express the claim that S is true in all models.

There are a number of problems with this mode of representation (one of which is the need to capture the idea of varying domains). The most important for the issue at hand can be illustrated by using Etchemendy's system of representation to interpret the passage just quoted. The sentence C in the passage is just our sentence A. Our claim that A is true in all models is identified by Etchemendy with (10) in the passage. At this point, one further fact, not explicitly mentioned by Etchemendy, should be noted. As Gomez-Torrente has pointed out in "Tarski's Definition of Logical Consequence," 101–3, the relevant second-order sentence A (which is such that the claim that it is true in all models is "equivalent" to the continuum hypothesis) can be formulated using no nonlogical constants. But then Etchemendy's C and his (10) turn out to be the same sentence, so he in effect ends up identifying A with the claim that A is true in all models.

Now look at the last sentence of the quoted passage. According to Etchemendy's conventions for representing claims of the form *s is true in all models*, what that sentence says, in contraposed form, is that if s is logically true, then the claim that s is true in all models is logically true. Applying this to the example at hand, we get the claim that if A is a logical truth, then the claim that A is true in all models is a logical truth. But then since the claim that A is true in all models has been identified with A, what we have is an utter triviality. No wonder no argument was given for it.

This illustrates the perils of Etchemendy's method of canonically representing claims of the form *s is true in all models* as certain related higher-order generalizations (interpreted in a suitably large domain). When variations in the size of the domains makes a crucial difference, as with the sentences in $\sigma_2, \sigma_3, \ldots$, which contain no logical constants, the claim that s is true in all models may not even be materially equivalent to Etchemendy's canonical representation of that claim. (Since σ_n contains no nonlogical symbols, it is identical with Etchemendy's canonical representation of the claim that it is true in all models. But each σ_n is true, whereas the claim that σ_n is true in all models is false.) Even putting this problem aside and focusing on the case he is concerned with in the quoted passage—where the claim that A is true in all models and his representation of that claim (namely, A itself interpreted in a suitably large domain) are materially equivalent—a fundamental problem remains. The fact that the claim that s is true in all models is materially equivalent to Etchemendy's canonical representation of that claim does not guarantee the stronger forms of equivalence — logical or analytic equivalence — that his argument requires. For this reason, when evaluating principles like $(S5_1)$ and $(S5_2)$, one should cling to the literal and avoid Etchemendy's nonstandard shortcut for representing claims of the form *s is true in all models*.

64. In *The Concept of Logical Consequence* 104–5, Etchemendy gives an argument that if s is a genuine logical truth and so is true in virtue of the meanings of its logical vocabulary, then s is true in all models. Since the argument is entirely conceptual in nature, it is reasonable to take it as expressing the view that it is (virtually) analytic that if s is a logical truth, then s is true in all models. From this, together with the claim that if s is a logical truth, then it is virtually analytic that s is a logical truth, one gets the conclusion that if s is a logical truth, then it is virtually analytic that s is true in all models — that is, the claim $(S5_1)$. For a useful discussion of Etchemendy's argument, see Gomez-Torrente, "Tarski's Definition of Logical Consequence," 70–79.

65. This argument is given in Gomez-Torrente, "Tarski, Etchemendy, and Logical Consequence," and "Tarski's Definition of Logical Consequence," 110–11.

66. An early version of some of the material in this appendix was presented in my truth seminar at Princeton University in the spring of 1993. The material was presented again in the fall of 1995, this time as a joint presentation with Mario Gomez-Torrente, who gave his reconstruction of Etchemendy's argument that the model-theoretic account of second-order logical truth is extensionally incorrect. I presented the material again at the City University of New York in the spring of 1997.

Lessons of the Liar

A Dilemma

In chapter 3, we outlined Tarski's proof that the language L_A of arithmetic does not contain its own truth predicate — that is, there is no formula in L_A that applies to all and only the Gödel numbers of true sentences of L_A. One of the most interesting things about this proof is the use it makes of the Liar paradox. We prove that the language of arithmetic does not contain its own truth predicate by showing that the assumption that it does contain such a predicate entails a contradiction due to the presence of Liar sentences in the language.

Suppose that L_A does contain its own truth predicate True(y). Then since it contains classical negation, it will also contain a formula $^\ulcorner(\sim\text{True}(y))^\urcorner$ that applies to a number n iff it is not the Gödel number of a true sentence of L_A. To show that a Liar sentence would be constructible using this formula, we need simply to ensure that L_A contains sufficient resources for self-reference (or simulated self-reference). To this end, we defined a predicate of L_A to be a formula containing exactly one free variable and a self-ascription of a predicate P to be the sentence that results from replacing occurrences of its free variable with the numeral denoting the Gödel number of P. We next noted that there is a formula of L_A that applies to a pair of numbers n and m iff m is the Gödel number of a predicate P of L_A and n is the Gödel number of a self-ascription of P. But this means that

L_A will contain both the predicate (1) and the self-ascription (2) of that predicate that results from substituting for 'x' the numeral [m] denoting the Gödel number m of (1).

1. $\exists y$ (y is a self-ascription of x & $\sim$True (y))
2. $\exists y$ (y is a self-ascription of [m] & $\sim$True (y))

Formula (1) is true of those Gödel numbers of predicates whose self-ascriptions are not true. Sentence (2) is true iff the self-ascription of (1)—that is, sentence (2) itself—is not true. But then since every sentence of L_A is either true or not true, it follows that sentence (2) is true and not true. Thus the assumption that L_A contains its own truth predicate leads to a contradiction and must be rejected.

A striking feature of this proof is its extreme generality. The only significant assumptions about the language of arithmetic needed for the argument are the following:

A_1. The language contains the usual logical operators, including classical negation. Moreover, a conjunction is true in the language iff both conjuncts are true; the negation B of a sentence A is true iff A is not true, and so on.[1]

A_2. The language contains sufficient resources for self-reference (or simulated self-reference). (As we have seen, it suffices for simulated self-reference if the language contains quantification over the natural numbers, a name for zero, plus the notions of addition, multiplication, successor, and identity.)

A_3. Every sentence of the language is either true or not true.

Given any language L for which these assumptions hold, we can construct a proof, analogous to the proof for L_A, that shows that L does not contain any predicate applying to all and only the true sentences of L (or to all and only the Gödel numbers of true sentences of L). In short, no bivalent language with a certain minimum expressive power can contain its own truth predicate.

This is a strong result and also a perplexing one, for surely English and other natural languages have the minimum expressive power required by (A_1) and (A_2).[2] Thus if natural languages are bivalent—that is, if (A_3) holds for them—then they cannot contain their own truth predicates. But this seems incredible. It is undeniable that English contains the predicate 'is a true sentence of English.' If this expression is not a truth predicate for English, then either (i) there is some true sentence of English that the predicate 'is a true sentence of English' does not apply to or (ii) there is something that the predicate applies to that is not a true sentence of English. But both these alternatives seem impossible.

Perhaps, then, we should conclude that English *does* contain its own truth predicate but that not every sentence of English is either true or not true and so (A_3) fails. But this also seems impossible, for if not every sentence of English is either true or not true, then there must be some sentence of English that is neither true nor not true. And if some sentence of English is neither true nor not true, then there must be a sentence of English that is both not true and also not not true. But this is a contradiction. Thus it seems that we cannot maintain that (A_3) is untrue of English.

We have now reached an intolerable position. We have apparently *proven* that English *cannot* contain its own truth predicate, even though we seem to have no choice but to admit the obvious fact that the English expression 'is a true sentence of English' *is* a truth predicate for English. In order to determine what the Liar paradox shows about English and other natural languages, we must find a way out of this dilemma.

The Claim That Natural Languages are Inconsistent

One well-known response is that of Alfred Tarski. It was, of course, Tarski himself who proved that the language of arithmetic could not contain its own truth predicate. Since he regarded English and other natural languages to be bivalent in the sense of (A_3), while recognizing that they contain the standard logical operators plus devices for self-reference, one would expect him to have extended his theorem about the language of arithmetic to natural languages as well. However, he did not, for the simple reason that he took it to be obvious that natural languages *do* contain their own truth predicates:

> A characteristic feature of colloquial language (in contrast to various scientific languages) is its universality. It would not be in harmony with the spirit of this language if in some other language a word occurred which could not be translated into it; it could be claimed that 'if we can speak meaningfully about anything at all, we can also speak about it in colloquial language'. If we are to maintain this universality of everyday language in connexion with semantical investigations, we must, to be consistent, admit into the language, in addition to its sentences and other expressions, also the names of these sentences and expressions, and sentences containing these names, as well as such semantical expressions as 'true sentence', 'name', 'denote', etc.[3]

Tarski recognized, of course, that his assumptions about natural languages were sufficient to give rise to paradoxical results. However, instead of taking these results to show that one or more of the assumptions should be rejected, he took them to show that natural languages are inconsistent: "But it is presumably just this universality of everyday language which is the primary source of all semantical antinomies, like the antinomies of the liar or of heterological words. These antinomies seem to provide a proof that every language which is universal in the above sense, and for which the normal laws of logic hold, must be inconsistent."[4]

The first question to ask about this position is, "How does it help with our dilemma?". Our problem is that although we can prove that no language satisfying (A_1)–(A_3) can contain its own truth predicate, we do not see any way to deny that English both satisfies (A_1)–(A_3) and contains its own truth predicate. If the theorem were that no *consistent* language satisfying the three assumptions can contain its own truth predicate, then the claim that English is inconsistent would at least tell us that the theorem does not apply. However, the theorem is about *all* languages.

As a result, labeling English inconsistent does not resolve the dilemma unless claiming inconsistency allows us to reject (A_1), (A_2), or (A_3).

In chapter 2, we examined Tarski's argument that English and other natural languages are inconsistent. We saw that the premises of his argument entail that (i) some sentence s of English and its negation are jointly true; (ii) English contains true contradictions; and indeed (iii) every sentence of English is true. With this is mind, we characterized the perplexing notion of an inconsistent language as a language in which some sentence and its negation are both true. If this is what it means for a language to be inconsistent, then we can at least see the extraordinary claim that English is inconsistent as being directed at our dilemma, for (A_1) requires that the negation of any sentence s is true iff s is not true. Since the combination of this assumption and the claim that English is inconsistent entails a contradiction, (A_1) will be rejected and the result that English cannot contain its own truth predicate will thereby be blocked.

Nevertheless, this is not an acceptable response to the problem. The reason it is not is that Tarski's characterization of English as inconsistent is simply not credible. As we have seen, if English is inconsistent, then it contains true contradictions. Contradictions, are, of course, never rationally acceptable, as Tarski would have been the first to admit. What makes the claim that a contradiction is true so hard to accept is the disquotational inference from ⌜'S' is true⌝ to S. In order for one who maintains that a contradiction ⌜(A & ~A)⌝ is true to avoid committing oneself to a contradiction, one must repudiate this inference. However, it seems impossible to do this if 'true' is used with its normal meaning. In addition, such a repudiation would tend to undermine the rationale for a crucial premise in Tarski's argument. In order to derive the result that English is inconsistent, Tarski requires the premise that all instances of the schemata *If 'S' is true, then S* and *If S, then 'S' is true* are true sentences of English. But the pretheoretic intuition that these are true is tied to the intuition that they are assertable. As a result, once assertability is rejected—as it must be by one who maintains that English is inconsistent—the claim that instances of *If 'S' is true, then S* are true loses its intuitive justification and the argument for the inconsistency of English becomes untenable.

The Claim That English Does Not Contain Its Own Truth Predicate: The Hierarchical Approach

Having rejected the claim that English is inconsistent, we have little reason to doubt (A_1). Since (A_2) clearly holds for English, this leaves us with the choice of rejecting (A_3) or accepting the conclusion that English does not contain its own truth predicate. The most well known and widely accepted of these alternatives is the latter, which, in its most familiar form, is inspired by Tarski's definitions of truth for formalized languages. As we have seen, Tarski insulates his definitions from paradox by using a metalanguage M to talk about a formal object-language L and then defining within M a restricted truth predicate T applying to sentences of L. Since L does not contain a truth predicate, no Liar sentences are constructible in it. Since any sentence S of M containing the predicate T is not a sentence of L, the predicate contained in S is not one that applies to S itself, and thus the sentence cannot be seen as asserting or denying its own truth. If a truth predicate for M is wanted, then the process is repeated in a metametalanguage M' and so on ad infinitum.

When applied to formal languages, Tarski's hierarchical approach is a way of avoiding the paradoxes by ensuring that they will never arise. However, the hierarchical idea can also be applied to natural languages as a diagnosis of the paradoxes they give rise to. This view is often expressed by saying that there is no single truth predicate for all of English. Instead of containing a single (unambiguous) word *true* (applying to sentences), English is thought of as containing an infinite hierarchy of (sentential) truth predicates: $true_0$, $true_1$, $true_2$, and so on.[5] Moreover, English itself is treated as an infinite hierarchy of languages:

E_0 = English minus semantic predicates.

E_1 = E_0 plus $true_0$, where $true_0$ applies to all truths of E_0 and does not apply to anything else.

E_2 = E_1 plus $true_1$, where $true_1$ applies to all truths of E_1 and does not apply to anything else, and so on.[6]

Each truth predicate $true_i$ may be thought of as totally defined over the entire universe of discourse (including all English sentences) in the sense that for any object the predicate either applies to that object or it does not. However, each is a truth predicate for only one of the sublanguages in the hierarchy. The extensions of the different truth predicates are, of course, related. When n is greater than m, a sentence may fail to be $true_m$ while being $true_n$; however, whenever a sentence is $true_m$, it will be $true_n$ for all n greater than m. More specifically, the extension of $true_i$ is always a proper subset of the extension of $true_{i+1}$.

When proper attention is paid to the indexing of truth predicates, instances of schema T turn out to be unproblematic. For each level n, there is an acceptable version

'S' is $true_n$ iff S

of schema T whose instances result from replacing each occurrence of the letter 'S' with a sentence of level E_n. Each such instance is a sentence of E_{n+1} that is $true_{n+1}$.

With this in mind, one can see how the paradoxes are blocked. For example, consider what we called version 1 of the Liar in chapter 2. That version was based on the Liar-paradoxical sentence (1) (where the expression *sentence* [1] was understood as synonymous with and an abbreviation for *the sentence that is the first numbered example in the section "Truth and Paradox" in chapter 2 of the book by Scott Soames on truth*).

1.   Sentence (1) is not true.

Version 1 of the paradox was stated as follows:

Version 1 of the Liar
P1.   'Sentence (1) is not true' is true iff sentence (1) is not true.
P2.   Sentence (1) = 'Sentence (1) is not true'.
C1.   Sentence (1) is true iff sentence (1) is not true.
C2.   Sentence (1) is true and sentence (1) is not true.

In analyzing this version of the paradox in accordance with the hierarchical approach, we must add subscripts to the truth predicates that occur in it. There are two possibilities to consider. The first way of subscripting would construe sentence (1) and (P1) as follows:

1.   Sentence (1) is not true$_n$.
P1.   'Sentence (1) is not true$_n$' is true$_n$ iff sentence (1) is not true$_n$.

In this construal, (P1) is not a proper instance of schema T since the sentence that replaces both occurrences of 'S' in the schema—namely, sentence (1)—is not a sentence of E_n. Thus it may safely be rejected. Since *true$_n$* does not apply to anything that is not a sentence of E_n, the left-hand side of (P1) is false$_{n+1}$ and the right-hand side is true$_{n+1}$, making (P1) unproblematically false$_{n+1}$. This way of blocking the paradox by rejecting (P1) is possible because, in this construal, sentence (1) is simultaneously true$_{n+1}$ and untrue$_n$, thereby illustrating the fact that *true$_n$* is not a truth predicate for all of English, even though it is a truth predicate for E_n.
   A different way of subscripting would treat sentence (1) as before but would formulate (P1) as follows:

P1.   'Sentence (1) is not true$_n$' is true$_{n+1}$ iff sentence (1) is not true$_n$.

This is a proper instance of schema T and is therefore acceptable. Its right-hand side is both true$_{n+1}$ and true$_{n+2}$; its left-hand side is true $_{n+2}$. As a result, the sentence as whole is true$_{n+2}$. With this formulation we derive

C2.   Sentence (1) is true$_{n+1}$ and sentence (1) is not true$_n$.

However, this conclusion is harmless because the truth predicates on the two sides are different. As a result, the hierarchical approach is able to dispose of version 1 of the Liar.[7]
   In chapter 2, we reconstructed Tarski's argument that English is inconsistent as version 2 of the Liar. Its major premises were the following:

Version 2 of the Liar
A1.   Sentence (1) is a sentence of English.
A2.   All instances of schema T are true in English.
A3.   'Sentence (1) = "Sentence (1) is not true"' is true in English.
A4.   The usual laws of logic hold in English—that is, all standard logically valid patterns of inference are truth preserving in English.

Since this is essentially a metalinguistic formulation of version 1, the same considerations that applied before apply here as well. For example, if we let the truth predicate in sentence (1) be $true_n$, then we may reformulate (A2)–(A4) as follows:

A2.   All (proper) instances of the schema — 'S' is $true_{n+1}$ iff S—(which result from substituting a sentence of E_{n+1} for each occurrence of 'S') — are $true_{n+2}$.

A3.   'Sentence (1)= "Sentence (1) is not $true_n$," ' is $true_{n+2}$.

A4.   The usual laws of logic hold in E_{n+2}—that is, all standard logically valid patterns of inference are truth $_{n+2}$ preserving.

Given this, we can derive the result that (C2)—Sentence (1) is $true_{n+1}$ and sentence (1) is not $true_n$—is $true_{n+2}$. However, since the right-hand conjunct is not a negation of the left-hand conjunct, (C2) is not a contradiction, and we avoid the paradoxical result that English is inconsistent.

As before, the basic point is that since there is no truth predicate for all of English, any use of a truth predicate must be indexed and thereby restricted. Thus when one says (in the original [A_2] of version 2) that all instances of schema T are true, one must restrict the truth predicate to a particular level i. Once this is done, the only chance of saving the assumption is to adopt corresponding restrictions of schema T, in which case, one does not get a paradoxical result. If one does not restrict the instances of schema T in this way but instead one allows instances to be constructed with truth predicates of any level m (so long as both occurrences of 'S' are replaced by a sentence of E_m), the assumption will fail because there is no restricted notion of truth in the hierarchy according to which all such instances are $true_i$.

Problems with the Hierarchical Approach

There is no doubt that the hierarchical approach is an effective means of avoiding the Liar paradox. The paradox is avoided by adopting restrictions that make it impossible to construct Liar sentences. It is impossible to construct within the hierarchy any sentence that assesses its own truth value, any pair of sentences, each of which assesses the truth value of the other, and so on. Since there are no problematic sentences, the paradoxes cannot get off the ground.

The fundamental worry about this approach is whether the restrictions it imposes on the use of semantic notions are too severe. This worry may take two different forms. One is a concern that there may be unparadoxical things we want to be able to assert that are inexpressible in the hierarchy. The other is a concern that the hierarchy simply may not be an accurate description of English and other natural languages. Although different, these concerns are clearly related. If we can give examples of certain unparadoxical things we would like to be able to assert that are inexpressible in the hierarchy, then presumably those examples can be given in English. Conversely, if there are things expressible in English but not in the hierarchy, then there may be things we want to be able to assert that the hierarchy cannot accommodate.

There are several reasons to believe that the restrictions in the hierarchy are too severe and are not an accurate account of English. One obvious point is that the truth predicate in English is not limited to applying only to sentences of English. In addition, it applies to propositions and to sentences of other languages. Thus, at best, the hierarchy is an account of only a limited set of uses of the predicate *true*.

A related point involves the relational nature of the English truth predicate of sentences. When we predicate truth of sentences in English, we do not use separate truth predicates — *true*$_{Japanese}$, *true*$_{Greek}$, and so on — for different languages but rather employ a single relational notion — *true in L* — for variable L. Even if we put other natural languages aside, the relational notion is virtually irresistible as a device for characterizing sentences at different levels of the hierarchy as being true in the different sublanguages that supposedly make up English. In fact, we have already made repeated use of this relational predicate in setting up and describing the hierarchy.

For example, we made implicit use of the relational predicate when we said (i) that when n is greater than m, a sentence may fail to be true$_m$ while being true$_n$; (ii) that whenever a sentence is true$_m$, it will be true$_n$ for all n greater than m; (iii) that the extension of *true*$_i$ is always a proper subset of the extension of *true*$_{i + 1}$; (iv) that for each level n, there is an acceptable version 'S' *is true*$_n$ *iff* S of schema T whose instances are truths$_{n + 1}$ that result from replacing each occurrence of the letter 'S' with a sentence of level E_n; and so on. In all of these cases, we implicitly treated the subscript on the truth predicate as an independent variable capable of being bound by a quantifier whose range included all the languages in the hierarchy. However, if the hierarchical approach is correct, then there can be no such sentences in English, for if there were, they would have to exist at some level of the hierarchy that would then contain truth predicates for all the other levels and even a single predicate — *s is true*$_i$ *at some level i of the hierarchy* — that could properly be regarded as a truth predicate for the whole of English. Since the point of the hierarchy is to avoid this, it is clear that we have transgressed its essential bounds in attempting to describe it.

It is important not to misunderstand the import of this objection. The hierarchy can be fully, accurately, and coherently described provided the language we use to describe the hierarchy is not itself a member of the hierarchy.[8] Incoherence arises from (i) the claim that the hierarchy includes all of English; (ii) the apparent fact that in setting up and describing the hierarchy we are speaking English; and (iii) the conclusion just established — namely, that the language we use in describing the hierarchy cannot itself be a member of the hierarchy. One way to avoid this incoherence would be to content ourselves with merely partial and incomplete characterizations of the hierarchy from within the hierarchy. There need be nothing incoherent about (i) characterizing E_0 as the fragment of English that contains no semantic predicates; (ii) characterizing E_1 as consisting of E_0 plus a predicate applying to all truths$_0$; and (iii) maintaining that English is a collection of languages generated by continuing this process so long as we never specify precisely what this amounts to. However, even such a partial characterization requires an independent notion of $truth_0$ that is not just an instance of a general relational notion of truth. Moreover, one must maintain that English speakers grasp and apply a series of independent notions $truth_1$, $truth_2$, and so on, even though there is no single relational definition capable of generating them all. Finally, if this basic conception is correct, then there are many things we would ordinarily regard as expressible and would like to express that must be condemned as inexpressible nonsense. The very fact that we find so many such things in our attempts to describe basic features of the hierarchy suggests that it is not an accurate account of our ordinary notion of truth in English but may instead be parasitic on that notion.

It is worth noting in this connection that even the central claim that the hierarchical approach is often invoked to support—namely, that English as a whole does not contain its own truth predicate—becomes problematic if the hierarchy is taken seriously. To say that a language L does not contain its own truth predicate is to say that there is no predicate in L that applies to all and only the true sentences of L. Thus to say that English does not contain its own truth predicate should be to say that there is no predicate in English that applies to all and only the true sentences of English. But this cannot be quite right since in making this claim we are presumably speaking English, and it is a central tenet of the hierarchical approach that all legitimate uses of *true* in English must be regarded as implicitly indexed. The problem, of course, is that once we index the truth predicate in our theoretical statement about English, our claim that there is no predicate in English that applies to all and only the $true_n$ sentences of English must be rejected.[9] Although this does not refute the hierarchical approach, it does show that the temptation to go beyond it is remarkably persistent and may well reflect the fact that the hierarchy does not provide a correct account of the meaning of *true* in English.

Another feature of the hierarchy that does not fit well with our ordinary use of the word *true* involves the way in which one determines the levels of the hierarchy at which particular sentences of English belong. I have presented the hierarchy as containing different subscripted "truth predicates," with the level of a sentence being determined grammatically by which of the different indexed predicates it contains. If we imagine that the word *true* in English is ambiguous, with the subscripted predicates representing its different possible meanings, then we may take the meaning of a predicate to be included in its identity conditions and treat the ambiguity as a case of homonymy. In this view, English does in fact contain infinitely many predicates $true_0$, $true_1$, . . . with different meanings, each spelled and pronounced the same. Here again, the level of any *sentence* will be determined grammatically by which of these predicates it contains. An utterance may then be assigned to a sentence type on the basis of which subscripted predicate the speaker intends to be using.

This picture works reasonably well in simple cases in which one knows precisely which sentences one wishes to assess for truth value. For example, if one wants to say that *Snow is white* is true, one simply selects $true_0$. Similarly, if one wishes to predicate untruth of Bill's statement that the sentence *Ronald Reagan did not play an important role in ending the Cold War* is true, then one will select $true_1$. However, many of our claims about truth are not like this. For example, someone with faith in the integrity and competence of a witness who has gone before the grand jury might say

1.   Every sentence uttered by the witness to the grand jury is true

without knowing what the witness actually said—and, in particular, without knowing whether the witness assessed the truth value of anyone else's statement (which may in turn have characterized every sentence in some document as true and so on). In such a case, there may be no way for one to know in advance which truth predicate in the hierarchy will be high enough to fulfill one's intention of assessing everything said by the witness. Nevertheless, there are cases like this in which we do coherently and unparadoxically assert something like (1) without selecting any level of the hierarchy as providing the intended interpretation of the truth predicate.[10]

Saul Kripke's example, (2), illustrates a related problem.[11]

2a.   No Watergate-sentence uttered by Nixon is true.
 b.   No Watergate-sentence uttered by Dean is true.

In this example, we are to imagine that Dean utters (2a), that Nixon utters (2b), that both are Watergate-sentences, and that each intends to include the other's sentence within the scope of his statement. The first point to notice is that although we are bound to reject the claim that these sentences are jointly true, the pair need not be paradoxical. For example, if Nixon and Dean have both previously uttered the sentence

3.   Nixon's handling of Watergate was inept,

then (2a) and (2b) are unparadoxically false. A more interesting case is one in which Dean has uttered (3) and Nixon has uttered exactly 100 Watergate-sentences—99 that are demonstrably false plus (2b). In such a case, (2b) is false and (2a) is unparadoxically true, with the evaluation of (2a) depending on the prior and independent evaluation of (2b).

Now notice that (2a) and (2b) cannot be placed on any levels of the hierarchy without losing their intuitive force. If they are placed on the same level, then both must contain the same predicate $true_n$. But then neither assesses the truth value of the other, and we get the result that it is possible for them to be jointly $true_{n+1}$. This may happen if all the other Watergate-remarks of the two men are $false_n$. Then the mere fact that (2a) and (2b) are not sentences of level n will be sufficient for both to be $true_{n+1}$. But this violates our ordinary, intuitive understanding of these sentences.

Suppose, then, that one is placed above the other in the hierarchy. Let Dean's sentence, (2a), contain $true_{n+1}$ and Nixon's sentence, (2b), contain $true_n$. Now we get the result that Nixon's sentence does not really assess Dean's for truth value, but Dean's sentence does assess the truth value of Nixon's sentence. Thus if all the other Watergate-statements by the two men are $false_n$, then (2b) gets declared $true_{n+1}$ and Dean's gets declared $false_{n+2}$. But this violates our ordinary understanding of these remarks as symmetrical in this sort of case.

Difficulties like these suggest that the hierarchical approach does not capture our ordinary understanding of the truth predicate in English. They do not, however, absolutely refute the hierarchy as an account of English. The extremely puzzling character of the Liar paradox and the ease with which intuitively obvious assumptions about truth can be shown to lead to contradiction make it plausible to suppose that any effective treatment of the paradox may lead us to revise some of our intuitive judgments about truth. Thus it is not out of the question that one might argue that the difficulties we have found with the hierarchy are based on erroneous intuitions that need to be revised. However, in order to be successful, such an argument would have to provide good reasons to believe that there is no alternative nonhierarchical treatment that more closely corresponds to our intuitive judgments about truth, for if there is such an account, then it clearly ought to be preferred. Thus the problems we have found with the hierarchy provide a strong incentive to look for an alternative solution that is more effective in capturing our pretheoretic understanding of how the predicate *true* works in English.

The Possibility of Rejecting Bivalence

Our dilemma is that we remain reluctant to give up the claim that English contains its own truth predicate, even though we can prove that no language satisfying (A_1)–(A_3) can contain such a predicate. Since the claim that English satisfies (A_2) seems undeniable and the prospects of rejecting (A_1) do not appear promising, it is time to reconsider our initial acceptance of (A_3), here applied to English and renumbered as (1).

1. Every sentence of English is either true or not true.

Our initial reason for accepting this claim was simply that its negation, (2), is logically equivalent to (3) and (4) and hence is unacceptable.

2. Not every sentence of English is either true or not true.
3. Some sentence of English is neither true nor not true.
4. Some sentence of English is not true and also not not true.

However, there are grounds for thinking that the unacceptability of (2) is not a persuasive reason for accepting (1), for anyone who takes seriously the possibility of rejecting (1) must take seriously the possibility that there is a sentence S of English such that both the claim that S is true and its negation—namely, the claim that S is not true—ought to be rejected. But if there are claims that may be rejected even though their negations are also rejected, then the mere fact that claim (2) is rejected may not require us to accept (1).

What we must do is examine (1) in its own right and determine whether and in what circumstances one might be justified in rejecting both the claim made by a certain sentence and the claim made by its negation. This will be done in chapter 6, where I will argue (i) that where P is a certain kind of partially defined predicate, there are pairs consisting of a meaningful sentence, ⌜α is P⌝, and its negation, ⌜α is not P⌝, neither of which may be accepted; (ii) that there is a natural way of understanding the truth predicate according to which *true* is such a partially defined predicate; and (iii) that in this way of understanding truth, (2) may be rejected without accepting (1), and the claim that a Liar sentence is true may be rejected without accepting the claim that it is not true.

Before doing this, however, it is important to clarify how rejecting (1) would resolve our dilemma and block the paradoxical results. The dilemma over our acceptance of both Tarski's theorem and a truth predicate for English would be resolved by giving up the claim that (A₃) of the theorem is satisfied by English. The way in which rejection of this claim would block contradictory results based on Liar sentences is illustrated by the following version of the paradox.

5.   Sentence (5) is not true.

Version 3 of the Liar
A.   Since all sentences are either true or not true, either sentence (5) is true or it is not true.
B.   Suppose that sentence (5) is true—that is, 'Sentence (5) is not true' is true.
C.   Since one can always infer S from ⌜'S' is true⌝, it follows that sentence (5) is not true.
D.   Thus the supposition that sentence (5) is true leads to the contradictory result that sentence (5) is true and sentence (5) is not true.
E.   Suppose then that sentence (5) is not true.
F.   Since one can always infer ⌜'S' is true⌝ from S, it follows that 'Sentence (5) is not true' is true and hence that sentence (5) is true.
G.   Thus the supposition that sentence (5) is not true leads to the contradictory result that sentence (5) is true and sentence (5) is not true.
H.   Since the same contradiction can be derived from each of the alternatives contemplated in (A), it follows that sentence (5) is true and sentence (5) is not true.

Without the assumption, (A), that all sentences are true or not true, the final, contradictory conclusion could not be derived. Rather, we would have an argument, (B)–(D), showing that the supposition that sentence (5) is true must be rejected and a related argument, (E)–(G), showing that the supposition that sentence (5) is not true must also be rejected. Since in giving up (A), we allow for the possibility of such joint rejection, no contradiction is forthcoming.

Giving up the assumption that Liar sentences, like sentence (5), are true or not true is also effective in blocking version 1 of the Liar paradox (even though the assumption is not explicitly stated in the argument).

Version 1 of the Liar
P1.   'Sentence (5) is not true' is true iff sentence (5) is not true (that is, 'S' is true iff S).
P2.   Sentence (5) = 'Sentence (5) is not true'.
C1.   Therefore, sentence (5) is true iff sentence (5) is not true.
C2.   Therefore, sentence (5) is true and sentence (5) is not true. (From [C1])

The crucial premise is (P1), which is an instance of schema T. Let us assume that *iff* is the material biconditional and that $\ulcorner(\sim \sim S)\urcorner$ is equivalent to S. Then $\ulcorner(A \text{ iff } B)\urcorner$ is equivalent to $\ulcorner(A \& B) \text{ or } (\sim A \& \sim B)\urcorner$ and (P1) is equivalent to (P1*).

P1*.   ('Sentence (5) is not true' is true & sentence (5) is not true) or ('Sentence (5) is not true' is not true & sentence (5) is true).

If we give up the assumption that sentence (5) is true or not true, then we will reject each of the following claims:

6a.   Sentence (5) is true.
  b.   Sentence (5) is not true.
7a.   'Sentence (5) is not true' is true.
  b.   'Sentence (5) is not true' is not true.

Since rejecting these claims involves rejecting both disjuncts of (P1*), we will therefore reject (P1*) (given the usual meaning of *or*) and also (P1). Thus giving up the assumption that Liar sentences must be either true or not true blocks version 1 of the paradox by providing grounds for rejecting problematic instances of schema T.

This result depends on assuming that *iff* is the material biconditional. However, a similar result can be gotten even if this connective is given an interpretation in which $\ulcorner(A \text{ iff } B)\urcorner$ is assertable and true whenever both A and B "have the same status"—including the case in which both are claims that must be rejected. In this interpretation, (P1), (P2), and (C1) are unobjectionable, but the contradictory (C2) cannot be derived without the assumption that sentence (5) is either true or not true. Thus giving up this assumption blocks version 1 of the paradox on either interpretation of *iff*. (Exactly analogous reasoning applies to version 2 of the paradox as well.)

What this means is that all the problematic results we have looked at up to now can be avoided if we can find a convincing rationale for rejecting the claim that all sentences, and in particular Liar sentences, are either true or not true. Since I have so far said nothing about what this rationale might be, the idea that one may reject the claim that a sentence is true while also rejecting the claim that it is not true might seem utterly mysterious. The next chapter is devoted to dispelling this mystery.

Notes

1. Assumptions about the truth conditions of conjunctions, negations, and existential quantifications are needed in order to characterize (1) as being true of all and only the Gödel numbers of predicates whose self-ascriptions are not true, and (2) as being true iff it is not true.

2. In considering the question of whether (A_1) holds for English (and other natural languages), we need to introduce a slight qualification. Since natural languages contain imperatives, interrogatives, and other nondeclarative sentences that are not true even though their negations are also not true, and since they may also contain meaningless sentences whose negations are also meaningless, we need to amend the clause of (A_1) that says that the negation B of a sentence A is true iff A is not true so as to exclude such (for our purposes) irrelevant examples. If we understand (A_1) as being qualified in this way, then it seems very plausible to suppose that English and other natural languages satisfy the assumption. Moreover, if they satisfy (A_2) and (A_3) as well, then the reasoning behind Tarski's proof of the arithmetical indefinability of arithmetical truth will lead to the conclusion that these natural languages do not contain their own truth predicates.

3. Alfred Tarski, "The Concept of Truth in Formalized Languages," in *Logic, Semantics, and Metamathematics*, 2d ed., ed. John Corcoran (Indianapolis, Ind.: Hackett, 1983), 152–278, at 164.

4. Ibid., 164–65.

5. There are in principle two ways of understanding the claim that English contains an infinite hierarchy of truth predicates. According to the first, what we ordinarily call the single word *true* is systematically ambiguous, with the subscripted truth predicates representing its different meanings. According to the second, *true* is indexical, with the indexed truth predicates representing the different contents it can take in different contexts of utterance. The first of these is probably the more orthodox conception and the one that fits most naturally with the characterization of English as a collection of languages. However, the second has also been explored; see, for example, Tyler Burge, "Semantical Paradox," in *Recent Essays on Truth and the Liar Paradox* ed. Robert L. Martin, (New York: Oxford University Press, 1984), 83–118. Although I will not try to decide between these two approaches, my exposition will tend to follow the more orthodox approach in treating English as if it contained an infinite hierarchy of distinct but homonymous truth predicates.

6. In addition to containing a truth predicate, each level should be thought of as containing related semantic predicates (applying to the immediately preceding level).

7. In this view, the reason we tend to be puzzled by the paradox is presumably that the word *true* in English lacks subscripts and we fail to attend to the fact that different uses of it have different extensions.

8. Suppose we use a language M outside the hierarchy to set up and describe the hierarchy. In M we will have a relational predicate s *is a true sentence of level n*, which we use when we characterize an arbitrary level n + 1 of the hierarchy as containing a predicate T that applies to an object iff that object is a true sentence of level n. In such a case, the object-language predicate T is not relational, although the metalanguage predicate used in describing it is.

9. It is worth noting that (A_1) on page 149 fails if the truth predicate in it is indexed since for any level n there will be sentences A and B at higher levels such that B is the negation of A even though neither is *true$_n$*.

10. This point is emphasized by Saul Kripke in "Outline of a Theory of Truth," in *Recent Essays on Truth and the Liar Paradox*, ed. Martin, 53–81, at 59–60.

11. Ibid., 60.

S I X

Truth, Paradox, and Partially Defined Predicates

A Philosophical Model of Partially Defined Predicates

Our task is to construct a model of partially defined predicates according to which, for certain things, both the claim that these predicates apply to those things and the claim that they do not apply to them must be rejected. The key to this model is the contention that a predicate may be introduced into a language by rules that provide sufficient conditions for it to apply to an object and sufficient conditions for it to fail to apply but no conditions that are both individually sufficient and jointly necessary for it to apply or for it to fail to apply to an object. Since the conditions are mutually exclusive but not jointly exhaustive, there will be objects for which there are no possible grounds for accepting either the claim that the predicate applies to them or the claim that it does not.

In addition to illustrating how a language could come to contain such predicates, I will argue that truth predicates may naturally be understood as conforming to this model. To this end, I will articulate an unremarkable set of instructions that could plausibly be used to introduce a truth predicate into a language and govern its use. It will be shown that, first appearances to the contrary, these instructions do not provide necessary and sufficient conditions but rather define sufficient conditions for a sentence to be true and sufficient conditions for a sentence not to be true. Although mutually exclusive, these conditions turn out not to be jointly exhaustive. Thus there will be sentences, including Liar sentences like *This sentence is not true*, about which the instructions are silent. As a result, there will be no possible grounds for accepting either the claim that the truth predicate applies to them or the claim that it does not. Because of this, both the claim that such sentences are true and the claim that they are not true must be rejected, thereby blocking the usual paradoxical results.

In order to see how a language might come to contain a partially defined predicate, it is useful to imagine an idealized situation in which a person has been given the authority to introduce a new word. Imagine that I am to be the authority on what the word is to mean and that you are willing to accept that. Imagine further that I have assembled two groups of adults in the room to serve as examples in my introduction of the word. Group A consists of adults who are abnormally short. Some are around four feet tall, some are a little taller, and others are a little shorter. Group B consists of adults whose height is at the low end of the normal range. Some are around five feet tall, a few are a little taller, and a few are a little shorter. Moreover, each member of group B is perceptibly taller than any member of group A.

In this situation, I make the following stipulation:

i.   Every member of group A is (now) a smidget. Further, for any adult whatsoever (and time t), if the height of that adult (at t) is less than or equal to the (present) height of at least one member of group A, then that adult is a smidget (at t).

ii. Every member of group B is not (now) a smidget. Further, for any adult whatsoever (and time t), if the height of that adult (at t) is greater than or equal to the (present) height of at least one member of group B, then that adult is not a smidget (at t).

iii. Nonadults (and nonhumans) are not smidgets.

My stipulation consists of a *sufficient* condition for something to be a smidget and a *sufficient* condition for something not to be a smidget. It does not give *necessary and sufficient* conditions. In certain circumstances, there might be a reason for this. For example, the point of introducing the term may be to set up a gross categorization of two groups easily distinguishable from each other by casual observation. Because of this, there may be no need to define a sharp and finely discriminated boundary requiring precise measurement to distinguish the smidgets from the nonsmidgets. The price we pay for this convenience is, of course, our inability to use the instructions introducing the predicate to characterize certain individuals as smidgets or as nonsmidgets. However, if adults whose heights are in the intermediate range between group A and group B are rare and not often encountered, this may well be a price that we are willing to pay. Surely there is no a priori reason why the advantages of introducing a predicate by stipulations of the sort just illustrated must always be outweighed by the potential disadvantages. Language is an institution designed to meet various practical contingencies. As such, it is not required that linguistic conventions be framed in terms of all imaginable circumstances.

Thus my stipulation may be successful in introducing a new term. On the basis of it, there will be clear cases in which one is justified in characterizing someone as a smidget and clear cases in which one is justified in characterizing someone as not being a smidget. Moreover, these characterizations will convey information to other members of the linguistic community. In short, the word *smidget* may enter the language as a useful and meaningful predicate.

There are, of course, other ways in which one could achieve similar results. For example, one might first point to group A and say, "Those people are smidgets. Further, for any adult whatsoever, if the height of that adult is *not noticeably (or significantly) greater than* that of each member of group A, then that adult is a smidget." One might then point to group B and say, "Those people are not smidgets. Further, for any adult whatsoever, if the height of that adult is *not noticeably (or significantly) less than* that of each member of group B, then that adult is not a smidget." The difference between this definition of smidget and the original one is that although both provide *partial* specifications of the term, the conditions specified by the second definition are, in addition, *vague*. Our concern in this chapter is with *partiality*. Since vague predicates are typically also partial, most of what is said here will apply to them. However, I will postpone the discussion of the specific features of vagueness until chapter 7, and I will assume, for the sake of simplicity, that the word 'smidget' has been introduced by the original definition and is not vague.[1]

Suppose now that the word *smidget* has become entrenched in the language. We next consider the question of whether an adult whose height is precisely halfway between that of the tallest person in group A and the shortest person in group B is or is not a smidget. It is important to emphasize that the question I am asking is *not* the practical one of whether the concept of a smidget should be *extended* so as to include or exclude the relevant individual. Rather, the question is theoretical. Given the concept of a smidget as it already exists in the language, is the individual a smidget or not?

Since our linguistic conventions provide no basis for answering this question, no answer to it can be accepted as correct. To characterize the individual as not being a smidget would be just as arbitrary and unjustified, on the basis of the meaning that has been given to the predicate, as to characterize that person as being a smidget. Since the individual fits neither the conditions in the definition for being a smidget nor the conditions for not being a smidget, neither claim (1a) nor claim (1b) can be accepted.

1a.   Mr. Smallman is a smidget.
  b.   Mr. Smallman is not a smidget (where 'Mr. Smallman' names an adult of intermediate height).

Does this mean that (1a) and (1b) are not true? In the conception of truth I wish to defend, it does not. I maintain that there is a natural way of understanding the truth predicate according to which saying that (1a) is not true would be just as unjustified as saying that Mr. Smallman is not a smidget. In this conception of truth, neither (2a) nor (2b) can be accepted.[2]

2a.   (1a) is true.
  b.   (1a) is not true.

The reason for this can be seen by imagining a process by which semantic terms like *true* might be introduced into a language that did not previously contain them. If, to begin with, we focus just on atomic sentences and their negations, we could think of the semantic terms *true* and *apply* being introduced by the rules in (3). Instruction (3a) tells us what it is for any one of the meaningful, antecedently understood predicates already in the language to apply (or fail to apply) to an object.

3a.   The predicate 'red' applies (does not apply) to an object $\equiv$ it is (is not) red.
  The predicate 'smidget' applies (does not apply) to an object $\equiv$ it is (is not) a smidget.
  (And so on, one clause for each predicate in the language)

Instruction (3b) uses the notion of a predicate applying to an object to explain what it is for an atomic sentence to be true; (3c) extends the explanation to negations of such sentences.

3b.   For any n-place predicate P and terms $t_1, \ldots, t_n$, $\ulcorner Pt_1, \ldots, t_n \urcorner$ is true (not true) $\equiv$ P applies (does not apply) to the n-tuple $<o_1, \ldots, o_n>$ of referents of the terms.
  c.   For any sentence S, $\ulcorner \sim S \urcorner$ is true (not true) $\equiv$ S is not true (true).

At this point, a word should be said about the connective, symbolized as '$\equiv$' and pronounced "just in case," used in these biconditionals. Since the biconditionals in (3) introduce and give content to the truth predicate, I cannot use the notion of truth to define the connective. However, I can illustrate its meaning by giving examples of how it is used. If Bill and Mary are both adults who are as short as or shorter than someone in group A or if they are both either nonadults or adults as tall or taller than someone in group B or if both are taller than everyone in group A but shorter than everyone in group B, I will say that Bill is a smidget $\equiv$ Mary is a smidget. Otherwise I will say that it is not the case that Bill is a smidget $\equiv$ Mary is a smidget. With this understanding, the principles in (3) may be used to introduce the truth predicate.

Since these principles are biconditionals, it might appear that they provide necessary and sufficient conditions for atomic sentences and their negations to be true or to be not true. However, this appearance is misleading. When an atomic sentence contains the predicate *smidget*, it will be true just in case *smidget* applies to the referent of the accompanying term; otherwise the sentence will not be true. Moreover, *smidget* will apply to an individual just in case that individual is a smidget. Thus if 'Mr. Smallman' is a name, the biconditionals in (4) will be logical consequences of the instructions in (3) (plus a homophonic axiom specifying the referent of the name).

4a. 'Mr. Smallman is a smidget' is true ≡ Mr. Smallman is a smidget.
 b. 'Mr. Smallman is a smidget' is not true ≡ Mr. Smallman is not a smidget.

However, we have only *sufficient* (not individually sufficient and jointly necessary) conditions for something to be a smidget, and *sufficient* (not individually
sufficient and jointly necessary) conditions for something not to be a smidget. As
a result, in the case in which 'Mr. Smallman' names an adult of intermediate
height, we have no basis for accepting the right-hand sides of these biconditionals
and hence no basis for accepting their left-hand sides either. This means that we
have only sufficient (not individually sufficient and jointly necessary) conditions
for sentences (1a) and (1b) to be true (or not to be true). Thus we are in the same
position regarding *true* as we are regarding *smidget*. Just as we must reject both
(1a) and (1b), so we must reject both (2a) and (2b) — and for the same reason. In
each case, the instructions governing the use of the predicate are silent about and
provide no justification for the predication in question.

How shall we think about this? It might seem natural to characterize the sentences in (1) and (2) as giving rise to truth-value gaps. However, if we do characterize them in this way, it is crucial to note that the gaps they give rise to are
different from those most often discussed in the logical and philosophical literature. In particular, these gaps must be distinguished from both the Fregean and
the Strawsonian paradigms, which have played prominent roles in philosophical
discussions of presupposition, and the semantic paradoxes.[3]

Truth Value Gaps and Partially Defined Predicates

Let us say that a proposition P *logically presupposes* a proposition Q iff for all
possible circumstances w, if Q is not true in w, then P is neither true nor false in
w. For example, the proposition that the king of France is bald has been held by
some theorists to logically presuppose (the proposition) that there is a (unique)
king of France. According to Gottlob Frege, the presupposition arises from a com-
positional account of the truth conditions of this proposition. The individual concept expressed by *the king of France* picks out different individuals in different
possible circumstances, and in some circumstances, it picks out no individual at
all. In Frege's analysis, the proposition that the king of France is bald is true in
w iff the concept picks out an individual in w and that individual is bald in w; it
is false in w iff the concept picks out an individual in w who is not bald in w. In
circumstances in which the concept fails to pick out any individual — that is, in
circumstances in which there is no (unique) king of France — the proposition is
neither true nor false.

Sentences bear logical presuppositions in a derivative sense. A sentence S logically presupposes a proposition Q relative to a context of utterance C iff S expresses a proposition in C that logically presupposes Q. In this account, the
sentence *The king of France is bald* logically presupposes a falsehood with respect
to any actual present context and hence is neither true nor false. The same can
be said for *The king of France is not bald*, if we assume that the proposition it

expresses is true (false) in a circumstance just in case the proposition that the king of France is bald is false (true) in that circumstance.

Thus the proponent of this analysis will reject both (5a) and (5b).

5a. The king of France is bald.
 b. The king of France is not bald.

In this respect, the present example is like the smidget case, in which we rejected both (1a) and (1b). However, there is a crucial difference between the two cases. Since Fregeans characterize (5a) and (5b) as being neither true nor false, they are committed to the claim that they are not true.[4] This contrasts with the smidget case, in which the claim that (1a) and (1b) are not true must be rejected on the same grounds as (1a) and (1b) themselves. Thus the truth-value gaps illustrated by (1a) and (1b) are not Fregean gaps and do not arise from logical presupposition failure.

Whereas the bearers of logical presuppositions are, in the first instance, propositions, there is another kind of presupposition, discussed by Peter Strawson in "On Referring," that applies directly to sentences or utterances of sentences, which we may think of for present purposes as sentence/context pairs.[5] The basic idea is that a sentence presupposes a proposition Q relative to a context C iff Q must be true in order for S to (semantically) express a proposition in C. This idea finds its natural home in a theory in which the meaning of a sentence is taken to be a compositional function from contexts of utterance to propositions expressed. Meanings of subsentential constituents are then seen as functions from contexts to propositional contents — namely, that which the constituents contribute to the propositions expressed by sentences containing them. Suppose now that failure of a constituent to express a content in a context results in failure of a sentence containing it to express a proposition in that context. Then conditions semantically necessary for constituents of S to express a content become Strawsonian presuppositions of S.

An example of this is given in "On Referring": "I advance my hands, cautiously cupped towards someone, saying, as I do so, 'This is a fine red one.' He, looking into my hands and seeing nothing there, may say: 'What are you talking about?' Or perhaps, 'But there's nothing in your hands.' "[6] The natural thing to say about this utterance is, I think, that it is untrue, not because it expresses a proposition that is neither true nor false but rather because it fails to express any proposition at all.[7]

This point is supported by the contrast between (6) and (7).

6. Bill says/believes that the king of France is bald.
7. Bill says/believes that this is a fine red one.

Whereas (6) may be true even if *the king of France* fails to denote anyone, an utterance of (7) in which the demonstrative *this* fails to refer is as problematic as Strawson's original example. This may readily be explained on the assumption that *say* and *believe* express relations to the propositions expressed by their sentential complements. Since the complement in (6) expresses a proposition, there is some-thing for Bill to say or believe. Since the complement in (7) fails to express a proposition (in a context in which *this* fails to refer), it cannot be true.

We have already seen that the smidget examples, (1a) and (1b), are not bearers of false logical presuppositions. They are also not bearers of false Strawsonian presuppositions, as is shown by the following considerations.

First, if they were, they would not express propositions and so would not be true sentences. But we have seen that the claim that (1a) and (1b) are not true cannot be accepted. Second, consider a case in which Ralph is an adult who is four feet tall. The sentence *Ralph is a smidget* will then be true and will certainly express a proposition. Let us call this proposition "P". Now consider a counter-factual circumstance in which Ralph has been given a growth hormone and is four feet six inches tall (exactly halfway between the actual heights of the tallest member of group A and the shortest member of group B).[8] Is the proposition P true in this circumstance, or is it not true in this circumstance? This is the same question, in modified form, as our original question about (1a) and (1b). Just as it would be incorrect to characterize (1a) or (1b) as true or as not true (in the original circumstance), so it would be incorrect to characterize P as true or as not true in the counterfactual circumstance. Moreover, in the latter case, it is no good claiming that there is no proposition to evaluate. We already have the proposition; it is just that the proposition cannot correctly be evaluated for truth value in every possible circumstance. But then the same thing should be said about (1a) and (1b). Once it is admitted that there are propositions that resist evaluation in certain circumstances, there are no longer grounds to suppose that (1a) and (1b) do not express propositions in the context originally imagined.

On the contrary, there are good reasons to think that they do. For example, just as (6) may truly describe the beliefs or assertions of Bill, so (8) may truly describe the beliefs or assertions of an agent, Mary, who is misinformed about Mr. Smallman's height. (Surely an agent can say or believe that someone is a smidget even if, unknown to the agent, the individual is an adult whose height is in the intermediate range.)

8.   Mary says/believes that Mr. Smallman is a smidget.

Thus if propositional attitude ascriptions report relations to the propositions ex-pressed by their complement sentences, then (1a) must express a proposition.

In light of this, it is not surprising that utterances of (1a) and (1b) succeed in accomplishing another of the central tasks that propositions are standardly used to explain. The proposition P expressed by a sentence S relative to a context C determines in which possible circumstances S, as used in C, is true and in which it is not true. In effect, P determines a function from possible circumstances to truth values. This function must not be confused with one that assigns possible contexts of utterance the value truth iff in that context S expresses a truth. For example, if S contains a demonstrative, then the latter function will assign truth to only those contexts in which one individual demonstratively refers to another. However, S, as used in any particular context, may well be true in circumstances in which no one is referring to anything. The sentence *You are tired* expresses a truth only in contexts in which someone is referred to, but the fact that someone is referred to is no part of *what is said* on these occasions.

Suppose now that α is a demonstrative that refers, on some occasion of utterance of ⌜α is a smidget⌝, to an adult o whose height is midway between that of the tallest person in group A and the shortest person in group B. What are the circumstances in which what is said on this occasion is true (not true)? The answer is clear. The truth-making circumstances are those in which o is an adult whose height is less than or equal to the actual height of the tallest person in group A (i.e., the circumstances in which o is about four feet tall or shorter); the untruth-making circumstances are those in which o's height is greater than or equal to the actual height of the shortest person in group B (i.e., the circumstances in which o is about five feet tall or taller). The utterance therefore succeeds in specifying a function from circumstances to truth values that constrains the way the world is represented to be. This, along with serving as objects of the attitudes, is just what propositions are needed for in the first place. Thus if any utterances express propositions, those of (1a) and (1b) do. The fact that the functions determined by these propositions are partial just shows that there are "truth-value gaps" of a non-Fregean and non-Strawsonian kind.[9] I propose to call this new partiality paradigm the Kripke-Salmon paradigm after Saul Kripke, whose discussion in "Outline of a Theory of Truth"[10] inspired it, and Nathan Salmon, who first brought it to my attention as a way of understanding Kripke's construction in that essay.[11] The question before us is, What can we learn about truth from the Kripke-Salmon paradigm?

Truth, Determinate Truth, and Ungroundedness

I have said that we must reject the claim that (1a) and (1b) are true. We must also reject the claim that they are false or even not true. Thus we must reject bivalence, both in the strong form expressed by (9) and in the weak form expressed by (10).

> 9. Every sentence (proposition) is either true or false.
> 10. Every sentence (proposition) is either true or not true.

However, rejecting (9) and (10) does not commit us to accepting (11) and (12).

> 11. Some sentence (proposition) is neither true nor false.
> 12. Some sentence (proposition) is neither true nor not true.

There might, of course, be independent reasons for accepting the weak non-bivalence thesis (11). If there are genuine instances of Strawsonian presupposition, then the sentential version of (11) is correct since there are some meaningful sentences that fail to express propositions on certain occasions of use and therefore are neither true nor false on those occasions. If there are genuine instances of

Fregean, logical presupposition, then both the sentential and the propositional versions of (11) are correct since there are sentences and propositions that are neither true nor false.

The strong nonbivalence thesis (12) is another matter. Given a classical understanding of quantification, negation, and disjunction (which I assume), we must reject (12). And indeed, our *smidget* examples give us no reason to think otherwise. Just as we reject (2a) and (2b), so we reject (2c) and (2d).

2c. (1a) is either true or not true.
 d. (1a) is neither true nor not true.

Thus we reject not only (weak) bivalence but also its negation.

In what sense do we reject these claims? At a minimum, we must not assert them. However, there is more to it than that. We must also hold that it would be a mistake to assert them. But what kind of mistake?

It is not that one can never be justified in believing or asserting the kind of proposition expressed by (1a). If all available evidence indicates that Mr. Smallman's height would place him among the members of group A, one may be justified in believing that Mr. Smallman is a smidget even if he is really taller than everyone in group A and shorter than everyone in group B. It is striking, however, that all such cases involve some kind of ignorance. A person who was omniscient about nonlinguistic facts would not be justified in believing or asserting that such an individual was (or was not) a smidget. On the contrary, to assert that such an individual was (or was not) a smidget would be to go beyond what can in principle be justified by linguistic convention plus nonlinguistic fact. Moreover, it is not just these assertions that fail to be licensed. Since attributions of truth or untruth to such assertions are themselves ungrounded, linguistic convention also fails to license them.

One may think of the matter in the following way. Let the *determinate-extension* and *determinate-antiextension* of 'smidget' be as follows:

Determinate-extension: The determinate-extension of a predicate P is the set S of things such that the linguistic conventions of the language stipulate that P applies to members of S. Where P is 'smidget', S is the set of adults whose height is less than or equal to the height of at least one member of group A.

Determinate-antiextension: The determinate-antiextension of a predicate P is the set S of things such that the linguistic conventions of the language stipulate that P does not apply to members of S. Where P is 'smidget,' S is the set of nonadults plus adults whose height is greater than or equal to the height of at least one member of group B.

These are contrasted with the *extension* and *antiextension* of 'smidget'.

Extension: The extension of a predicate is the collection of things it applies to. The extension of 'smidget' is the collection of smidgets.

Antiextension: The antiextension of a predicate is the collection of things it does not apply to. The antiextension of 'smidget' is the collection of things that are not smidgets.

Note that all members of the determinate-extension of 'smidget' are members of its extension and all members of the determinate-antiextension of 'smidget' are members of its antiextension. However, the converse of these claims cannot be accepted. Adults who are taller than every member of group A but shorter than every member of group B are not members of the determinate-extension or the determinate-antiextension of 'smidget'. Since we cannot say this about the extension and antiextension, the former pair cannot be identified with the latter.

If an individual i is in the determinate-extension or the determinate-antiextension of *smidget*, then linguistic conventions will ground the attribution of the predicate to i, as well as the denial of that attribution. But if i is in neither the determinate-extension nor the determinate-antiextension of the predicate, then neither the assertion that i is a smidget nor its negation will be grounded. Our linguistic conventions are simply silent about these cases. We can say, if we like, that the predicate 'smidget' is *undefined* for individuals in the intermediate range and hence that the corresponding assertions and their negations are *ungrounded*. However, if we say this, we must *not* conclude that an individual for which a predicate is *undefined* is an individual the predicate *does not apply to* or that an *ungrounded* sentence (or proposition) is one that *is not true*. To assert something ungrounded is to make a kind of mistake. But the mistake is not correctly described as that of saying something untrue. Rather, it is in saying something that cannot, in the end, be sanctioned by the linguistic conventions that give one's words their meaning.

We could, of course, introduce a theoretical semantic notion that would allow us to treat ungrounded sentences on a par with untruths. This is done in (13).[12]

13a.   A sentence $\ulcorner Pt_1, \ldots, t_n \urcorner$ is determinately true (determinately false) $\equiv$ the n-tuple $\langle o_1, \ldots, o_n \rangle$ of referents of the terms is a member of the determinate-extension (determinate-antiextension) of the predicate.

  b. $\ulcorner \sim S \urcorner$ is determinately true $\equiv$ S is determinately false.
       $\ulcorner \sim S \urcorner$ is determinately false $\equiv$ S is determinately true.

Examples (1a) and (1b) are not determinately true. However, truth and determinate-truth cannot be identified. To explore this difference further, we need to look more closely at the linguistic conventions responsible for introducing the predicate *true*.

Extending the Truth Predicate

Up to now, I have been assuming that the word *true* is introduced by the conventions in (3). But (3) is highly simplified. As it stands, it tells us only what it is for atomic sentences and negations to be true. Fortunately, it is easily expanded to include standard truth-functional and quantificational structure as well. For example, consider disjunction. Given the standard meaning of 'v' (i.e., 'or') plus the classical identification of being false with not being true, we want a disjunction with a true disjunct to be true and a disjunction with a false disjunction to receive the same evaluation as its other disjunct.[13] Thus the truth table for disjunction is (14), and the clause needed in the truth characterization is (3d).

14. A v B

		B		
		T	F	*
	T	T	T	T
A	F	T	F	*
	*	T	*	*

3d. ⌜A v B⌝ is true ≡ A is true or B is true.
     ⌜A v B⌝ is not true (i.e., false) ≡ A and B are not true.

Similar reasoning leads to clauses (3e)–(3h) for conjunction, material implication, and quantification (where, in giving the latter, I pretend, for the sake of simplicity, that every object is named and every name names an object).

3e. ⌜A & B⌝ is true ≡ A is true and B is true.
     ⌜A & B⌝ is not true ≡ A is not true or B is not true.
 f. ⌜A ⊃ B⌝ is true ≡ A is not true or B is true.
     ⌜A ⊃ B⌝ is not true ≡ A is true and B is not true.
 g. ⌜∃v F(v)⌝ is true ≡ Fv/a is true for some name a
     ⌜∃v F(v)⌝ is not true ≡ for all names a, Fv/a is not true.
 h. ⌜∀v F(v)⌝ is true ≡ Fv/a is true for all names a.
     ⌜∀v F(v)⌝ is not true ≡ for some name a, Fv/a is not true.

Note that these clauses present exactly the classical understanding of these logical constructions. Not only are no new truth values introduced, but also being false is identified with not being true. Truth tables for the connectives do, of course, show three possibilities. However, it is important not to be misled by this. The reason for the three entry tables is that some of our linguistic conventions are partial in the manner illustrated by *smidget*. As a result, they are silent about examples like (1) and (2). Clauses (3c)–(3h) pass this silence on to certain logically complex sentences. Thus '*' in tables like (14) does not mean '*untrue without being false*' but rather '*ungrounded*' (or '*undefined*'), where it is understood that the claim that S is not true does *not* follow from the claim that S is ungrounded (or undefined). Ungroundedness is not a truth value.

Imagine then the semantic predicates *true* and *apply* being introduced by the instructions in (3). These instructions allow one to establish results corresponding to those in (15) while rejecting problematic examples like (2a) and (2b).

15a.   '∀x [(x is an adult & x is under three feet tall) ⊃ x is a smidget]' is true.
   b.   'Ronald Reagan is a smidget' is not true.

Nevertheless, the instructions are incomplete. The clause, (3a), covering *apply* does not tell us what it is for the predicate *true* to apply to something or for the predicate *apply* to apply. The reason it does not is that when we invoked (3a) to introduce the semantic predicates, the only resources at our disposal were the antecedently understood expressions already in the language. Since the predicates *true* and *apply* were not among them, they were not mentioned in (3a). Hence the instructions governing *true* do not tell us what it is for a sentence containing *true* (or *apply*) to be true.

Fortunately, this incompleteness is easily remedied by adding the clauses in (3a+) to (3a).

3a+.   The predicate 'true' applies (does not apply) to an object ≡ it is (is not) a true sentence.
   The predicate 'apply' applies to a pair <o, o'> ≡ o is a predicate that applies to o'; otherwise it does not apply.

Let us concentrate on the part of (3a+) that mentions the truth predicate. What allows us to introduce this new instruction is the fact that our previous instructions have already given sense to the idea of sentences not containing the truth predicate being true or not being true. Because of this, we now have a grasp of the right-hand side of the initial biconditional in (3a+) that is sufficient to fix the interpretation of the left-hand side. The end result is an expanded set of instructions, (3), governing the use of the truth predicate both in sentences that contain the predicate and in sentences that do not. Although this set of instructions does not have the form of an explicit definition, it does define an inductive procedure sufficient to give sense to the predicate *true*, which it introduces.

The first stage of the procedure covers sentences that do not contain the truth predicate. The original, unexpanded instructions tell us what it is for one of these sentences to be true or to be untrue. It is at this stage that results like (15) are established.[14] At the next stage, we use the results of the first stage plus the expansion (3a+) of our original instructions to make sense of attributions to certain sentences that contain the word *true*. For example, at this stage, we use the facts in (15) to establish those in (16), and, thereby, those in (17).[15]

16a.   The predicate 'true' applies to the sentence whose quote-name appears in (15a).
   b.   The predicate 'true' does not apply to the sentence whose quote-name appears in (15b).
17a.   (15a) is a true.
   b.   The sentence '*Ronald Reagan is a smidget*' *is true*, of which (15b) is the negation, is not true.
   c.   (15b) is true.

These results then become available at the next stage of the process, and so on ad infinitum, with more and more sentences containing the truth predicate coming to be counted as true or as not true.

How long should this process be thought of as continuing? The natural answer is that it should continue indefinitely or until it stops having an effect—that is, until no further sentences are able to be characterized as true or as not true. It must be noticed, however, that no matter how long the process continues, certain sentences will never be characterized one way or the other. This is true of the sentences in (1) and (2) plus a variety of similar sentences involving (or parasitic upon) attributions of *smidget* to individuals for which it is not defined. However, it is also true of a number of examples in which the original partially defined predicate is *true* rather than *smidget*.

For example, consider the so-called Truth Teller (18).

18. Sentence (18) is true.

Since (18) is an atomic sentence whose predicate is the word *true*, the instructions in (3) can be used to characterize it as true or as not true at some stage of the inductive process only if (19) has already been established at that stage.

19. The predicate 'true' applies (does not apply) to sentence (18).

But in order for (19) to have been established, the truth or untruth of sentence (18) must already have been determined at an earlier stage. The effect of our instructions then is that sentence (18) can be characterized as true or as not true at a given stage only if it has already been determined to be true or to be not true at a prior stage. Since it is not determined to be true or to be not true at the first stage, it follows that it will never be determined at any stage. The instructions introducing the truth predicate are silent about it in the same way that our instructions introducing *smidget* are silent about (1a). Just as our linguistic conventions do not license the assertion of (1a) or its negation, so they do not license the assertion of (18) or its negation. Just as neither truth nor untruth can correctly be predicated of (1a), so neither truth nor untruth can correctly be predicated of (18).

The same point can be made about Liar sentences like (20).

20. Sentence (20) is not true.

Our linguistic conventions do not allow us correctly to say either that (20) is true or that it is not true. In this case, it is fortunate that they do not since either characterization leads swiftly, together with obvious assumptions, to contradiction. However, the reason our conventions do not sanction these characterizations is *not* that they have been crafted with an eye to avoiding paradox. The reason is that the procedure for introducing the truth predicate makes the status of the claim that S is true (or not true) dependent on the prior status of S and ultimately on the status of sentences that do not contain the truth predicate at all. When this dependence can be traced from a sentence containing the truth predicate all the way back to (grounded) sentences that do not contain it, the original sentence will either be determined to be true or be determined not to be true. When the dependence cannot be traced back in this way, the rules for characterizing sentences as true or as not true will simply be inapplicable. Thus the instructions governing the truth predicate provide sufficient conditions for a sentence to be true and sufficient conditions for a sentence not to be true. However, these conditions are not jointly exhaustive because there is a class of sentences that the instructions are silent about.

It should be evident that what we have here is a philosophical justification of a certain kind of "gappy" treatment of the Liar paradox. The justification amounts to a demonstration that the proposed treatment of the paradox satisfies the following three desiderata: First, the gaps are not technical artifacts cooked up just to avoid the paradox; rather, they exist independently in language and arise from a process that applies to semantic and nonsemantic notions alike. Second, the gaps result from a plausible set of instructions for introducing the truth predicate; the gappy character of Truth Tellers and Liars is an automatic and unpremeditated consequence of these instructions. Third, the gaps provide an explanation of how we can (and indeed must) reject the claim that the Liars are true while also rejecting the claim that they are not true (thereby avoiding the Strengthened Liar).

Limitations of the Model

Despite the attractiveness of this treatment of the Liar, it is important not to carry our enthusiasm over these results too far. Given the model of partially defined predicates outlined, one can see how a language can come to contain its own truth predicate. However, there are definite limits to this treatment of semantic notions.

Earlier, I distinguished the notion of *truth* from that of *determinate-truth*. These notions differ regarding the status of sentences for which the truth predicate is *undefined*. Although such sentences are not determinately true, we cannot accept the claim that they are therefore not true. Moreover, although a reasonably rich object-language, with the capacity for self-reference and the usual logical operators, can contain its own truth and untruth predicates, it cannot contain a predicate that applies to precisely those of its sentences that are not determinately true and, for that reason, cannot contain its own determinate-truth predicate.

This is easily shown. If a language contained its own determinate-truth predicate plus self-reference and classical negation, then it would allow the construction of Liar sentences like (21).

21. Sentence (21) is not determinately true.

Since the determinate-truth predicate is totally defined, (21) must either be determinately true or not. But it cannot, on pain of contradiction, be either. If we assume that sentence (21) is determinately true, then we can use rule (22), which allows us to infer a sentence from the claim that it is determinately true, to derive the contradictory result that sentence (21) is not determinately true.

22. 'S' is determinately true ⊢S.

Similarly, if we assume that sentence (21) is not determinately true, then we can use rule (23)

23. S ⊢ 'S' is true.

to derive the result that sentence (21) is true. But then since (21) is both true and defined, it must be determinately true, thereby contradicting our previous assumption. In short, the assumption that the language contains both classical negation and its own determinate-truth predicate leads to contradiction. Given that it does contain classical negation, we therefore conclude that it cannot contain its own determinate-truth predicate.

The same considerations show that if such a language contains its own truth predicate, then it cannot contain its own ungroundedness (or undefinedness) predicate, for if it did, then determinate-truth could be defined in the language as in (24).

24. ∀x [x is determinately true ↔ x is true & ~ (x is ungrounded)].

Finally, a (reasonably rich) language that contains its own truth predicate cannot contain one of the connectives I have been using up to now. If one examines the instructions in (3) that I used to introduce the truth predicate, one will notice two things. First, the clauses in the inductive characterization are biconditionals containing the "just in case" connective symbolized by '≡'. Second, none of the clauses in the characterization of truth has as its subject matter sentences containing this connective. Straightforward material conditionals are covered in (3f). Material biconditionals are definable in terms of (3e) and (3f). However, my "just in case" biconditionals involving '≡' are not standard, material biconditionals.

The reason they are not is indicated in (25).

25a. ⌜A ↔ B⌝ is ungrounded (undefined) when both A and B are.
  b. ⌜A ≡ B⌝ is (determinately) true when A and B are both ungrounded (undefined).[16]

In order to understand what is at issue, it is important to realize that clauses like those in (3d)–(3h), as well as those in (25), are not regarded as giving the meanings of the connectives. We are not presupposing truth and using it to define the connectives. Rather, we are presupposing the connectives and using them to introduce the truth predicate. Thus one might wonder why we do not simply add (26) to our specification of truth in the object-language.

26. ⌜(A ≡ B)⌝ is true ≡ (A is true ≡ B is true).

The problem with such an addition is not that it is circular; it is not. The problem is that it would render the whole account incoherent, for suppose the object-language contained both its own truth predicate and the connective in (26). Since it also contains negation, it would then contain its own ungroundedness predicate, given in (27).

27.   x is ungrounded: [x is true $\equiv$ $\sim$ (x is true)].

But we have seen that it is impossible for our language to contain its own ungroundedness predicate (together with its own truth predicate).

Therefore I did not include (26) as one of the clauses in the truth characterization. As a result, the language I used to introduce the truth predicate was slightly more extensive than the language into which the truth predicate was introduced. The former contains the "just in case" connective, '$\equiv$'; the latter does not. Although this does not affect the validity of our results, it does limit their scope. There is no possibility of a universal language in which everything is expressible, and there seems to be no avoiding a Tarski-like hierarchy for certain semantic concepts like *determinate-truth* and *ungroundedness*.

Still, one might wonder whether one could introduce a truth predicate into a language without going beyond the resources available in the language. One possibility would be to reinterpret the instructions in (3) as rules of inference, inviting us to infer what appears to the left of '$\equiv$' from what appears to the right and vice versa.[17] In this conception, the clauses introducing the truth predicate would not be statements and so could not be evaluated for truth value. Instead, they would be instructions licensing us to infer S from ⌜'S' is true⌝ and vice versa, and to infer ⌜~S⌝ from ⌜'S' is not true⌝ and vice versa, while not licensing anything when we are not given S or ⌜~S.⌝ With this, we could introduce a truth predicate into a language we speak. This achievement is not negated by the fact that later, when we seek to describe what we have done, we will have to start speaking an expanded language.

The Resiliancy of the Liar

Let us suppose, then, that we have a language that contains its own gappy truth predicate, governed by instructions of the sort I have indicated. Although the language allows the construction of Liar sentences, which characterize themselves as being untrue, the instructions governing the truth predicate do not apply to them, and because of this, one can reject the claims they make without accepting their negations. As a result, these sentences do not lead to paradox. In this sense, we have what might be called a solution to the Liar paradox as it arises in the language under consideration.

Do we have a general solution to the Liar paradox as it arises in English and other natural languages? Unfortunately we do not. Although much of what we have said can, I think, be applied to these languages, our discussion is incomplete in two important respects. The first involves ways in which our original instructions might consistently be supplemented to eliminate some of the truth-value gaps to which they initially gave rise. The second involves the introduction of semantic terms that have the effect of extending the language beyond the reach of the previously introduced truth predicate.

Both of these points can be illustrated by imagining a process involving an idealized group of people who speak a language of the sort I have been describing up to now, with a truth predicate introduced by instructions like those in (3). Initially, we may imagine them speaking the language, unaware of any paradox. Later, they discover the Liar paradox and are puzzled by it. At some point, they come up with the correct solution; they realize that their truth predicate is partially defined and that there are many sentences, including Liar sentences, that the instructions governing it simply do not apply to. Having noticed these truth-value gaps, they also notice that they have a significant degree of freedom in supplementing their original instructions governing the truth predicate so as to eliminate some of these gaps.

To this end, they distinguish four types of gappy sentences. The first type are *paradoxical sentences* like (28a).

28a.   ~ Sentence (28a) is true.

Any attempt to assign truth values to these sentences will be inconsistent with the instructions governing the truth predicate and thus will lead to contradiction. As a result, these gaps cannot be eliminated (while retaining the original instructions).

The second type of gappy sentence are those like (28b).

28b.   Sentence (28b) is true.

Although these sentences can consistently be assigned a truth value, the value they are assigned is completely arbitrary. If they choose to do so, speakers can supplement their original instructions in a way that makes these sentences come out true or in a way that makes them come out untrue. Moreover, nothing in the original instructions provides a reason for making one choice rather than the other.

The third type of gappy sentence are those like (28c).

28c.   (Sentence (28b) is true) v ~ (sentence (28b) is true).

If these sentences are assigned any truth value at all, they have to be assigned a particular truth value—in the case of (28c), the value truth. However, even though the truth values assigned to these sentences are nonarbitrary, in order for them to receive a truth value at all, some arbitrary assignments must be made to other sentences. For example, in order to make the nonarbitrary assignment of truth to (28c), one must arbitrarily assign either truth or untruth to (28b).

The final type of gappy sentence are those like (28d).

28d.   (Sentence (28d) is true) v ~ (sentence (28d) is true).

These sentences can be assigned a nonarbitrary truth value without making any arbitrary assignments of truth values to other gappy sentences. If (28d) is given any truth value, it must be given the value truth; moreover, this can be done without making arbitrary decisions about other sentences. Thus if speakers wish to eliminate some truth-value gaps by supplementing the original instructions governing the truth predicate, the most conservative addition they can make is one that limits itself to such nonarbitrary assignments.[18]

The lesson to be learned is that even if we imagine a group of speakers who have correctly diagnosed and resolved the Liar paradox as it arises in their language, the position they arrive at is one that leaves open various decisions about how they might choose to augment the conventions governing their truth predicate. Suppose now that we try to apply this lesson to English.[19] It is, of course, clear that English speakers have not made any collective decision about the gappiness of their truth predicate, let alone about the various ways in which some of those gaps could be eliminated. Nevertheless, it is not implausible to hold that one of their central intentions is to use the truth predicate in accord with instructions analogous to those in (3) of our discussion. If so, then the English truth predicate may be gappy. Most likely, however, English speakers have other intentions as well—for example, the intention to make maximally many assignments of truth value or perhaps the intention to make as many nonarbitrary assignments of truth value as possible. What we need is a principled means of extracting some precise and specific characterization of the truth predicate from the welter of ordinary intentions and intuitions. Even if we succeed in justifying the claim that the English truth predicate is gappy and that Liar sentences are ungrounded, the question of locating the scope and extent of such gaps may remain. This is one of the two respects mentioned earlier in which our discussion of the truth predicate and the Liar paradox is incomplete.

The other respect in which it is incomplete has to do with the dynamic character of the paradox. What I mean by this is that the very activity of solving the paradox in a particular language provides the material for re-creating another version of it in a broader context. Imagine again our idealized group of speakers who have solved the Liar paradox as it arises in their language by noting that Liar sentences are ungrounded because the truth predicate is undefined for such sentences. In coming to this solution, the speakers have had to expand their initial language L_1 by introducing new semantic terms like *determinate-extension, determinate-anti-extension, is undefined* and *is ungrounded*. This results in an expanded language L_2 consisting of the original language L_1 plus the new semantic terms applying to expressions of L_1. Initially, the speakers may see nothing amiss in this and may regard their language as now containing both its own partially defined truth predicate and its own ungroundedness predicate. However, before long they will realize, as we have, that this cannot be. Thus if an ungroundedness predicate is introduced in the process of diagnosing and solving the Liar paradox, then either the initial truth predicate for the unexpanded language L_1 or the newly introduced ungroundedness predicate *must be restricted to* L_1. This means that if one wishes to be able to assess the new sentences of L_2 for both truth and ungroundedness, one must extend the language again by introducing *new* semantic predicates applicable to sentences of L_2. This process can be repeated over and over, without end.

In and of itself, this ascent through a hierarchy of languages is perfectly coherent. However, it does raise questions about the analysis of the truth predicate in English. If English has a gappy truth predicate of the sort I have described here, does it also have an ungroundedness predicate? Since I have been speaking English all along, one would certainly think so. But this means that if claims about ungroundedness can be assessed for truth in English and claims about truth can be assessed for ungroundedness in English, then English must contain higher semantic predicates in addition to its initial gappy truth predicate. Indeed, it would seem that, in this analysis, what we call English is really a hierarchy of languages and what we call the "truth predicate" in English really represents a hierarchy of truth predicates.

The virtue of this analysis then is not that it allows us to completely avoid a Tarski-like hierarchy but rather, first, that it arises from a plausible account of how the notion of truth might be introduced into a language and understood by its speakers and, second, that it makes room for a lot of expressive power at the very first level of the hierarchy (which contains a gappy truth predicate). Because of this, it maximizes the portion of English that can be analyzed free of the rigidity and expressive limitation inherent in the Tarski hierarchy.

Kripke's Theory of Truth

The philosophical conception of truth given in the previous section is an interpretation of the central aspects of Saul Kripke's theory of truth, presented in his 1975 article, "Outline of a Theory of Truth." In that article, Kripke provides a precise mathematical framework in which different views about truth can be investigated and in which intuitive notions like "paradoxical" and "ungrounded" can be formally defined. A guiding intuition behind Kripke's formal construction is the idea that the status of the claim that a sentence S is true or that S is not true is dependent on the prior status of S or $\ulcorner \sim S \urcorner$.

Kripke describes this intuition as follows:

> We wish to capture an intuition of somewhat the following kind. Suppose we are explaining the word 'true' to someone who does not yet understand it. We may say that we are entitled to assert (or deny) of any sentence that it is true precisely under the circumstances when we can assert (or deny) the sentence itself. Our interlocutor then can understand what it means, say, to attribute truth to (6) ('snow is white') but he will still be puzzled about attributions of truth to sentences containing the word 'true' itself. . . .
>
> Nevertheless, with more thought the notion of truth as applied even to various sentences themselves containing the word 'true' can gradually become clear. Suppose we consider the sentence,

(7) Some sentence printed in the *New York Daily News*,
      October 7, 1971, is true.

(7) is a typical example of a sentence involving the concept of truth itself. So if (7) is unclear, so still is

(8)   (7) is true.

However, our subject, if he is willing to assert 'snow is white', will according to the rules be willing to assert '(6) is true'. But suppose that among the assertions printed in the *New York Daily News*, October 7, 1971, is (6) itself. Since our subject is willing to assert '(6) is true', and also to assert '(6) is printed in the *New York Daily News*, October 7, 1971', he will deduce (7) by existential generalization. Once he is willing to assert (7), he will also be willing to assert (8). In this manner, the subject will eventually be able to attribute truth to more and more statements involving the notion of truth itself. There is no reason to suppose that *all* statements involving 'true' will become decided in this way, but most will. Indeed, our suggestion is that the "grounded" sentences can be characterized as those which eventually get a truth value in this process.[20]

Intuitively, it should be clear that, as Kripke says, although many sentences containing the word *true* can be evaluated by the process he describes, some sentences will never receive any evaluation. In particular, the process will provide no basis for characterizing Liar sentences and Truth Tellers, like (28a) and (28b) of the last section, either as true or as not true. Thus the intuition that Kripke sets out to capture in his mathematical framework is one that gives rise to "gappy" truth predicates. Later I will argue that although Kripke's formal construction is compatible with different philosophical interpretations of the nature of these gaps, the Kripke-Salmon gaps discussed in the first half of this chapter provide the best interpretation.

Kripke's formal construction involves a hierarchy of first-order languages with the same syntax and vocabulary, with sufficient resources to refer to their own expressions,[21] and differing from one another only in the interpretation of a common predicate 'T'. With the exception of 'T', all the other predicates in the languages are totally defined and retain the same interpretation from language to language. By contrast, 'T' is partially defined and has different interpretations in different languages of the hierarchy.

The predicate 'T' is a potential truth predicate, and its varying interpretations in the different languages in the hierarchy are reflected in the truth theories for those languages. These theories can be presented in different ways, depending on whether one formulates them in a gappy or a nongappy metalanguage. Since I believe that the gappy approach is the most illuminating, I will begin by stating Kripke's basic results in terms of it.

The truth theory for a language can be thought of as being divided into a denotation theory and a characterization of truth in terms of denotation. The denotation theory associates an object with each name and a set of n-tuples with each n-place predicate other than 'T'. Each of these predicates is totally defined in the sense that for each n-tuple of elements in the domain of discourse, the predicate either definitely applies or definitely fails to apply to that n-tuple. 'T', on the other hand, is only partially defined. The denotation theory associates it with a pair of mutually exclusive but not jointly exhaustive sets, S_1 and S_2.

These sets may be thought of either as the *extension* and the *antiextension* of 'T', respectively, or as the *determinate-extension* and the *determinate-antiextension* of 'T', in the sense that these terms are defined in the first half of this chapter. If we think of them as extension and antiextension, then membership in S_1 and S_2 will be indeterminate for sentences for which 'T' is undefined and the denotation theory will include the following statements (where '≡' is the "just in case" connective discussed earlier).

1a.   The predicate 'T' applies to an object $o \equiv o \in S_1$.

 b.   The predicate 'T' does not apply to an object $o \equiv o \in S_2$.

If we think of S_1 and S_2 as the determinate-extension and determinate-antiextension of 'T', then membership in them will be determinate for all objects and the denotation theory will include (2a) and (2b).

2a.   If $o \in S_1$, then 'T' applies to o.

 b.   If $o \in S_2$, then 'T' does not apply to o.

Either way, the denotation theory will provide sufficient but not individually sufficient and jointly necessary conditions for 'T' to apply to an object and sufficient but not individually sufficient and jointly necessary conditions for 'T' to fail to apply to an object. Although Kripke uses the terminology *extension* and *antiextension* in connection with S_1 and S_2, he implicitly assumes that membership in these sets is determinate and so seems to mean by these terms what I mean by *determinate-extension* and *determinate-antiextension*. In the interest of clarity, I will follow Kripke in treating membership in the sets as determinate while substituting my terminology for his. In any case, the characterization of truth in terms of denotation may be taken to consist in the clauses (3b)–(3h) in the first half of this chapter.[22]

The first language, L_0, in the hierarchy is one in which both S_1 and S_2 are empty. This corresponds to the first stage of the inductive process described previously for ascribing truth values to sentences. The fact that S_1 and S_2 are empty reflects the fact that prior to invoking the instructions in the truth theory, no sentences have yet been characterized as true or untrue. Therefore the determinate-extension and the determinate-antiextension of the potential truth predicate 'T' are empty in L_0. The truth theory for L_0 will then determine the members of a certain set S_1' as being true sentences of L_0 and the members of a certain set S_2' as not being true sentences of L_0. S_1' will contain true sentences of L_0 that do not contain the predicate 'T' plus sentences analogous to *Either snow is white or what Bill said is T*, whose truth is determined independent of any assumptions about the interpretation of 'T'. S_2' will contain nonsentences plus untrue sentences of L_0 that do not contain 'T' and sentences containing 'T' whose untruth is fixed independent of any assumptions about its interpretation. Since neither S_1' nor S_2' is empty, $S_1' \neq S_1$ and $S_2' \neq S_2$. Thus 'T' is not a truth predicate for L_0 because its determinate-extension does not coincide with the set of sentences determined to be true by the truth rules of L_0 and its determinate-antiextension does not coincide with the set of things determined not to be true sentences by the truth rules of L_0.

We now move to the next language, L_1, in the hierarchy, which corresponds to the second stage in the inductive process described previously. At this stage, we add the truths and untruths determined at the previous stage to the determinate-extension and determinate-antiextension of 'T', respectively. Thus the sets S_1 and S_2 that give the interpretation of 'T' in L_1 are identical with the sets S_1' and S_2' of determinate-truths and determinate-untruths of L_0. In general, if L_α (S_1, S_2) is any language in the hierarchy, the successor of that language is the language $L_{\alpha + 1}$ $(S_{1, \alpha}', S_{2, \alpha}')$, which results from taking the determinate-extension of 'T' to be the set of sentences determined to be truths of L_α and the determinate-antiextension of 'T' to be the set of things determined not to be true sentences of L_α.[23]

The hierarchy also includes limit levels. For each natural number n, we have seen how to characterize the language L_n in the hierarchy. We can also characterize a language L_ω, which is the limit of the previous languages. We simply take the determinate-extension S_1 of 'T' in L_ω to include all sentences in the determinate-extension of 'T' at lower levels and similarly for the determinate-antiextension of 'T'. Now notice that our definition of the successor of a language applies to L_ω, thus giving us $L_{\omega + 1}$, $L_{\omega + 2}$, and so on. We can then characterize another limit level, just as before. In general, where B is a limit ordinal, the language $L_B = L(S_{1, B}, S_{2, B})$, where $S_{1, B}$ = the union of all $S_{1, \alpha}$ for $\alpha < B$ and $S_{2, B}$ = the union of all $S_{2, \alpha}$ for $\alpha < B$. In this way, the hierarchy is extended to include nondenumerably many levels.[24]

Having defined the hierarchy, our next task is to show that the determinate-extension and determinate-antiextension of 'T' will grow as one moves up the hierarchy until they stabilize at a certain point and cease to change thereafter. We begin by stipulating that a pair (S_1+, S_2+) *extends* (S_1, S_2) iff S_1 is a subset of S_1+ and S_2 is a subset of S_2+. Next we need to establish the following result:

3. If (S_1+, S_2+) extends (S_1, S_2), then the pair (S_1+', S_2+'), consisting of the set of sentences determined to be truths of $L(S_1+, S_2+)$ and the set of elements determined not to be truths of $L(S_1+, S_2+)$, respectively, extends the pair (S_1', S_2'), consisting of the set of sentences determined to be truths of $L(S_1, S_2)$ and the set of elements determined not to be truths of $L(S_1, S_2)$.[25]

This will mean that if the interpretation of 'T' at a higher level of the hierarchy agrees with the interpretation of 'T' at a lower level, for all sentences for which 'T' is defined at the lower level, then every sentence determined to be true at the lower level will remain true at the higher level and every sentence determined not to be true at the lower level will remain untrue at the higher level (in which case the higher level will differ from the lower level at most by assigning a definite truth value to some sentences not evaluated at the lower level).

In order to establish (3), we may reason as follows. If (3) does not hold, then there must be some sentence s such that either $s \in S_1'$ but $s \notin S_1+'$ or $s \in S_2'$

but $s \notin S_2+'$. If s is atomic, then $s = \ulcorner T\alpha \urcorner$ for some term α (since the interpretations of all other predicates remain fixed). But if $\ulcorner T\alpha \urcorner \in S_1'$ (and hence is determined to be true in $L[S_1, S_2]$), then the referent of α must be a member of the determinate-extension S_1 of 'T' at $L(S_1, S_2)$. Since S_1 is a subset of S_1+, it follows that the referent of α is also a member of the determinate-extension S_1+ of 'T' at $L(S_1+, S_2+)$ and hence that $\ulcorner T\alpha \urcorner \in S_1+'$ (the set of sentences determined to be true at $L[S_1+, S_2+]$). Identical reasoning shows that s cannot be a member of the set S_2' of elements determined not to be true in $L(S_1, S_2)$ without being a member of the set S_2+' of elements determined not to be true in $L(S_1+, S_2+)$. Thus s cannot be an atomic sentence.

To show that s cannot be a nonatomic sentence either, we reason by induction on the complexity of formulas. Let atomic formulas be of complexity 0; let the complexity of $\ulcorner \sim S \urcorner, \ulcorner \exists v S \urcorner$, and $\ulcorner \forall v S \urcorner$ be 1 + the complexity of S, and let the complexity of a disjunction be 1 + the complexity of its most complex disjunct (similarly for the other truth-functional connectives). We have just shown that sentences of complexity 0 cannot falsify (3). We now show that for any n, if no sentences of complexity n falsify (3), then no sentences of complexity n + 1 do either—from which it will follow that no sentences at all falsify (3) and hence that (3) is true.

Suppose that $\ulcorner \sim P \urcorner$ is of complexity n + 1. Since P is of complexity n, either $P \in S_1'$ and $P \in S_1+'$ (in which case $\ulcorner \sim P \urcorner \in S_2'$ and $\ulcorner \sim P \urcorner \in S_2+'$) or $P \in S_2'$ and $P \in S_2+'$ (in which case $\ulcorner \sim P \urcorner \in S_1'$ and $\ulcorner \sim P \urcorner \in S_1+'$) or $P \notin S_1'$ and $P \notin S_2'$ (in which case both P and $\ulcorner \sim P \urcorner$ are undefined at $L[S_1, S_2]$ and so cannot falsify [3]). Thus no negation of complexity n + 1 falsifies (3). Similar reasoning shows that no disjunction (conjunction, etc.) of complexity n + 1 falsifies (3). Finally, suppose that $\ulcorner \exists v S \urcorner$ is of complexity n + 1. Continuing with our simplifying assumption that every object in the domain of discourse is named, we know that $\ulcorner \exists v S \urcorner$ can be a member of S_1' without being a member of S_1+' only if one of its instances Sv/α is a member of S_1' without being a member of S_1+', which is impossible since Sv/α has complexity n. We also know that $\ulcorner \exists v S \urcorner$ can be a member of S_2' without being a member of S_2+' only if all of its instances are members of S_2' even though at least one such instance is not a member of S_2+', which is again impossible. Analogous reasoning applied to universal quantifications shows that no quantified sentence falsifies (3). Since we have covered all the different sentences there are, we conclude that no sentences falsify (3) and hence that (3) is true.

It should be noted that the simplifying assumption used here—namely, that every object in the domain is named—is not in any way essential to this result. Dropping the assumption and reformulating the truth rules so as to characterize the truth of a formula relative to an assignment of objects to variables, we could easily recast the above argument to establish (3').

3'. If (S_1+, S_2+) extends (S_1, S_2), then for any formula F and assignment A of objects to variables, (i) if F is determined to be true relative to A in $L(S_1, S_2)$, then F is determined to be true relative to A in $L(S_1+, S_2+)$, and (ii) if F is determined not to be true relative to A in $L(S_1, S_2)$, then F is determined not to be true relative to A in $L(S_1+, S_2+)$.

Since (3) follows from (3'), it can be established independent of our simplifying assumption.

We now use (3) to establish (4).

4.   For any finite level α in the hierarchy, the interpretation $(S_{1, \alpha + 1}, S_{2, \alpha + 1})$ of 'T' in $L_{\alpha + 1}$ extends the interpretation $(S_{1, \alpha}, S_{2, \alpha})$ of 'T' in L_α.

For the case in which $\alpha = 0$, the thesis is obvious since the interpretation of 'T' at level 0 is empty and every pair of sets extends the pair consisting of the empty set and itself. Next suppose that (4) holds for L_n. This means that the interpretation of 'T' in $L_{n + 1}$ extends the interpretation of 'T' in L_n. But then from (3) it follows that the pair $(S_{1, n + 1}', S_{2, n + 1}')$ consisting of the set of sentences determined to be truths of $L_{n + 1}$ and the set of elements determined not to be truths of $L_{n + 1}$ extends the pair $(S_{1, n}', S_{2, n}')$ consisting of the set of sentences determined to be truths of L_n and the set of elements determined not to be truths of L_n. Since $(S_{1, n + 1}', S_{2, n + 1}')$ is the interpretation of 'T' in $L_{n + 2}$ and $(S_{1, n}', S_{2, n}')$ is the interpretation of 'T' in $L_{n + 1}$, this means that the interpretation of 'T' in $L_{n + 2}$ extends the interpretation of 'T' in $L_{n + 1}$ and hence that (4) holds for $L_{n + 1}$. Thus we have established (4) by showing both that it holds at the 0 level and that if it holds at an arbitrary level n, then it holds at the next level as well.

In addition to the 0 level and successor levels, the hierarchy also contains limit levels. Since the interpretation of 'T' at a limit level is gotten by taking the union of its interpretations at lower levels, it follows that the interpretation of 'T' at higher levels always extends its interpretation at lower levels. Thus as one moves up the hierarchy, the interpretation of 'T' always either grows or stays the same.

In fact, Kripke observes, there must come a point at which the interpretation of 'T' stops growing. Recall that the languages in the hierarchy are all made up of the same sentences. If, as is standard, each sentence is of some finite length, then the totality of these sentences constitutes a denumerable set. However, since the hierarchy contains nondenumerably many levels, new sentences cannot be added to the interpretation of 'T' at each level.[26] Thus there must be a language L_α such that the interpretation $(S_{1, \alpha}, S_{2, \alpha})$ of 'T' in L_α = the interpretation $(S_{1, \alpha + 1}, S_{2, \alpha + 1})$ of 'T' in $L_{\alpha + 1}$ = the pair $(S_{1, \alpha}', S_{2, \alpha}')$ consisting of the set of sentences determined to be truths of L_α and the set of elements determined not to be truths of L_α. Such a language, in which the determinate-extension (and determinate-antiextension) of 'T' = the set of determinate-truths (and the set of determinate-untruths) of the language, is called a *fixed point*. When, as we have assumed, the hierarchy is based on a language L_0 in which the determinate-extension and determinate-antiextension of 'T' are empty, the fixed point L_α reached from this starting point is called the *minimal fixed point*.

If $L(S_1, S_2)$ is the minimal fixed point, then the sets S_1 and S_2 are mutually exclusive but not jointly exhaustive since, for example, Liar sentences and Truth

Tellers are not members of either. This observation supports Kripke's formal definition (5) of the notion of ungroundedness.

5. A sentence s is ungrounded iff s is not a member of either the determinate-extension or the determinate-antiextension of 'T' at the minimal fixed point (i.e., iff it is neither determined to be true nor determined not to be true at the minimal fixed point).[27]

A sentence is grounded iff it is not ungrounded—that is, iff it has a determinate-truth value at the minimal fixed point.

In addition to the minimal fixed point, there are also other fixed points. Non-minimal fixed points are fixed points reached from *sound starting points* $L_0(S_1, S_2)$ in which either S_1 or S_2 is nonempty. A pair (S_1, S_2) is a sound starting point iff the pair (S_1', S_2') consisting of the set of sentences determined to be true and the set of elements determined not to be true (at the initial level) extends (S_1, S_2). For example, there are sound starting points in which the Truth Teller (6) is a member of S_1, and there are other sound starting points in which (6) is a member of S_2.

6. Sentence (6) is true.

However, there are no sound starting points in which a Liar sentence such as (7) is a member of either S_1 or S_2, for if $(7) \in S_1$, then $(7) \in S_2'$ (rather than S_1'), and if $(7) \in S_2$, then $(7) \in S_1'$ (rather than S_2').

7. Sentence (7) is not true.

As the reasoning used to establish (3) and (4) indicates, it is a feature of Kripke's construction that if it is based on a sound starting point, then the interpretation of 'T' at higher levels always extends the interpretation of 'T' at lower levels. Thus there are nonminimal fixed points in which (6) is a member of the determinate-extension of 'T' (and hence is determined to be true) and fixed points in which (6) is a member of the determinate-antiextension of 'T' (and hence is determined not to be true). Moreover, for any sound starting point P, the fixed point reached from P extends the minimal fixed point.[28] However, there are no fixed points in which Liar sentences are members of the interpretation of 'T' (and hence there are no fixed points in which Liar sentences are determined to be true or are determined not to be true). In light of this, Kripke is able to give the following formal definition of the intuitive notion a paradoxical sentence.

8. A sentence s is paradoxical iff s is not a member of either the determinate-extension or the determinate-antiextension of 'T' at any fixed point (i.e., iff there is no fixed point in which it is either determined to be true or determined not to be true).

In addition to making definitions such as this possible, the existence of multiple fixed points also has an important philosophical significance. The minimal fixed point represents the interpretation of the truth predicate that arises from the basic instructions governing the truth predicate — instructions licensing the assertion of the claim that s is true (not true) whenever the assertion of s (the negation of s) is legitimate and the assertion of s (the negation of s) whenever the assertion that s is true (not true) is legitimate.[29] Other fixed points represent interpretations of the truth predicate that arise from supplementing these basic instructions so as to assign truth values to various ungrounded sentences.

We have seen that there are fixed points in which the basic instructions are supplemented with an arbitrary decision to make (6) true, as well as fixed points in which (6) is arbitrarily taken to be untrue. More interesting are those fixed points that supplement the basic instructions by making entirely nonarbitrary assignments of truth values to ungrounded sentences. Kripke calls these *intrinsic fixed points*. Formally, a fixed point (S_1, S_2) is intrinsic iff it never assigns a sentence a truth value that conflicts with the truth value assigned to that sentence at any other fixed point — that is, iff for every sentence s and fixed point $(S_1\#, S_2\#)$, if s $\in S_1$, then s $\notin S_2\#$, and if s $\in S_2$, then s $\notin S_1\#$. A sentence has an intrinsic truth value iff it has a truth value at some intrinsic fixed point.

One example of such a sentence is (28d) of the first half of this chapter, here renumbered as (9). This sentence is true in any fixed point in which it has a truth value and may be assigned a truth value without making arbitrary assignments of truth values to other sentences.

9.   (Sentence (9) is true) v $\sim$ (sentence (9) is true).

An example of an intrinsic fixed point is the fixed point reached from the starting point $L_0(S_1, S_2)$ in which S_2 is empty and S_1 contains only (9) ([9] is not a member of S_2 at any sound starting point). Other intrinsic fixed points assign truth values to other sentences. Of special interest is the maximal intrinsic fixed point, which extends all other intrinsic fixed points. It represents the interpretation of the truth predicate that makes as many assignments of truth value as possible while being consistent with the basic instructions and never making an arbitrary evaluation. Thus if speakers of a language with a partially defined truth predicate wish to eliminate some truth-value gaps by supplementing the original instructions governing the predicate, they may adopt the interpretation given in the maximal intrinsic fixed point without having to agree on arbitrary assignments of truth values to any sentences.

The most elementary fact about all fixed points is, of course, that they are languages that contain their own partially defined truth predicates. However, there is more than one way in which this fact can be understood, and the way in which one understands it has important philosophical consequences. Let us say that 'T' is a truth predicate for a language L_α (S_1, S_2) in the hierarchy iff 'T' applies (in L_α) to a sentence s just in case s is a truth of L_α. Suppose further that L_α is a fixed point. Does it contain its own truth predicate? Well, it contains the predicate 'T', whose determinate-extension S_1 = the set of sentences S_1' determined to be true by the rules determining truth in L_α. If we accept both (10a) and (10b),

10a. For all sentences s of L_α, 'T' applies (in L_α) to s $\equiv$ s $\in$ the determinate-extension S_1 of 'T' in L_α

b. For all sentences s of L_α, s is true (in L_α) $\equiv$ s $\in$ the set S_1' of sentences determined to be true by the rules determining truth in L_α,

then we may conclude that 'T' is a truth predicate for L_α and hence that L_α contains its own truth predicate.

However, if we reason in this way, then we must also conclude that L_α does *not* contain its own untruth predicate—that is, it does not contain any formula that is true of an object o just in case o is not a true sentence of L_α.[30] Consider any sentence s for which the truth predicate 'T' is undefined in L_α. Since s $\notin$ of the determinate-extension S_1 of 'T' in L_α, it follows from (10b) plus the identity of S_1 and S_1' that s is not true in L_α. However, since s $\notin$ of the determinate-antiextension S_2 of 'T', $\sim Tx$ is not determinately true of s and so, by (10b), is not true of s either.[31] This means that $\sim Tx$ and *is not true in L_α* are not coextensive and hence express different notions. Either 'T' does not express the notion of truth in L_α, or '$\sim$' does not capture the standard sense of negation, expressed by *not* in the expression *is not true in L_α*, or both.

This is disappointing. The most basic form of the Liar paradox involves self-attribution of the property of not being true. The standard Tarskian response to the paradox is to claim that such self-attribution is really illusory. No language, we are told, can contain both self-reference and a predicate expressing the property of not being true (in the language). As a result, no language can contain a Liar sentence.[32] But how can that be? Surely English contains the predicate *is not true (in English)* while containing devices for self-reference. Surely there are Liar sentences in English. The thought that this cannot be entirely illusory has been one of the main driving forces behind non-Tarskian, gappy approaches to the paradox. Thus it would be disappointing if Kripke's elegant construction provided no genuine alternative to Tarski's negative conclusions.

However, this is not the only, let alone the preferred, interpretation of Kripke's formal construction. Instead of being primary objects of study, the languages in the hierarchy should be seen as corresponding to stages in the inductive process of interpreting the notions of truth and untruth illustrated in the first half of this chapter. This process arises from instructions governing the truth predicate that are represented by gappy truth theories for languages in the hierarchy. These instructions provide sufficient but not jointly necessary and sufficient conditions for a sentence to be true and sufficient but not jointly necessary and sufficient conditions for a sentence not to be true. Since the conditions are not jointly exhaustive, some sentences satisfy neither the sufficient conditions for being true nor the sufficient conditions for not being true. As a result, the instructions determining truth and untruth are silent about these sentences, and the claim that they are not true must be rejected as just as unjustifiable, in principle, as the claim that they are true.

In this interpretation, both (10a) and (10b) are incorrect, for if s is a sentence for which 'T' is undefined, then the left-hand sides of the instances, (11a) and (11b), of these claims are indeterminate (undefined) even though the right-hand sides are clearly false (not true).

11a.   'T' applies (in L_α) to $s \equiv s \in$ the determinate-extension S_1 of 'T' in L_α.
   b.   s is true (in L_α) $\equiv s \in$ the set $S_1{}'$ of sentences determined to be true by the rules determining truth in L_α.

Since the two sides of these biconditionals do not have the same status, the biconditionals are untrue, as are (10a) and (10b). But without (10a) and (10b), there is no argument that the formula $\sim Tx$ of L_α fails to be true of precisely those things that are not true sentences of L_α, and hence no argument that either 'T' fails to express the notion of truth in L_α or '$\sim$' fails to capture the sense of negation expressed by *not* in *is not a true sentence of L_α*.

On the contrary, 'T' does express the notion of truth in L_α, and $\sim Tx$ expresses the notion of not being a truth of L_α, as indicated in (12) and (13).[33]

12a.   The extension (antiextension) of 'T' in L_α = the set of true sentences (things that are not true sentences) of L_α.
   b.   The determinate-extension (determinate-antiextension) of 'T' in L_α = the set $S_1{}'$ of sentences determined to be true in L_α (the set $S_2{}'$ of things determined not to be true sentences of L_α).

13a.   The set of things that $\sim Tx$ is true of in L_α = the set of things that are not true sentences of L_α.
   b.   The set of things z such that $\sim Tx$ is determinately true of z in L_α = the set $S_2{}'$ of things determined not to be true sentences of L_α.

In this interpretation, then, the fixed-point language contains its own truth predicate and its own untruth predicate, both of which are partially defined in the manner illustrated previously by *smidget*. It does not, however, contain its own determinate-truth or determinate-untruth predicate.

It is important to realize that although this interpretation is the one that best fits the intuition guiding Kripke's intuitive characterization of the hierarchy, there is nothing in his formal construction that requires it. If one wished, one could view the languages in the hierarchy as stages in the determination of totally defined truth predicates[34] that give rise to Fregean or Strawsonian truth-value gaps. However, to do so would be to rob the Kripke construction of much of its philosophical significance.

For example, consider the Fregean interpretation. In this construal, S_1 and S_2 are determinate sets, and the clauses specifying the denotation of 'T' plus the inductive characterization of truth for languages in the hierarchy are as indicated in (14).[35]

14a.   The predicate 'T' positively applies to an object o iff o ∈ S_1; it negatively applies to an object o iff o ∈ S_2; and it neither positively nor negatively applies to an object o iff o ∉ S_1 and o ∉ S_2.

 b.   For any n-place predicate P and terms $t_1, \ldots, t_n$, $\ulcorner Pt_1, \ldots, t_n \urcorner$ is true iff P positively applies to the n-tuple $<o_1, \ldots, o_n>$ of referents of the terms; $\ulcorner Pt_1, \ldots, t_n \urcorner$ is false iff P negatively applies to the n-tuple $<o_1, \ldots, o_n>$ of referents of the terms; and $\ulcorner Pt_1, \ldots, t_n \urcorner$ is neither true nor false iff P neither positively nor negatively applies to the n-tuple $<o_1, \ldots, o_n>$ of referents of the terms.

 c.   For any sentence S, $\ulcorner {\sim}S \urcorner$ is true (false) iff S is false (true); $\ulcorner {\sim}S \urcorner$ is neither true nor false iff S is neither true nor false.

 d. $\ulcorner A \vee B \urcorner$ is true iff A is true or B is true; $\ulcorner A \vee B \urcorner$ is false iff both A and B are false; otherwise $\ulcorner A \vee B \urcorner$ is neither true nor false.

 e. $\ulcorner A \mathbin{\&} B \urcorner$ is true iff both A and B are true; $\ulcorner A \mathbin{\&} B \urcorner$ is false iff either A is false or B is false; otherwise $\ulcorner A \mathbin{\&} B \urcorner$ is neither true nor false.

 f. $\ulcorner A \supset B \urcorner$ is true iff A is false or B is true; $\ulcorner A \supset B \urcorner$ is false iff A is true and B is false; otherwise $\ulcorner A \supset B \urcorner$ is neither true nor false.

 g. $\ulcorner \exists v\, F(v) \urcorner$ is true iff Fv/a is true for some name a; $\ulcorner \exists v\, F(v) \urcorner$ is false iff for all names a, Fv/a is false; otherwise $\ulcorner \exists v\, F(v) \urcorner$ is neither true nor false.[36]

 h. $\ulcorner \forall v\, F(v) \urcorner$ is true iff Fv/a is true for all names a; $\ulcorner \forall v\, F(v) \urcorner$ is false iff for some name a, Fv/a is false; otherwise $\ulcorner \forall v\, F(v) \urcorner$ is neither true nor false.

Evaluation rules of this sort characterize every sentence as being either true, false, or neither true nor false (and every predicate as either positively applying, negatively applying, or neither positively nor negatively applying to any given object). In this interpretation, the minimal fixed point is a language L_α containing a predicate that positively applies to exactly the truths of L_α, negatively applies to exactly the falsehoods (plus nonsentences) of L_α, and neither positively nor negatively applies to sentences of L_α that are neither true nor false. Since these latter include (what look like) Liar sentences and Truth Tellers, such examples are assimilated to sentences with failing logical presuppositions.

Although the fixed point, L_α, can then be seen as containing its own truth predicate, it cannot, in this interpretation, contain its own untruth predicate. There simply is no formula of L_α that is true of exactly those things that are not true sentences of L_α. (Similarly, there are no sentences of L_α that say of themselves that they are not true.) This is problematic since it leads to the disappointing conclusion that $\sim Tx$ and *is not true in* L_α are not coextensive and hence express different notions. Thus in the Fregean interpretation, either 'T' does not express the notion of truth in L_α, or '$\sim$' does not capture the sense of negation expressed by *not* in the expression *is not true in* L_α, or both. As a result, this interpretation provides no alternative to Tarski's negative conclusions that languages capable of self-reference cannot contain their own untruth predicates and that our ordinary understanding of the expression *is not a true sentence of English* as being just such a predicate is incoherent. At best, all the interpretation provides is a weakened substitute for our original notion.

Moreover, the substitute is parasitic on the concept it is supposed to supplant. In providing a Fregean truth characterization for the languages of Kripke's hierarchy, we used the metalinguistic *not true* to interpret object-language sentences containing $\sim$ and T.[37] Had we not already understood what it was not to be true, we could not have used the rules in (14) to interpret these sentences. What rules, then, could a speaker of L_α who was innocent of metalinguistic semantic concepts use to interpret sentences of the speaker's language containing $\sim$ and T? When the truth predicate is understood on the model sketched in the first half of this chapter, we have an idea of how it could be introduced into the object-language without assuming an antecedently understood metalinguistic semantic scheme.[38] When truth is thought of as giving rise to Fregean truth-value gaps, we have no explanation of this.

It is significant, in light of this, that Kripke does not endorse a Fregean interpretation in which sentences for which the truth predicate is undefined are characterized as being neither true nor false. He indicates this in a discussion of his incorporation of the strong Kleene valuation system into truth characterizations of languages in the hierarchy. (This valuation system assigns truth [falsity] to precisely those sentences that are assigned truth [falsity] by the rules in [3] of the first half of the chapter and [14] of this section. The issue in question is how to characterize sentences that are not declared to be true or declared to be false, by these rules. Are they to be treated as being neither true nor false—where this is tantamount to a third truth value—or are they to be treated in some other way?)

I have been amazed to hear my use of the Kleene valuation compared occasionally to the proposals of those who favor abandoning standard logic "for quantum mechanics," or positing extra truth values beyond truth and falsity, etc. Such a reaction surprised me as much as it would presumably surprise Kleene, who intended (as do I here) to write a work of standard mathematical results, provable in conventional mathematics. "Undefined" is not an *extra* truth value, any more than—in Kleene's book—u is an extra *number* in sec. 63. Nor should it be said that "classical logic" does not generally hold, any more than (in Kleene) the use of partially defined functions invalidates the commutative law of addition. *If* certain sentences express propositions, any tautological truth function of them expresses a true proposition. Of course formulas, even with the forms of tautologies, which have components that do not express propositions may have truth functions that do not express propositions either. (This happens under the Kleene valuation, but not under the van Fraassen.) Mere conventions for handling terms that do not designate numbers should not be called changes in arithmetic; conventions for handling sentences that do not express propositions are not in any philosophically significant sense "changes in logic."[39]

Since the category of being neither true nor false can, trivially, be made to correspond to an extra truth value, the Fregean interpretation of the hierarchy's truth-value gaps is not Kripke's.

His own (official) interpretation assimilates undefined sentences to those with failing Strawsonian rather than Fregean presuppositions. Following Strawson, Kripke sees (utterances of) sentences as attempts to make statements or express propositions, each of which is either true or false. Whenever a sentence expresses a proposition, the sentence itself will be either true or false. However, in certain cases, sentences fail to express propositions because specific conditions (presuppositions) necessary for them to do so are not fulfilled. Strawson's original examples of such conditions were those whose truth was necessary in order for referring uses of singular terms to successfully pick out referents. Although Kripke takes no position on these motivating examples, he extends the idea of failing Strawsonian presuppositions to undefined sentences of the hierarchy. In this interpretation, the most basic result concerning the hierarchy is that the minimal fixed point contains a predicate, T, that applies to precisely the sentences of the language that express truths and a formula, $\sim Tx$, that is true of precisely the sentences of the language that express propositions that are not true. The explanation of how this is possible is that Liar sentences and Truth Tellers do not express propositions.

Unfortunately this interpretation is at least as problematic as the Fregean account. Kripke grants that we can truly say in the metalanguage that Liar sentences, Truth Tellers, and other ungrounded sentences do not express propositions in the minimal fixed point L_α and therefore are not true in L_α. Of course, in this interpretation, they are not false either. Thus they are neither true nor false. But this seems little different from the extra truth value that Kripke does not want. Moreover, having characterized ungrounded sentences as not being true in L_α while rejecting the claim that $\sim Tx$ is true of them in L_α, one is forced to admit that the formula $\sim Tx$ of L_α does not express the same notion as the metalinguistic *is not a true sentence of L_α*. As before, one must then acknowledge that L_α does not contain its own untruth predicate and either '$\sim$' fails to capture the sense of negation expressed by *not* or Tx fails to capture the notion of truth in L_α or both.[40] As I have indicated, this is disappointing.

It is also based on a doctrine that is incorrect. It is simply not true that all Liar sentences, Truth Tellers, and other ungrounded sentences fail to express propositions at the minimal fixed point. We have already demonstrated something analogous to this by showing that ungrounded *smidget* sentences do express propositions. Several of the same considerations used there can be used to support the claim that certain Liar sentences and Truth Tellers do too.

For example, consider the potential Liar sentence (15).

15.   Some sentence written in place P is not true.

Whether or not this is a Liar sentence depends on which, if any, sentences are written in place P. Suppose, for the sake of argument, that (15) is the only sentence written in place P and therefore is a Liar sentence. Still, it accomplishes the two main tasks for which propositions are needed. First, it determines a function (albeit partial) from possible circumstances to truth values that constrains the way the world is represented to be; circumstances in which either no sentences, or determinate-truths, and only determinate-truths, are written in place P are assigned the value untruth; circumstances in which a determinate-untruth is written in place P are assigned the value truth. Second, (15) expresses a possible content of propositional attitudes. For example, suppose that a sincere, reflective agent A assertively utters (15), not realizing that it is the only sentence written in place P and is therefore a Liar sentence. Intuitively, it seems that one should be able to truly describe such a person using (16).

16.   A says/believes that some sentence written in place P is not true.

But then if propositional attitude ascriptions report relations to the propositions expressed by their complements, some Liar sentences express propositions.

All of this might seem contentious if it had not already been shown that there are *propositions* that cannot correctly be evaluated for truth value in certain possible circumstances. In the first half of this chapter, we saw that if Ralph is a member of group A (the smidgets), then the *true proposition* that he is a smidget resists evaluation in counterfactual circumstances in which his height is in the intermediate range (i.e., exactly halfway between the actual heights of the tallest member of group A and the shortest member of group B). But then since *propositions* can resist evaluation for truth value, there is no compelling reason to think that such resistance on the part of Liar sentences like (15) shows that they do not express propositions.

This is fortunate, for any attempt to spell out semantic mechanisms preventing ungrounded (undefined) sentences from expressing propositions would, I think, be hopelessly ad hoc and implausible. In the case of the Strawsonian *This is a fine red one*, uttered in a context in which the demonstrative fails to refer, there is a plausible semantic theory that explains the intuition that no proposition is thereby expressed. The theory is one in which the proposition expressed by a sentence in a context is a structured complex consisting of the semantic contents of the constituents of the sentence relative to the context. In this theory, contexts in which demonstratives fail to refer are contexts in which they lack semantic contents and hence have nothing to contribute to the formation of a proposition. As a result, no proposition is expressed.[41]

Of course, this Strawsonian example is not ungrounded (undefined) in the sense that Liar sentences, Truth Tellers, and *smidget* sentences like (1a) and (1b) in the first half of the chapter are. The point is that for such cases there is no independently motivated semantic theory that characterizes them as not expressing propositions. On the contrary, the same theory of structured propositions that correctly predicts Strawsonian presupposition failure in examples like *This is a fine red one* will characterize the *smidget* sentence (1a) at the beginning of this chapter as expressing a proposition containing an individual plus the property of being a smidget and (15) as expressing a proposition consisting of the function that assigns to each object o the proposition that o is a sentence written at place P and o is not true, together with the property of propositional functions of being "sometimes true."[42] In short, a plausible semantic theory needed on independent grounds will assign propositions as a matter of course to many ungrounded (undefined) sentences of the Kripke hierarchy.

In light of this, it is not surprising that ungrounded (undefined) sentences behave differently from sentences that fail to express propositions with regard to various logical constructions, such as disjunction.

17a.   Either this is a fine red one or the earth is round.
  b.   Either Mr. Smallman is a smidget or the earth is round.
  c.   Either some sentence written in place P is not true or the earth is round.

If (17a) is uttered in a context in which *this* fails to refer, its left disjunct will fail to express a proposition. What about the sentence as a whole? Surely it does not express the proposition that the earth is round; someone who assertively utters (17a) does not assert that. Nor is any other proposition a reasonable candidate for being semantically expressed by the sentence as a whole. The natural conclusion, then, is that the entire disjunction fails to express a proposition in this context.

This, in turn, has consequences for the semantic scheme used to evaluate sentences containing the connectives. In "Outline of a Theory of Truth," Kripke adopts Kleene's strong "three-valued" truth tables, with 'undefined' occurring in the tables at positions not occupied by 'true' and 'false'.[43] However, if 'undefined' signifies failure to express a proposition, then this choice conflicts with the natural conclusion that (17a) fails to express a proposition (when *this* fails to refer), for in the strong Kleene scheme, (17a) is true. In the construal in which 'undefined' indicates failure to express a proposition, the most plausible treatment of the connectives is not Kleene's strong tables but his (or Frege's) weak scheme, in which assignment of the third "value" to a constituent clause of a compound sentence (negation, disjunction, etc.) always results in the assignment of that "value" to the compound sentence as a whole.

In fact, I think Kripke was right in not adopting the weak scheme. Unlike (17a), (17b) and (17c) do express true propositions, even when their initial disjuncts are undefined. This supports the view that 'undefined' should not be interpreted as indicating failure to express a proposition.

Although this conclusion conflicts with Kripke's explicit Strawsonian interpretation of undefined sentences, it is very much in harmony with the spirit and substance of his analysis. The rejection of undefinedness as an extra truth value, the use of the strong Kleene tables, the intuitive presentation of the inductive process interpreting the object-language truth predicate, and the discussion of the notion of truth expressed by that predicate (at the minimal fixed point) as conceptually prior to the notion of (determinate) truth (at the minimal fixed point) expressed in the metalanguage all suggest an implicit grasp of truth as gappy, not according to the Fregean or Strawsonian models but according to the Kripke-Salmon model illustrated by the *smidget* examples in the first half of this chapter.

Notes

1. I here ignore as irrelevant for present purposes the fact that words used in the original definition are themselves vague.

2. It is important to note that (1b), (2b), and the negative clause (ii) in the definition of *smidget* are assumed to be instances of standard, sentential negation. In particular, it is assumed that the negation of a sentence S is equivalent to the claim ⌜It is not the case that S⌝.

3. For further discussion of the Fregean and Strawsonian accounts of presupposition and truth-value gaps, see Scott Soames, "Presupposition," in *Handbook of Philosophical Logic*, vol. 4, *Topics in the Philosophy of Language*, ed. F. Guenthner and D. Gabbay (Dordrecht: Reidel, 1989), 553–616.

4. In the case of (5a), this commitment is uncontroversial. Since there is no king of France, (5a) cannot be true. Whereas in the case of the smidget example, (1a), we feel that it is as problematic to say that it is not true as to say that it is true, we do not feel that it would be as wrong to say that (5a) is not true as to say that it is true.

5. P. F. Strawson, "On Referring," *Mind* 59 (1950): 320–44. The theory of presupposition that follows is a modified version of Strawson's original proposals, designed to remove certain conflicts and ambiguities in his discussion. A more detailed account of Strawson's actual analysis can be found in Soames, "Presupposition."

6. Strawson, "On Referring," 333.

7. This will result if the demonstrative *this* is directly referential—that is, if its propositional content in a context is its referent in the context. In contexts in which it fails to refer, it will therefore lack a content and a sentence continuing it will (arguably) fail to express a proposition in that context. The result will also obtain if the content of a demonstrative in a context is a sense that is dependent (for its existence) on its referent.

8. The stipulation introducing *smidget* is to be understood in such a way that an adult is a smidget in a possible circumstance w just in case the height of that adult in w is less than or equal to the height in the actual world of the tallest person in group A; the individual is not a smidget in w just in case the height of that individual in w is greater than or equal to the height in the actual world of the shortest person in group B.

9. The terminology, *partial function*, must here be understood in a somewhat special sense. Normally we think of a partial function as one that fails to assign a value to some argument. *In this sense* a partial function from circumstances to truth values would be such that for some circumstance w, the function *does not* assign the value truth or any other truth value. If we further assume that a proposition P is true at a circumstance w only if the function f from circumstances to truth values determined by P assigns w the value truth, then P could correctly be characterized as *not true* in any circumstance w for which f was not defined. This is *not* the result we want for the proposition expressed by $\ulcorner \alpha$ is a smidget.$\urcorner$ One way to get what we want is to characterize the function f determined by this proposition as being such that for some circumstances w as argument we cannot accept the claim that f(w) = truth or the claim that f(w) = untruth.

10. Saul Kripke, "Outline of a Theory of Truth," *Journal of Philosophy* 72 (1975): 690–716. Although I believe that the philosophical conception behind Kripke's theory of truth requires a partiality paradigm distinct from those of Frege and Strawson, Kripke himself characterizes the paradigm in Strawsonian terms (699–700). I therefore take his comments to that effect to be a misstatement of the central philosophical insight underlying his analysis. (This point will be discussed further later.)

Another article that is relevant to the characterization of the needed partiality paradigm is Terrence Parsons, "Assertion, Denial, and the Liar Paradox," *Journal of Philosophical Logic* 13 (1984): 137–52. Parsons correctly characterizes the kind of partiality needed for Kripke-type analyses. In my view, however, he is guilty of wrongly assimilating traditional examples of (Fregean) logical presupposition to this kind of partiality. This is just the converse of the widespread error in truth-gap solutions to the Liar paradox of assimilating what are in fact instances of the Kripke-Salmon paradigm to instances of logical presupposition.

11. The seminal idea that a new kind of partially defined predicate is needed to understand Kripke's theory of truth was suggested to me by my former colleague Nathan

Salmon in one of my spring-term seminars at Princeton University in 1981. At the time, I was trying to determine whether Kripke's theory of truth really escaped the Strengthened Liar and whether his fixed-point language really contained its own *untruth* predicate. Salmon suggested that if it did, then Kripke's object-language truth predicate must be partially defined in a sense essentially like that illustrated by the previous stipulative definition of *smidget*.

In this chapter, I develop this basic idea and explore the extent to which truth, as we ordinarily understand it, can be seen as conforming to this model. Although the points I will make arose out of reflection on Salmon's initial insight, they have been developed independently and should not be assumed to reflect views that Salmon would endorse.

12. In order to simplify matters, I am ignoring the possibility that any t_i might fail to refer to an object. Various treatments of the effects of reference failure are possible.

13. In order to simplify matters, I here put aside the question of whether there are more than two truth values, and I adopt the standard classical assumption. This does not affect the discussion of the kind of truth-value gaps illustrated by the sentences in (1) and (2) since these gaps may be incorporated into two valued systems or many valued systems.

14. Also determined at this stage are the truth values (as opposed to truth conditions) of those complex sentences containing the truth predicate whose truth values are determined independently of any consideration of what the predicate *true* applies to—for example, sentences like *The earth is round v every sentence in tomorrow's* Wall Street Journal *is true*, whose truth follows from the truth of its initial disjunct alone.

15. (16a) and (16b) follow directly from (15a) and (15b) plus clause (3a+). (17a) is then derived from (16a) using the truth instruction (3b) for atomic sentences. (17b) is derived in the same way, while (17c) comes from (17b) plus the truth instruction, (3c), for negations.

16. This characterization of sentences of the form $A \equiv B$ is required by the role that the connective '$\equiv$' plays in the instructions introducing semantic predicates. For example, in order to ensure the truth of the clause *For all individuals i, 'smidget' applies to i $\equiv$ i is a smidget* in (3a), we must treat *'smidget' applies to i $\equiv$ i is a smidget* as true relative to all assignments of individuals to the variable *i*, including assignments of individuals for which the predicate 'smidget' is undefined and for which the formula *i is a smidget* is therefore ungrounded. Similarly, the truth of the clause (3c), *For any sentence S, $\ulcorner\sim S\urcorner$ is true (not true) $\equiv$ S is not true (true)*, requires that the formula $\ulcorner\sim S\urcorner$ *is true (not true) $\equiv$ S is not true (true)* be true even when the variable 'S' is assigned an ungrounded sentence as value (and hence when both the claim $\ulcorner\sim S\urcorner$ *is true* and the claim *S is not true* are also ungrounded).

17. This suggestion parallels Kripke's discussion in "Outline of a Theory of Truth," 701, regarding how one could explain the word *true* to someone who does not understand it by indicating that for any sentence S, (i) one is entitled to assert that S is true in exactly those circumstances in which one is entitled to assert S and (ii) one is entitled to assert that S is not true in exactly those circumstances in which one is entitled to assert the negation of S. If *true* is introduced in this way, then assertability conditions for claims to the effect that something is or is not true will standardly be grounded in assertability conditions for sentences not involving truth at all. However, the instructions will be silent in the case of ungrounded sentences (Liars, Truth Tellers, etc.).

18. The distinctions illustrated by the sentences in (28) are discussed and formally characterized in ibid., 708–9. Sentences like (28d) are said by Kripke to have *an intrinsic truth value*.

19. More specifically, suppose we try to apply it to the predicate *is a true sentence of English*. In this discussion, I am putting aside the fact that the English predicate *true* seems to apply in the first instance to propositions rather than sentences.

20. Kripke, "Outline of a Theory of Truth," 701; emphasis in original.

21. Or to refer to Gödel numbers of their own expressions.

22. I here continue the simplifying assumption that all objects in the domain are named. This simplification is not essential to Kripke's construction.

23. Using the notions of extension and antiextension, we say that the successor of $L_{\alpha+1}$ of L_α is the result of taking the extension of 'T' in $L_{\alpha+1}$ to be the set of truths of L_α and the antiextension of 'T' in $L_{\alpha+1}$ to be the set of untruths of L_α (i.e., the nonsentences plus the sentences that are not true in L_α).

24. This is an understatement. Since there is no set of all ordinals, Kripke's hierarchy includes "more" levels than there are members of any set.

25. Kripke defines a function f as follows. Given a pair of disjoint subsets (S_1, S_2) of the domain to serve as the interpretation of 'T', $f(S_1, S_2) = (S_1', S_2')$—that is, the pair consisting of the set of sentences determined to be truths of $L(S_1, S_2)$ and the set of elements determined not to be truths of $L(S_1, S_2)$. (3) expresses the result that f is a monotone (order-preserving) function on the *extends* relation defined previously—that is, if (S_1+, S_2+) extends (S_1, S_2), then $f(S_1+, S_2+)$ extends $f(S_1, S_2)$.

26. Kripke makes the stronger point that as long as the sentences eligible for inclusion in the interpretation of 'T' constitute a set, new sentences cannot be added at each level because the levels of the hierarchy exceed the contents of any set.

27. The concept of ungroundedness defined here is related to but slightly different from the intuitive notion of ungroundedness appealed to in the first half of this chapter. According to the intuitive notion, an ungrounded sentence is one about which linguistic conventions are silent. Because of this, it is impossible in principle to justify accepting such a sentence or its negation even if one is given all relevant nonlinguistic facts. The relationship between this notion and the one defined by Kripke may be illustrated as follows. If L_α is the minimal fixed point, then the set of sentences of L_α that are ungrounded in the intuitive sense = the set of sentences that are ungrounded in Kripke's sense. However, if L_β is a nonminimal fixed point that arises from an explicit convention to assign determinate-truth values to some previously "gappy" sentences, then those sentences will still count as ungrounded in Kripke's sense, although they will not be ungrounded (in L_β) in the intuitive sense because the conventions of the language will no longer be silent about them. (The intuitive notion makes ungroundedness relative to particular interpreted languages so that a sentence can be ungrounded in one language while being grounded in another. The formal notion defined by Kripke does not relativize the notion in this way.)

From now on, in order to avoid confusion, I will use the term *ungroundedness* in Kripke's formal sense, and I will use the term *undefined sentence* for the intuitive notion of ungroundedness in a language characterized previously. If L is a fixed point, then the undefined sentences should be precisely the sentences for which the truth predicate 'T' is undefined.

28. This is shown as follows. Let $(S_{1,F}, S_{2,F})$ be a fixed point reached from a sound starting point. Let (S_1, S_2) be the pair consisting of the empty set and itself, which constitutes the starting point from which the minimal fixed point is reached. $(S_{1,F}, S_{2,F})$ extends (S_1, S_2). From (3) it follows that $(S_{1,F}', S_{2,F}')$ extends (S_1', S_2'). Since $(S_{1,F}, S_{2,F})$ is a fixed point, $(S_{1,F}, S_{2,F}) = (S_{1,F}', S_{2,F}')$. Thus $(S_{1,F}, S_{2,F})$ extends (S_1', S_2'). By the same token, $(S_{1,F}, S_{2,F})$ extends all finite levels and hence the first limit level reached from (S_1, S_2). Similarly for succeeding successor and limit levels. Since $(S_{1,F}, S_{2,F})$ extends all levels in the construction starting from (S_1, S_2), it extends the minimal fixed point, which is reached from (S_1, S_2). Hence all fixed points extend the minimal fixed point.

29. We assume here that s is a meaningful declarative sentence and so an appropriate candidate for assertion or denial.

30. Here we need the notion of a formula containing a single free variable being *true of* an object relative to an assignment of values to variables or of an object *satisfying* the formula relative to the assignment. If we maintain our simplifying assumption that each object is the referent of some (closed) term in the language, then we can say that such a formula F is true of an object o ≡ for some term α designating o, the result *Fv/α* of replacing all free occurrences of the single free variable v in F with the term α is a true sentence of the language. Dropping the simplifying assumption would not affect the final result, but it would require rewriting the truth characterizations in terms of the notion of a formula being true relative to an assignment of objects to variables (or, equivalently, of a sequence of objects satisfying a formula).

31. The characterization of a formula being determinately true of an object is parallel to the characterization in note 30 of a formula being true of an object, except for the substitution of *determinately true* for each occurrence of *true*. (We continue to maintain the simplifying assumption that all objects are referents of closed terms of the language. In the absence of this assumption, we could recast the argument by reformulating [10b] to say that a formula is determinately true of an object ≡ it is true of the object.)

32. I am here ignoring, as inadequate, Tarski's views about inconsistent languages.

33. The sets mentioned in (12a) and (13a) are, of course, "fuzzy" in the sense that for some sentences s, it is indeterminate whether s is a member of them.

34. I call a predicate P "totally defined" iff for each object o, either it is determinate that P is true of o or it is determinate that P is not true of o.

35. I call this interpretation "Fregean" because according to it, sentences (and propositions) receive one of three determinate truth values—truth, falsity, and neither truth nor falsity. Which sentences are characterized as being neither true nor false is determined by the specific contents of the truth theory. (The specific contents of the clauses in [14] are not due to Frege.) Kripke's formal construction is compatible with many different choices in this regard. I have chosen (14) so as to parallel truth theories based on the instructions in (3) in the first half of this chapter. The two give rise to the same hierarchy with the same minimal fixed point, $L_\alpha(S_1, S_2)$. The difference between them is in how sentences not in S_1 and S_2 are characterized. Since the instructions in (3) are silent about these sentences, they cannot correctly be characterized as true or as not true. Rather, they are undefined, where being undefined is not equivalent to having a third truth value. (See note 27.) According to (14), sentences not in S_1 or S_2 do have a third truth value—they are neither true nor false and hence not true.

36. Again, in (14g) and (14h), I invoke the simplifying assumption that all objects are named and all names refer to objects.

37. The clauses in (14) speak of sentences being neither true nor false—that is, being not true and not false.

38. Here it is necessary to keep in mind the qualification regarding the possibility of viewing clauses of the form A ≡ B not as statements that can be evaluated for truth value but as instructions licensing us to infer S from ⌜'S' is true⌝ and vice versa, and to infer ⌜~ S⌝ from ⌜'S' is not true⌝ and vice versa, while not licensing anything when we are not given S or ⌜~S⌝.

39. Kripke, "Outline of a Theory of Truth," 700–701; emphasis in original.

40. Kripke seems to be ambivalent about this: "There are assertions we can make about the object language which we cannot make in the object language. For example, Liar sentences are *not true* in the object language, in the sense that the inductive process never makes them true, but we are precluded from saying this in the object language by our interpretation of negation and the truth predicate" (ibid., 714; emphasis in original). If, in understanding this comment, one emphasizes that Liar sentences are *not true in the object*

language, then one is led to think that Kripke's construction has failed to provide us with a genuine untruth predicate and hence failed either to capture the notion of truth in the object-language or to capture our ordinary sense of negation. On the other hand, if one emphasizes his comment that Liar sentences are not true only *in a sense*, then one may hold out hope that the sense in question is somehow secondary or derivative from what are really the genuine and fundamental senses of truth and negation.

Some support for the latter emphasis is given by Kripke's continuation of the discussion quoted previously. He says: "If we think of the minimal fixed point, say under the Kleene valuation, as giving a model of natural language, then the sense in which we can say, in natural language, that a Liar sentence is not true must be thought of as associated with some later stage in the development of natural language, one in which speakers reflect on the generation process leading to the minimal fixed point" (ibid.). This emphasis is welcome. However, it does not harmonize well with Kripke's official view that Liar (and other undefined) sentences do not express propositions, for it would seem that if they do not, then they are *not true* in as fundamental and primary a sense as there is. We do not, I think, generally feel that there is some sense of *true* and *not true* in which the claim that

(i)   Sentences that fail to express propositions are not true

is just as incorrect, unacceptable, and impossible to justify as the claim that

(ii)   Sentences that fail to express propositions are true.

41. See Nathan Salmon, *Frege's Puzzle* (Cambridge: Massachusetts Institute of Technology Press, 1986); and Scott Soames, "Direct Reference, Propositional Attitudes, and Semantic Content," *Philosophical Topics* 15 (1987): 47–87, reprinted in *Propositions and Attitudes*, ed. N. Salmon and S. Soames, (New York: Oxford University Press, 1988) 197–239.

42. See Salmon, *Frege's Puzzle*, and Soames, "Direct Reference, Propositional Attitudes, and Semantic Content," for details and variations.

43. Although Kripke clearly regards Kleene's strong scheme as a plausible system for handling undefined sentences, he does not endorse it or any other scheme as *the unique correct system*. See in particular his qualifying remarks in "Outline of a Theory of Truth," 711–12.

PART III

Extensions

SEVEN

Vagueness, Partiality, and the Sorites Paradox

Vague Predicates and the Sorites Paradox

In this chapter, I will present a semantic model of vague predicates from which an account of the Sorites paradox can be extracted. This paradox is a puzzling instance of mathematical induction, a common form of argument in logic and mathematics. Arguments involving mathematical induction typically come in the following forms:

Positive Version
P1. Zero is F (has property P).
P2. For all natural numbers n, if n is F (has property P), then n + 1 is F (has property P).
 C. Thus all natural numbers are F (have property P).

Negative Version
P1. Zero is not F (does not have property P).
P2. For all natural numbers n, if n is not F (does not have property P), then n + 1 is not F (does not have property P).
 C. Thus no natural numbers are F (have property P).

Although considered in the abstract, these argument forms seem clearly to be truth preserving, there is an important class of paradoxical cases involving vague predicates in which the premises appear to be true even though the conclusion is false.

Example 1: Heaps; P is the property of being a number of grains of sand sufficient to make a heap of sand

P1. Zero is such that a mass consisting of exactly zero grains of sand is not a heap of sand. (Something that consists entirely of zero grains of sand is not a heap of sand.)

P2. For any natural number n, if a mass consisting of exactly n grains of sand is not a heap of sand, then a mass consisting of exactly n + 1 grains of sand is not a heap of sand. (Adding a single grain of sand to something that is not a heap of sand does not result in a heap of sand.)

C. No number of grains of sand is sufficient to make a heap of sand. (No matter how many grains of sand have been brought together, they do not constitute a heap of sand.) So there are no heaps of sand.

Example 2: Baldness; P is the property of being a number of hairs on one's head sufficient for one to be bald

P1. Zero is such that people with exactly that number of hairs on their heads are bald. (People with no hair on their heads are bald.)

P2. For any natural number n, if those with exactly n hairs on their heads are bald, then those with exactly n + 1 hairs on their heads are also bald.

C. All people are bald, no matter how much hair is on their heads.

Example 3: Poverty; P is the property of being an amount of money such that someone with that amount of money is poor (not rich)[1]

P1. Someone who has no money is poor (not rich).

P2. If someone who has exactly n pennies is poor (not rich), then someone who has exactly n + 1 pennies is poor (not rich).

C. All people are poor (not rich), no matter how much money they have.

Each of the above examples is an instance of the Sorites paradox, which is characteristic of vague predicates. In each case, (P1) is clearly true and (C) is clearly false, even though (P2) seems highly plausible and the inference appears to be truth preserving. But it cannot be that (P1) and (P2) are true, and (C) is false if the inference is truth preserving. Hence the paradox.

Another well-known instance of the paradox involves patches of color. In constructing this example, we let G be a patch of color that clearly and definitely looks green; we let Y be another patch of color that clearly and definitely looks yellow and so does not look green; and we let S be a progression of patches of color beginning with G and ending with Y such that any two adjacent patches in the progression are perceptually indistinguishable in color from each other in the following sense: a normal, competent observer when presented with both patches, by themselves, in good light and otherwise normal conditions cannot perceive any difference in color between the two.[2] In this situation, one can move from something that clearly and definitely looks green to something that clearly and definitely does not look green by a series of gradual, imperceptible changes. This gives rise to the version of the paradox given in example 4.

Example 4
P1.   G looks green, and Y does not look green.
P2.   There is a progression, S, containing Y whose first member is G such that for all members s_i and s_{i+1} of S, s_i is perceptually indistinguishable in color from s_{i+1} to competent observers in good light under normal conditions. For any two patches of color x and y that are perceptually indistinguishable in color to competent observers in good light under normal conditions, x and y look to be the same color and so one looks green if the other looks green. Hence for each s_i, s_{i+1} looks green if s_i looks green.
C.   Therefore each member of the progression S looks green. Since this includes Y, which does not look green, Y both looks green and does not look green.

This example, as well as the earlier three, are all instances of the following basic argument form:

Generalized Sorites Paradox
P1.   A is (is not) F.
P2.   There is a progression S whose first member is A such that for all members s_i and s_{i+1} of S, s_{i+1} is (is not) F if s_i is (is not) F.
C.   All members of the progression are (are not) F.

In order to comprehend this paradox, we need to understand the role of vagueness in generating it. If a predicate is vague, then there are clear cases in which it applies, clear cases in which it does not apply, and a range of indeterminate cases in which it is unclear to varying degrees whether it does or does not apply. Often, although not always, the range of potential application of such a predicate forms a natural continuum starting with clear cases of application, moving gradually to cases in which it seems defensible but less clear to suppose that the predicate applies, continuing to cases in which there seems to be little guidance one way or the other about the application of the predicate, extending to cases of more and more doubtful application, and culminating in clear cases in which the predicate does not apply. A crucial feature of the continuum is that adjacent items are so closely related that, intuitively, it seems incredible that the rules governing the application of the predicate should dictate that it applies to one member of the pair but not the other. It is this fact that gives the inductive premise of the paradox its appeal.

The strength of this appeal can be gauged by our reluctance to accept the negation of the inductive premise. One can scarcely deny that there are progressions of the relevant sort connecting things that are F with things that are not F. Given this, one can accept the negation of the inductive premise only if one maintains that there is a pair s_i, s_{i+1} of the progression such that s_{i+1} is not F even though s_i is F (or s_{i+1} is F even though s_i is not). However, there are serious problems with this. For one thing, any choice of such a pair seems arbitrary; for any such choice, there are other pairs that have as much claim of marking the supposed dividing line as the one selected. For another, it is hard to imagine how the meanings of these predicates, which we have all learned, incorporate a sharp dividing line between being F and not being F even though no competent speaker observes such a dividing line or knows where it is. Here it is important to notice that vague predicates like these are not like the term *one meter*, which is stipulated to designate the length of some standard, fixed example (which can be measured to a degree of precision that far surpasses ordinary, unaided observation). Nor do they seem to be like those natural kind terms that allow the question of whether the term applies to an object to be determined by hidden internal structure posited by our most advanced and successful scientific theories. Unlike these terms, ordinary vague predicates seem not to be associated with any authoritative source we can identify that would decisively settle questions of application or nonapplication based on distinctions that go well beyond the sort of casual observation that accompanies ordinary use. For this reason, it is important that in ordinary life, when we learn and employ vague predicates, we do not notice and often cannot even recognize individual grains of sand in a heap, individual hairs on a person's head, each penny of a person's assets, or physical differences in colored patches that are imperceptible to the naked eye (in the sense defined). Consequently, there seems to be no ordinary context of utterance in which a speaker would assert that one of two indistinguishable patches of color looks green while the other does not look green, that one of two masses of sand that differ by a single grain is a heap while the other is not a heap, and so on. This is a serious obstacle to accepting the negation of the induction premise, for if one claims that there is an s_i and s_{i+1} such that one is F and the other is not F, then one would naturally think that if we were presented with the pair and asked to characterize it, we would speak truly iff we said that one was F and the other is not. The problem is that we do not normally think that such a remark would be true. Rather, we are inclined to accept as true a remark that characterizes both in the same way and to reject any other characterization as incorrect.

So the situation we are in with regard to the paradox is as follows. We know that (P1) of the argument is true while (C) is false. Therefore we must reject either the inductive (P2) or the inference from (P1) and (P2) to (C). Since the inference seems to be truth preserving, the strategy of rejecting (P2) is attractive. However, for the reasons just indicated, we are loath to accept the negation of (P2). If the strategy of rejecting the inductive premise is to be successful, we must find a way of dealing with this difficulty. The semantic model of vague predicates presented here is intended to do this.

Vague Predicates Are Partially Defined

The first step in the construction of the model is to treat vague predicates as partially defined. As we saw in chapter 6, when F is partially defined, there will be objects to which it applies, objects to which it does not apply, and objects for which it is undefined. The latter are objects for which the linguistic rules governing the predicate and giving it meaning have nothing to say about whether or not F applies to them. To say of any such object ⌐it is F⌐ or to say ⌐it is not F⌐ is to say something that goes beyond what can be justified by the rules that give F its meaning. Therefore, where F is undefined for object o, we must reject both ⌐it is F⌐ and ⌐it is not F⌐, when said of o.

Given a natural understanding of quantifiers and truth-functional connectives (provided by the strong Kleene tables), we can extend this point to sentences of arbitrary complexity. In particular, where o_i and o_{i+1} are adjacent items in a Sorites progression involving the predicate F and F is undefined for both items of the pair, the conditional

$$Fx_i \supset Fx_{i+1},$$

which is equivalent to the disjunction

$$\sim Fx_i \vee Fx_{i+1},$$

will not receive any evaluation for truth value by the rules of the language (relative to an appropriate assignment). More generally, if F is undefined for some items in a Sorites progression that begins with an object to which F applies and ends with an object to which it does not apply, then some instances of the universal generalization[3]

$$(x_i)\,(Fx_i \supset Fx_{i+1})$$

will be undefined and the rest will be true. Since this renders the universal generalization undefined, we are required to reject it while also rejecting its negation. Standardly, the inductive premise in a Sorites argument is a universal generalization of this sort. Hence if vague predicates are only partially defined, we typically can avoid the conclusions of Sorites arguments by rejecting the inductive premises without being forced to accept their negations.

This is an attractive feature of the analysis. There is, however, more at work in Sorites paradoxes, and also more to vagueness, than just partiality. If partiality were the whole story and o were an object in the undefined range of a predicate F, then we would have no choice regarding how to characterize o. We would have to reject the claim expressed by ⌐it is F⌐ as well as the claim expressed by ⌐it is not F⌐. But if we think of actual vague predicates, like *green*, *looks green*, *bald*, *rich*, and so on, we do not feel this way. Given some object in the intermediate ranges of these predicates, we can imagine circumstances in which it is perfectly correct to characterize the predicate as applying to the object or as failing to apply to it. If these predicates were only partial, there would be no such circumstances. In addition, if they were simply partial and nothing more, then presumably there would be a pair of objects o_i and o_{i+1} in a Sorites progression which, if they were presented to us, we would have to characterize by saying of o_i ⌐it is F⌐ while rejecting the corresponding claim about o_{i+1}, despite the fact that the two objects were indistinguishable or virtually indistinguishable to us. Typically, however, we would not do this. For example, given two perceptually indistinguishable patches of color, normally we would not be willing to assert that one looked green while rejecting the claim that the other did. So far, we have no explanation for this.

Vague Predicates Are Context-Sensitive

In order to illustrate the need to attribute more to the semantics of vague predicates than just partiality, it is helpful to focus on a slightly different form of the paradox in which the universally quantified inductive premise is replaced by a finite series of particular conditionals or biconditionals. For this purpose, we let F be some vague predicate like *bald* or *looks green*. We let a_0 through a_n be a (large) finite set of individuals, and we stipulate that F applies to a_0, that F does not apply to a_n, and that each a_i bears a certain relation R to a_{i+1}. Where F is the predicate *bald*, we may suppose that x bears R to y iff y has exactly one more hair on his head than x.[4] Where F is the predicate *looks green*, x bears R to y iff the two are perceptually indistinguishable in color (in the previously defined sense) to suitably situated observers. The paradox may now be formulated as follows:

Particularized Version of the Sorites
P1. a_0 is F.
P2. a_n is not F.
P3. a_0 is (is not) F iff a_1 is (is not) F.
      a_1 is (is not) F iff a_2 is (is not) F.

.
.
.

      a_{n-1} is (is not) F iff a_n is (is not) F.
C. a_n is F and a_n is not F.

Since the conclusion is a contradiction that follows from the premises,[5] at least one premise must be rejected. Since (P1) and (P2) are clearly true, at least one of the biconditionals in (P3) must be given up. ([P3] is a set of individual premises, not a conjunction.) If F were totally rather than just partially defined, then exactly one of these biconditionals would be false and the rest true, which seems wrong.[6] Given that F is partially defined, we avoid this problem since some of the biconditionals will be undefined and the rest true. However, we have still left out an important fact. For each of the biconditionals in (P3), we can imagine using F in a way that would make it true. Where a_i and a_{i+1} are individuals in the intermediate range of the predicate, we can imagine situations in which conversational participants agree to apply the predicate to both or to apply it to neither, thereby treating the relevant biconditional as true. For example, if two greenish patches in the intermediate range of the predicate *looks green* are perceptually indistinguishable in color, speakers who agree on a particular occasion to count both as looking green or both as not looking green need not be making any error and may even speak truly. If this is right, then although we can never accept all the biconditionals in (P3), each of the biconditionals can be accepted in the right sort of situation. This suggests that the vague predicates that appear in these paradoxes are not only partial but also context-sensitive. We need a dynamic model of vagueness that incorporates this.

Proposed Model of Vague Predicates

The model I propose treats vague predicates as partially defined predicates that have the following characteristics.

  i.   They are partially defined.
  ii.   They have default determinate-extensions and antiextensions. The default determinate-extension of F is the set of things that the communitywide rules or conventions of the language (plus relevant nonlinguistic facts) determine that the predicate applies to. The default determinate-antiextension consists of the things that the conventions of the language (plus nonlinguistic facts) determine that the predicate does not apply to.
  iii. Speakers have the discretion of adjusting the (determinate-) extension and antiextension of a vague predicate by including initially undefined cases — objects not in the default determinate-extension or antiextension — in the predicate's contextually determined extension or antiextension.
  iv.   This discretion typically is exercised by explicitly characterizing an object for which the predicate is initially undefined as being F or as being not F. When such an object o is explicitly characterized by a speaker as being F and other conversational participants accept this, the (determinate-) extension of the predicate is conversationally adjusted so as to include o plus all objects that bear a certain similarity relation R_e to o. Similarly, when such an object o is explicitly characterized by a speaker as not being F and other conversational participants accept this, the (determinate-) antiextension of the predicate is conversationally adjusted so as to include o plus all objects that bear a certain related similarity relation R_a to o.
  v.   The meaning of the predicate constrains the similarity relations R_e and R_a. Within those constraints, the identity of the relations R_e and R_a may vary from conversation to conversation depending on the intentions of the conversational participants.

These points can be illustrated by the way we come to understand a vague predicate. Often we are shown clear and unproblematic examples of its application and nonapplication. We are shown some clear cases and told, ⌜These things (individuals) are F⌝ and ⌜Those things (individuals) are not F.⌝ From these instructions, we learn both how to characterize the particular examples shown to us and how to generalize the use of the predicate to characterize many items outside the original sample.[7]

For example, in coming to understand the predicate *bald*, we learn that whether or not people are bald depends on how much hair they have on their heads. People with little or no hair—no more than the bald individuals in our original sample—are bald. People with a lot of hair—at least as much as the "not bald" individuals in the original sample—are not bald. Our ability to generalize beyond the samples we are initially exposed to depends on our being able to determine whether people have as much hair on their heads as someone we have already explicitly characterized as bald or as not bald. How do we do this? We certainly do not count individual hairs, nor do we make precise measurements about the proportion of a person's skull that has hair growing on it. Instead, we rely on ordinary perceptual judgments. These perceptual judgments, together with the initial samples of paradigmatically bald individuals and individuals who are para-digmatically not bald, give rise to the default (determinate-) extension and the default (determinate-) antiextension of the predicate in essentially the following way: (i) The predicate is applied to certain specific individuals who are taken as paradigmatic examples of baldness, and it is denied of other specific individuals who are taken as paradigmatic examples of people who are not bald. (ii) It is resolved that other individuals, y, are to be taken as determinate instances of bald-ness if they bear the relation R_e—*y has a perceptually equivalent amount of hair as x or less hair than x*—to someone, x, in the initial sample of paradigmatically bald individuals. (iii) It is further resolved that still others, z, are to be taken as determinate instances of individuals who are not bald if they bear the related relation R_a—*z has a perceptually equivalent amount of hair as w or more hair than w*—to someone, w, in the initial sample of individuals who are paradigmatically not bald.

In this way, the predicate becomes semantically associated with two distinct and easily distinguishable classes of individuals: those to which it determinately applies and those to which it determinately does not apply. These two classes are mutually exclusive, though not jointly exhaustive. Individuals in neither class are those about whom the semantic rules of the language governing the predicate issue no verdict. However, this does not mean that the predicate can never cor-rectly be used to characterize them. Rather, this is a realm of discretion reserved for individual speakers and hearers. If on a particular occasion one wishes to characterize an individual x in the intermediate range as bald, one is free to do so provided that others in the conversation are prepared to accept this character-ization. Having characterized x as bald, one is then committed to a standard that counts as bald all individuals with an equivalent amount of hair as x or less hair than x. A corresponding story holds for conversational characterizations of x as not bald.

Similar accounts can be given for other vague predicates. Where F is such a predicate, linguistic rules in the language governing its use determine certain clear cases in which it applies and certain clear cases in which it does not apply, thereby establishing default settings for its (determinate-) extension and antiextension. These settings are adjustable on the basis of additional standards that vary from one conversation to another. Occasionally the new standards may be explicitly announced—we might say something like "For purposes of this discussion, any family with an annual income of less than $12,000 will be counted as poor." Often, however, the new standards are implicit. Some individual x in the indeterminate range is considered, F is explicitly characterized as applying to x, and it is assumed that F applies to anything relevantly similar to x. In such cases, we can think of the determinate-extension and-antiextension of F as governed by rules of the following sort: *If an individual x not already in the determinate-extension of the predicate is explicitly considered and characterized as F, then anything that bears R_e to x is added to the determinate-extension of the predicate and so is counted as F. If an individual x not already in the determinate-antiextension of the predicate is explicitly considered and characterized as not F, then anything that bears R_a to x is added to the determinate-antiextension of the predicate and so is counted as not F.*

This raises the question of what is it for one thing to bear R_e or R_a to another in specific cases. The answer varies from one predicate to another and from one context of utterance to another. For example, suppose we are characterizing adult Americans as having high incomes or not. Let us grant that individuals with incomes over $100,000 have high incomes while individuals with incomes under $50,000 do not have high incomes. Suppose now that I characterize Bill, who earns $78,000, as having a high income. What is the relation R_e that determines which other individuals, whom I have not explicitly mentioned, count as having high incomes according to the conversational standards established by my characterization of Bill? The answer depends on my present dispositions, as well as perhaps those of the other participants in the conversation, to judge one individual as earning at least as much as another. Normally when we say that x earns as much money as y, we do not mean that x's earning must either strictly exceed y's or match y's down to the last penny. Although contexts vary regarding the degree of precision presupposed, typically we would be safe in regarding individuals as earning as much as Bill, in our present example, if their total earnings were within $1 of Bill's. If this were the relevant conversational standard, then anyone earning more than $77,999 would count as having a high income according to the conversational standards governing the predicate in the context of my utterance.

In this example, the relation R_e used in drawing contextually adjustable boundaries of application and nonapplication of the predicate is defined in terms of an objective amount of money—$1. In other cases, the relation is determined more subjectively in terms of the perceptions or experiences of subjects. One particularly interesting class of cases involves predicates defined in terms of the tendency of some things to produce a certain kind of response in subjects. Such predicates include appearance predicates like *looks green*.[8] It is natural to suppose that this is a vague (hence partially defined and context-sensitive) predicate that is defined in terms of an object's disposition to produce a certain sort of visual experience in observers or to elicit a certain sort of judgment from them. If this is right, then it may be part of the meaning of the predicate that one who explicitly characterizes something x as looking green is thereby committed to a standard that counts all objects that look greener than x plus objects perceptually indistinguishable in color from x as also looking green. In this model, the rule governing contextual adjustments of the predicate *looks green* should be roughly as follows:

If in a context C something x is explicitly judged to look green, then the extension of *looks green* in C includes everything perceptually indistinguishable in color from x, as well as everything that looks greener than x. If in C something y is judged not to look green, then the antiextension of *looks green* in C includes everything perceptually indistinguishable in color from y, as well as everything that looks less green than y.

With this analysis in place, we are now ready to look at a dynamic version of the Sorites paradox.

Dynamic Version of Sorites

In constructing this version of the paradox, we will use the predicate *looks green* and take the rule determining its application to new cases to be the one just given. We will also suppose that two stimuli can be perceptually indistinguishable for greenness even though they differ slightly in the feature that causes them to look green (or not green). In such a case, we can construct a chain connecting x_1, which definitely looks green, to x_n, which definitely does not look green, in which each link in the chain is a pair of items that are perceptually indistinguishable in color.

In this version of the paradox, we imagine a subject being presented with the colored patches in the chain one by one and being asked to characterize them as looking green or not. To avoid extraneous complications, we make sure that the conditions of observation are normal, the lighting is good, and the subject is a suitable observer: the subject has good vision, is not color-blind and so on. We start with x_1, which the subject correctly asserts to look green. The rule for the application of the predicate to new cases will then determine that, by current conversational standards, x_2, which is perceptually indistinguishable from x_1, also looks green. Keeping x_1 in sight, we next present the subject with x_2 and ask whether it looks green. Since all the subject is being asked to do is explicitly to characterize something as looking green that already counts as looking green by previously accepted standards, fidelity to those standards dictates that the subject agree that x_2 looks green. But once the subject has perceived x_2 and explicitly characterized it as looking green, the rule for the application of the predicate to new cases will classify x_3 as looking green. Thus when we remove x_1, keep x_2 in sight, and present x_3, the dynamic of the situation will be just as before.

After repeating this process a number of times, we might start at the other end with x_n, which the subject will correctly characterize as not looking green. The rule for application of the predicate to new cases will then determine that, by current standards, x_{n-1} also does not look green. Thus when we present x_{n-1} to the subject (keeping x_n in sight), fidelity to those standards will dictate that the subject agree that x_{n-1} does not look green. But once the subject has agreed to this, the rule for the application of the predicate to new cases will classify x_{n-2} as not looking green. Thus when we remove x_n, keep x_{n-1} in sight, and present

x_{n-2}, the dynamic of the situation will be repeated, and the subject will feel pressured to move further down the chain.

It is clear that by continuing this process long enough, we may arrive at a point in which the subject characterizes some x_i as not looking green that previously the subject has characterized as looking green. Is this paradoxical? On the one hand, no claim to the effect that something both looks green and does not look green can possibly be correct, so the subject may seem to have made a mistake. On the other hand, when we consider the subject's individual judgments, none of them seems to be in error. On the contrary, each such judgment was straightforwardly sanctioned by the semantic rules governing the predicate *looks green* and so, it seems, could not be in error. What, then, is going on?

The answer, in our analysis, is that there is no contradiction here at all. According to the analysis, when x_i is initially characterized as looking green, this is done with respect to a certain set of standards, S. Later, when it is characterized as not looking green, this is done with respect to a new set of standards S^*.[9] But there is no contradiction in the observation that something may look green with respect to one set of standards and not look green with respect to a different set of standards. The dynamic version of the Sorites is just the particularized version of the paradox in which each premise in (P3) is evaluated with respect to its own conversational standards, according to which it comes out true. Nevertheless, there is no single context of utterance in which the standards governing the predicate determine that all the premises are true and no context in which the contradictory conclusion can be established.

What makes this easy to miss and gives the dynamic version of the paradox its force is the fact that at each stage in the sequence from x_1 to x_i (or from x_n to x_i), it does not seem to us as if we are changing conversational standards. This is, of course, an illusion. Each time we move one step further along the scale, the (determinate-) extension or antiextension of the predicate changes, and therefore the standards for further application or nonapplication of the predicate do too. What hides this fact from us is that the adjustment of standards is the minimum possible change and one for which there is a powerful justification built into the semantics of the predicate itself. All one is doing in each case is explicitly recognizing something as F (or not F) that has already been determined to be F (or not F) by one's previously established standards. Consequently, the most conservative thing one can do when presented with the new case is to accept it as F (or not F) as well. Although this will result in a subtle, indeed imperceptible, shift in standards, any other judgment about the new case (including a failure to characterize it as being either F or not F) will involve a more substantial shift. Thus speakers have a powerful reason in each case to move further along the scale from the characterization of one member of the sequence as F to the characterization of the next as F (or from the characterization of something as not F to the characterization of its immediate predecessor as not F).

Because of this, the boundary lines fixing the (determinate-) extensions and antiextensions of certain vague predicates are inherently unstable. In the kind of case we are imagining, speakers have every reason for starting down the road from

x_1 to x_n, characterizing more and more items as F. At some point, as they approach x_n, they will feel uneasy about the fact that the things they are now judging to be F are perceptually quite different from the things they originally judged to be F and indeed are closer to the things they previously judged not to be F. When this happens, they can be expected to resist characterizing some new example x_k as being F. They may characterize the new example as not F, or they may resist characterizing it one way or the other.[10] In doing either of these things, they are perfectly within their rights; they are not contradicting themselves and are not violating any semantic rule. They are, indeed, changing the standards for Fness they had previously adopted when they characterized x_{k-1} as being F. However, there is no requirement that standards never be changed in this way. It is even possible that subjects may find themselves forced back down the scale toward x_1, recanting along the way their previous characterizations of many items as being F, after which point they may start up the scale again (recanting the recantations), and so on.

The lesson here is that there is no stable stopping point for subjects to establish a boundary between the things they are willing to characterize as F and the things they are not willing to characterize as F. Any commitment to a standard S, underwritten by the judgment that something x_k is F, will carry with it the obligation to explicitly characterize x_{k+1} to be F on pain of eliminating something from the extension of the predicate already determined to be there by S. Continued fidelity to obligations of this sort cannot be maintained indefinitely. This is the inherent instability in the application of certain vague predicates that is revealed by the dynamic version of the Sorites and that is correctly predicted by the analysis given here. Although this inherent instability is not a practical problem for speakers in ordinary situations and although it does not represent any theoretical incoherence in the semantics of the relevant vague terms, it does explain the discomfort one feels when presented with the dynamic version of the paradox. We are uncomfortable because we feel pressured into doing something that cannot be done — namely, establishing a stable boundary line for the application of the predicate. The solution to this paradox is to recognize that there is no such boundary line and no requirement for there to be one.

Lessons for the Generalized Version of the Sorites Paradox

In the dynamic version of the paradox, the analysis predicts that we have no contradiction but rather a change of conversational standards over time. What does the analysis tell us about the corresponding generalized version of the paradox? Consider again example 4.

Example 4
P1. G looks green, and Y does not look green.
P2. There is a progression, S, containing Y whose first member is G such that for all members s_i and s_{i+1} of S, s_i is perceptually indistinguishable in

color from s_{i+1} to competent observers in good light under normal conditions. *For any two patches of color x and y that are perceptually indistinguishable in color to competent observers in good light under normal conditions, x and y look to be the same color and so one looks green if the other looks green. Hence for each s_i, s_{i+1} looks green if s_i looks green.*

C.   Therefore each member of the progression S looks green. Since this includes Y, which does not look green, Y both looks green and does not look green.

We know that the inductive premise, (P2), must be rejected. Why then are speakers initially tempted to accept it? The semantic analysis offered here provides a plausible answer. We are tempted to accept (P2) because we confuse the italicized portion of it with a closely related metalinguistic principle, (P2*), which really is true.

P2*.   For any two patches of color x and y that are perceptually indistinguishable to competent observers under normal conditions, if someone who is presented with x characterizes the predicate *looks green* as applying to it, then that person is thereby committed to a standard that counts the predicate as applying to y as well.

The intuitive line of reasoning connecting (P2) and (P2*) may be put as follows:

i.   If (P2) were false, then some patch of color x_i would look green even though a perceptually indistinguishable patch x_{i+1} did not look green.

ii.   Therefore if, upon being presented with those patches, one said of x_i *it looks green* while saying of x_{i+1} *it does not look green*, one would have spoken the truth and only the truth.

iii.   But (P2*) tells us that this cannot be, for any characterization of x_i as looking green will carry with it a characterization of x_{i+1} as also looking green.

iv.   Thus (P2) cannot be false and so must be true.

It is important to realize that although this line of reasoning is extremely natural, it is also confused. First, step (iv) contains an error: even if we must reject the claim that (P2) is false, it does not follow that we must accept the claim that it is true; instead, (P2) may be undefined and hence rejectable. As I have stressed, this is in fact the case in most normal contexts. Second, and even more important, step (ii) does not follow from step (i): the truth of (P2*) does not in fact rule out the possibility that (P2) might be false. To see this, imagine a situation in which a subject is presented with two items x_{i-1} and x_{i+2}, drawn from a Sorites progression, the colors of which are just barely distinguishable perceptually. Imagine further that the subject is not shown any other items in the progression. (P2*) allows for the possibility that the subject might legitimately characterize x_{i-1} as looking green and x_{i+2} as not looking green, thereby committing to a standard that classifies x_i as looking green and x_{i+1} as not looking green even though these two are perceptually indistinguishable. In such a context, the standards governing the predicate *looks green* implicitly classify members of a perceptually indistinguishable pair in opposite ways, thereby falsifying (P2) even though any attempt to present the falsifying pair for explicit characterization will result in a change of standards that classifies them in the same way.[11] Failure to notice this extremely subtle and unusual possibility encourages us to confuse (P2) with (P2*) and helps generate an air of paradox.

An Objection

Dispelling this confusion also defuses a potential objection to the semantic analysis presented here. The analysis predicts that when a predicate is vague, normally there will not be a sharp line distinguishing things that it applies to from things that it does not apply to; however, it also predicts that in such cases there may well be a sharp line distinguishing things that the predicate applies to from things for which it is undefined. The critic objects to this, citing the fact that we can typically construct a Sorites progression for which the following holds.

> Obj.   When presented with a pair of adjacent items in the progression, we will not be content to assert of one of them that it is F, while simultaneously rejecting the claim that the other is F—either because we think the other is not F or because we take the predicate to be undefined for it.

From this, the critic concludes that there can be no sharp lines distinguishing cases in which the predicate applies to an object from cases in which the predicate is undefined. In addition, the critic argues that the truth of Obj leaves us no grounds for rejecting the weakened inductive premise WIP.

> WIP.   For all members s_i and s_{i+1} in a Sorites progression, if s_i is F, then s_{i+1} is neither not F nor undefined for the predicate.

But then since, according to the analysis, every member of the progression is either F, not F, or undefined for the predicate, the critic concludes that the paradox can be reconstructed and the analysis fails to provide a solution.

The critic is wrong on both counts. First, the truth of Obj is quite compatible with the existence of sharp lines distinguishing cases in which the predicate is defined from cases in which it is not. Indeed, the explanation of Obj is provided by (P2*), which, we have just seen, allows for sharp lines as long as they are systematically movable. Second, recognition of the truth of Obj does not commit one to WIP, so the paradox does not arise again.

The salient facts about the analysis are these:

> i.   Often there will be a sharp line separating things that are F, according to a given conversational standard, from things for which, according to the standard, the predicate is undefined.

ii.   Attempts to display that sharp dividing line for inspection will result in a change of standards, according to which the pair of adjacent items in the progression come to be characterized in the same way (with respect to the predicate).

The critic wrongly takes the inability to *display* a sharp dividing line between things that are F and things for which the predicate is undefined, according to some conversational standard, to imply that there is no sharp dividing line, according to that standard. This ignores the dynamic feature of the model. Once this feature is recognized, the objection is defused.

Varieties of Vagueness

If this analysis is right, then vague predicates are partially defined, with context-sensitive boundaries and standards of precision. To say that a predicate P is partially defined is to say that it has a determinate-extension and-antiextension that do not exhaust its potential range of application. Hence there will be a range of undefined cases not covered by the existing standards governing the predicate. To say that the predicate has context-sensitive boundaries is to say that speakers are allowed the latitude to characterize previously undefined cases as being either in the extension or in the antiextension of the predicate, depending on their conversational purposes. Finally, to say that the standards of precision for P are context-sensitive is to say that the relations R_e and R_a for adjusting the extension and antiextension of P as a result of new characterizations of previously undefined cases are capable of being made finer or coarser, depending on the intentions of the conversational participants. Vague predicates typically have all these characteristics.

However, not all vague predicates are Sorites predicates. Predicates that generate compelling versions of the paradox are vague predicates whose application or nonapplication is governed by the position of items on an underlying scale that forms a natural continuum. The particular vague predicates we have so far considered fit this picture. However, this is not an essential feature of vagueness. Predicates like *vehicle, machine,* and so on are vague even though there is no natural underlying continuum semantically connected to them. As a result, compelling versions of the Sorites paradox are much harder to construct using such terms.

The difference between Sorites predicates and other vague predicates shows up in the constraints at work when speakers conversationally adjust the extensions and antiextensions of their terms. The meaning of a Sorites predicate like *poor* or *bald* constrains the way in which the conversational characterization of a previously undefined item results in a new standard that implicitly classifies other previously undefined items. For example, if in a particular context we decide to characterize a family with n-dollars in total wealth/income as poor, then we are automatically committed to characterizing other families with less than (or equal to) that total as poor. The reason for this is that the meaning of *poor* ties its application or nonapplication to positions on a continuum of wealth/income.

Vague predicates that are not Sorites predicates do not have this feature. Consider, for example, the predicate *vehicle*. Are skateboards vehicles or not? The best thing to say, I think, is that the question is not settled by the communitywide linguistic rules that govern its use. If this is right, then the predicate is initially undefined for skateboards. This leaves speakers free to characterize them one way or the other in particular situations. Such characterizations may turn out to be important in special cases, such as when a judge is called upon to interpret a statute that prohibits vehicles in a park.[12] In facing such a choice, the judge cannot simply locate skateboards along a single semantically determined continuum from vehicles to nonvehicles and draw a line. Rather, he must articulate some general principle that is justifiable in practice. It is important to note that there is no way of telling in advance what such a principle will say about other cases — unicycles, for example. The meaning of the vague predicate *vehicle* allows speakers in a given context the freedom to characterize skateboards as vehicles and unicycles not or unicycles as vehicles and skateboards not or to leave the predicate *vehicle* undefined for both.[13] The two are simply not related to one another along any continuum semantically encoded in the meaning of the predicate.[14]

A further fact about Sorites predicates is that the continuum semantically associated with such a predicate can be broken down into units fine enough so that once one has characterized one item as F (or not F), it is virtually irresistible to characterize the next item in the same way. One way in which this may come about was illustrated with appearance predicates. The idea in these cases is that it is part of the meaning of the predicate that whenever one considers and explicitly characterizes something as F (or not F), one implicitly classifies everything that bears a certain relation R_e (R_a) to it (characterized in terms of perceptual discriminations and perceptual indistinguishability) as also being F (or not F). Since the relations R_e and R_a can be used to construct a chain running from things that are F to things that are not F, the Sorites paradox is, for all intents and purposes, encoded in the semantics of the predicate itself. As I have emphasized, it does not follow from this that such predicates are incoherent, that semantic theories describing their meanings are inconsistent, or that speakers using them in accord with their meanings can inevitably be made to contradict themselves. None of these things is true. What is true is that the (determinate-) extensions and antiextensions of Sorites predicates of this sort have inherently unstable boundaries.

All Sorites predicates have natural uses in which their (determinate-) extensions and antiextensions have unstable boundaries. However, this instability is not always inherent in the meaning of the predicate itself, therefore it is sometimes theoretically avoidable. Take, for example, the predicate *poor*. Given any normal purpose for which we might want to characterize a family as poor or not, we would have no reason explicitly to characterize one family (in the previously undefined range of the predicate) as poor while implicitly classifying an otherwise identical family with a single penny more in total wealth/income as not poor. Nevertheless, we probably could stipulate such a fully precise boundary if we wished without violating any semantic principle governing the predicate. If, in some particular context, we were to make such a decision and firmly stick to it, the Sorites argument would have no force since it would be clear that one of the premises was straight-forwardly false. In normal contexts, however, we do not impose such precise standards, and the diagnosis of the Sorites given previously carries over.[15]

Types of Higher-Order Vagueness

Let F be some ordinary vague predicate like *green*, *poor*, or *bald*. I have said that the communitywide rules governing such a predicate in the language determine a default setting for its extension and antiextension. An object is in the default extension of F just in case it is in the extension of F and hence "counts as F" in all contexts sanctioned by the rules of the language. Similarly for the default antiextension. Objects in neither of these classes are objects that speakers have discretion to characterize differently in different contexts. Speakers have no discretion about how to classify objects in the default extension and antiextension.

Now consider the predicate ⌜is a member of the default extension of 'F'.⌝[16] Is this predicate fully precise, or is it, too, a vague predicate? Is it fully precise which individuals count as green, poor, or bald in any context in which these predicates are used with their standard meanings? If so, what is the precise spot on the spectrum at which something will count as green in any context? What is the maximum number of pennies or hairs that one may possess while still qualifying as poor or bald in any legitimate context? Faced with these questions, one is hard-pressed to imagine that they have fully precise answers. Thus where F is an ordinary vague predicate of the sort we have been talking about, it appears that the higher-order technical predicate ⌜is a member of the default extension of 'F'⌝ typically will also be vague.

This means that at least some of the concepts I have used in my account of vague predicates are themselves vague.[17] Since the account is intended to be comprehensive, it ought to apply even to them. And it does. Suppose, for example, that the vague predicate F satisfies the following three conditions: (i) For some objects x, x is in the extension of F in every context sanctioned by the rules of the language; (ii) for some objects y, there is at least one context C such that y is in the antiextension of F in C (and so is not in the extension of F in C); and (iii) for some objects z, (a) F is undefined for z in at least one context, and (b) for all contexts C, either z is in the extension of F in C or F is undefined for z in C. If these conditions are fulfilled, then the predicate ⌜is a member of the default extension of 'F'⌝ will be partially defined, with a nonempty default extension and default antiextension plus a (typically rather small) range of indeterminate cases in which speakers may have the discretion to apply the predicate or not.[18] Thus the model presented previously makes room for one kind of higher-order vagueness.

Although this sort of higher-order vagueness does not undermine the account given here, it does have an important consequence for our understanding of how vagueness arises. If our account of vagueness is correct, it ought to be possible to use a set of fully precise and totally defined concepts and intentions to introduce a new vague predicate. To do this, one might simply provide fully determinate and precise specifications of a pair of mutually exclusive but not jointly exhaustive classes to serve as the default extension and antiextension, while stipulating that speakers are free to extend these classes to include new objects in particular contexts on the basis of certain specified and fully precise principles. The result would be a fully precise specification of a new vague predicate.

This, it seems to me, is a genuine theoretical possibility. However, it is not the way in which most ordinary vague predicates we are familiar with were introduced; the genesis of these predicates normally does not lie with some conceptually prior set of fully precise concepts and intentions. Rather, there is vagueness "all the way down (or up)." How this can be remains an unanswered question, as does the more general question of how the use of a predicate by a community determines its central semantic properties, including its extension and antiextension, whether vague or not.

A related question that so far has not been addressed concerns a different sort of higher-order predicate. Let us say that an object o is in the default determinate-extension of a predicate F iff for all contexts C sanctioned by the rules of the language, o is in the determinate extension of F in C. As we have seen, the determinate-extension of a predicate F (in a context C) is the set S of things such that the linguistic conventions of the language that govern F (together with special facts about the use of F in C and the relevant nonlinguistic facts) determine that F applies (in C) to members of S. Thus if

    i.   what counts as a linguistic convention governing the use of F

is fully precise and totally defined and if

    ii.   what such conventions (plus the relevant extra nonlinguistic and contextual facts) determine that F applies to

is also fully precise and totally defined, then the higher-order predicate ⌜is a member of the determinate-extension of 'F' (in C)⌝ will itself be fully precise and totally defined. Finally, if it is fully precise and totally defined which contexts count as legitimate, it will follow that the higher-order predicate ⌜is a member of the default determinate-extension of the predicate 'F'⌝ is totally defined and so cannot be vague.

If all this is right, then for some vague predicates, a certain sort of higher-order vagueness simply is not possible. However, before we draw this conclusion in any particular case, we must satisfy ourselves that (i) and (ii) really are precise and totally defined. Sometimes, as when we artificially introduce a vague predicate using precise and fully defined concepts, we may be able to do this. However, when F is an ordinary vague predicate like *green, poor,* or *bald,* either (i) or (ii) or both may themselves be vague, in which case the corresponding higher-order predicates ⌜x is in the determinate-extension of the predicate 'F' (in C)⌝, ⌜x is determinately F (in C)⌝, and ⌜x is a member of the default determinate-extension of the predicate 'F'⌝ may inherit this vagueness.

Finally, it is important to distinguish this class of predicates from a different but related class including ⌜x is definitely F⌝ and ⌜x is clearly F⌝. To say ⌜x is clearly or definitely F⌝ is to say ⌜Clearly or definitely x is F⌝. These are epistemic claims that, roughly speaking, assert both the proposition expressed by ⌜x is F⌝ and that the evidence or justification for this proposition is obvious or beyond serious question. Although *clearly* and *definitely* are often used with a vague or partially defined predicate, there is no requirement that the predicate be such. For example, if someone expresses doubt about a certain calculation, one can appropriately respond "3,978 + 8,596 is definitely 12,574," despite the fact that the 'is' of identity is already precise and totally defined. This suggests that there is nothing special about the semantics of ⌜x is definitely F⌝ when F is vague; it is just the combination of the ordinary semantics for vague predicates plus the epistemic claim carried by the word *definitely*. Thus it is no surprise that the predicate ⌜x is definitely F⌝ is often itself vague.

In order to understand how such a predicate is used, however, it must be noted that in many contexts there is some further, special information communicated by an utterance of ⌜x is definitely F⌝ over and above the information it semantically expresses. This may be seen by imagining a situation in which we are confronted with two men, Bob and Bill, both of whom are candidates for being bald. Looking at Bob, who has lost a lot of hair but still has a fair amount remaining, we are unsure whether to characterize him as bald. About Bill, who has much less hair, we feel no doubt, and so we say, "Bill is definitely bald." What we are saying is that it is beyond question that Bill is bald. Although in principle there are many reasons why a given claim might be beyond question, in a context like this the obvious reason is that Bill can be seen to be located at a point near the hairless end of the continuum determining the application of *bald*—a point well within the boundaries of the (determinate-) extension of the predicate. Consequently, this information is carried (implicated) by the utterance.

The implicated information is like that (semantically) expressed by ⌜x is very F⌝ or ⌜x is really F⌝, where F is vague and *very* and *really* are understood as intensifiers. The effect of adding one of these intensifiers to F is to locate the boundary of the (determinate-) extension of the compound predicate (in the context) down the continuum a substantial distance to a point well within the (determinate-) extension of F (in the context). Of course, the boundary of the (determinate-) antiextension of the compound predicate also is located down the continuum, but there is no reason to think that the newly arrived at (determinate-) extension and (determinate-) antiextension exhaust all the cases. Standardly, the predicates ⌜x is very F⌝ and ⌜x is really F⌝ are themselves vague just as F is; they just occupy different portions of the underlying continuum than F does.[19]

Notes

1. I ignore here complicating factors like the difference between wealth and income. Similarly, in discussing baldness, I ignore the distinction between determining baldness by counting hairs on someone's head and determining baldness by calculating the percentage of the skull on which hair is growing.

2. It is compatible with the claim that two patches are perceptually indistinguishable in color in this sense, that they might be (indirectly) perceptually distinguishable from one another in other ways. For example, it is not incoherent to suppose that x and y might be perceptually indistinguishable in the sense defined in the text, even if there is a third patch z such that x is perceptually distinguishable from z (when the two are considered in isolation) whereas y is perceptually indistinguishable from z (when the two are considered in isolation). When in the text I speak of two patches of color being perceptually indistinguishable, I will always mean perceptually indistinguishable in the narrowly defined sense. Hence I allow that two perceptually indistinguishable colors might be indirectly distinguishable by perception in more complicated ways.

3. Think of this universal generalization as involving a single variable ranging over the members of a Sorites progression and saying that for any such member, if it is F, then its successor in the progression is F. (Think of 'x_{i+1}' not as a variable distinct from 'x_i' but rather as a complex singular term in which the sign for a function taking one member of the progression to its successor is applied to the variable 'x_i'.)

4. To simplify matters, we are assuming, for purposes of this example, that for each number less than or equal to n, we actually have a person with exactly that number of hairs on the person's head.

5. A biconditional of the form A *iff* B is logically equivalent to one of the form ~A *iff* ~B.

6. One of these biconditionals will be false just in case one side is true and the other is false.

7. Of course, we are not always given explicit instructions at all, let alone of this specific kind. In many instances, we simply observe other speakers applying the word to certain individuals and denying it of other individuals, sometimes with accompanying reasons or explanations, sometimes not. From this, we get an idea of paradigmatic examples to which the word applies and similarly paradigmatic examples to which it does not, and we generalize from there.

8. The same may be said for color predicates themselves, like *green*, if, as some philosophers maintain, they are dispositional predicates that apply to an object just in case it has the disposition to produce certain sorts of visual experiences in appropriate observers. I will not explore the nuances of this view, nor do I wish to take a position on whether or not it is ultimately correct. However, I do want to explore the consequences of applying the present model of vague predicates to an appearance predicate, like *looks green*.

9. When the subject first considers x_i and characterizes it as looking green, the subject has adjusted the (determinate-) extension of the predicate to include it without having made any such corresponding adjustment of the (determinate-) antiextension of the predicate. When later the subject is led to characterize x_i as not looking green, the subject adjusts the (determinate-) antiextension of the predicate to include it. Standardly, in this sort of situation, we should think of the inclusion of an item in the (determinate-) antiextension or extension as carrying with it an intention to exclude the item from the (determinate-) extension or antiextension of the predicate, and an appropriate conversational adjustment of such will be made if necessary. So at this later point, the current standards of application of the predicate exclude x_i from the (determinate-) extension of *looks green*.

10. Where in the progression this happens is a psychological, not a semantic, matter.

11. The possibility that a subject presented with perceptually distinguishable items x_{i-1} and x_{i+2} from a Sorites progression might be legitimately characterize them as looking green and as not looking green, respectively (whether or not they were presented to the subject in the course of running through a Sorites progression), reveals a potential conflict between the following two putative semantic principles:

i. For any two perceptually indistinguishable patches of color x and y and acceptable context of utterance C, if the conversational participants adjust the (determinate-) extension of the predicate *looks green* by explicitly stipulating that it applies to x, then the conversational standards in C governing the application of the predicate will count it as also applying to y, as well as all other patches of color that look at least as green as x; similarly for adjustments of the (determinate-) antiextension of the predicate.

ii. For any two perceptually indistinguishable patches of color x and y and acceptable context of utterance C, the standards governing the predicate *looks green* cannot include x in the (determinate-) extension of the predicate and y in its (determinate-) antiextension.

The second of these principles, unlike the first, rules out the possibility that the predicate could ever be totally defined over the entire Sorites sequence in any context. Thus if it is semantically legitimate to characterize x_{i-1} in one way while characterizing x_{i+2} in the opposite way, then (i) and (ii) cannot jointly be maintained.

I do not see any credible alternative to (i). Surely we do not want to say that in stipulating that x looks green one is committed to a standard according to which only things that look visibly *more* green than x, and so not even physical duplicates of x or perceptually indistinguishable items *preceding* x in a Sorites progression, count as looking green. Where x is the ith item in a Sorites progression, such a standard would give rise to the bizarre result in which the patches of color in an initial stretch of f items preceding x in the progression are characterized as looking green, the patches in the stretch of items following f and preceding i are classified as being things for which the predicate is undefined, while the ith patch, x, is characterized as looking green. Given both that we want to avoid this result and that we want the newly adjusted (determinate-) extension of the predicate to be determined by how other previously undefined items *appear* in relation to the item, x, newly stipulated to be look green, we seem to be required to accept something like (i). Thus either (ii) cannot be regarded as a genuine semantic principle governing the use of the predicate, or the characterization of x_{i-1} as looking green and x_{i+2} as not looking green, described previously, must be rejected as not giving rise to a coherent and legitimate conversational standard. Since such a characterization does seem legitimate, the rejection of (ii) seems called for.

12. See H. Hart, *The Concept of Law* (Oxford: Oxford University Press, 1961), 124, for a discussion of this type of case.

13. The concept of speech, as it occurs in the legal interpretation of the First Amendment to the U.S. Constitution, seems to be vague in the way in which *vehicle* is. The range of indeterminate cases seems to include things like displaying or burning flags; wearing clothing containing various symbols; nonverbal but nevertheless expressive artistic performances; nonverbal, nonartistic forms of behavior; and so on. Since these candidates for falling under the concept do not form an obvious or natural continuum, justices cannot simply draw a line but need to articulate some substantive principle to discriminate among them.

14. The difference between Sorites predicates and other vague predicates, like *vehicle*, seems itself to be a matter of degree rather than a fundamental difference in kind. Even in the case of ordinary Sorites predicates, the postulation of a natural underlying continuum (with the structure of a complete linear ordering) often involves substantial idealization. For example, in the case of *green*, there may be several different ways of making a color appear more or less green: changing it hue, its saturation, its brightness, and so on. In some cases, changing these different dimensions may leave us with colors that cannot easily be compared in terms of how green they appear. In such cases, we may be free to characterize

one as being or looking green, while making any stipulation we like about the other. The same sort of situation may arise with *bald*, where both the number of hairs and their distribution probably play a role. If this is right, then clear Sorites predicates like *bald* and *looks green* share some of the "messiness" of a vague predicate like *vehicle*. In this account, the difference between clear Sorites predicates and other vague predicates involves the extent of such "messiness." The more the potential range of application of the vague predicate approaches a complete linear ordering along some natural, semantically relevant dimension, the easier it will be to construct clear Sorites progressions and the more of a Sorites predicate it will be.

Thanks to John Barker and Neil Delaney for drawing my attention to this point.

15. In such cases, analogues of the principle (P2*) of the previous section are not guaranteed to be true by the inherent meanings of the predicates themselves but rather are supported by ordinary standards of precision present in normal contexts.

Even with appearance predicates, a case might be made for invoking a stricter notion of perceptual indistinguishability than the one I have relied upon for adjusting contextually determined extensions and antiextensions. Instead of characterizing two things as perceptually indistinguishable in color iff suitable observers when presented with both, by themselves, in good conditions cannot perceive any difference in color between them, we might insist that two things are perceptually indistinguishable in color iff they are indistinguishable in color by any combination of observations, including those in which other objects are brought in for comparison. If, as seems likely, there is some latitude in the strictness of the standards of perceptual indistinguishability that can be incorporated into R_e and R_a, then the theoretical situation with appearance predicates like *looks green* parallels that with other vague predicates like *poor* and *bald*.

16. Here I treat 'F' as a metalinguistic variable ranging over vague predicates. For example, where the value of 'F' is *bald*, the new predicate is *is a member of the default extension of 'bald.'*

17. Speakers' discretionary conversational adjustments of the extension and antiextension of a vague predicate often involve standards—the relations R_e and R_a—with a certain amount of vagueness, with the result that the conversational extensions and antiextensions thereby established may also be vague.

18. The result should not be surprising. We already know that when F is vague, the predicate ⌜is a member of the extension of 'F' (in context C)⌝ is partially defined (and also vague). When F is undefined for an object z in a context C, we cannot correctly say that z is not in the extension of F (even though we can correctly say that z is not in the determinate-extension of F). If for all contexts C', either z is in the extension of F in C' or F is undefined for z in C', then the predicate ⌜is in the extension of 'F' in every context⌝ is undefined for z, as is the predicate ⌜is in the default extension of 'F'⌝.

19. The material in this chapter grew out of my thoughts about partially defined predicates, prompted initially by a consideration of Saul Kripke's "Outline of a Theory of Truth," *Journal of Philosophy* 72 (1975): 690–716. The conception of vague predicates given here was developed intermittently between 1984 and 1995, and some of the ideas were presented in my seminars at Princeton University during that period. Versions of the paper were presented in May 1995 at the Instituto de Investigaciones Filosóficas of the Universidad Nacional Autónoma de Mexico and in October 1995 at Wayne State University.

Although I did not, for the most part, consult the philosophical literature on vagueness in formulating my view, since finishing the chapter I have become aware of important previous work on the subject developing some of the central themes presented here. Three of the most important of these are Kit Fine, "Vagueness, Truth, and Logic," *Synthese* 30

(1975): 265–300; Hans Kamp, "The Paradox of the Heap," in *Aspects of Philosophical Logic*, ed. U. Monnich (Dordrecht: Reidel, 1981), 225–77; and Jamie Tappenden, "The Liar and Sorites Paradoxes: Toward a Unified Treatment," *Journal of Philosophy* 90 (1993): 551–77.

The closest of these in conception to mine, and the only one I was familiar with prior to writing the chapter, is Tappenden's insightful article. Both of us see vague predicates as partially defined predicates with default (determinate-) extensions and antiextensions that are contextually extendable at the discretion of speakers in ways constrained by the meanings of the predicates. Both of us employ the strong Kleene method of assigning truth values to logically compound sentences containing constituent sentences that may lack determinate-truth values, and both of us reject the orthodox use of van Fraassen–style supervaluations to assign truth to those sentences containing vague predicates that come out true for all admissible classical extensions of their default settings (where the predicates are totally defined) and to assign falsity to all sentences that come out false in all such extensions. (Sentences in neither of these categories are characterized as not being true and not being false.) An elementary but nevertheless important objection to this view is that it violates fundamental truths about the meanings of various logical terms—for example, the platitude that if P is not true and Q is not true, then ⌜P or Q⌝ cannot be true either. (It should also be noted that supervaluations do not come into play in any significant way in explaining the particularized and dynamic versions of the Sorites paradox presented earlier, as opposed to the generalized version.)

An important area of disagreement between Tappenden and me, and one closely connected to our differing explanations of Sorites paradoxes, concerns the constraints on vague predicates governing conversational adjustments of their (determinate-) extensions and antiextensions. My discussion focuses on the fact that typically such adjustments are made by explicitly considering some new item and characterizing it one way or the other. But this raises the question, How does the explicit characterization of one item affect the classification of other items for which the predicate may have been undefined? I answer the question by positing rules that classify these new items on the basis of the relations they bear to items explicitly considered and characterized as F or as not F in the conversation. Tappenden takes a different approach. Instead of positing rules of this sort, he sees constraints on conversational adjustments of vague predicates arising from a set of sentences containing the predicate that are not allowed to come out false in any admissible extension of the predicate. (Extensions in which they would come out false are ruled inadmissible.)

There are, I think, several problems with this approach. The first is illustrated by Tappenden's discussion of the vague predicate, *heavy*, about which he says the following: "Anyone who understands the meaning of 'heavy' and who knows that a is heavier than b knows that new boundaries may not be stipulated in such a way that 'If b is heavy then a is heavy' becomes false. . . . Sentences that constrain increases in precision as S does in this example will be called pre-analytic: a sentence S is pre-analytic if anyone who understands S knows not to draw more precise boundaries to any of the expressions in S in such a way that S would be false in any circumstances. . . . An example of a pre-analytic sentence is 'If a is heavier than b and b is heavy then a is heavy'. Even if a and b are borderline cases of heavy things, so that it is acceptable to specify new boundaries on which 'a is heavy' comes out true or on which it comes out false, and similarly for 'b is heavy', there is a restriction on how one may resolve both at once. When sharpening the predicate to resolve application to both a and b, boundary drawing is constrained at least in that 'If a is heavier than b and b is heavy then a is heavy' must not come out false" ("The Liar and Sorites Paradoxes," 557). The problem here is that the constraint is too weak; it allows for admissible extensions in which b is counted as heavy even though the predicate remains undefined for things heavier than b. This is wrong: anyone who knows the meaning of *heavy* and who knows that a is heavier than b knows that new boundaries may not be stipulated in such a way that *b is heavy* comes out true unless *a is heavy* also comes out true. Tappenden's treatment misses this.

The reason it does is that Tappenden limits consideration of constraints on conversational adjustments of the predicate to those of a certain form—namely, those that require every member of a certain set of sentences to be true or those that require every member of a certain set of sentences never to be false. Given the strong Kleene tables, one simply cannot put the proper constraint on *heavy* in this form. By contrast, it is statable in the form I advocate—that of a rule according to which the characterization as heavy of one item for which the predicate was previously undefined automatically carries with it the classification of all heavier items as heavy as well.

The second problem with Tappenden's discussion concerns what he calls local consistency rules for essentially vague predicates. He says: "Say that a pre-analytic sentence is a local consistency rule if it is of the form 'If Qab then $(Pa$ iff $Pb)$'. Pre-analytic sentences of this type ensure that, if some condition holds, boundaries will not be drawn in such a way as to separate a and b by assigning different values to Pa and Pb. So, for example, . . . note that if a and b are color samples 'If a and b are observationally indistinguishable to me in respect of color, then a looks red to me if and only if b looks red to me' is a local consistency rule. Call a predicate P essentially vague if there is a sequence $a_1, a_2, \ldots, a_n$, and a relation Q, such that a_1 is a clear case of P, a_n is a clear countercase, for each $i < n + 1$, $Q\,a_i, a_{i+1}$ is true, and each instance of 'If $Q\,a_i, a_{i+1}$ then $(Pa_i$ if and only if $P\,a_{i+1})$' is a local consistency rule. . . . No admissible elaboration [extension] can make an essentially vague predicate completely precise, because any sharp boundary would violate one of the local consistency rules." (ibid., 567–68). The problem with this view is that it cannot accommodate the observations in note 11 and in the section "Lessons for the Generalized Version of the Sorites Paradox." Although the issues here are subtle and philosophical in nature, they are real and seem to me to provide a reason for stating constraints on conversational adjustments of vague predicates in terms of rules indicating how the classification of some new items affects the classification of others, rather than in terms of restrictions on acceptable assignments of truth values to all members of certain classes of object-language sentences.

For these reasons, I prefer the approach given in the text to Tappenden's closely related treatment. Nevertheless, I want to acknowledge his influence. In writing this chapter, I was aware of his work from his dissertation and from a 1989 draft of his 1993 paper. Although by that time I had developed many of my own thoughts on the subject, I found his work stimulating and was influenced by it—most of all, I think, by being pressed to try to determine how conversational adjustments of vague predicates are in fact made and how they might be constrained by the meanings of those predicates. Tappenden, more than anyone else, got me to appreciate the importance of this question. (Once working on it, however, I pursued the problem independently, and only after developing the approach in the text did I come to notice the differences between Tappenden and me and to articulate the objections to his treatment given here.)

Finally, I would like to mention Diana Raffman's interesting article, "Vagueness without Paradox," *Philosophical Review*, 103, (1994), 41–74, which I read only after finishing a draft of this chapter. Although Raffman emphasizes the psychology of Sorites judgments whereas I concentrate on using partiality and context-sensitivity to provide a semantic model of vague predicates, there seem to be some significant similarities (as well as important differences) in our views. Because of our different theoretical perspectives on the problem, I am not sure how much of my semantic model she would accept. However, I believe that many of her observations can be incorporated in that model.

I would like to thank John Barker, Neil Delaney, Chrys Gitsoulis, Mark Richard, Diana Raffman, David Sosa, and Jamie Tappenden for reading and commenting on earlier drafts of this chapter.

EIGHT

What Is Truth?

The Deflationary Perspective

In chapter 1, we identified propositions as the primary bearers of our ordinary, prephilosophical notion of truth; utterances and sentences (taken in contexts) were characterized as true iff they express true propositions. In chapter 2, we considered various forms of truth skepticism and argued that none is conclusive. Having dismissed such skepticism, we were ready to take seriously the idea that the notion of truth has a significant role to play in our logical, mathematical, and empirical theories and that something useful and informative can be said about it. To this end, we looked in some detail at two of the most influential, well-developed, and promising theories of truth in the philosophical literature—those of Alfred Tarski and Saul Kripke.

Despite the rich formal development of these theories, both deal with truth in a sharply restricted sense. Neither applies to propositions, and both limit their attention to eternal (non-context-sensitive) sentences of specified formal languages. In Tarski's case, this restriction originally reflected a conception of analysis in which the ordinary (paradox-generating) notion of truth was to be replaced by formally defined substitutes capable of playing the roles demanded of truth predicates in our mathematical and scientific theories. In this respect, we saw that despite the considerable theoretical utility of Tarskian truth predicates, they cannot play the roles reasonably demanded of semantically significant notions of truth in theories of meaning and interpretation. For this reason, Tarski should not be viewed as having successfully replaced or analyzed our ordinary notion. Instead of providing a definition, his theory can be seen as presupposing the notion of truth as we ordinarily understand it and stating certain laws governing its application to sentences of certain restricted formal languages. A similar point applies to Kripke's theory, although in his case the restricted nature of his truth predicate resulted from a simple pragmatic acknowledgment that sentences of formal languages and the predicates applying to them have received more attention and are better understood than other truth bearers and the predicates applying to them.[1] Still, the lessons of his formal construction are broadly applicable and should be seen as illuminating truth as we ordinarily conceive of it. In particular, I argued that ordinary uses of natural-language truth predicates may plausibly be viewed as partially defined and that they share this feature with uses of familiar vague predicates, which are, in addition, context-sensitive.

It is time now to sketch a broader and more philosophical (though less detailed) conception of truth that incorporates the important insights of Tarski and Kripke without artificial restrictions on relevant truth bearers. Among these insights, none is more important than their essentially deflationist conception of truth. For Tarski and Kripke, truth is not a contentious metaphysical or epistemological notion, and a successful analysis of it should not be laden with controversial philosophical consequences. Rather, the content of the claim that a putative truth bearer is true is equivalent to that of the truth bearer itself, a fact that endows the truth predicate with an important practical and theoretical utility. Because the claim that x is true is equivalent to the claim made by x itself, one can get the effect of committing oneself to each member of a class of putative truth bearers by predicating truth of them, even if one is not able to produce, display, or assert the members of that class one by one.

The view that truth is a philosophically uncontentious concept, the content of which is grasped by recognizing the equivalence of a putative truth bearer with the claim that it is true, has come to be known as *deflationism*. This view has attracted a number of philosophers who have developed various versions of the doctrine. In this chapter, we will assess deflationism as a general perspective and evaluate several of its different forms.

We begin with the following observation from Gottlob Frege:

> We cannot recognize a property of a thing without at the same time finding the thought *this thing has this property* to be true. So with every property of a thing there is tied up a property of a thought, namely truth. It is also worth noticing that the sentence 'I smell the scent of violets' has just the same content as the sentence 'It is true that I smell the scent of violets'. So it seems, then, that nothing is added to the thought by my ascribing to it the property of truth. And yet is it not a great result when the scientist after much hesitation and laborious research can finally say 'My conjecture is true'? The meaning of the word 'true' seems to be altogether *sui generis*.[2]

As we saw in chapter 2, there are two points to notice here. First, according to Frege, truth is ascribed to thoughts (propositions), which are the semantic contents of sentences, as well as the objects of propositional attitudes, like belief and assertion. He correctly notes in other places that truth can also be ascribed to sentences, but such ascriptions are derivative; a true sentence is one that expresses a true thought or proposition. Second, in the passage, Frege draws an important contrast between two different linguistic environments in which the truth predicate is used to talk about propositions.

Environment 1.   It is true that S / The proposition that S is true.
Environment 2.   Everything John says is true.
There are true propositions that are not supported by available evidence.
Every proposition is such that either it or its negation is true.

When, in the passage, Frege talks about the sentences *I smell the scent of violets* and *It is true that I smell the scent of violets,* he is concerned with a use of the truth predicate in the first kind of environment. When he talks about the scientist's remark *My conjecture is true,* he is concerned with a use of the truth predicate in the second sort of environment.

Frege observes that when we use the truth predicate in the first sort of environment—to say ⌜It is true that S⌝—we do not seem to be adding anything significant to what we could assert by simply saying S. We may express this cautiously by saying that instances of ⌜It is true that S⌝ and S are trivially equivalent. The propositions they express are necessary and a priori consequences of each other; indeed, each is trivially inferable from the other.[3] Corresponding to this, the proposition expressed by the biconditional ⌜It is true that S iff S⌝ is necessary, a priori, and capable of being known, on the basis of one's linguistic knowledge, by anyone who understands the sentence. Frege also seems to suggest that when the truth predicate is used in the second sort of linguistic environment—as in *My conjecture is true*—it does add something and is not eliminable in the way it is when used in the first kind of context. Although Frege does not elaborate on the importance of this contrast, it turns out to be significant. We may sum it up this way: Environments of type 2 are important because they provide a reason for having a truth predicate of propositions; environments of type 1 are important because they play a privileged role in explaining what such a notion of truth consists in.

What does this mean? First consider environments of type 2. These are cases in which we predicate truth of some proposition or set of propositions that we do not explicitly assert, display, or produce. For example, we might assert that everything John says is true on the basis of our assessment of John's character and intellect even if we do not know everything he says and do not believe the conjunction of everything he has in fact asserted. Similarly, we might claim that every proposition or its negation is true without having to produce an infinite list of disjunctions. In cases like these, we are able to use the truth predicate to say something that we would not be in a position to say without it.[4] By contrast, if we never wished to say of a proposition that it is true without displaying it, as we do with ⌜It is true that S⌝ or ⌜The proposition that S is true⌝, then we could get along reasonably well without a truth predicate by just saying S instead. Thus it is the use of the truth predicate in environments of type 2 that provides the reason we need it.

Now consider environments of type 1. These are involved in the equivalence schemata *It is true that S iff S* and *The proposition that S is true iff S*, which are crucial in explaining what truth consists in. For example, in explaining what it is for the proposition that snow is white to be true, one can scarcely do better than to point out that it is true iff snow is white. In explaining what it is for an arbitrary proposition to be true, it would seem to be enough to note that the same sort of explanation could be given in any individual case. Thus in order to know what truth is, it seems to be enough to know that the proposition that snow is white is true iff snow is white, that the proposition that the earth is round is true iff the earth is round, and so on for propositions generally.[5]

This brings us to the leading idea behind deflationism about truth—namely, that claims of the sort ⌜It is true that S⌝ and ⌜The proposition that S is true⌝ are trivially equivalent to S and that this equivalence is in some sense definitional of the notion of truth. Different versions of deflationism take the form of different variations of this general idea. Among these variations are (i) the claim that there is no such property as truth and that the propositions expressed by sentences of the form ⌜It is true that S⌝ and ⌜The proposition that S is true⌝ are identical with the proposition expressed by S itself; (ii) the view that what is needed for a definition of truth to be adequate is that it entail (appropriate) instances of the above schemata or some closely related schema; (iii) the claim that whether or not it is possible to give an adequate definition of truth, the content of the truth predicate is given by the totality of (appropriate) instances of these truth schemata; and (iv) the idea that one's grasp of the notion of truth consists in one's knowledge of or disposition to accept the propositions expressed by those instances.

Other variations could be added. Even then, however, the general characterization of deflationism would remain somewhat vague and imprecise. The reason for this is that deflationism is not itself an analysis of truth nor a specific thesis about truth; rather, it is a general approach encompassing a variety of more specific proposals. Thus some vagueness at the general level is to be expected. Still, it is fairly clear what sort of thing is to be ruled out. According to deflationism, sweeping, philosophically contentious doctrines about reality and our ability to know it cannot be established by analyzing the notion of truth. Examples of such doctrines are the thesis that a statement is true iff it corresponds to a mind-independent fact that makes it true and the rival thesis that a statement is true iff it would be rational for beings like us to believe it under ideal conditions of inquiry. These are independent philosophical doctrines that cannot be derived from an adequate analysis of truth. The doctrines are compatible with deflationist analyses of truth. However, deflationism is neutral regarding them.

I believe that deflationism, characterized in this admittedly vague and general way, is correct. Demonstrating this is another matter. Short of producing a specific analysis and showing it to be correct, it is unclear how to do this. The problem is that no existing deflationist analysis is completely adequate. With this in mind, I will discuss the leading varieties of deflationism with an eye to separating their virtues from their vices. We will look briefly at representatives of classical redundancy theories of truth, Peter Strawson's performative theory, the semantic theories of Tarski and Kripke, and Paul Horwich's minimal (propositional) theory. In considering these proposals, it is important that we distinguish two ways in which a theory may be deflationist. First, it may attempt to give a deflationary interpretation of our ordinary notion of truth, often in the form of a deflationary account of the content of one or another ordinary use of the word 'true' in English. Second, a theory may offer a deflationary notion of truth as a replacement or substitute for our ordinary notion of truth; if this route is taken, the burden of the analysis is to show that the replacement notion is capable of performing all the legitimate theoretical tasks we require of a notion of truth.

Once we have surveyed a variety of different versions of deflationism, we will take up the question of whether deflationism, properly understood, has significant philosophical consequences. In this connection, we will look at Paul Boghossian's[6] arguments that (i) deflationism about truth is incompatible with philosophical nonfactualism about a given domain of discourse; (ii) nonfactualism about psychological and linguistic content presupposes deflationism about truth and thus is inconsistent; and (iii) deflationism about truth is itself a form of nonfactualism and so is internally inconsistent. I will argue that these contentions are incorrect.

Varieties of Deflationism

The Classical Redundancy Theory

According to the classical redundancy theory,[7] there is no such property as truth, and the predicate *is true* is not used to describe anything. Thus to say that the proposition that the earth is round is true is *not* to refer to a proposition and to describe it as being a certain way; rather it is simply to assert that the earth is round. In general, to say ⌜It is true that S⌝ or ⌜The proposition that S is true⌝ is just to choose a redundant or long-winded way of saying S. The word *true* in such sentences may have the practical function of signaling one's agreement with something that has already been said or conceding a point that one expects to come up. But it does not play any logical role; it has no descriptive content of its own and so does not contribute to the content of what is said.

This theory is most naturally applied in linguistic environments of type 1, in which what one ostensibly predicates truth of is presented or displayed. However, the truth predicate also occurs in linguistic environments of type 2, in which what is said to be true is not directly presented. As we saw in "Nihilism about Truth" in chapter 2, these environments pose serious problems for the redundancy theory.

There we considered (1a), which is naturally understood in the manner suggested by (1b).

    1a. Everything Maria asserted is true.
      b. (p)(Maria asserted p ⊃ p is true)

(1b) involves ordinary, first-order quantification over propositions. Since it contains a truth predicate, redundancy theorists cannot make use of it. Instead such theorists typically resort to the higher-order quantification in (1c).

1c.   (P)(if Maria asserted that P, then P)

Here variables occupy the position of sentences rather than that of singular terms. As a result, instances of (1c) are formed not by replacing variables with names of propositions but rather by replacing variables with sentences.

1d.   If Maria asserted that power corrupts, then power corrupts.

In chapter 2, we considered two standard options for interpreting the quantification in (1c): substitutional and objectual. The most obvious problem with the substitutional interpretation had to do with inherent limitations on the substitution class associated with the variable 'P'. Since (1a) is an English sentence, that class must itself be a set of English sentences. However, English does not have the resources to express every proposition. Thus there are some propositions not expressed by any sentence in the substitution class associated with 'P' in the redundancy analysis (1c) of (1a). Since these propositions are relevant to the truth or falsity of (1a), the substitutional interpretation of (1c) cannot provide a correct analysis of it.

Another problem with substitutional versions of the redundancy theory involves propositions which, although expressed by sentences of English, are expressed by different sentences at different times. These propositions create difficulties in cases in which we want to say that a person continues to believe something that person asserted or believed at an earlier time. The problem is that, intuitively, an ascription such as

2a.   Ralph now believes something he previously asserted (believed)

may be true even if there is not any English sentence S such that

2b.   At (some earlier) t, Ralph asserted (believed) S

and

2c.   Ralph now believes S

are jointly true. If the quantification in (2a) is objectual quantification over propositions, no such sentence will be required. However, if the quantification is substitutional, the truth of (2a) will require such a sentence. Since the facts of English seem to indicate that no such sentence is required, it seems that the quantification found in these examples is not substitutional.

If this is right, then no redundancy analysis involving higher-order substitutional quantification can be correct. This leaves the redundancy theorist with the alternative of interpreting the proposed analysis (1c) of (1a) as involving higher-order quantification over propositions. However, this runs counter to the central motivations of most redundancy theorists since such quantification, if intelligible, not only carries with it an ontological commitment to propositions but also allows one to define a genuine predicate expressing the property of being a true proposition.[8]

In addition, we found other, related problems with the redundancy theory. One type of case involves referring demonstratively to a proposition and saying, "That's true." In the type of case for which the theory was designed, the proposition said to be true is expressed by an assertive utterance or inscription present in the context, making it clear what proposition has been referred to. However, not all instances of referring to a proposition and saying it is true are like this. Just as we can refer to a proposition using an ordinary demonstrative, so we can nondemonstratively refer to a proposition using a proper name. In chapter 2, we considered a case in which a proposition p gets named *Extensionality* and is so inscribed in *The Encyclopedia of Philosophical Logic*. In such a case, one can use the sentence *Extensionality is true* to predicate truth of p even in contexts in which there is no assertive utterance or inscription that expresses p. Since, in general, one can use a name to say something about its referent even if one is unable to identify the relevant entity in any other way, one should be able to use the sentence *Extensionality is true* to predicate truth of the proposition p even in cases in which one is not in a position to state or assert that proposition. In such a case, one has asserted the proposition that Extensionality is true without asserting the proposition p. Therefore, the two propositions, though necessarily equivalent, cannot be identical, and the redundancy analysis fails to account for this type of example.

Because of these difficulties, the redundancy theory cannot be accepted. Although initially tempting as an account of uses of *is true* in environments of type 1, it cannot account for its uses in those environments of type 2 in which what is said to be true is not directly displayed or presented. To account for such cases, *is true* must be treated as a genuine predicate expressing the property truth. Once this is admitted, this analysis applies to ⌜That is true⌝, ⌜The proposition that S is true⌝, and ⌜It is true that S⌝ as well. In other words, there is such a thing as truth; it is a property of things that are said, asserted, and believed; and the predicate *is true* is used to describe these things.[9]

Strawson's Performative Theory

A view sharing much in common with the classical redundancy theory was developed by Peter Strawson in 1949 and 1950.[10] Like redundancy theorists, Strawson held that someone who assertively utters (3a), (3b), or (3c)

   3a. It is true that the earth is round
    b. The proposition that the earth is round is true
    c. That is true (said in response to an assertion that the earth is round)

does not refer to a proposition and predicate truth of it. There is no property truth, and the phrase *is true* never functions to describe anything. Why, then, do we have the predicate, and how does it function? According to Strawson, to say ⌜It is true that S⌝ is to assert the proposition expressed by S and only that proposition; however, it is also to *do* something other than make an assertion: it is to perform the speech act of confirming, endorsing, or conceding the proposition expressed by S. It is in its contributions to these speech acts that Strawson locates the central function of the truth predicate.

There is, I think, no denying that there are subtle conversational differences of the sorts Strawson has in mind between uses of ⌜It is true that S⌝ and ⌜That S is true⌝, on the one hand, and S, on the other.[11] However, these differences do not provide the chief rationale for the truth predicate. Rather, that is provided by examples in which what is said to be true is not directly displayed or presented. One example of this type is (4).

4. What the policeman said is true.

Strawson says that someone who utters (4) can be regarded as implicitly making what he calls the "second order, existential meta-statement" (5).

5. The policeman made a statement.

According to Strawson, (5) can be regarded

> as part [but not all] of the analysis of [(4)]. . . . To complete the analysis, then of the entire sentence [(4)] "What the policeman said is true," we have to add, to the existential meta-assertion, a phrase which is not assertive but (if I may borrow Mr. Austin's word) performatory. We might, e.g., offer, as a complete analysis of one case, the expression: "The policeman made a statement. I confirm it"; where, in uttering the words "I confirm it," I am not describing something I do, but *doing* something.[12]

This view, though admirably clear, fails in two fundamental respects. First, it gives an incorrect account of what is and what is not done when one utters sentences like (4). Second, even when its account of the speech acts performed in uttering certain sentences is substantially correct, its analysis of their meaning is not. This is shown by three counterarguments to the theory.

The first counterargument is directed against claim (A), which slightly extends Strawson's remarks about (4).

A. In uttering *What the policeman said is true*, one confirms, endorses, or concedes what the policeman said (provided that he said something); in uttering *Several/some/many things the policeman said are true*, one confirms, endorses, or concedes several/some/many things the policeman said (providing that he said a number of things).

In showing this claim to be false, it is useful to note the contrast between the following pairs of sentences.

6a.   John is caring for several/some/many kittens.
  b.   There are several/some/many kittens that John is caring for.
7a.   John is looking for several/some/many kittens.
  b.   There are several/some/many kittens that John is looking for.

Whereas (6a) entails (6b), (7a) does not entail (7b). The verbs used in Strawson's performative theory—*confirm, endorse, concede*—are like *care for* and unlike *look for* in this respect. One cannot confirm, endorse, or concede something unless there is something that one confirms, endorses, or concedes. Thus (8a) entails (8b).

8a.   John has confirmed several/some/many statements in the report.
  b.   Several/some/many statements in the report are such that John has confirmed them.

This fact can be used to show the falsity of claim (A). Imagine that John has some but not complete confidence in a certain policeman who has written a report; the policeman typically gets most of what he says right but from time to time makes mistakes. John, not knowing the contents of the report, might nevertheless feel confident enough to claim that many statements in the report are true. Despite this, there is not even one statement in the report such that John has said that it is true. So there is not even one statement in the report that John has confirmed. Therefore, it is not the case that many statements in the report are such that John has confirmed them. But then since (8b) is false, (8a) is also false. John has said that many statements in the report are true, but he has not confirmed any of them.[13]

This argument shows that many sentences in which *is true* occurs (in linguistic environments of type 2) are not standardly used to perform the speech acts specified by the performative theory. The next argument shows that a primary function of the predicate in such sentences is descriptive. The idea is simple. Utterances of sentences containing *true* are used to assess statements. Since such utterances can themselves be assessed by further uses of *true*, they must also make statements.

For example, suppose that a person x, testifying before a legislative committee, says several things, including something false. The next day y, testifying before the committee, makes several true claims plus the claim (9).

9.   Every assertion made by x to the committee was true.

What is the status of y's remark that every assertion made by x was true? Clearly it is false. Strangely, the performative theory does not allow this. According to it, the only assertion made by y's utterance of (9) was the assertion (10), which is true.

10.   x made some assertions to the committee.

Hence according to the performative theory, all of y's *assertions* were true, and none was false. Hence the performative theory is committed to (11).

11.   Every assertion y made to the committee is true.

Since this is incompatible with the datum that y said something false, the performative theory fails.

If these arguments are correct, then the performative theory gives the wrong account of both the use and the meaning of sentences in which the truth predicate occurs in linguistic environments of type 2. However, its central error is even more general: the theory systematically fails to distinguish meaning from use. For example, it is correct to observe that ⌜The proposition that P is true⌝ is often used, when uttered assertively, to endorse, confirm, or concede the proposition expressed by P. However, it is a mistake to think that this observation provides an analysis of the meaning of such a sentence. To suppose otherwise is to ignore a crucial requirement placed on analyses of meaning—that of specifying the contributions made by expressions to larger sentences or discourses in which they may be embedded. When these larger linguistic contexts are considered, it becomes obvious that a sentence like ⌜The proposition that P is true⌝ may be used with its literal meaning even though its content has nothing to do with the speech acts with which the performative theory associates it.

This point is illustrated by the following pairs of examples.

12a.   Either the proposition that there are 3 consecutive 7's in the decimal expansion of π is true, or the proposition that there are not is true.
  b.   Either I endorse/confirm/concede that there are 3 consecutive 7's in the decimal expansion of π, or I endorse/confirm/concede that there are not.
13a.   I do not know whether the proposition that budget deficits cause inflation is true.
  b.   I do not know whether I endorse/confirm/concede that budget deficits cause inflation.
14a.   The ancients believed that the proposition that Hesperus was a star was true.
  b.   The ancients believed that I endorsed/confirmed/conceded that Hesperus was a star.
15a.   The proposition that the earth is round would have been true even if I had not endorsed/confirmed/conceded it.
  b.   I would have endorsed/confirmed/conceded that the earth is round even if I had not endorsed/confirmed/conceded it.

The (a) and (b) sentences of these pairs clearly differ in meaning and even truth value. Since the members of the pairs are alike except for containing corresponding grammatical variants of (16a) and (16b), these sentences must themselves differ in meaning.

16a.   The proposition that P is true.
  b.   I endorse/confirm/concede that P.

The same holds for other constructions involving the truth predicate. Thus the performative theory's analysis of truth is a nonstarter.[14]

Semantic Versions of Deflationism

Tarski   We now turn to the most famous and influential version of deflationism: Tarski's semantic conception of truth. Unlike the accounts just sketched, Tarski's conception was concerned with truth predicates of sentences—in particular, sentences of precisely specified object-languages of certain well-known kinds. His achievement was to show how to define a truth predicate for each such language using only nonsemantic concepts already expressible in the object-language, purely syntactic concepts applying to expressions in that language, and elementary set theory plus logic. As we have seen, in standard cases, the definitions can be shown to be materially adequate and so to introduce a truth predicate coextensive, over the object-language, with our ordinary notion of truth.

It is important to be clear about what this involves. To say that a truth definition is materially adequate is to say that it entails an instance of schema T for each sentence of the object-language.

Schema T.   s is true (in L) iff P.[15]

Why are we so confident that a definition of truth that is materially adequate in this sense introduces a truth predicate that is extensionally equivalent, over the object-language, with our ordinary notion of truth? The answer, I think, is that it is part of our ordinary concept of truth, of what we mean by the predicate *true*, that the claim that a sentence is true is materially equivalent to the sentence itself and hence to any sentence with the same meaning. We may express this by noting that, given our ordinary concept of truth, we take all instances of schema (17) to be trivial, a priori, and necessary.

17.   If s means in L that P, then s is true in L iff P.[16]

It is because we are justified in taking (17) for granted that we are justified in assuming that any definition that is materially adequate in Tarski's sense introduces a predicate that applies to all and only the truths (in the ordinary sense) of the object-language.

Because of this, there should be no question that a Tarskian truth predicate for a language L is coextensive over L with our ordinary truth predicate. However, one might well question whether Tarski provides an *analysis* of the notion of truth. In general, mere coextensiveness is not sufficient for an analysis, nor will it help to appeal to synonymy. Since our ordinary notion of truth applies to propositions and, derivatively, to sentences of arbitrary languages whereas Tarski's truth predicates do not, his predicates are not synonymous with our ordinary notion. In what sense then does it make sense to claim that he provided an analysis of truth? The answer, as I suggested in chapter 4, involves conceiving of a Tarskian definition of truth for a particular language in the way that Tarski himself did—namely, as a stipulative definition that introduces a new, restricted truth predicate designed to do the theoretical work, over a limited domain, of our unrestricted, pretheoretic notion of truth. The claim that Tarski provided an adequate analysis of truth can then be taken to be the claim that his formally defined truth predicates are, in principle, capable of doing all the theoretical work that can legitimately be demanded of a notion of truth.

Earlier I indicated that this claim derives support from the fact that Tarski's definition of truth has proven to be theoretically fruitful. A striking feature of the definition is that it links the truth or falsity of a sentence to properties of its structurally significant parts. Because of this, it provides both the tools needed for systematic metatheoretical investigations of object-language sentences and the basis for compelling analyses of logical truth and logical consequence. This shows that Tarski's notion of truth performs some of the legitimate theoretical functions required of a notion of truth. But why might one think that it can perform them all? The answer, I suspect, lies in the thought that a Tarskian truth predicate for L captures not only the extension but also the meaning of our ordinary truth predicate when restricted to L. If that were indeed so, then one could be sure that any theoretical work involving L that could be done by the ordinary notion of truth could be done by Tarski's notion as well.

In chapter 3, I pointed out that Tarski regarded individual instances of schema T—like 'Snow is white' is true in English iff snow is white—as partial definitions that give the meaning of the word true as applied to particular sentences. Because of this, he took the problem of giving a general definition that captures the meaning of true to be that of finding a generalization that entails each partial definition. Here is a representative passage:

> We begin with a simple problem. Consider a sentence in English whose meaning does not raise any doubts, say the sentence 'snow is white'. For brevity we denote this sentence by 'S', so that 'S' becomes the name of the sentence. We ask ourselves the question: What do we mean by saying that S is true or that it is false? The answer to this question is simple: in the spirit of Aristotelian explanation, by saying that S is true we mean simply that snow is white, and by saying that S is false we mean that snow is not white. By eliminating the symbol 'S' we arrive at the following formulations:
>
> (1) 'Snow is white' is true if and only if snow is white
>
> (1') 'Snow is white' is false if and only if snow is not white.
>
> Thus (1) and (1') provide satisfactory explanations of the meaning of the terms 'true' and 'false' when these terms are referred to the sentence 'snow is white'. We can regard (1) and (1') as partial definitions of the terms 'true' and 'false', in fact, as definitions of these terms with respect to a particular sentence. Notice that (1), as well as (1'), has the form prescribed for definitions by the rules of logic, namely the form of logical equivalence. It consists of two parts, the left and the right side of the equivalence, combined by the connective 'if and only if'. The left side is the definiendum, the phrase whose meaning is explained by the definition; the right side is the definiens, the phrase that provides the explanation.[17]

If individual instances of schema T are regarded as partial definitions that give the ordinary and recognized meaning of the word *true* when applied to particular sentences, then it is natural to regard the problem of giving a general definition that captures the ordinary and recognized meaning of the word as that of finding an appropriate generalization that entails each partial definition. This is how Tarski conceived of the problem.[18] In short, his view was that since instances of schema T using our ordinary truth predicate are definitional, a formal definition that has all these partial definitions as consequences will capture the meaning of our ordinary notion. This, I believe, is what stands behind his remark in "The Semantic Conception of Truth and the Foundations of Semantics" that his definition "does not aim to specify the meaning of a familiar word used to denote a novel notion; on the contrary, it aims to catch hold of the actual meaning of an old notion."[19] Since Tarski took himself to have succeeded in this, it is only natural that he should have thought that his formally defined truth predicate could play all the legitimate theoretical roles for which we need a notion of truth for the object-language. It is therefore no surprise that he should express his confidence in this position, as he does in section 13 of "The Semantic Conception of Truth and the Foundations of Semantics," where he says that his notion of truth (satisfaction) can be used to define central concepts in the theory of meaning.

Surprising or not, this position is demonstrably incorrect. In particular, (i) an instance of '*S' is true (in L)*, in which a sentence s replaces the symbol '*S*', does not mean the same thing as s; (ii) instances of schema T are not definitional of the ordinary notion of truth; (iii) Tarski's formally defined truth predicates differ substantially in meaning from our ordinary truth predicate, even when restricted to the relevant object-languages; and (iv) this difference in meaning has significant theoretical consequences: whereas our ordinary notion of truth can play a substantial role in providing semantic interpretations of sentences of formal languages and in developing theories of meaning for natural languages, Tarski's truth predicates cannot.

Let us review these points one by one. (i) If the English sentence *The earth is round* meant the same as the metalinguistic sentence *'The earth is round' is true (in English)*, then they would express the same propositions; hence anyone who believed one would believe the other. In point of fact, however, someone who does not know English, or at least does not know the meaning of the English sentence *The earth is round*, might believe either of these propositions without believing (or having any basis for inferring) the other. Hence the propositions are different. They may even fail to be necessarily equivalent. If expressions could have meant something other than what they actually mean or if they could have failed to exist (if there had never been any speakers, say), then the proposition that the earth is round could have been true even if the proposition that 'The earth is round' is true (in English) was not. As a result, an instance of '*S' is true*, in which a sentence s replaces the symbol '*S*', does not mean the same thing or express the same proposition as s.

Next consider point (ii), instances of schema T are not definitional of our ordinary notion of truth. In order to simplify matters, let us restrict our attention to homophonic instances of the form '*S' is true in English iff S* (or '*S' is a true sentence of English iff S).* The idea that these instances are definitional of the notion of truth is deceptively seductive and far too widespread. Here is a rational reconstruction of the reasoning behind it.

The Argument That Homophonic Instances of Schema T Are Definitional of the Notion of Truth

a.   If one is a competent speaker of English who knows what quotation, *iff*, and the phrase *is true in English* mean, then one has all the information one needs to conclude that all instances of 'S' *is true in English iff P* that result from replacing the letter 'S' with a "normal" (unparadoxical, non-indeterminate, non-context-sensitive) declarative sentence of English and the letter 'P' with a sentence that means the same as the sentence that replaces 'S' are true.

b.   So if one is a competent speaker of English who knows what quotation, *iff*, and the phrase *is true in English* mean, then one has all the information one needs to conclude that all instances of 'S' *is true in English iff S* are truths of English, where an instance is the result of replacing both occurrences of the letter 'S' with a "normal" (unparadoxical, nonindeterminate, non-context-sensitive) declarative sentence of English.

c.   If, in addition, e is such a sentence and one understands e, then one has all the information needed to accept the instance of 'S' *is true in English iff S* that results from substituting sentence e for each occurrence of the letter 'S' and to conclude that it is true.

d.   Given that one understands this instance, accepts it, and knows it to be true, one knows the proposition p it expresses.

e.   It follows that each (normal, nonindeterminate, non-context-sensitive) instance of schema T for English expresses a proposition p that competent speakers of English can be expected to know solely on the basis of their understanding *is true* together with the expressions occurring in the instance.

f.   Because of this, the relevant instances of schema T are definitional of the ordinary truth predicate for English in the following sense: accepting these instances is necessary and sufficient for understanding the predicate, and any (consistent, formally correct) definition that entails all these instances captures the ordinary meaning of the predicate.

Since I have already indicated that the conclusion (f) is false, the argument must go wrong at some point. Where? Aside from worries about problematic sentences, such as those that are vague, ungrounded, or paradoxical, step (a) is alright. If one knows what 'S' *is true in English iff* means, then one knows that any instance of the schema 'S' *is true in English iff P* which results from replacing 'P' with some sentence (of one's language) that means the same as the English sentence that replaces 'S' will express a truth (in one's language). The main problem with the argument occurs at steps (b) and (c). The case of (c) is particularly clear and can be illustrated by comparing the sentences (18a) and (18b).

18a.   'Snow is white' is true in English iff snow is white.
  b.   'Snow is white' is true in my language iff snow is white.

Suppose that my language is English but that I do not know that the word *English* refers to my language. I understand the word and know a number of things about it—for example, that it designates a language spoken in England, North America, Australia, and New Zealand. However, I do not know that it designates the language I speak. This is clearly possible, just as it is possible for me to understand the name *Japanese* without knowing that it is the language I hear on channel 25, to understand the name *Boston* without knowing that I am presently located in the city it designates, or to understand the name *October* without knowing that it designates the current month. If I am in this situation and I do not know that *English* designates my language, then my attitudes toward the sentences (18a) and (18b) may be different.

We may suppose that I know that (18b) is a true sentence of my language, that I accept it, and that I believe the proposition it expresses. Sentence (18a) is also a sentence of my language; moreover, it is one I understand. Do I know that it expresses a truth? Do I accept it? Do I believe the proposition it expresses? Let us suppose not only that I understand the construction '*S*' *is true in L iff* but also that I know that both it and the word *English* are parts of the language designated by *English* and that their meanings in that language are precisely what I take them to be (in my language).[20] We may then suppose that I accept (19a) and (19b).

19a.   All sentences of the form '*S*' *is true in English iff S* that result from substituting a (proper) declarative sentence of English for each occurrence of '*S*' are truths of English.
  b.   All sentences of the form '*S*' *is true in my language iff S* that result from substituting a (proper) declarative sentence of my language for each occurrence of '*S*' are truths of my language.

The sentence *Snow is white* is a sentence of my language that I understand and recognize as a sentence of my language. However, I may not realize that it is a sentence of the language designated by the name *English*. Thus I may fail to assent to or I may even dissent from (20a) while accepting (20b).

20a.   'Snow is white' is a sentence of English.
  b.   'Snow is white' is a sentence of my language.

Because of this, I may fail to accept or I may even dissent from (21a) while accepting (21b).

21a.   '*Snow is white*' *is true in English iff snow is white* is a truth of English.
  b.   '*Snow is white*' *is true in my language iff snow is white* is a truth of my language.

Next consider (22).

22. *'Snow is white' is true in English iff snow is white* is a truth of my language.

We may imagine that I accept this sentence iff I accept its disquotational version (18a) (which is just the italicized part of [22]). One reason for failing to accept these sentences has already been covered: although I may believe that snow is white, I may not realize that the words *Snow is white* constitute a sentence of the language designated by *English*. Moreover, even if I do realize this, there is another reason why I may fail to accept (22) and (18a): I may not believe that the sentence *Snow is white* means in the language designated by *English* what it means in my language. Indeed, I may suspect that it means something in the language designated by *English* that has a truth value different from the truth value it has in my language. All this goes to show that understanding and reflecting about homophonic instances of schema T of the sort illustrated by (18a) do not guarantee that one has a sufficient basis for accepting them, believing them to be true, or believing the propositions they express. Hence homophonic instances of schema T of this sort are *not* definitional of the notion of truth, as we ordinarily understand it.[21]

There are, of course, other T-sentences one might consider—for example, instances of 'S' *is true in my language iff* S. There is an obvious sense in which these T-sentences are properly regarded as trivial by any English speaker who understands them. They are trivial in that anyone who uses and understands them on a given occasion will have reason to accept them and believe the propositions they express on that occasion. But even if some version of (e) in the previous argument could be established for these highly special instances, the conclusion (f) still could not. Since the propositions expressed by S and ⌜'S' is true in my language⌝ are obviously neither necessary nor epistemic consequences of one another, the relevant instances of schema T are not definitional in the required sense.[22]

Next consider point (iii), which states that a Tarskian truth predicate for L differs substantially in meaning from our ordinary truth predicate, even when restricted to L. The correctness of this point was established in chapter 4, where it was shown that T-sentences containing the two predicates carry different information. For example, let us take 's' to name some particular sentence, (23a) to contain our ordinary truth predicate, and (23b) to contain the definiens, T, of Tarski's formal definition.

23a. s is true in L iff P.
  b. s is T in L iff P.

As we saw, if one does not already know the meaning of s but one does grasp our ordinary notion of truth, then one can learn something about the meaning of s by being given (23a). For example, one can use the relevant, trivial, a priori instance of schema (17) to conclude from (23a) that s does not mean that $\sim$P.

Not so with (23b). If one does not already understand s but one does understand Tarski's definiens, one cannot learn anything about s's meaning simply by being given (23b). The reason for this is that the analogue of (17) that results from substituting Tarski's definiens for the ordinary predicate *is true* is not a trivial a priori schema and so is not available for drawing conclusions about meaning.[23]

Another way to bring out the same point involves the notion of material adequacy. Given a Tarskian definition of a putative truth predicate T plus knowledge of the meanings of object-language sentences, we can show that the definition is correct by demonstrating that it is materially adequate. However, the definition itself does not say anything about its own material adequacy and does not include any claims about the meanings of object-language expressions. Hence given the definition alone without an antecedent understanding of the object-language, one would have no basis for concluding that the predicate introduced by the definition applied to all and only the truths of the language as opposed to the falsehoods or some arbitrary class of sentences. As a result, T-sentences like (23b) carry no information about meaning even though T-sentences like (23a) do. Hence Tarski's truth predicate does not mean the same thing as our ordinary truth predicate, restricted to the object-language (point [iii]). Because of this, his truth predicate cannot be used to interpret sentences or to play a substantial role in a theory of meaning in the manner of our ordinary truth predicate (point [iv]).

As a consequence, Tarski cannot be regarded as having provided an adequate analysis of truth. Moreover, there is reason to believe that any adequate analysis will have to recognize truth as primarily a property of propositions and derivatively a property of sentences. Only then, in my view, can we explain why statements of truth conditions carry information about meaning. The crucial fact is that our ordinary notion of truth is conceptually connected to the notion of meaning in a way that makes instances of schema (17) trivial, a priori necessities. In chapter 4, I suggested that (where no indexicality is involved and s expresses the same proposition on different occasions of use) these properties of instances of (17) are the result of the fact that (i) a sentence s means in L that P iff s expresses in L the proposition that P and (ii) s is true in L iff the proposition expressed by s in L is true. Given this, (17) amounts to (24).

24.   If s expresses the proposition that P in L, then the proposition expressed by s in L is true iff P.

Instances of this schema inherit their obviousness from trivial, a priori, and necessary instances of the propositional schema PT.[24]

PT.   The proposition that P is true iff P.

If this is right, then the semantic bite of statements that give the truth conditions of sentences comes from and is explained by the implicit commitment to propositions carried by our ordinary notion of truth.

Kripke's Theory   Before leaving the topic of semantic theories of truth, I want to add a word about the broader significance of the theory expounded in chapter 6, based on Saul Kripke's "Outline of a Theory of Truth." For present purposes, what is important is that Kripke's work on the Liar contains important deflationist lessons that ultimately must be incorporated into any adequate analysis. The guiding deflationary intuition behind his formal construction is the idea that the status of the claim that a sentence s is true or not true is dependent on the prior status of s or its negation. Roughly put, the truth predicate is governed by rules that license one to assert that s is true in precisely those cases in which one is licensed to assertively utter s and to assert that s is not true in precisely those cases in which one is licensed to assertively utter the negation of s.

As we have seen, although many sentences containing the word *true* can be evaluated using these rules, some sentences never receive any evaluation. Examples of these are the paradoxical (25a) and the puzzling (and ungrounded) but unparadoxical (25b).

25a.   Sentence (25a) is not true.
  b.   Sentence (25b) is true.

The linguistic rules governing Kripke's truth predicate do not license either the claim that these sentences are true or the claim that they are not true. The reason for this is that the procedure for introducing the truth predicate makes the status of the claim that s is true (or not true) dependent on the prior status of s and ultimately on the status of sentences that do not contain the truth predicate at all. When this dependence can be traced from a sentence containing the truth predicate all the way back to (grounded) sentences that do not contain it, the original sentence will either be determined to be true or be determined not to be true. When the dependence cannot be traced back in this way, the rules for characterizing sentences as true or not true will simply give no result. Because of this, the instructions governing the truth predicate can be seen as providing sufficient conditions for an arbitrary sentence to be true and sufficient conditions for an arbitrary sentence not to be true. However, these conditions are not jointly exhaustive because there is a class of sentences that the instructions are silent about. The truth predicate is therefore "gappy" or partially defined.

In chapter 6, we saw that this alone does not constitute a final solution to the Liar paradox. Nevertheless, Kripke's account illustrates an important lesson: Any successful analysis of truth must provide both an explanation of pathological sentences like (25a) and (25b),[25] and a treatment of the corresponding pathological T-sentences that saves the analysis from contradiction or incoherence. In particular, it is not enough for a deflationist simply to maintain that nonpathological instances of schema T (or of related schemata involving propositions) give the content of the truth predicate. On the contrary, we need some antecedent account of the content of the truth predicate to identify which sentences (or propositions) and corresponding instances of T-schemata are pathological and to explain what the pathology amounts to in particular cases. It is not as if the needed T-equivalences were given to us antecedently and we then decide to use them to give content to a truth predicate. Rather, we possess some rules that determine the content of the truth predicate, and we use these rules both to explain the obviousness of the normal T-equivalences and to separate them from the pathological ones. It is a virtue of Kripke's account that it provides a broadly deflationary model for doing this.

Horwich's Minimal Theory

According to Paul Horwich, truth is an indefinable but trivially transparent property of propositions.[26] Its content is exhausted by what he calls the "minimal theory": the collection of all nonparadoxical T-propositions. These are biconditional propositions in which one side consists of a proposition p and the other consists of a proposition that attributes truth to p. This collection of propositions is uncountable; in fact, it is too large even to constitute a set. Hence there can be no question of exhaustively formulating the minimal theory in a single language. The portion that is formulatable in English is expressed by the totality of nonparadoxical instances of schema PT.

PT.   The proposition that P is true iff P.

The content of the property truth is taken to be given by the totality of nonparadoxical propositional equivalences of this sort. Since there is nothing more to be grasped about it than its role in this vast collection of equivalences, to grasp the property is to be disposed to believe these equivalences. Horwich adds that to understand the word *true* in English is to be disposed to accept, without evidence, any instance of schema PT that is obtained by replacing 'p' with a declarative sentence of English that one understands.[27]

It should be clear from this that Horwich is a deflationist. However, he is not a redundancy theorist. He does not hold that *true* fails to express a property or that the proposition that p is true is the same as the proposition that p.[28] It should also be noted that although he takes the T-equivalences to give the content of the notion of truth, he emphasizes that the reason the notion is important to us and the reason we have a truth predicate is that it allows us to generalize, or commit ourselves to propositions that we are not in a position to state. Thus his minimal conception fully recognizes the importance of what I earlier characterized as uses of the truth predicate in linguistic environments of type 2.

In my opinion, there is much about Horwich's minimal conception of truth that is correct. Nonpathological T-propositions are both necessary and a priori. In addition, it is plausible to suppose that they are trivial — that is, that anyone who grasps the notion of truth and is familiar with the propositional constituents of one of these T-propositions will be inclined to accept it (when presented in an appropriate way). Corresponding to this, the sentences of English that constitute nonpathological instances of schema PT may well be analytic in the sense that any person who understands the truth predicate and is presented with one of these instances that the person fully understands would be justified in accepting it.[29]

The question then is not whether the minimal conception of truth is correct on many basic points; it is. The crucial question is whether the minimal theory explains everything about truth that needs explaining.

It should be clear from the previous discussion of Kripke that I do not think it does. Our grasp of the property truth is not exhausted by our dispositions to accept T-propositions about ground-level propositions, which do not themselves contain the concept of truth. On the contrary, we find some T-propositions about "higher-level" (truth-attributing) propositions fully acceptable, even trivial; others we find puzzling and pathological; while still others are outright paradoxical. These reactions are not arbitrary. There is something about our grasp of the notion of truth that guides them. No account that leaves this out can be complete. Rather, an adequate theory of truth must correctly identify the different classes of T-propositions — unproblematic, pathological, and paradoxical — and it must explain why these different classes have the characteristics they do. An important constraint on such an account is that it treat unproblematic T-propositions and the sentences that express them as having modal, epistemic, and semantic properties that Horwich suggests. But this is a constraint on an adequate theory, not the theory itself.

The minimal theory is also incomplete in another respect. There are many generalizations about truth that the minimal theory alone does not suffice to explain. Consider, for example, the elementary claim (26).[30]

26. For any propositions p and q, the conjunction of p and q is true iff p is true and q is true.

Since the minimal theory consists entirely of T-propositions, it does not contain (26) or any other generalization. (26) is also not a logical consequence of the theory. To see this, interpret the quantifiers in (26) as ranging over propositions expressed by sentences of a language L, and imagine we are speaking in a meta-language containing the fragment of the minimal theory applying to propositions expressible in L — namely, the totality of instances of schema PT involving sentences of L. Each instance of (26) is a logical consequence of the instances of PT plus some statement of what counts as a conjunction — for example, the proposition expressed by a sentence ⌜P and Q⌝.[31] However, (24) is a universal generalization, and universal generalizations are not logical consequences of the set of all their instances. Thus although the minimal theory restricted to L gives us each instance of (26), it cannot give us (26) itself.[32]

I take this to be a genuine problem. Because the minimal theory is just a collection of instances, it is conceivable that one could know every proposition in the theory and still be unable to infer (26) because one is ignorant about whether the propositions covered by one's instances are all the (relevant) propositions there are. For example, given only the minimal theory, one might think: Perhaps there are more propositions and the predicate *true* applies differently to them. A person in such a position has no guarantee of (26) and might lack sufficient justification for accepting it. It seems doubtful that such a person should be credited with understanding the word *true* or with grasping the notion of truth. On the contrary, it seems that grasp of the notion of truth (plus an understanding of what a conjunction is) should be sufficient for knowing (26). Since in the minimal theory this would not be sufficient, the minimal theory does not give us an adequate account of what truth is.[33]

One could, of course, simply add (26) to the minimal theory as a separate proposition. But where would this end? Lots of other generalizations about truth are equally good candidates for inclusion. Perhaps there is some small finite number of them from which the rest follow, and perhaps these could be added. However, such a strategy would mean the end of the minimal theory and its replacement by some sort of propositional version of Kripke's approach or some other. Such a theory might even turn out to contain generalizations strong enough to entail the T-equivalences of the minimal theory and to distinguish them from T-equivalences involving pathological truth ascriptions. If so, this would be all to the good, for if such a theory is possible, it is the sort of thing we should be after.

This point is connected with another aspect of Horwich's discussion that I find problematic. He defines falsity for a proposition as its not being true; he accepts the law of the excluded middle; and he denies that there can be truth-value gaps of any kind.[34] Although related, these issues are separable. Particularly problematic, in my view, are the acceptance of the law of the excluded middle and the denial of truth-value gaps. A central question here is whether there exist partially defined predicates (and properties) of the sort discussed in chapters 6 and 7. When a predicate F is partially defined, there will be objects to which it applies, objects to which it does not apply, and objects for which it is undefined. The latter are objects for which the linguistic rules governing the predicate have nothing to say about whether or not it applies to them. To assert of any such object ⌜it is F⌝ or to assert ⌜it is not F⌝ is to do something that goes beyond what can be licensed by the rules that give the predicate its meaning. Therefore, when F is undefined for o, we must reject both ⌜it is F⌝ and ⌜it is not F⌝.

In chapter 7, I argued that vague predicates are partially defined in this way and require rejection of certain instances of the law of the excluded middle. In chapter 6, I presented two reasons for thinking that the truth predicate is also partially defined. First, if ⌜Fn⌝ is a sentence in which a partially defined predicate is applied to an object for which it is undefined, then the claim expressed by ⌜It is true that Fn⌝ or ⌜It is not true that Fn⌝ should have the same status as the claim made by ⌜Fn⌝ or its negation. But then since both of these latter claims must be rejected, both of the former claims must also be rejected, thereby indicating that the truth predicate is undefined for this case. Second, I argued that the proper philosophical interpretation of the intuition guiding Kripke's formal approach to the Liar paradox is one that treats the truth predicate as being partially defined in the sense indicated here. Since I regard this as a promising approach, I take it to provide a reason to believe in truth-value gaps of this special kind.

It is not my intention to reargue these points of controversy with Horwich here. However, I do want to emphasize that deflationism is not an issue in the controversy. Neither deflationism nor Horwich's proposed definition of a proposition's being false iff it is not true[35] favors one side or the other regarding the possibility of partially defined predicates, the rejection of certain instances of the law of the excluded middle, or the existence of truth-value gaps of this special sort. Horwich's own position on these issues is dictated neither by a commitment to deflationism in general nor by the minimal theory. Hence for present purposes, we can set these positions aside.

The final point in Horwich's discussion I want to touch on concerns the broader philosophical implications of deflationism. In section 29 of chapter 5, he considers the following objection to his minimal conception of truth: "There is a substantive issue in meta-ethics as to whether evaluative utterances purport to assert truths or whether they are merely expressions of feeling; but this question would be trivialized by minimalism."[36]

In response to this objection, Horwich says the following:

> There has indeed been a tendency for ethical emotivists (also known as 'non-cognitivists'), to want to use the notion of truth-value to distinguish 'genuine descriptions' from syntactically similar sentences whose linguistic role is arguably non-descriptive. And this practice certainly is at odds with a minimalist perspective, from which ethical propositions are perfectly good and useful instances of the equivalence schema.

After noting this apparent incompatibility between minimalism and the usual formulations of emotivism, Horwich goes on to suggest that emotivism be reformulated so as to eliminate the conflict.

I will not be concerned with the proposed reformulation. Rather, the question I want to address is whether there is a genuine conflict between deflationism on the one hand and emotivism or other varieties of nonfactualism on the other. It is helpful to begin with a sketch of a hypothetical position that really does conflict with deflationism. (i) Suppose a philosopher maintains that ethical sentences of the sort *Act A is right/wrong/obligatory* express propositions that speakers assert. (ii) Suppose further that the philosopher is willing to use, seriously and sincerely, some of these sentences—to say that certain acts are right, wrong, or obligatory. (iii) Finally, suppose that the philosopher maintains that no ethical statements are true or false and hence that none is true.

This hypothetical position really does conflict with deflationism. Given (i), the philosopher will assert some claims of the form (27a).

27a. X said (asserted) that A is right/wrong/obligatory.

Given (ii), the philosopher will also assert corresponding claims of the form (27b).

27b. A is right/wrong/obligatory.

However, given (iii), the philosopher will deny (27c).

27c. What x said—namely, that A is right/wrong/obligatory—is true.

This does conflict with deflationism since according to deflationism acceptance of a pair of premises (28a) and (28b) commits one to the conclusion (28c).

28a.   X said (asserted) that S.
 b.   S.
 c.   What x said (asserted) — namely, that S — is true.

However, this is not a substantive philosophical consequence of one particular approach to truth; rather, it is a feature of any acceptable theory.[38]

Is there some further, special relationship between deflationism and emotivism that goes beyond this? I do not see one. The classical emotivist denies that evaluative sentences express propositions that are either true or false on the grounds that they do not express propositions at all. Rather, the emotivist maintains that evaluative sentences have something like the force of imperatives such as (29a) or explicit performatives such as (29b).

29a.   Don't perform acts of that type!
 b.   I recommend not doing that.

It is part of his view that someone who uses evaluative sentences in the normal way does not assert any evaluative proposition, just as one who uses (29a) does not assert any special (truth-valueless) imperative proposition and one who uses (29b) does not assert any proposition about oneself. But if no proposition is asserted, then there is no candidate for being true and hence no need for any special, inflationist doctrine about truth.

It must be admitted that the classical emotivist view that normal indicative, evaluative sentences do not express and are not used to assert evaluative propositions is extremely implausible. From the point of view of ordinary use, evaluative sentences have all the linguistic marks of ordinary, proposition-expressing sentences and none of the marks of imperatives, interrogatives, or explicit performatives.[39] For example, normal indicative sentences containing evaluative terms are routinely embedded in truth-functional and other clearly proposition-taking constructions such as antecedents of conditionals in ways that imperatives, interrogatives, and explicit performatives are not. They are also used as linguistic objects of propositional attitude verbs such as *assert*, *believe*, and *realize*, whereas sentences like imperatives, which clearly do not express propositions, are not possible linguistic objects of such verbs. Such facts make a strong prima facie case for the view that ordinary indicative sentences containing evaluative words do express propositions after all.

The case for this view does not come from deflationism. Deflationism is perfectly compatible with the claim that some grammatically indicative sentences do not express propositions and are not used to make assertions. What makes systematic nonfactualism implausible is that the usual domains selected as covertly non-proposition-expressing have all the normal semantic and syntactic properties of ordinary fact-stating discourse and few of the semantic and syntactic properties of non-fact-stating discourse. One could say, I suppose, that deflationism is helpful in illuminating the basic dilemma of classical emotivism — namely, that of being caught between the absurdity of asserting (28a) and (28b) while denying (28c) on the one hand and the implausibility of maintaining that normal indicative sentences containing evaluative words are not used to assert propositions on the other. But this does not show that deflationism has significant philosophical consequences any more than arithmetic has significant philosophical consequences in virtue of being inconsistent with the (revisionary) philosophical view that there cannot be infinitely many numbers. Systematic nonfactualism fails on its own. It does not need any help from a special approach to truth.

Boghossian's Account of the Philosophical Consequences of Deflationism

I now turn to a recent discussion of the philosophical implications of deflationism about truth that takes quite a different view of the matter. In "The Status of Content," Paul Boghossian argues for a number of sweeping theses about the philosophical character of deflationism and its relationship to other philosophical doctrines. Among these theses are the following:

Thesis 1: Deflationism about truth is incompatible with nonfactualism about any substantial or systematic range of discourse.

Thesis 2: Nonfactualism about psychological and linguistic content presupposes deflationism about truth and so is inconsistent. (Other versions of irrealism about content are also inconsistent.)

Thesis 3: Deflationism about truth is a form of nonfactualism and so is internally inconsistent or incoherent.

These theses are startling. I have been arguing that deflationism is obvious and philosophically innocuous; Boghossian takes it to be philosophically contentious and incoherent. Why?

Boghossian begins with a characterization of irrealism about a domain of discourse. Irrealism about a domain is taken to be the view that the predicates in the domain either (i) fail to express properties at all or (ii) express properties that do not apply to anything. In case (ii), this means that atomic sentences formed with such predicates are uniformly false. In case (i), it means that atomic sentences containing such predicates do not make descriptive claims and so do not have truth conditions. The classical example of such irrealism is ethics. J. L. Mackie's error theory is of type (ii).[40] Emotivism is of type (i). Boghossian notes that these characterizations make heavy use of the notions of truth and falsity, and he raises the question of what we mean by them.

He contrasts two different conceptions of truth: deflationary and robust. This division is apparently intended to be exhaustive, and the only characterization of robust conceptions is that they are not deflationary. What then is a deflationary conception of truth? Boghossian says that "it is characterized by the claim that there is no such thing as the property of truth, a property that sentences or thoughts may enjoy, and that would be named by the words 'true' or 'truth'."[41] This view is supposed to come in two varieties: Strawson's performative variety and the disquotational variety (illustrated by particular Tarski-style definitions of truth-in-L for various Ls). Disquotational theories are said to reject the idea of a general notion of truth and to view truth predicates simply as devices for "semantic ascent."[42] One important problem here is that Horwich's minimal theory, or indeed any theory that takes truth to be a genuine but trivially transparent property of propositions, does not qualify as deflationary for Boghossian. Since such theories are not robust in any interesting sense, his characterization of deflationism should be modified to accommodate them.[43]

For the most part, Boghossian's discussion of deflationism focuses on cases in which the truth predicate is applied to sentences. He asks what conditions must be satisfied if a sentence is to be truth assessable and suggests that it must be meaningful, declarative, and embeddable "within negation, the conditional, and other connectives, and within contexts of propositional attitude."[44] The basic idea is that according to deflationism the effect of asserting that a sentence is true is the same as that of assertively uttering the sentence itself, so any assertoric sentence should be truth assessable.

We now get an argument for thesis 1. Consider a nonfactualist treatment of some domain of discourse. It says that all atomic sentences in the domain fail to have truth conditions and so are not truth assessable. But typically sentences in the domain are meaningful, declarative sentences that are embeddable in all the standard ways. Thus they are sentences that must be counted as truth assessable by a deflationary account of truth. Since nonfactualism takes them not to be truth assessable, nonfactualism presupposes a robust rather than a deflationary account of truth. In short, philosophical nonfactualism about any domain of discourse presupposes a nondeflationary conception of truth.

This argument is misleading for reasons noted in my discussion of emotivism in the previous section. The nonfactualist has two apparent options. (i) Like the traditional emotivist, the nonfactualist can claim that sentences in the domain are not used to assert propositions. If, despite all appearances to the contrary, this option could be established, then the deflationist could consistently maintain that we have no genuine candidates for truth assessability.[45] (ii) The nonfactualist could admit that sentences in the domain are used to assert propositions, which the nonfactualist is willing to assert, while denying that these propositions have truth value. This is, indeed, incompatible with deflationism but only because it is incompatible with any adequate account of truth, requiring, as it does, a willingness to assert (28a) and (28b) while denying (28c).[46] So the nonfactualist faces a dilemma. The nonfactualist must either deny trivial facts about truth or find a way of rebutting the overwhelming linguistic evidence that sentences in the domain of discourse do express and are used to assert propositions. Deflationism can be seen as playing a role in clarifying this dilemma, but its role should not be seen as contentious.

Next we turn to the argument for thesis 2.

Boghossian's Argument That Nonfactualism about Content Presupposes
Deflationism about Truth and So Is Inconsistent[47]

   i.   Assume that ascriptions of psychological content (e.g., belief ascriptions)
        are nonfactual; they do not have truth conditions and so are not true and
        not false.

   ii. Since the same considerations that would lead to nonfactualism about
        psychological content would lead to nonfactualism about the linguistic
        contents of sentences, ascriptions of linguistic content are also nonfactual.

  iii. But the linguistic contents of sentences are (or are explained by) their
        truth conditions.

   iv. So ascriptions of truth conditions are nonfactual.

    v.   These could be nonfactual only if the predicate *true* fails to express a
        property and sentences that ascribe truth to other sentences are nonfactual
        (and thus are neither true nor false). Thus truth is deflationary.

   vi. From thesis 1, we know that any version of nonfactualism presupposes
        that truth is not deflationary but robust.

  vii. Thus we have from (v) that truth is deflationary and from (i), (v), and (vi)
        that truth is nondeflationary. Since this is incoherent, (i) is not just im-
        plausible, it is incoherent.

There are two main problems with this argument. First, since thesis 1 was not
successfully established, steps (vi) and (vii) are questionable. Second, the move
from the linguistic contents of sentences to their truth conditions expressed by
step (iii) raises difficulties. In making this move, Boghossian notes that there is
controversy about whether truth conditions, by themselves, can completely account for linguistic content or whether something additional is needed as well.
But, he adds, "what is not controversial, however, is that the essential core of the
ordinary notion of content does consist simply in the idea of a truth condition."[48]
However, this is deeply problematic. Any account in which truth conditions are
central to meaning is an account in which the truth predicate is applied to sentences. This is not true of either the classical redundancy theory or Strawson's
performative theory. Although it is true of Tarski's version of deflationism, it is
transparent that statements of truth conditions employing Tarskian truth predicates
carry no information whatsoever about linguistic meaning. So if Boghossian is
right that it is uncontroversial that linguistic meaning is to be explained in terms
of truth conditions,[49] then it ought to be uncontroversial that the notion of truth
employed in this enterprise is not any of the different notions that he explicitly
characterizes as deflationary.

   This point carries over to any proper characterization of deflationary truth for
sentences. If the truth predicate in ⌜'s' is true iff s⌝ were genuinely deflationary,
then the claim expressed by the sentence ⌜'s' is true⌝ would have to be trivially
equivalent to the claim expressed by s.[50] However, this is impossible if the biconditional is to express any information about meaning. Otherwise someone who
knew that snow is white but did not understand any English could trivially infer
from a knowledge of snow that 'Snow is white' is true and hence that 'Snow is

white' is true iff snow is white, thereby obtaining information about the meaning of the English sentence. Since this is absurd, no sentential truth predicate in any statement of truth conditions that carries implications about meaning can be a deflationary truth predicate.

So there is an incoherence here after all, though not the one Boghossian had in mind. The incoherence comes from the combination of steps (ii) and (iii) in the argument. It is incoherent to characterize the meanings of sentences in terms of their truth conditions while simultaneously holding that the relevant notion of truth for sentences is deflationary.[51] This does not mean that all forms of deflationism about truth are inconsistent with the view that statements of the truth conditions of sentences provide information about their meanings. Suppose, for example, that one defines the relevant sentential truth predicate in terms of a deflationary truth predicate of propositions—a sentence is true iff it expresses a true proposition (where the expression relation between sentences and propositions is a substantive one). Then ⌜'s' is true iff s⌝ will provide information about the meaning of s by (implicitly) providing information about the truth conditions of the proposition it expresses, even though (propositional) truth is ultimately deflationary. Not only is this position consistent, but I believe it is correct.

We now come to Boghossian's argument for thesis 3.

Boghossian's Argument That Deflationism about Truth Is Self-Defeating[52]
   i.   Deflationism about truth is the view that *true* does not express a property.
  ii.   To hold that a predicate F does not express a property is to be a nonfactualist about F.
 iii.   But nonfactualism about anything is incompatible with deflationism about truth.
 iv.   So deflationism about truth is self-defeating.

This is remarkable. How could the positions of F. P. Ramsey, Strawson, Tarski, Horwich, and others be incoherent in this way? For Boghossian, nonfactualism about F is supposed to have the consequence that a sentence ⌜x is F⌝ does not have truth conditions and so is not true. But deflationists do not hold that sentences of the form *x is true* cannot be true. So deflationism about truth cannot be a version of nonfactualism.

Where then does the argument go wrong? At steps (i), (ii), and (iii). Step (iii) is just thesis 1, which, we saw, was not established. Step (i) is also incorrect. There are versions of deflationism that hold that *true* does refer to a property—for example, Horwich's version, Tarski's version, and Kripke's version. In the case of Tarski, there is no one property that all legitimate uses of truth predicates express. Still, each such use does express a property; moreover, a claim of the form *Sentence s is true* can always be assessed using a truth predicate at a higher level.[53]

Even step (ii) is problematic. Consider classical redundancy theorists who say that *true*, in sentences in which it apparently is ascribed to a proposition, does not express a property. In saying this, they do not intend to deny that these sentences state facts or that the sentences can be characterized as true or false. Rather, they distinguish between grammatical form and logical form. For them, *true* is a grammatical predicate that does not have the logical or semantic function of a predicate. For example, the sentence *The proposition that snow is white is true* is thought to have the same simple logical form as the sentence *Snow is white*, and the sentence *Everything he said is true* is assigned the logical form of the sentence *For all P, if he said that P then P* involving higher-order quantification. All of these statements are regarded as factual.

Moreover, in evaluating the so-called platitude '*x is P' is true iff the object denoted by 'x' has the property expressed by 'P'*, the redundancy theorist will distinguish between logical and grammatical form. If instances of *x is P* are restricted to logical forms, then predicates replacing *P* will never be truth predicates and the platitude may be accepted without giving the unwanted result that sentences containing the grammatical predicate *true* fail to be true. If instances of *x is P* in the platitude are allowed to be any grammatical sentences, then the truth predicate may replace *P* but the platitude will be rejected. The idea that if a predicate does not express a property, then grammatically simple atomic sentences containing it cannot be fact-stating is at base the idea that to be fact-stating these sentences would have to state facts, one of whose constituents was the property expressed by the predicate. But that is just to ignore the difference between logical and grammatical form that the classical redundancy theory postulates.[54]

I conclude from all this that deflationism about truth survives Boghossian's attempt to discredit it. Moreover, I doubt that any philosophical argument with that aim will ever succeed.[55] This is partly due to the fact that deflationism is somewhat vague, being a general approach rather than a specific theory. Mostly, though, it is because deflationism is obvious, uncontentious, and, I suspect, without substantial philosophical consequences. That is not to say that it will be easy or philosophically insignificant to come up with a precise and specific deflationist analysis that adequately deals with the paradoxes and related issues. On the contrary, such a task is both difficult and important. Truth is a central notion, and clarifying it can be expected to improve our grasp of related logical and semantic notions while indirectly illuminating a number of broader philosophical concerns. Throughout the history of philosophy, the notion of truth has occupied a corner into which all manner of problems and confusions have been swept. One may take heart from the fact that we have at last begun to dispel those confusions.

Notes

1. See Saul Kripke, "Outline of a Theory of Truth," *Journal of Philosophy* 72 (1975): 690–716, at 691, n. 1.

2. Gottlob Frege, "Thoughts," in *Propositions and Attitudes*, ed. N. Salmon and S. Soames (New York: Oxford University Press, 1988), 33–55, at 36–37.

3. A proposition p is a priori iff there is a way of grasping p such that it is possible to come to know p, when grasped in that way, without appeal to empirical evidence. A priori consequence can be defined in either a stronger or a weaker sense. According to the strong characterization, a proposition q is a (strong) a priori consequence of p iff for any

way G of grasping p, there is a way G' of grasping q such that it is possible, in principle, to reason deductively from p under G to q under G' without appeal to empirical evidence. According to the weak characterization, a proposition q is a (weak) a priori consequence of p iff there is some way G of grasping p and some way G' of grasping q such that it is possible, in principle, to reason deductively from p under G to q under G' without appeal to empirical evidence. The claim in the text—that the propositions expressed by S and ⌜It is true that S⌝ are a priori consequences of each other—may be taken in the strong sense.

4. More precisely, we say something we would not be in a position to say without either a truth predicate or some complex, higher-order quantification in terms of which a truth predicate could be defined.

5. I am here putting aside paradoxical instances of the relevant schemata.

6. Paul Boghossian, "The Status of Content," *Philosophical Review* 99, no. 2 (1990): 157–84.

7. Versions of the theory can be found in F. P. Ramsey, "Facts and Propositions," *Proceedings of the Aristotelian Society*, suppl., 7 (1927): 153–70; A. J. Ayer, *Language, Truth, and Logic*, 2d ed. (New York: Dover, 1946), chap. 5; A. N. Prior, *Objects of Thought* (Oxford: Oxford University Press, 1971); and Dorothy Grover, Joseph Camp, and Nuel Belnap Jr., "A Prosentential Theory of Truth," *Philosophical Studies* 27 (1975): 73–125. The Prior and Grover (plus descendants of Grover) are quite interesting, but they employ certain nonstandard logical devices that I do not have space to present or evaluate here.

8. Lack of space prevents me from discussing accounts of quantification other than the standard objectual and substitutional versions. One of the most interesting is presented, in connection with the redundancy theory, in Prior, *Objects of Thought*. Other accounts have been presented in connection with the prosentential theory. (For present purposes, I am ignoring restrictions needed to block the Liar and related paradoxes.)

9. Since the redundancy theory is first and foremost an attempt to do away with the notion of truth for propositions, I have not considered the status of truth predicates of sentences from that point of view. There are two points to make. First, since one can believe, for example, the proposition that the earth is round without believing the proposition that the English sentence 'The earth is round' is true and vice versa, the propositions are different, and the redundancy theory of truth for sentences is a nonstarter. Second, insofar as redundancy theorists are willing to talk at all about the truth of sentences, they typically hold that a sentence is true iff it expresses a true proposition—that is, s is true iff $(\exists P)$(s expresses the proposition that P & P). But then all the difficulties with their analysis of true propositions come into play again.

10. Peter Strawson, "Truth," *Analysis* 9, no. 6 (1949), 83–97 and "Truth," *Proceedings of the Aristotelian Society* supp. vol. 24, (1950) 129–56.

11. Utterances of sentences containing *true* often carry suggestions that are not carried by utterances of corresponding sentences that do not contain *true*. For example, imagine the following questions being asked at a presidential press conference: *Is it true that you are considering sending troops to Latin America? Are you considering sending troops to Latin America?* The first question carries the suggestion that it has been reported, predicted, or suggested that the president is considering sending troops to Latin America. Because of this, the question is naturally understood as a request for the president to confirm or deny these reports, predictions, or suggestions. Although the second question asks for the same information, it does not carry this suggestion that the questioner is merely following up a previous remark rather than perhaps placing an issue on the public agenda.

Another example: The president says, *We have proposed a comprehensive program to reduce the deficit while stimulating the economy. It is true that unemployment has already begun to drop but not fast enough, so we still need the stimulus package.* Or *Yes, unemployment has already begun to drop but not fast enough.* . . . In this context, *it is true that* and *yes* are rhetorical devices used to indicate that the speaker is aware that people have said or thought that unemployment is already dropping without the stimulus package and to concede the point while trying to deny the further implication that the stimulus package is unnecessary. Again, *true* is used to suggest the existence of something to which a response is called for.

12. Strawson, "Truth" (1949), 92–93.

13. Ironically, this result alone does not show that sentences of the form (i) differ in meaning from those of the form (ii).

i. I (hereby) endorse (confirm, etc.) some/several/many statements in the report.
ii. Some/several/many statements in the report are true.

The reason it does not show this is that utterances of sentences of the form (i) typically do not themselves constitute endorsements, confirmations, and so on. To see this, consider an analogy. Imagine a duly constituted authority standing before several new ships at a christening ceremony. At the proper moment, the authority utters the sentence *I hereby name at least one of these ships the* J. L. Austin and sits down. The authority does not go on to specify which ship is supposedly being named but simply lets the performance stand. In such a case, the authority has not named anything; the performance is flawed, even absurd.

In the absence of special stage setting (specifying which statements are being endorsed or confirmed), utterances of sentences like (i) share these defects. They are not endorsements or confirmations of anything; rather, they are flawed, even absurd, performances (unless they are construed as straightforward descriptions). Of course, this is not the case with utterances of (ii), which suggests that sentences of type (ii) do not have the meanings of sentences of type (i).

14. This type of argument against the performative theory can be found in Peter Geach, "Ascriptivism," *Philosophical Review* 69, no. 2 (1960) 221–25, and in John Searle, "Meaning and Speech Acts," *Philosophical Review* 71, no. 4 (1962) 423–32. For an argument of the same type directed against the emotivist view of the meaning of *good*, see David Ross, *The Foundations of Ethics* (Oxford: Oxford University Press, 1939), 33–34.

It should be noted that the argument based on examples (12)–(15) cannot be avoided by modifying the (b) sentences of those pairs. One might think, for example, that the analysis of (13a) should not be (13b) but the following: *I do not know whether I should endorse/confirm/concede that budget deficits cause inflation.* However, this suggestion runs up against the datum that sentences of the form (16a) do not change meaning when they are embedded in one or another linguistic environment. Thus if *I should endorse/confirm/concede that P* is to be the analysis of (16a) in a case like (13), it must serve as the analysis across the board. Since it cannot do so in all examples, it cannot be the correct analysis.

One uniform analysis that might be suggested is the following: ⌜The proposition that P is true⌝ means ⌜The proposition that P is worthy of endorsement⌝. But to adopt this view would be to give up the performative aspect of the theory altogether. To say that a proposition is worthy of endorsement is to assert that it has a certain property. Thus in this view, *true* would function as a genuine predicate, and the property of truth would be identified with the property of being worthy of endorsement, contrary to both the performative and redundancy theories. Moreover, the identification would be incorrect. Although P is obviously equivalent to ⌜The proposition that P is true⌝, it is not obviously equivalent to ⌜The proposition that P is worthy of endorsement⌝.

15. Instances are obtained by replacing 's' with a name—for example, a quote-name—of a sentence of L and 'P' with a sentence of the metalanguage that means the same thing as the sentence the name of which replaces 's'.

16. Instances are obtained by replacing 's' with a name of a sentence of L and 'P' with an arbitrary sentence of the metalanguage (English).

17. Alfred Tarski, "Truth and Proof," *Scientific American*, June 1969, 63–77, at 64.

18. He says: "Thus our main problem is: can we establish an adequate use of the term 'true' for sentences in English and, if so, then by what methods? We can, of course, raise an analogous question for sentences in any other language. The problem will be solved completely if we manage to construct a general definition of truth that will be adequate in the sense that it will carry with it as logical consequences all the equivalences of the form (3) ['p' is true iff p]. If such a definition is accepted by English-speaking people, it will obviously establish an adequate use of the term 'true' " (ibid., 65).

19. Alfred Tarski, "The Semantic Conception of Truth and the Foundations of Semantics," *Philosophy and Phenomenological Research* 4 (1944): 341–75, reprinted in *The Philosophy of Language*, ed. A. P. Martinich (New York: Oxford University Press, 1985), 48–71, at 48.

20. The need for these extra conditions is shown by the following considerations. First, if I did not know that 'S' *is true in English iff* was a construction in the language designated by the word *English*, then I would not know that instances of 'S' *is true in English iff* S were themselves sentences of the language designated by that word. Second, if I did know that these were sentences of the language designated by *English* but I had the wrong idea about what 'S' *is true in English iff* meant in that language—for example, if I wrongly thought it meant what 'S' *is false in English iff* means in my language—then I would not know that instances of 'S' *is true in English iff* S were truths of the language designated by *English*. In either of these cases, I would not accept sentence (19a). Since no other sentence I am guaranteed to accept expresses the same proposition as (19a), I might also fail to believe or know that proposition. This is the problem mentioned previously with step (b) of the argument. That step, which did not include the extra conditions noted here, is false, as stated. I am indebted to Doug Cannon for a discussion of these issues.

21. I have occasionally been asked whether this conclusion could be avoided if sentences were thought of not simply as syntactic objects (sequences of shape or sound types) but rather as syntactic objects together with their interpretations. In this conception, the English sentence *Snow is white* is thought of as a pair, the first member of which is a sequence of syntactic elements and the second member of which is the proposition that snow is white. It is sometimes further suggested that quotation-mark names of sentences like 'Snow is white' name the pair consisting of the sequence of syntactic elements together with the proposition it expresses in English. In this conception, the truth predicate that occurs in instances of schema T is not relational (it does not hold between sentences and languages), nor is it indexed to a particular language. Rather, a sentence like 'Snow is white' *is true in English* is understood as 'Snow is white' *is a sentence of English that is true*, with the truth predicate expressing a nonrelational property of "interpreted sentences" (propositions really). Now, I do not accept this account of quotation or of what sentences are. However, it is worth noting that accepting the account would not change our results. In the conception sketched, knowing that 'Snow is white' is a sentence of English would involve knowing that the pair consisting of a certain syntactic object and the proposition that snow is white was a sentence of English, which in turn

would require knowing that the syntactic object expressed that proposition in English. This means that, for all the reasons given in the text, understanding the T-sentences (when construed in this way) would not guarantee that one accepted them or believed the propositions they expressed.

22. For further discussion, see Scott Soames, "T-Sentences," in *Modality, Morality, and Belief: Essays in Honor of Ruth Barcan Marcus*, ed. Walter Sinnott-Armstrong, Diana Raffman, and Nicholas Asher (Cambridge: Cambridge University Press, 1995), 250–70. That discussion includes much of the material just presented, plus further related issues.

23. Ibid., 252–55, and note 8.

24. In the case of schemata PT, (17), and (24), I am continuing to defer any consideration of paradoxical or other pathological instances.

25. As we saw, pathological sentences involving the truth predicate come in several varieties that need to be distinguished. It is an important virtue of the Kripke construction that it provides conceptual resources for making these distinctions.

26. Paul Horwich, *Truth* (Oxford: Blackwell, 1990).

27. Ibid., 36.

28. See ibid., 38–40.

29. Examples provided by Mark Richard have persuaded me that it would be too strong to maintain that anyone satisfying ordinary standards for being a competent speaker of English would actually assent to every relevant instance of schema PT, no matter what his or her philosophical views about truth. Nevertheless, it still seems to me that one's linguistic competence is enough to incline one to accept and to justify one in accepting each such instance. Cases in which an ordinarily competent speaker ends up dissenting from a particular instance are, I suspect, cases of linguistic confusion, which can be brought about by holding false philosophical and semantic views. (No precise definition of analyticity is intended here.)

30. In discussing this objection, I will ignore pathological propositions and restrict myself to the class of unproblematic propositions that Horwich talks about.

31. For simplicity, we may suppose that L is a fragment of English containing *and* as a sentential connective. We may also use David Kaplan's meaning marks to express (26). Where 'p' and 'q' are (first-order) variables ranging propositions and P and Q are sentences of L that express, respectively, the propositions designated by 'p' and 'q' (relative to an assignment), we let *p and q* be a singular term directly designating (relative to the appropriate assignment) the proposition expressed by ⌜P and Q⌝ in L. (26) may then be expressed as follows: For any propositions p and q (of L), *p and q* is true iff p is true and q is true. For all sentences P and Q of L, this generalization (together with subsidiary background assumptions) will have the proposition expressed by ⌜The proposition that P and Q is true iff the proposition that P is true and the proposition that Q is true⌝ as a consequence.

32. I am indebted to George Boolos for initially directing my attention to this problem. After finishing the chapter, I discovered, thanks to Paul Horwich, that Anil Gupta points out a version of essentially the same problem in "A Critique of Deflationism," *Philosophical Topics* 21, no. 2 (1993): 57–81, esp. 65–67.

33. The objection based on (26) can be used to undercut Horwich's attempt to show in section 3 of chapter 2 of *Truth* (22–24) that the collection of T-equivalences is sufficient to explain all facts about truth. In particular, Horwich tries to show that the minimal theory is sufficient to explain the following generalization: If one proposition materially implies another and the first one is true, then so is the second. He gives a five-step "proof" of this, which appeals at two points (steps 2 and 5) to the minimal theory (23). The problem with the proof is illustrated by the final step, which Horwich expresses as follows:

    4.   We have every instance of: $<[<\text{p}> \text{ is true } \& <\text{p}> \text{ implies } <\text{q}>] \to <\text{q}>$ is true$>$

    5.   Therefore (from the minimal theory) every proposition of the form $<[<\text{p}>$ is true $\& <\text{p}>$ implies $<\text{q}>] \to <\text{q}>$ is true$>$ is true.

  ('$< \ldots >$' is read 'the proposition that . . .')

The only justified reading of (4) is one that asserts each instance of the relevant schema (on the basis of logic and the minimal theory). But it is not a logical (or a priori) consequence of all these instances plus the minimal theory that every instance of that schema is true. This is obscured by Horwich's use of the words "we have every instance of" in (4). True, from all the instances plus the separate claim that they are all the instances there are, we can get (5). But that separate claim does not follow from the minimal theory or from the minimal theory plus the other assumptions (logic and the definition of material implication) explicitly appealed to earlier in the proof.

34. Ibid., 80–87.

35. As opposed, for example, to defining a proposition to be false iff its negation is true, a definition that leaves open the possibility of treating certain propositions (like the proposition that the present king of France is bald) as neither true nor false. I take no stand on this question.

36. Horwich, *Truth*, 87.

37. Ibid.

38. That is, I see any acceptable theory of truth as recognizing that acceptance of (28a) and (28b) commits one to (28c).

39. By an explicit performative, I mean examples like *I hereby name this blimp the Hillary* and *I pronounce you man and wife*.

40. J. L. Mackie, *Ethics* (New York: Penguin, 1977).

41. Boghossian, "The Status of Content," 161. This passage is a direct comment on Ayer's version of the redundancy theory of truth. However, Boghossian seems to regard it as at least loosely applicable to deflationism in general.

42. Ibid., 162–63.

43. Other problems with Boghossian's characterization of deflationism are (i) that classical redundancy theories typically are neither performative nor concerned with attribution of truth to sentences and (ii) that disquotational Tarskian truth predicates each express properties, even though, according to Tarski, there is no coherent general notion of truth.

44. Boghossian, "The Status of Content," 163.

45. This is obvious in the case of propositional versions of deflationism. However, a version of it could be established even for sentential versions of deflationism that attempt to replace our ordinary notion of truth for sentences with an explicitly deflationary substitute. For example, there is no reason why a Tarskian revisionist has to apply the truth predicate to sentences that are not used assertively.

46. What is Boghossian's view of this matter? Unfortunately, he says so little about propositions that the issue is not explicitly addressed. However, he does address a corresponding issue about truth predicates of sentences in a way that leaves little room for any conception of truth in which acceptance of examples analogous to (28a) and (28b) is deemed not to commit one to (28c).

For example, in giving an argument against an irrealist conception of linguistic content according to which all ascriptions of contents to sentences are characterized as false, Boghossian says the following: "Consider first an error conception. As the preceding discussion has argued, this amounts finally to the claim that (4) All sentences of the form 'S has truth condition p' are false, where S is to be understood as ranging over sentences in the language of thought, or neural structures, as well as over public-language sentences. But, now, (4) would seem to have the immediate consequence that *no sentence* has a truth condition. *For whatever one's conception of 'true'—whether robust or deflationary—a sentence of the form 'S has truth condition p' will be true if and only if S really does have truth condition p; this is, of course, nothing but a reflection of the truth predicate's disquotational properties, properties it possesses on any conception of truth.* And so, since 'S has truth condition p' is true if and only if S has truth condition p, then, since *all* sentences of that form are held to be *false*, for no S and for no p does S have truth condition p" ("The Status of Content," 171; emphasis added). In this passage, Boghossian seems to be saying that any conception of truth for sentences—whether deflationary or robust—is committed to all (nonparadoxical) instances of the schema *'s' is true iff s.* The corresponding claim about propositions is that any conception of truth for propositions—whether deflationary or robust—is committed to all instances of the schema *The proposition that p is true iff p.* But if this claim is correct, then to assert (28a) and (28b) while denying (28c) (which is tantamount to denying an instance of the propositional schema) is to do something incompatible with any conception of truth—whether deflationary or robust.

47. The argument is a reconstruction of Boghossian's discussion in ibid., 171–75. He presents a different argument for the version of thesis 2 concerning the error theory version of irrealism. That argument is as follows: (i) According to the error theory, the claim that a sentence has content is always false. (ii) Since content is truth conditions, all sentences of the form *s has truth condition p* are false. (iii) Therefore according to the error theory, no sentence has a truth condition or a truth value. (iv) But this contradicts (ii), which says that sentences of the form *s has truth condition p* are false.

The argument is clear enough provided one can make sense of what it means to say that a sentence has truth condition p or that a sentence has a truth condition. (I take it that 'p' is being used as a schematic letter to be replaced with ordinary 'that'-clauses and that 's' is to be replaced by a name of a sentence.) Presumably, Boghossian's *s has truth condition p* cannot be regarded as equivalent to *s is true iff p* (where 'p' is replaced by a sentence) since the claim that all such biconditionals are false, plus the fact that the negation of a false sentence is true, entails that a pair of contradictory sentences are jointly true. (Note that where 's' is replaced by the name of an interrogative sentence, presumably *s has truth condition p* should really turn out false, for any replacement of 'p', even though *s is true iff p*, will be true for many such replacements.) So it is not entirely clear to me what his predicate—*x has truth condition p*—is supposed to mean.

48. Ibid., 173.

49. One person who denies this allegedly uncontroversial view is Horwich.

50. In the terminology of note 3, the claims made by s and ⌜'s' is true⌝ would have to be strong a priori consequences of one another (which they are not).

51. Boghossian, "The Status of Content," 176–78, seems to indicate that he misses this point. There he presents as a live option the idea that deflationism (nonfactualism) about truth coupled with the admission that sentences have truth conditions could itself be viewed as a version of content irrealism. This ignores the incoherence just noted of using a deflationary truth predicate in a theory that treats the meanings of sentences as given by their truth conditions.

52. This is a reconstruction of the argument in ibid., 180–81.

53. Even classical redundancy theories may hold that when 'true' is applied to sentences, it expresses a property—s is true iff for some P, s expresses the proposition that P and P.

54. The same point applies to the prosentential theory.

55. For further argument on this score, see Mark Richard, "Deflating Truth," 57–78 (which is a response to my "The Truth about Deflationism," on which the present chapter is based), and Scott Soames, "Reply to Garcia-Carpintero and Richard," 79–93 *Philosophical Issues* 8 1997.

Index

263